European

Architecture

and the

American Challenge

1893–1960

Scenes of the World to Come

Jean-Louis
Cohen

European
Architecture
and the
American
Challenge
1893–1960

Scenes of the World to Come

Preface
by Hubert Damisch

Flammarion

Canadian Centre
for Architecture

Published in conjunction with the exhibition
"Scenes of the World to Come: European Architecture and the American Challenge, 1893–1960"
at the Canadian Centre for Architecture in Montreal, 14 June–24 September 1995
and the Centre de Cultura Contemporània in Barcelona from February to April 1996.
Exhibition Curator: Jean-Louis Cohen

The French Consulate in Montreal has generously contributed to the transportation costs.

Canadian Centre for Architecture, Montreal
Phyllis Lambert, Director

Centre de Cultura Contemporània, Barcelona
Josep Ramoneda, Director

Director of publications (CCA): Christine Dufresne
Photo Editing (CCA): Jocelyne Gervais
Designed by: Frédéric Célestin
Editor: Claire Rouyer

English edition:
Edited by Christa Weil
Research and proofreading by Christine Schultz-Touge
Additional research by Kathleen Fleming
Typesetting by Octavo Editions, Paris
Origination by Pack Edit, Paris
Printed by Clerc SA, Saint-Amand-Montrond
Translated by Kenneth Hylton

Flammarion
26, rue Racine
75006 Paris

ISBN: 2-08013-576-7
Numéro d'édition: 0977
Dépôt légal: June 1995
Printed in France

F O R E W O R D

This publication accompanies the first in a series of exhibitions organized by the Canadian Centre for Architecture (CCA) on the American Century, a series which will examine the character and ascendancy of North American architectural culture in its varied manifestations over the twentieth century. Tracing the origins of Americanism back to the late nineteenth century, this study focuses on the European discovery of the North American city—with its grand hotels, skyscrapers, and massive industrial plants; its new-found sense of efficiency and mobility; its infatuation with domestic appliances and mechanization.

Jean-Louis Cohen demythologizes the mixture of dread and enthusiasm, imitation and contention with which Europeans welcomed this New World. He also brings into focus processes of adoption and reaction between different cultures, processes that are far more complex than initially assumed. Above all, he leads us to discover in the European reception of the American vision the evolution of the principal tenets of European avant-gardes, often well ahead of their American models, allowing us to trace the efforts of the modernists to shield their new models from appropriation—examples are found in Sant'Elia's *Città Nuova*, Le Corbusier's *Ville contemporaine*, the first towers of glass by Mies van der Rohe and Leonidov, the Taylorized factories of Italy and Czechoslovakia, and the "plug-in cities" and "instant houses" of the 1950s and 60s. Coincident with these developments is the periodic re-emergence of a certain formal conservatism in the adoption of American models, as in Paris in the 1890s and 1930s and in Stalinist Moscow, revealing how New World sources have been used to serve a retrograde, authoritarian, or monumentalist architectural aesthetic.

By linking the roots of the American ascendancy to the European dialectic which it informed, we hope that this study will begin a re-evaluation of the most important cultural exchange in the architectural history of the twentieth century—and hence of the ideological foundations of the built world in which we live.

I wish to thank Jean-Louis Cohen who initiated this project, and followed it through every stage with rigor and perseverance. The participation from the initial phases of development of Josep Ramoneda and his team at the Centre de Cultura Contemporània de Barcelona enabled us to expand the scope of the exhibition and the research that underlies it. Finally, assistance with transportation costs by the French Consulate in Montreal provided needed support for this exhibition.

Phyllis LAMBERT
Director, Canadian Centre for Architecture

C O N T E N T S

P R E F A C E

And if America were not only an immense source of myths, forms, and images, but also of the kinds of vogues, fetishes, and products we are inclined to see in her; if these myths, these forms, and these images contributed to her sway, if not her supremacy, in the form of exportable goods, items which afford glimpses of the inherent contradictions of their origins, a play of opposing forces which are never quite resolved or surmounted, and which indeed maintain their full strength? This is the case (at least in my hypothesis) by virtue of the elemental relationship they hold with the American scene: either because the myths, objects, and images in question are inseparable from the American landscape (as is the case with skyscrapers) or because they make it what it is (which is also the case with skyscrapers).

The characteristic process of urbanization in America, passing abruptly as it often does from horizontal to vertical, from the scattered to the concentrated, from diffuse to congested, merits our attention. To the extent that it works invariably, and spectacularly, in two contradictory dimensions, and insofar as we can use the term without lending it the dramatic connotation found in Le Corbusier's writings, America can be viewed as the scene of "catastrophe." (For René Thom, the term implies that which has phenomenological discontinuity, for instance unmediated 90° shifts from the horizontal to the vertical).[1] The American model—which is not to say Americanism in all its forms—is most effective when it imposes itself more or less surreptitiously on that which is called the "European consciousness," setting off a change that rattles, that moves, that riots through its foundations. In this way, as in many others, America serves as Europe's unconscious.

I shall illustrate this thesis by citing three experiences.

1/ (*Aerial View*). Landing at Chicago airport from Montreal on a late afternoon in winter. As the airplane loses height in the dazzling light of the setting sun, the broad lines of the urban grid seem to fuse with the crisscross Jeffersonian layout of the great midwestern plains stretching far away to the horizon, as if etched in the snow. The aerial view of Daniel Burnham and Edward Bennett's plan for greater Chicago (1907–09), drawn and watercolored by Jules Guérin, expresses the way the city fits into the surrounding territory fairly well, except that a star-shaped pattern is superimposed onto the perpendicular grid of the city center, while the Loop (which, then as now, encircles the first tall buildings constructed in iron and steel) seems to loosen and take on the appearance of a meandering river, thus achieving integration with the overall monumental and geographical device of the "Paris of the Great Prairies" as conceived by conscientious École des Beaux-Arts pupils. And if, paradoxically, the band of yellow stretching across the horizon evokes both sunrise and sunset, this double orientation harmonizes with the notion of a "frontier" continually pushed westward. In America, the East (including the Far East, notably China and Japan) is to be found in the West.

2/ (*Skyline*). At the Dallas-Fort Worth airport exit, the International Parkway enters the vast, deserted plain at a point precisely equidistant between the two cities, as signposts symmetrically placed on either side of the intersection indicate: to the right, "Dallas, 20 miles"; to the left, "Fort Worth, 20 miles." Of the approach to Dallas I recall only a tangle of hangars and shopping malls with their restaurants and movie theaters. At the time (1986), the tall Hotel Hyatt stood apart from the rest, aloof, caught between the desert and an urban agglomeration with which it appeared reluctant to compromise; yet its showy architecture was certainly more effective in this no-man's-land set against the city skyline than it would have been within the strangely discreet and elusive center of Dallas, where what architecture there is (including a Frank Lloyd Wright theater) does not spring immediately to the eye. Fort Worth is something quite different. As we reach the end of the dead-straight turnpike from Dallas, we are surprised to see a dotted skyline against a background of darkest night; the city vanishes behind its neon signs, amid thousands of lights in regular array that outline the silhouette of the skyscrapers. An effect à la Saul Steinberg (*The Discovery of America*), as if the city drew itself in the two dimensions of a plane.

3/ (*Manhattan*). Finally, this—an experience so banal that one would hardly dare describe it, were it not for the fact that is not so self-evident today, given that one is forced to use tourist networks (the Circle Line, the excursion to Brooklyn Heights, the Staten Island ferry, perhaps even a helicopter ride) to recapture some of the emotion that earlier discoverers of Manhattan must have felt from the deck of an ocean-going liner or an airplane porthole, at a time when such means of transport were authorized to get close enough. Postcards have taken over, showing head-on or aerial views such as few tourists are ever likely to get, restricted as they are to more or less panoramic vistas from the observation decks of the Empire State Building, Rockefeller Center, or World Trade Center. By fusing "real" and "virtual" (as witnesses the cinematographic treatment of Manhattan-as-object), such images vie with the multiple views that the city reveals to itself.

The city's image has long been a virtual one—and not only for the Americans. The *vedute* or silhouettes of riverside settlements have long since been replaced with aerial overviews. Well before the invention of the aerostat, architects and artists learned the essentially graphic techniques of the "bird's-eye" view, whereby the viewpoint, continually shifting, seemed to stretch away to infinity. When New York was still New Amsterdam, the Dutch painter Jan Micker painted a famous *View of Amsterdam* depicting the network of canals not so much in terms of a ground-level plan as a sort of axonometric one (this before the term was invented), its reference point hidden somewhere beneath a bank of clouds whose shadow covers the city.[2] Manhattan hardly existed at this time, even if a line of fortifications already marked the northern limits of the agglomeration. One of today's busiest streets, a focus for traffic and commerce of all types stretching away to the Holland Tunnel, preserves in its name the memory of canals carved in the rock, which small shipping plied at high water. Representations of this, the East India Company's first trading post on American soil, were highly romanticized in plan and elevation so as to reflect the traditional imageries of a walled riverside settlement.[3]

Whether seen head-on or from the air, much of the impact of modern Manhattan certainly springs from its geographical and monumental outline; the invention of the skyline reinforces that of the site. The contours of the city are as sharp at ground level (the clear-cut demarcation between the island and its surrounding waters must have pleased the Dutch) as in elevation; yet far from being mere silhouette or façade, Manhattan soars skyward as a sequence or concatenation of *profiles*—what Le Corbusier termed a "spectacle of plasticity." Manhattan does not peer into its waters any more than Chicago. But where Burnham and Bennett's Chicago, as visualized by Jules Guérin, was reflected less in the waters of Lake Michigan, which dominates its foreground, than in the plains to the West in the background, Manhattan's Narcissus, having multiplied his own self-images, discovered the only mirror to suit him: architecture, whose effects came to rival those of photomontages claiming to embody the dynamic, high-contrast image of the city of the future. The glass curtain wall, as exemplified by Gordon Bunshaft's Lever House (though others, such as Eero Saarinen's CBS Building stand in opposition to these) mirrors not only the façades of the surrounding buildings but the sky itself. The clouds that pass are "impelled by the wind," as Antonio di Tuccio Manetti wrote concerning the first demonstrations of mathematical perspective associated with Brunelleschi—demonstrations reflecting an eminently narcissistic impulse, to the extent that they rejected city-oriented visions in favor of a mirror-image. In Brunelleschi's Florence, as in Bunshaft's Manhattan, Narcissus of course runs the risk of what might be termed symbolic death—what the poet of *The Metamorphoses* called "dying through one's own eyes."[4]

If I touch on Brunelleschi's experimental demonstrations here, it is because they relate to the question of the subject, in the modern, if not the western, sense of the term. To the extent that the subject is involved in the perspective device—as its "origin," at the *punto dell'occhio* corresponding to the viewpoint reflected in a design—he fuses with the so-called vanishing point. Yet given that the role of perspective is directly bound up with that of architecture, above all the architecture of the city, the subject finds himself involved in the urban mechanism considered as a focus par excellence for the exercise of his function, if not for its emergence.[5] The discovery of America in 1492—when another great theorist of perspective, Piero della Francesca, died—imposed on that same subject an equally radical conversion. It was not merely that Christopher Columbus was immediately transformed by the tropism so characteristic of subsequent American culture and decided of his own accord to follow the Western route to the Orient; the discovery, along the way, of American "savages" led the European subject, struggling with the question of his own identity, to a self-questioning that was in no way narcissistic. Thus Rousseau (like Montaigne) wrote that "in order to study man one must learn to look far afield," and above all "to observe the differences so as to discover what the properties are." Lévi-Strauss felt this view of things signaled the birth of anthropology, and the architect Adolf Loos would adopt a comparable position in the course of his pioneering "grand tour" of America, before returning to Vienna to start up a review with only two issues, but with a title—*Das Andere*—that gave it programmatic status.[6] Classical antiquity did not grant "human" qualities to its Barbarians. Modern Europe would have its "savages"—a notion which made it necessary to reassess "humanity" in terms of the Other.

To varying degrees and in various guises, America has never ceased to play the role to which it was first assigned in the European imagination; urban America as much as (if not more than) in its rural counterpart, where Arcadian myths and community utopias went hand in hand with violent conquest. While in the first half of the nineteenth century, the Americans viewed the rampant urbanization accompanying European industrialization as the scourge to be avoided, this was soon to be stood on its head. People came to view the American city, for all its rigorously regular grid, as the crudest possible expression of a reputedly "wild" capitalism, in its achievements as well as its negative spin-offs.

The skyscraper was not the least of these heroic deeds (or misdeeds, as it was for some). The skyscraper has remained, in essence and in appearance, a profoundly American phenomenon, despite attempts to transplant, acclimatize, and hybridize it: in Milan, Paris, Frankfurt, or Tokyo, where a tall building, even one of American design (for example the Tour Montparnasse), is not a skyscraper but merely a tower. It can hardly be said that all skyscrapers are American (Norman Foster's Hong Kong and Shanghai Bank is a case in point), but we are nonetheless forced to admit that skyscrapers are to be found—and can only be found—in America, Hong Kong being the exception that confirms the rule. And it is easy to see why: skyscrapers constitute neither a type, nor an autonomous form, nor yet a model. As a species, they fit into any environment in which they can multiply (didn't Montaigne doubt the chances of "cannibals" surviving in Europe?). They found such an environment in northern America, just as they have found one in Hong Kong, and possibly in Brazil. As an economic environment, but above all a landscape, or better, an urban context, the city makes the skyscraper, not vice versa. Chicago, New York, Miami, and even Los Angeles, not to mention Hong Kong or Sao Paulo, are evidence of this, which the example of La Défense confirms *a contrario*. Some will say it is as much a matter of skyline as of situation, of elevation as of ground-plan; a question of site. Where the right conditions obtain, purely artificial elements of the skyline nurture something like a landscape (it is not for nothing that one speaks of the "cliffs" of Manhattan) within which the skyscraper can unfold its glories; whence the beauty of cities like Hong Kong and Rio de Janeiro, spectacular combinations of nature and artifice. The city enables the skyscraper; but it is architecture (and architecture, as Le Corbusier well understood, is the question) that "makes" the site, whether by *ex nihilo* or through its existing features.

New York is, as Paul Morand would have it, a "horizontal city," even if its extension in space (at least in the case of Manhattan) is strictly limited. This, as I have said, is one of the major reasons for its hold over the European imagination: Manhattan's sharply-drawn outline can be grasped at once, and is thus comparable to the fortified towns of the old continent, which could only grow by bursting successive perimeter walls. Yet it differs from the other American cities, with their ill-defined limits and their dilution into endless suburbs, whose centers can only be recognized where the mesh of its street-grid grows finer, as in Frank Lloyd Wright's *Broadacre City*. The exception is San Francisco, whose assertively European charms derive as much from the production of the site by the architecture as from the layout of its hills, which are literally assailed by its imperious grid. But downtown New York also has a horizontal skyline: by virtue of a "natural" process, the gaps created by each new summit are soon filled by others, creating an ever-higher, continuous façade (or "cliff").

European cities, in their form, are the products of operations supposed to be those of town planning, in which architecture is required to "fit" or fuse with its surroundings in the manner of monuments, spires, or domes. Formally speaking, American cities are checkerboards for the distribution of pieces whose urban effects are guaranteed; the "game" is purely architectural. No master plan or city plan could achieve, for the European high-rise block, that successful implantation at the monumental and urban levels which, both on the ground and in terms of the skyline, is so characteristic of the loveliest skyscrapers of New York or Chicago.

Here indeed is one of the paradoxes of "Americanism," at least at the architectural level. And we are speaking of an architecture that cannot be restricted to its (most obvious) urban incarnations; in many cases, it is to be found in the valleys of Pennsylvania, on the Wisconsin hills, in the innermost recesses of New England, lurking beneath the luxuriant vegetation of Santa Monica and Beverly Hills—or in the sere deserts of Arizona. I recall Richard Meier's reaction to an

article in the *New York Times*, complimenting him on the fact that he had never built skyscrapers. "It's not my fault," he confided to me, "I certainly wanted a commission!" I had just visited Meier's Atheneum at New Harmony near Kansas City, an introductory sequence to the community village conceived by Robert Owen as a first step towards the realization of his Utopia. The white-faced concrete walls furnish no clues as to the formwork, and bricks mask the wooden frames of the houses in the village. Here as elsewhere—in the indefinite expanses of the Midwest, or in the ever-increasing congestion of Manhattan—the image that is America draws its strength from an identical mythical gesture, one that runs counter to all notions of foundation or origins.

European notions of the city propound clear-cut horizontal demarcations as an immemorial principle, whether linked to ritual beginnings or seen as the products of necessity, as in the first fortified towns, which had to be enclosed for security reasons. Setting aside the case of Manhattan, the American city has no other outline than that of its vertically drawn skyline which, for all that, has nothing to do with façade or silhouette. I mean that its dynamic edges reflect the gestures of the pioneer (but this again is clearly an expression of the myth)—the first land-clearers and settlers. This corresponds to René Thom's example of phenomenological discontinuity: that of the sawing of a wooden plank, which produces a shift along its edges from vertical to horizontal. The saw introduces an elementary, static catastrophe, the result of the dynamic catastrophe which occurred when the plank was fashioned.[7] In this sense, the Manhattan skyline is a repository of successive catastrophes of which it is the product—one that is always provisional—just as the first dwellings of the pioneers preserved intact the memory of the trees of which they were made.

It is, therefore, not without good reason that Le Corbusier spoke of New York in terms of the positive sign +, one born of the encounter of two perpendicular straight lines in intersection. "The building sign," he called it, and this poses a problem. If America finds it hard to accept the disappearance of the last great sequoias along the northwest coastline, it is because she sees that disappearance—rightly—as marking the final stage in the land-clearing process and the end of the age of the "pioneer," and as heralding the beginning of a cycle in which the interplay between vertical and horizontal, dilution and concentration, diffusion and congestion, will no longer obey "natural" rules or allow clearly motivated decisions. At the fantasy level, this stems from the localization of the decision centers—which is becoming less and less dependent on the densification of communications networks owing to the "upright" status of cities—and to concomitant images of weightlessness, whereby pioneers of the new "frontier" are propelled vertically into space. Like it or not, America is a scene of future life—more so than ever perhaps, in that the scene no longer admits of self-evident parameters; there are no obvious sites, no irremediably dated ornaments, no constructions (in whatever sense) and thus no histories or descriptions that do not have to be called into question, or whose structural and narrative principles and definitions do not have to be permanently revalued.

1. See *Prédire n'est pas expliquer; René Thom à la question par Émile Noel*, Paris, 1991, p. 28

2. Svetlana Alpers, *The Art of Describing: Dutch Art in the Seventeenth Century*, Chicago, 1983, p. 157.

3. See John A. Kouwenhoven, *The Columbia Historical Portrait of New York: An Essay in Graphic History*, New York, Garden City, 1953.

4. "Perque oculos perit ipse suos," Ovid, *Metamorphoses*, Book III, p. 440.

5. See Hubert Damisch, *L'origine de la perspective*, Paris, 1987.

6. "Pour étudier l'homme, il faut apprendre à porter sa vue au loin." Here I take the liberty of referring the reader to my study of Adolf Loos, "L'autre 'Ich' ou le désir du vide," *Ruptures/Cultures*, Paris, 1976, pp. 143–159.

7. Thom, *op. cit.*, p. 49.

Hubert DAMISCH

INTRODUCTION

Americanism, which ushered in the political, economic, intellectual, and artistic cultures of contemporary Europe, emerged at the end of the 19th century as a constituent fact of modernity. Yet Europeans had discovered the American "scene" (to use the term Henry James coined upon returning to his native country after twenty years of self-imposed exile)[1] in its essentials a hundred years earlier. This found expression in a set of representations which—despite the condescending tone of certain authors—were rooted in a sense of inferiority, and even fear, given the formidable image of futuristic America (even if Goethe, writing at the outset of the 19th century, saw America's main chance in her very rootlessness). Georges Duhamel's *Scènes de la vie future* (1930), whose title I have referred to for the present work, is shot through with such anxieties. In this bestselling publication the author of the *Pasquier*, who had earlier assessed the dangers of the Soviet regime, warned of an America regarded as "omnipotent," and underlined the country's disturbingly totalitarian features.[2]

Unlike Orientalism, which, as Edward Said has shown, threw up discursive formations concerning a civilization deemed "inferior,"[3] Americanism involves collective discourses and practices rooted in an insidious sense of backwardness *vis-à-vis* the New World. The pan-European dimension of this phenomenon is apparent in the list of terminological variations, in particular the German *Amerikanismus* and the Russian *Amerikanizm* (recapitulating the Western-oriented attitudes of Peter the Great). Architecture, town planning, and visual culture in general were primary matrices of the phenomenon, which, however, also infiltrated the literary domain. Franz Kafka—who never visited America—espoused a latter-day myth when he had the hero of his unfinished novel *Amerika oder der Verschollene*, begun in 1912 and published in 1927 by his friend Max Brod, wander over an unlimited New World space crisscrossed by truck-filled highways and gigantic bridges.[4]

Since Manfredo Tafuri's remarks in 1973 on the architecture of America,[5] there have been numerous studies of Americanism, highlighting both its sectorial aspects and involving analysis of specific national representations.[6] In 1993 Hubert Damisch and I proposed a novel approach to the question in *Américanisme et modernité*.[7] The following pages extend that text's approach, attempt to systematize its problematics, and try to make good a number of its shortcomings (well-known figures such as Adolf Loos, Werner Hegemann, Erich Mendelsohn, and Richard Neutra were notable absentees in the work; Corbusian Americanism was not considered in all its aspects). The time frame is neither politically nor "stylistically" determined, but corresponds here to precise historical limits. It begins with the consolidation of Americanism following the first massive influx of European architects and engineers on the occasion of the 1893 Chicago World's Fair; it concludes with the Americanization of Europe in the 1950s, marked by the sweeping hegemony of American economics, politics, and culture across the old continent. The successive cycles caught between these historical limits were (as we shall see) largely determined by the two world wars, which together catalyzed both Americanism and Americanization. It is important at this point to distinguish Americanism—a set of individual and collective attitudes and representations—from Americanization, which is the actual transformation of European (and other) societies in the American image. Americanism rhymes often with Modernity, whereas Americanization is one of the principal modalities of modernization.

It should be understood at once that this book's aim is not so much to outline the incontestable "influences" of Henry Hobson Richardson, Louis Sullivan, Frank Lloyd Wright, Richard Neutra, or Richard Buckminster Fuller on the architects of Europe as it is to identify the global structures and thematic strategies that buttressed these formal influences. Today, Americanism is doubtless a planetary phenomenon. Its sway extends not only to the old socialist "camp," Russia included, but, in its architectural and urban models, to the "new dragons" of southeast

Asia. It would have been interesting to extend the present study to include Latin America, Japan, and China, where, from the 1930s, cities permeable to outside influences, such as Shanghai, began to bristle with Art Deco skyscrapers; yet the limitations of an as yet embryonic research precluded such extended coverage, which would have been less precisely documented than the European instance.

Far from existing solely in the age of Taylor and Ford and the initial phases of horizontal and vertical metropolitan growth, Americanism has experienced renewed impetus with the second industrial revolution. However, this text's scope is restricted to the first machine age, and focuses on specific European sites in which the most characteristic themes of Americanism emerged: Germany, the home of town planning, where social reform and modern architecture coincided; the Italy of Futurism and Fascism; France, whose cultural hegemony wavered with the influx of subversive avant-garde movements; and the Russia of industrialization, revolution, and cultural reaction. If we switch perspectives and consider the geographical sources of Americanism, the shifts in its discursive references, whether textual or iconic, become manifest. By a metonymic principle discussed elsewhere,[8] each city in turn encapsulated the substance of what Europe sought to reproduce. Thus, European interest shifted from Chicago to New York, and thence to Miami, before moving on to the great urban developments of the New Deal, Los Angeles, and the Southwest.

As will be grasped at once, the study involves scales and spheres as numerous as the vectors of Americanism itself. At the level of the city, the early planners looked for solutions to the problem of the extension of the centers and outskirts, while the manifestos of modern architects addressed the relations between architecture and industrial production. Elsewhere, planners and architects alike deployed their visions of mechanized cityscapes and tall buildings (freed henceforth from the constraints of masonry) right across the American territory. The theme of the tall building was a constant preoccupation well outside building circles, among travelers and readers of the popular press, but it was by no means the sole embodiment of Americanism. In all the processes of idealization or modelization, illustrations played a key role—so much so that the discovery of modern America might seem to proceed not from the invention of photography but from the spread of photoreproduction. Whether or not they were the fruits of first-hand experience, these images constituted an extraordinarily complex, living body of records, interpretations, and transpositions, with the clichés of the popular press supplemented by the critical notations of avant-garde photographers and the sketches of artists.

This vast corpus of images of the American metropolis transformed perceptions of its profile. In Manhattan, the Renaissance *veduta* (scenographic view) and the cavalier perspectives of 16th- and 17th-century albums were replaced by frontal views or views in profile.[9] The extraordinary complexity of the city's subterranean networks led to the general use of analytical cross sections. Faced with the vertical edifices of North America, photographers abandoned long-distance views for the dizzy delights of top-down and low-angle shots. Here it should be noted that architects gripped by American fever were both producers and consumers of photography. They supplemented their own travel notes, surveys, and snaps by buying commercial photographs and amassed reference collections which, though invariably intended for private use, became available to the public in a number of memorable publications. Aside from such architectural views, advertising imagery played a significant role in the spread of American products and consumer habits from the 1920s on; in 1950s Britain, it would inspire the critical acumen of the Independent Group and the dreamlike images of Archigram. In this latter phase, American mass culture as portrayed in magazines, movies, and comics played a key role (though detailed analysis of that role lies beyond the scope of the present work). In his 1939 publication *Usonie*, Jean Prévost intimated this when he made Frank Lloyd Wright ("a superb, ardent genius") and Walt Disney ("the man who never had a childhood") the two emblems of American art.[10]

Articulating both thematic and historical principles in which given national "scenes" are seen to predominate at given moments, the ensuing analyses reveal the existence of indirect modes of transmission from the United States to the various national spaces. Thus, Soviet perceptions of America in the period following 1917 were indissociable from Russia's special relationship with the Weimar Republic. Germany relayed the images which she reproduced and the documents which she translated, and German interpretations formed the basis for Soviet discussions and comparisons; at other times, it was the French scene that distorted, filtered, or boiled down these images and documents.

Despite the collective nature of the various currents of Americanism, individual experience strongly shaped them as well. Imported American themes and images reinforced the symbolic authority of certain practitioners, as in the case of Walter Gropius, whose early factories attracted notice as having already been made "available" in his 1913 article on American industrial construction. Conversely, Erich Mendelsohn's personality and his skill in appropriating and publishing unusual photographic documents (as in his *Amerika, Bilderbuch eines Architekten*) forced those involved in producing images of America to adopt new visual criteria.

The "Modern" movement's representations of America differed widely. Moisei Ginzburg hymned the "pioneers," whereas Sigfried Giedion placed the inventors on center stage, and Le Corbusier set the positive image of the American engineer against the poverty of architects practicing on both sides of the Atlantic.

In this respect, readers may be surprised to find works such as Kafka's *Amerika* and other less attractive but perhaps more effective documents side by side with projects and buildings on which the architectural historian must base his interpretations. The criterion is not merely a quantitative one, though the storehouse of publications on American buildings and cities is extraordinarily rich. More than skyscrapers, city plans, and constructional details (by which architects assimilated visions of the America that they rendered or consumed), it is the travel accounts, picture albums, manifestos, and theoretical texts which, in their indissociable intellectual and visual strategies, constituted major vectors of a shift in ideas, forms, and techniques without precedent since the Renaissance. Just as Walter Benjamin proposed, in his *Paris, Capital of the 19th Century*, a "literary montage" of scraps and tatters from the libraries,[11] the ensuing pages bring together texts, images, and project designs reflecting the rich abundance of ideal constructions, with a view to showing how America emerged as the capital territory of the twentieth century.

For many European architects, the curtain first rose on the American scene in 1893, when Chicago celebrated the 400th anniversary of Christopher Columbus's famous discovery with a grand Exposition. With it, a new vision of America began to emerge, though it was by no means the first. Some impressions already had been garnered from the centenary exhibition in Philadelphia in 1876, by fewer (though no less attentive) practitioners, and authors had already described the broad picture. The interest that Alexis de Tocqueville and François-René de Chateaubriand had shown in American monuments—reflecting in more ways than one their expectations and misgivings concerning America—focused above all on questions of scale. But even then, adverse reactions had set in. In the 1857 preface to his second volume of translations of Edgar Allan Poe's *Tales of Mystery and Imagination*, Charles Baudelaire denounced an "Americanism" which he considered at best to be "worthy of the nether spheres":

> It is a good thing to call attention, constantly, to these wonders of brutishness, at a time when Americano-mania has almost become a fashionable enthusiasm, to the extent where an archbishop has felt himself able to promise, in all seriousness, that Providence will soon call us to enjoy this transatlantic ideal.[12]

In the meantime, Americanism took on sharper focus through architectural production and metropolitan culture, with European critics and architects submitting their analyses to the professional public, as Arnold Dudley Lewis has shown.[13] The most eminent architectural journalist in 19th-century Paris, César Daly, who was director of the *Revue générale de l'Architecture et des Travaux Publics*, remarked on the novelty of America's buildings when he crossed the Atlantic in 1856, over twenty years after Abel Blouet had studied her prisons (the first type of building to be reformed by American architects). Daly viewed the United States as "the

This conception is somewhat like a modern mall

Drawing by Harvey Wiley Corbett (1873–1954) illustrating "La ville future: une solution hardie du problème de la circulation" (The city of the future: an innovative solution to the traffic problem), reprinted from *Scientific American* in *L'Illustration*, 9 August 1913. Canadian Centre for Architecture, Montreal

1. Jules-Louis-Édouard Deperthes, student architect. *Competition project for the Prix de Reconnaissance des Architectes Américains à l'École des Beaux-Arts: elevation of a "New York-style house,"* Paris, 1892. École nationale supérieure des beaux-arts, Paris

country to be studied as regards the advances of modern architecture."[14] Thirty years later, his son published the first important portfolio on American architecture.[15] Admiration and emulation were not, however, the only Parisian reactions. In 1886 the architect of the Printemps department store, Paul Sédille, who had already published his impressions of travels in England, expressed dissatisfaction at the "unjustified" picturesqueness of modern American architecture in the pages of *The American Architect*. On the other hand, he was seduced by American private housing, and predicted that "the rectangular and cold constructions will have their revenge on the charming habitations which please us so much today," and congratulated his American colleagues on the "unexpected" character of their buildings:

> . . . little troubled by tradition or the teachings of the schools, your architects have sometimes an audacity which is astonishing, but which also may lay the groundwork of a more modern style by presenting new solutions for new problems. It is the right, perhaps, of a young nation like yours to cast in the old archaic molds the elements of an architectural Renovation.[16]

The temptations of America found expression in architectural teaching towards the end of the century. In 1889, École des Beaux-Arts graduates living in the United States sponsored a prize "in recognition of American architecture," and in 1892 students were asked to design a "fifteen- or twenty-storey house or commercial hive." This height was not considered excessive, since Americans "practiced superimposition as if it cost nothing." Nonetheless, critics regretted that the jury was more attentive to "studies of a façade in the 'grand compositional manner'" than to the more interesting "floor-plan for offices," an example of which was taken from a real building and contrasted strongly with Jules-Louis-Édouard Deperthes's prize-winning entry, an eclectic post-

Haussmannian building rising more or less telescopically and cruciform in plan.[17] In the final analysis, *La Construction moderne* viewed Deperthes's project more as a caricature unrelated "to the habits of professors and pupils" than as a serious study.[18] A year later, the Chicago Exposition provided the framework for a radical shift in European attitudes to America, and rendered these early Parisian projects somewhat ridiculous.

1893: Chicago in Black and White

The architects, engineers, writers, and politicians visiting the shores of Lake Michigan in 1893 discovered not only the "white city" of the exhibition site and buildings, but also, behind them, a truly surprising "black city" of abattoirs, iron- and steel-frame buildings, and advanced mechanical and technical plants.[19] At the time, the temporary site, including both Midway Pleasance—a stage-set highlighting the world's racial and cultural diversity—and Daniel Burnham's White City on the lakeshore, was considered retrograde in comparison with the actual spatial and constructional innovations of the Chicago School. Louis Sullivan, its figurehead, thought the damage inflicted by the Exposition's "progressive meningitis" so bad that it might take half a century to recover from the blow. For his part, Henry-Russell Hitchcock considered the fair a contagious "white death."[20] Yet the view expressed by Claude Lévi-Strauss in *Tristes Tropiques* reveals the extent to which this "image of the Americas"—Chicago as the Europeans had discovered it—was still very much alive in the collective consciousness:

> No wonder the New World cherishes in it the memory of the 1880s; the only antiquity to which it can lay claim in its thirst for renewal is this modest gap of half a century, too short to be a criterion for our

ancient societies, but enough to give it, with its lack of temporal perspective, some little opportunity to sentimentalize about its transient youth.[21]

In no less trenchant explorations, as soon as Europeans ventured outside the Fair's perimeter, they quickly grasped the significance of changes taking place within the real city. Chicago's new buildings had already come under discussion in France, notably the "matchless" Auditorium Building by Adler and Sullivan, whose designs were published in 1890.[22] On this occasion, commentators remarked not only on the technical prowess of buildings where "electricity reigned supreme," but also on the potential of "a feeling for beauty" with the entry of women into the architectural profession.[23] French architects who made the trip

2. Title page of the article by Jacques Hermant, "L'Art à l'Exposition de Chicago," in the *Gazette des Beaux-Arts*, September 1893. Bibliothèque Nationale de France, Paris

included Maurice Yvon, Adolphe Bocage, and Jacques Hermant. Writing in the review *L'Architecture*, Bocage underlined the "advantage" that could be had "by following the meritorious efforts" and "the very real results achieved by this new, vigorous people, emancipated from servitude and prejudice alike," a people that could afford to indulge in fertile "experiments":

> And thus, we ought sincerely to admire the astounding feats accomplished by these pioneers in the city of Chicago alone, for having dared to build—upon a thankless soil, using unprecedented techniques and materials for their foundations and superstructure—buildings of such great height and such convenience in their internal arrangements and for having resolved the age-old problem of stability relative to economy of structure and weight by replacing iron with steel and stone with terra-cotta.

Could not their founding principle, i.e., rapid

3. Jacques Hermant, architect (1855–1930). *Residential and office building, 132 rue Réaumur: perspective,* Paris. From *La Construction moderne,* 1901. Canadian Centre for Architecture, Montreal

vertical communications, inspire us to similar experiments, in the business districts at the very least?

At the risk of being accused of utopianism, I would venture to predict the application, even to bourgeois housing, of a system of skyscrapers "reasonable" in height, dotted here and there along our thoroughfares like so many modern monuments.[24]

As author of an official report on the World's Fair, Hermant published his impressions in several periodicals.[25] He refused to consider the event as a "huge hoax," though he did express reservations about the showiness of its architecture, stating bluntly that each architect appeared to have "played at winning his own personal Prix de Rome [gold medal]." His unreserved praise went only to Sullivan's Transportation Building and Henry Ives Cobb's Fisheries Building. In his observations of the city he based his conclusions on the notion that "Chicago [was] America . . . the purest feature of a country where the preoccupation with money is everywhere manifested, concentrating the mind and reducing the acts of life to a single idea: one of profit." Hermant was fascinated by American practices, notably in the office, and singled out one type conceived "in a spirit of simple and somewhat savage grandeur" as characteristic:

> The [tall] *building* is construction *par excellence*, a temple of labor in which everything is designed, combined, and studied with a view to rendering work easy, agreeable, and as untiring as possible.[26]

Hermant also studied the "necessary adjuncts" of the tall building ("mail office, telegraph, telephone, and messenger services"), luxury hotels, and private housing. He was well aware of America's potential and predicted that "astonished Europeans" would one day "be forced to cross the Atlantic to witness the new expression (corresponding to new needs) which we are all seeking but which we have not yet found, paralyzed as we are by academic tradition and the mania of the collector, with his bric-a-brac and his needless repetitions."

On his return to Paris, Hermant strove to incorporate the new construction materials—he sat on the ministerial commission regulating the applications of reinforced concrete—and raised edifices based on his observations in America. His iron-skeleton building on the corner of rue Réaumur and Place de la Bourse was finished without partitions, "thus giving the department stores within a maximum of latitude, [in that] they can organize themselves according to their needs."[27] In this building, Hermant in fact initiated the search for what would later lead to Le Corbusier's "free plan." By comparison, the remarks which Julien-Azaïs Guadet included in his *Élements et théorie de l'architecture* were conservative, concerning typological and technical procedures only.[28]

Architects were not the only travelers to remark on the glaring opposition between the splendors of the Exposition and the dynamic character of the city. America's impact on the Parisian art dealer Samuel Bing during his 1893 travels is well documented. Bing saw in Tiffany's works his dream of "art nouveau," and saw architecture as the most original of America's contributions.[29] Like Octave Uzanne, the marquis de Chasseloup-Laubat, and others,[30] the society novelist Paul Bourget achieved great popular success with his travelogue *Outre-mer*, which ran to several editions and was even translated in America. Bourget's impression from New York harbor was that of "a pitch of intense collective effort" to the point where the city "[became] an element of nature itself." Looking down from the top of the Equitable Building and other "human beehives," he compared the city to a "table of contents of unique character." Not only did the Americans "make the streets walk," they also "made their floors fly" with their "sky-scrapers" and "cloud-pressers." In Chicago, on whose Porcopolis or abattoirs he expatiated at length, he looked down from the Audito-rium Building onto the city and saw new aesthetic principles embodied there:

> They scale the very heavens with their eighteen and twenty stories. The architect who built them, or rather, made them by machinery, gave up all thought of colonnades, moldings, classical decorations. He ruthlessly accepted the speculator's inspired conditions,—to multiply as much as possible the value of the bit of earth at the base by multiplying the superimposed "offices."
>
> One might think that such a problem would interest no one but an engineer. Nothing of the kind! The simple power of necessity is to a certain degree a principle of beauty; and these structures so plainly manifest this necessity that you feel a strange emotion in contemplating them. It is the first draught of a new sort of art,—an art of democracy made by the masses and for the masses, an art of science, where the invariability of natural laws gives to the most unbridled daring the calmness of geometrical figures.[31]

Following large-scale German immigration, America was visited from the 1850s on by German travelers such as the geographer Friedrich Ratzel.[32] In 1893 the Germans also discovered in Chicago the prodigies of modern industry and the new functional buildings within the Loop and on the city's outskirts, as witnessed by the voluminous literature devoted to their experiences.[33]

Deutsche Bauzeitung's coverage of the World's Fair, the city of Chicago, and American architecture[34] had a durable influence on German architects' attitudes.[35] From the turn of the century to the outbreak of war, Germany, as an emerging world power, would cast an increasingly specialized eye over a nation equally confident in itself and its future. The International Congress of Arts and Sciences, organized in 1904 during the St. Louis World's Fair by the German psychologist Hugo Münsterberg, who had been invited to teach at Harvard by William

NEW YORK
comme je l'ai vu

TEXTE ET DESSINS
PAR
CHARLES HUARD

PARIS
EUGENE REY, LIBRAIRIE-EDITEUR
8, BOULEVARD DES ITALIENS, 8
1906

4. Frontispiece and title page of Charles Huard, *New York comme je l'ai vu*, Paris, 1906. Collection Jean-Louis Cohen, Paris

James, led Max Weber and Werner Sombart to view the New World through their sociologists' eyes.[36] In the technical sphere, numerous articles by the engineer Karl Hinckeldeyn, a senior attaché at the Imperial Embassy in Washington, kept Germans informed of the edifying results of American innovation. But in purely architectural terms, it was the first skyscrapers and housing blocks that, as we shall see, attracted travelers' attention.[37]

The Russians also visited the Chicago Exposition and came away armed with stimulating lessons for the advocates of industrialization. The first studies, concerning American building techniques, urban hygiene, and housing, appeared from the early 1870s in Russia's major architectural review, *Zodchii,* and in its supplement, *Nedelia stroitelia,* both of which were published in St. Petersburg.[38] The topics covered in the pages of *Zodchii* were vast in scope. Cataclysms were a frequent feature, notably the fires of Baltimore and San Francisco and the new safety regulations they inspired; but metal construction techniques as applied to civil engineering works and public buildings, the transformations of domestic

construction, and the introduction of electricity were all regularly documented in articles, these often taken from German reviews such as *Deutsche Bauzeitung* or the *Zentralblatt der Bauverwaltung.*

Many of the Russian commentaries on the Chicago Exposition were written by advocates of industrialization, such as the founder of the Society for the Propagation of Technical Knowledge, A. I. Shuprov.[39] Specialist researchers into practical processes included Nikolai Melnikov, a polymath from Odessa who stressed the fair's importance for the industrial development of Russia. Some of his reflections concerned the exhibition envisioned for Nizhnii-Novgorod in 1896.[40] Russian architects and writers were commissioned by their editors to describe not only the Chicago Exposition buildings, but the city as a whole.[41] The radical author Vladimir Korolenko was highly critical of what he saw behind the scenes; like many European observers Korolenko viewed Chicago's abattoirs as a metaphor for the workings of American capitalism (in the manner of *The Jungle,* Upton Sinclair's novel of 1906).[42]

The publicist P. A. Tverskoi devoted some attention to the Exposition in his 1905 publication, *Ocherki,* in which he described the exponential growth and extreme diversity of the American population. He remarked on the number of lots still available in the city, adding that "with the exception of some of the new office buildings at its center, Chicago resembles most cities of the American West, in that recent additions of terrain seem more deserted and less built-upon than in most big cities." He was also puzzled by the inevitable contradictions between street capacity and density of construction, arguing in favor of a redefinition of public spaces. Prophetically, Tverskoi saw that "streets will soon act as a brake on human circulations and city authorities will be faced with the difficult task of reconciling the constant upward movement of the buildings with the ossification of street space."[43]

After 1900, Russian interest in America intensified rapidly as American business presence in Russia increased. However, Russian architects rarely traveled to the United States. Of the few available testimonies, the drawings published in 1905 by the St. Petersburg architect Aleksandr Dmitriev are especially remarkable.[44] Dmitriev was as much interested in the emergence of new architectural types as in the curricula of American schools of architecture. Yet Russian culture was divided over the American scene. While Symbolist poets such as Constantin Balmont (who made the trip), and Futurists like Aleksandr Blok (who did not)[45] vaunted the New World's industrial and urban potential, Maxime Gorky, writing in 1906, violently attacked the mercantile horrors of capitalism as typified in New York, which he termed "the city of the yellow devil."[46]

In Chicago, where he visited the Exposition before moving on to New York and Philadelphia, Adolf Loos conceived his idea of introducing "Western culture" to central Europe.[47] The exhibition left him feeling ashamed of the Austrian and German decorative arts exhibits.[48] It was the everyday landscapes and objects of America—and not her buildings—that Loos perceived as holding the New World's most useful lessons, as Robert Scheu reported in 1909:

> America was where he saw the light. He recounted how, saturated still with misrepresentations of beauty devoured in the art schools, he toured the artistic and industrial exhibits in search of the ornament he was sure he would find. But the country is young and treats technique with unselfconscious determination; it is a country where trees are felled in the virgin forests to make way for the railtracks. Human labor extends steel bands over cliffs and cataracts, throws telegraph wires across the great prairies. And it is beautiful. Dazzling in its

5. Gustave Umbdenstock, architect (1866–1940). *Two sketches of the St. Louis Exposition,* 1904. From an untitled album, 1904. Canadian Centre for Architecture, Montreal

beauty, the collision of extreme economy of technique with the wild green earth, with a word—style. But the whole task is indeed to extrapolate the principles of style, which can only be found in its elements, which the human spirit has first and foremost to assimilate and synthesize. And it is because we feel that Adolf Loos has accomplished this that we situate him at a level which his visible achievements have not yet confirmed. He glimpsed over there a style this country will not possess for a long time to come. Europe trails behind the Americans, just as our epoch trails behind theirs.[49]

On his return to Vienna, Loos shared his reflections on everyday life and social relations in New York with Rudolf Schindler and Richard Neutra, who later recalled the intensity with which the "Walt Whitman of Lower Manhattan"—his "first American father"—hymned the virtues of American plumbing and joinery.[50]

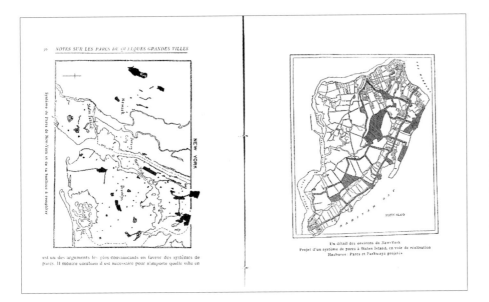

6. Two pages illustrating
the park system in and around
New York, in Jean-Claude-Nicolas
Forestier (1861–1930),
*Grandes villes et systèmes
de parcs*, Paris, 1906.
Collection Jean-Louis Cohen,
Paris

Americanism and Urban Art

Analyses of the American city were both architectural and urban in character. American architects were apparently perceived as "lifting" their latest compositional figures from the European Beaux-Arts practitioners in an attempt to embellish their cities,[51] while the practical modalities of urban growth and regulation in America began to interest the European pioneers of a new discipline, urban planning. The first years of the twentieth century marked the outset of a cycle of observations that went on for decades regardless of political events, insofar as they were largely unaffected by the First World War. A growing awareness of the specifics of the American scene, its buildings, and its protagonists—engineers, capitalists, adventurers, and liberated ladies—coincided with explicit proposals for the reform of European metropoles, to which observation of New York, Chicago, and theoretical urban schemes of American architects contributed.

Europeans focused their observations both on visible aspects of urban growth, as evident in the urban landscape, and on policies for the modernization of cities as expressed in urban plans and projects. The vertical momentum of New York and Chicago informed a new way of looking at cities: profile or aerial views replaced the Renaissance *veduta*, and the proliferation of subterranean levels brought the cross-section into play. The visual repertory of Americanist urban art thus involved new types of representation, which appeared in both general publications and professional reviews.

Major figures involved in the reform of European cities owed much of their familiarity with American urban operations after 1871 to direct experience. Between 1871 and 1879 the founding father of the Garden City Movement, Ebenezer Howard, visited New York and Chicago, where he was converted to spiritualism, learned shorthand, and witnessed the city's reconstruction. His correspondence testifies to an interest in the mechanization of urban space, notably that of public transportation systems.[52] Howard's "Social City"—a Middle Landscape designed to combine the advantages of urban center and countryside and eliminate their downfalls—was as much influenced by Edward Bellamy's novel *Looking Backwards*, or the land reforms advocated by Henry George in *Progress and Poverty*, as by the Chicago model.[53]

Another influential representative of the new British town planning movement, sociologist Patrick Geddes, discovered America in 1899 and 1900. His view of American cities and institutions was more that of a militant educator than of a journalist, though he did use American references in his subsequent reflections on urban and rural territory. Moreover, his project for the city of Dunfermline in Scotland, *Eu-topia*, was made possible by the generosity of Andrew Carnegie.[54] In 1905, the lawyer Georges Benoit-Lévy, secretary-general of the French Association des Cités-Jardins, was sent by the Musée Social to study American corporate employers' policies and union movements. Benoit-Lévy had already spoken of the "smiling life" of various American buildings in 1904,[55] but this time he wrote movingly of living conditions in Dayton, Ohio fostered by National Cash Register, or in Aurora, New York by Elbert Hubbard, plates of whose "vestals" he published in his *Cités-jardins d'Amérique*. Benoit-Lévy regarded industrial modernity as conditional to the success of these operations:

> I saw that the healthy, happy, beautiful cities were those where such model factories were to be found. *The factory's prosperity overflows into the City.* . . . Sound industrial organization and harmony between the various elements of production are reflected in increased prosperity at the level of the City and, subsequently, of the State. One of the key conditions for the success of garden-cities is a perfectly organized factory, which gives them their social life. The fact that model factories are widespread in America is one reason why I believe that garden-cities will soon emerge in this country.[56]

Occasionally based on readings of European, and especially Parisian, experiments (nonetheless reworked on a quite different scale),[57] urban modernization by the American Park Movement at the outset of the twentieth century found an attentive observer in the French landscape architect Jean-Claude-Nicolas Forestier. Curator of the Paris promenades, he investigated the park system design for Boston and other American cities,[58] and imagined a comparable layout for the French capital. In his comparative study, *Grandes villes et systèmes de Parcs*, Forestier explored the link between American experience (of which he acquired some knowledge in 1901, when the Senate Commission for the Development of Washington visited Paris) and the situation in Paris:

> Having dozed off in the wake of the admirable efforts of Haussmann and Alphand, who led us to believe that the perfect city had been achieved, we are now beginning to realize that Paris was wrong in breaking off its program of embellishments, of aeration, and in failing to foresee that its continual development would require a parallel development of open spaces, parks, and promenades.[59]

Forestier pointed out that the Americans saw Paris as a "finished" city, a view cited by Paul Bourget.[60] Holding up the example of America's garden cities and "park systems," whose hygienic virtues and positive effects on urban delinquency he celebrated, Forestier tackled the question of forward planning in metropolitan development. In the long-term global project he advocated, "avenue-promenades" connecting the various open spaces figured large. Forestier recommended close morphological definition of such avenues, distinguishing between the parkways and boulevards (which were often confused in America), and specified their role in the extended city:

> These avenue-promenades are key elements in any complete program or system of parks. They are pleasant means of access and communication. They allow for uninterrupted promenades. They can help to set off [the city's] viewpoints, riversides, and its interesting or picturesque landscapes.[61]

Referring explicitly to the park system of Boston, "programmed in two years and executed in seven," as well as those of New York and Chicago (the latter remarkable for its "wonderful increase")—Forestier cited a battery of statistics in an attempt to convince the Parisian authorities of their relative "backwardness." Twenty years later, while engaged in a study for the extension of Paris, he again praised the lucid and forward-looking Americans, citing the Boston parks system and the daring of the plan of the New York commissioners, regarding it "interesting to point out that American campaigns for park systems remained a dead letter as long as beauty and pleasure were the only criteria, but met with prodigious success as soon as health and utility were the arguments invoked."[62]

In 1875 the landscape architect Édouard André was sent to America by the Grand Duchy of Luxemburg as part of his study for the development of the capital, observing parks policies there.[63] The growth of the great American cities, as measured in real time by economists, statisticians, and professional reformers, furnished points of comparison with the situation in Russia or Germany, nations which

Semenov, who learned of American urbanization policies in the course of a stay in England, discussed the Park Movement and the City Beautiful in the pages of what became the first Russian urban planning manual.[65] As we shall see, Semenov was to be the principal author of the Stalinist plan for Moscow in the 1930s.

In his manual, Semenov published the 1907–09 plan drawn up by Burnham and Edward H. Bennett for Chicago's Commercial Club, a document

7. Ernest-Michel Hébrard, architect (1866–1933). *International World Center: general perspective and bird's-eye view*, 1912. Museo Andersen, Galleria nazionale d'arte moderna, Rome

underwent rapid urban growth from 1861 and 1871 respectively. The extension of Moscow following the abolition of serfdom was seen as "American" by contemporaries, and day-to-day aspects of urban management and domestic life in America became the subject of numerous publications, including those of Izaak Rubinov, whose comments were commissioned by the Moscow authorities created by the reforms of 1905.[64] In 1912 Vladimir

which had considerable impact on some theoretical productions of the first urban planners, including the Cité Mondiale, an American-funded project created in 1913 by the Frenchman Ernest Hébrard in association with the sculptor Henrik Christian Andersen.[66] In Germany, the New York parks network and the plan for Washington were cited as mandatory reference documents in the brief for the competition the societies of Berlin architects organized in 1908 for extending the Imperial capital, entries for which were submitted two years later.[67] But it was Werner Hegemann, nephew of Otto March, then president of the Ausschuss Gross-Berlin and chairman of the jury, who drew attention to the Burnham and Bennett plan. In 1911 Hegemann published *Amerikanische Parkanlage*, a general handbook on metropolitan policies, and an analysis of the plan of Chicago[68] in which he compared the prospects and tempos of Berlin's growth to those of the Illinois capital. In the field meanwhile, Hamburg's Stadtpark, executed by Fritz Schumacher as part of global transformations of the city, constituted the clearest response to the American experience. It is true that Schumacher had spent his youth in New York.[69]

With these two works, Hegemann ushered in a series of experiments and publications that were to make him not only one of the leading figures of German Americanism, but also a significant force in American urban planning. Consequently, the career of this eminently trans-Atlantic figure merits more detailed discussion. Actively committed to German intellectual life—his historical publications, in particular *Fridericus*, earned Nazi hatred—and to the international urban planning movement, Hegemann studied philosophy, political science, and history before his uncle by marriage, Otto March, oriented him towards architecture. In 1903–04 he was in Paris, attending lectures by the theorist of social economics and cooperation, Charles Gide, whose influence on Benoit-Lévy was equally considerable. He discovered America through the economics lectures of Simon N. Patten in Philadelphia, before returning to Strasbourg and Munich to prepare his doctorate under the supervision of Lujo Brentano, with a thesis concerning monetary policy in Mexico. This training left Hegemann with a sharp appreciation of public

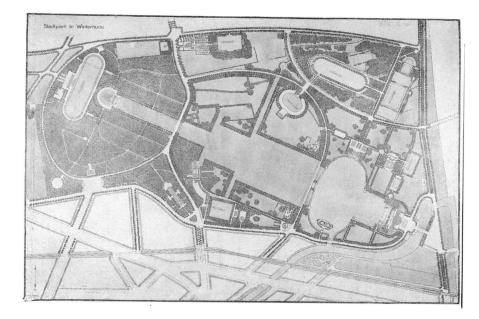

8. Fritz Schumacher, architect (1869–1947).
Project for the Stadtpark (municipal park):
general plan, Hamburg, 1909.
Staats– und Universitätsbibliothek, Hamburg

9. Two illustrations analyzing the plan of Chicago
by Daniel Burnham and Edward Bennett, in Werner
Hegemann, *Der Neue Bebauungsplan für Chicago*, Berlin,
1911. Collection Jean-Louis Cohen, Paris

10. "New York.
Fünf übereinanderliegende
Verkehrswege" (New York,
five superimposed traffic lanes).
Illustration published
in *Scientific American* in 1908,
reprinted in Werner Hegemann,
*Der Städtebau nach
den Ergebnissen der allgemeinen
Städtebau-Ausstellung in Berlin
nebst einem Anhang:
Die Internationale Städtebau-
Ausstellung in Düsseldorf*, Berlin,
1913. Canadian Centre
for Architecture, Montreal

intervention and economic realism.[70] Returning to America, he analyzed housing and participated in the activities of Edward A. Filene's "Boston 1915" movement,[71] about which he organized an exhibition in 1909. He next organized town planning exhibitions in Berlin (1910) and Düsseldorf (1912) which presented and elaborated on the competition for the plan for Berlin. At the same time he published two documentary works heavy with American references, in particular to parks and transportation systems, which were read with the utmost attention by young architects such as Charles-Édouard Jeanneret.[72] Elsewhere, he wrote of the "industrial district" as "an integral part of the organism" of the city.[73] Invited by Frederic C. Howe, founder of the People's Institute, to give a series of lectures in America, he declared that European urban planning was a fundamental source of American city projects.[74] Hegemann soon had a chance to put his ideas into practice. In 1915 he carried out detailed studies of Oakland and Berkeley before missing the boat back to Germany and settling in Milwaukee, where he worked until 1921, drawing up plans for the city with the young landscape architect Elbert Peets.

In 1913 Hegemann was involved in the debate sparked off by the 1910 Berlin competition over the usefulness of skyscrapers in that city.[75] Others joining forces with him included Peter Behrens, architect of the AEG factory.[76] The idea of a specialist City at the heart of the German capital had been voiced by several prizewinning teams, reflecting the visions of a specialist metropolis evinced by the partisans of the *Großstadt*. Writing in 1913, Karl Scheffler saw this business district as the heart of the "ideal *Großstadt*":

> . . . at the center, a logically constituted "City," a business zone which forms the nucleus of the metropolitan image, and which, beyond the forms immediately useful to commercial life, admits of no historical elements associated with the old city. In

this City, skyscrapers—office buildings comprising a large number of identical storeys—will have to predominate, if not completely, then in all essential points. It will be necessary to abandon regulations stipulating that the height of buildings must not exceed the width of the streets, and the most outstanding skyscrapers will have to be authorized around squares, on riverbanks, and wherever air and light encounter no obstacles.[77]

From then on, theorists and organizers (including the architect Bruno Möhring, who in 1914 founded a company intended to build a skyscraper next to the Friedrichstrasse station) strove to define these novel programs in detail.

The Vertical Dimension

Along with the skyscraper, America's infrastructure, whether theoretical designs or practical applications linked to railroad development, engaged engineers and architects. Superimposed street levels appeared simultaneously in the designs of imaginative architects and in popular publications. Reiterating ideas formulated a decade earlier, a sketch by Vernon House Bailey, drawn in accordance with Charles R. Lamb's instructions, proposed height differentiation for Manhattan—at a time when construction of the Singer Tower by Ernest Flagg, himself a visionary of the city of the future, sparked off considerable debate. This image showed sheer façades leading up to streets suspended in midair, moving from building to building on bridges, above which towers soared dizzily upward to eclectic summits. The drawing was published in the *New York Herald* in 1909.[78] Moses King's bestselling publications, *King's Views of New York*, included drawings by Harry M. Pettit and Richard W. Rummell, more lyrical versions of Lamb's principles in which impetuous airships hovered in the metropolitan skies.[79]

Five years later, Harvey Wiley Corbett elaborated on Lamb's idea. Instead of highlighting the upper levels of the city, he focused on the classification of traffic flow at street level and below. Two pedestrian walkways were superimposed above three levels for automobile traffic, a subway, and a goods railway. In the pages of *Scientific American*, Henry Harrison Suplee compared this to an assembly of ducts with various fluids flowing through them. Citing the example of the separate lanes of bridges over the East River, and of seaside boardwalks, Suplee imagined a systemic network of overhead and ground links between skyscrapers (whose employee capacity already constituted a headache for the highways department).[80] This idea set off an immediate echo in Europe. Some weeks later—at a time when the problem of traffic jams within Paris was becoming acute—the French weekly magazine *L'Illustration*, always quick to latch on to trans-Atlantic clichés apt to enthuse its *petit-bourgeois* readers, published an

11. Drawing by Harvey Wiley Corbett (1873–1954) illustrating "La ville future: une solution hardie du problème de la circulation" (The city of the future: an innovative solution to the traffic problem), reprinted from *Scientific American* in *L'Illustration*, 9 August 1913. Canadian Centre for Architecture, Montreal

LA VILLE FUTURE. — Une solution hardie du problème de la circulation.
D'après le « Scientific American ».

image both "complicated" and "highly amusing to study in detail":

Scientific American . . . has rightly observed how unreasonable and absurd it is to have mobiles (to use a mathematical term) of such divergent types and speeds move on the same plane. Do engineers, they ask, who have to build conduits for fluids of different types, have gas for lighting, steam for central heating, and water from the kitchen or bathroom circulate in a single duct? And would the railways have achieved their present state of perfection if, instead of building isolated tracks, they had been allowed to wander among the city's trucks or the country's oxcarts?

Division therefore: let us classify traffic in order to facilitate its flow. The street as such should be reserved for high-speed transport, trams, automobiles, and the few remaining horse-drawn vehicles (until such a time as these "animal engines" are sent back to the fields for good). For pedestrians, special overhead sidewalks. Heavy transport will travel underground, even below the level of the "métros" and "tubes." . . . We can imagine with pleasure what Paris might be like with one or two levels of sidewalks high above the boulevards, on rue de la Paix or rue Royale, and thus one or two floors of department stores—how different life would be, and of what increased value to buildings served in this way![81]

This type of solution had already been explored (though more modestly) by Eugène Hénard, an architect in the Paris Municipal Department, who in 1910 had presented his version of the "city of the future" during the London Town-Planning Conference, the proceedings of which received wide publicity.[82] In his own drawings of split-level boulevards for Paris, Louis Bonnier—another reformer of Parisian urban space—envisaged the vertical expansion of depth by superimposing terraces and underground roads.[83] In Moscow (where a project for an overhead railway was drawn up by

12. Louis Bonnier,
architect (1856–1946).
*Multi-level boulevard in Paris:
perspective*, c. 1913.
Institut Français d'Architecture.
Centre d'Archives d'Architecture
du xxᵉ siècle, Paris

N. Kazarin in 1902, complete with a viaduct crossing Red Square lengthwise to a station leaning up against the cathedral of Saint Basil), a series of postcard views of the "Moscow of the future" was printed in 1913, thus coinciding with King's *Views of New York*, with its ballet of airplanes and monorails.[84]

More plausible ideas for subterranean ingress included New York subway intersections, which Werner Hegemann presented in Germany,[85] and above all the construction of Grand Central Terminal. This monumental new station, which "recovered" railroad land by raising city blocks on foundations atop the train platforms, prefigured (on a smaller scale) the demarcation of human and goods traffic proposed by the visionaries.[86]

The sheer scale of the undertaking, completed only with the construction of the Waldorf-Astoria Hotel (which had its own underground rail access) attracted attention from all sectors. French analyses ranged from technical reports drawn up with engineers in mind to articles pointing to the fact that the station's architect, Warren Wetmore, was a Beaux-Arts graduate.[87]

These ideas and projects directly inspired the Italian Futurists. The terms of Antonio Sant'Elia's 1914 manifesto for Futurist architecture seemed literally to conjure up one of Corbett's spaces. Filippo Tommaso Marinetti's declarations landed not only speed, but "straight lines" and tunnels, while Apollinaire, in his "Futurist anti-tradition" manifesto, associated "Machine Age Eiffel Tower Brooklyn and skyscrapers." Writing in 1913, the painter and

13. Antonio Sant'Elia,
architect (1888–1916).
Railroad station and aerodrome,
1914. Musei Civici, Como

sculptor Umberto Boccioni sketched a general vision of an explicitly Americanized urban space born of speed:

Today we are beginning to have around us an architectural environment that develops in all directions: from the well-lighted basement floors of the big department stores, from the various levels of tunnels in the city subway systems, to the gigantic leap upward of the American skyscrapers.

The future will bring constant increasing progress to the architectural possibilities both in height and depth. Life itself will shape the age-old horizontal line of the earth's surface, with the infinite perpendicular in height and depth of the elevator, and with the spirals of the airplane and dirigible.

The future is preparing for us a sky invaded by architectonic scaffoldings.[88]

In 1914, Sant'Elia's considerations were fairly close to those of Boccioni. In his manifesto for Futurist architecture, he expressed disdain for "all the pseudo-architecture of the avant-garde, Austrian, German [i.e., Art Nouveau], and American" and defended every generation's right to "build its own city." The notion of permanent change—fundamental to his text—turned the city into an "immense, swirling construction site," and must be seen in the light of the rapid obsolescence of North American buildings, a fact underlined by all observers. Sant'Elia, too, cited Corbett's vision in a passage still famous today:

The house of concrete, glass, and iron, *without painting* and without sculpture, enriched solely by the innate beauty of its lines and projections, extremely 'ugly' in its mechanical simplicity, high and wide as prescribed by *local government regulations*, must rise on the edge of a tumultuous abyss: the street, which will no longer stretch like a foot-mat level with the porters' lodge, but will descend into the earth on several levels, will receive the metropolitan traffic and will be linked, for the necessary passage from one to the other, by metal walkways and immensely fast escalators. . . . Let us throw away monuments, sidewalks, arcades, steps; let us sink squares into the ground, raise the level of the city.[89]

While working on his *Città Nuova*, a project bringing together the threads of his architectural approach (two drawings of which were shown at the exhibition *Nuove Tendenze* and are clear illustrations of his manifesto), Sant'Elia designed a central railroad station in the manner of Grand Central, which had received press coverage in 1913.[90] In this project, the trains were buried deep underground, while the station building (whose roof doubled as an aerodrome) was hemmed in between the two edges of an urban space punctuated with regular blocks reminiscent of Park Avenue. It is, moreover, clear in other drawings leading to *Città Nuova* that the gangways linking Sant'Elia's vertical façades with stepped buildings and industrial

14. Antonio Sant'Elia,
architect (1888–1916).
*The Città nuova: terraced house
with elevators and four
street levels,* 1914.
Collection Consuelo Accetti, Milan

edifices also exhibited the diffuse marks of American imagery.[91]

The Futurist architects took Sant'Elia's cue and refined his initial hypotheses. In 1914 Mario Chiattone, a member of *Nuove Tendenze* who was in contact with Boccioni, designed his *Costruzioni per una metropoli moderna,* with its rows of streamlined skyscrapers linked by suspension bridges. His "volumetric studies" reproduced the alignments of grain silos earlier published in Germany.[92] Virgilio Marchi, a late arrival to the movement who was more a set designer than architect (despite his claims to the contrary), contributed a more impressionistic vision

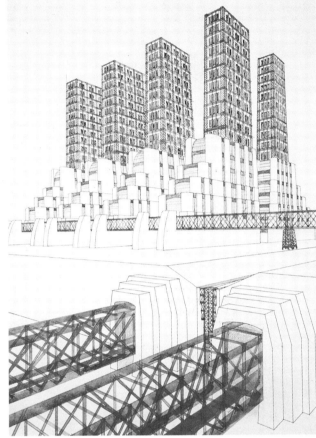

15. Hendricus Theodorus
Wijdeveld, architect
(1886–1940). *Millionenstad*
(city of millions): *an architectural
fantasy*, 1915. From *Architectura*,
1916. Library Nederlands
Architectuurinstituut, Rotterdam

16. Mario Chiattone, architect
(1891–1957). *Bridge and
volumetric study*, 1914. Università
degli Studi di Pisa, Pisa

17. Mario Chiattone, architect
(1891–1957). *Buildings for a
modern metropolis*, 1914.
Università degli Studi di Pisa, Pisa

of the subterranean city, one which exploited American models to the limit. His abyssal transport lines superimposed in the manner of Grand Central and his skyscrapers furnished the most striking images of the second Futurist movement. The multitalented inventor Fortunato Depero, who lived and worked in New York from 1928 to 1930, positioned a flurry of swaying skyscrapers above an intestinal subway network in his stage sets for *The New Babel*,[93] and reiterated this theme in one of his best-known canvases, *Grattacieli e Tunnel* (1930). Yet Italian projects inspired by the fragmentary research of the day (such as Tullio Crali's 1931 *Aeroporto Stazione*), by definitively dissociating transport infrastructure's elements, transformed them into autonomous machines with no real place in the city. Sant'Elia's approach was extended even further in Piero Martina's photographic portrait of Carlo Mollino, showing him in an aviator's helmet and goggles with a bird's-eye view of Manhattan in the background.[94]

Throughout the twenties Harvey Wiley Corbett, who had directly inspired many of these ideas, imagined traffic systems that would have made Manhattan a sort of Venice, with canals carrying vehicles and pedestrians moving along raised arcades. Redrawn by Hugh Ferriss and presented as a program that could be progressively implemented, these were included in the 1929 Regional Plan for New York and Environs.[95] Meanwhile, in what could be viewed as a new wave based on the aesthetics of the avant-garde, these ideas would inform Ludwig Hilberseimer's study for a high-rise city, *Hochhausstadt*.

MARIO CHIATTONE—1914

The United States' decision to enter the Great War, which quickly determined its outcome, had consequences that were as far-reaching in technical as in political or military terms. American industrial progress was first witnessed in the equipment used by the "Sammies," the perfection of which was much admired in European war theaters. The presence of American troops also directly affected popular culture, notably enabling the discovery of jazz music. In the industrial sphere, the consequences were less spectacular, to the extent that (as we shall see below) Frederick Winslow Taylor's efficiency theories had become influential even before the war. Yet America's role in the creation of the new European architecture was particularly important in specific crisis situations—especially the reconstruction of northwestern France, which had been devastated by the Germans—and was all the more decisive in that an intense period of observation and interpretation had preceded the outbreak of the war.

New Types, New Approaches

The artisans of new approaches to European architecture focused their attention on the new American architecture, revealed in part at the 1893 Chicago Exposition. As Leonard Eaton has shown, European opposition to Beaux-Arts eclecticism and the excesses of Art Nouveau in its various incarnations was nurtured by the work of the Americans, and led to the study of previously unknown types of constructions;[96] those of Henry Hobson Richardson and Louis Sullivan had come under discussion long before Frank Lloyd Wright's 1910 journey to Berlin and the publications which followed in its wake.[97] In an early German portfolio, Paul Graef contrasted Richardson's modernized Romanesque with the Beaux-Arts tradition.[98] Published in monthly installments from 1899, the 120 plates of Graef's *Neubauten in Nordamerika*

Charles-Louis Boussois, student architect.
Project for the Prix de Reconnaissance des Architectes Américains:
elevation of a major newspaper building for an American city, 1907.
École nationale supérieure des beaux-arts, Paris

The

Discovery

of

American

Buildings

targeted "practicing architects and craftsmen, who will find much to interest them in the ensuing pages, but also a wider public of art lovers, as furnishing lessons concerning one of the most significant branches of cultural development in America."[99] In his preface, Karl Hinckeldeyn pointed to several important buildings by members of the Chicago School, and to houses by J. Lyman Silsbee and Richardson:

> In architectural circles which have formed an opinion of American constructions either at first hand or by consulting professional reviews, contemporary architecture in the United States has long since been deemed worthy of observation and study. Given the number of those who in 1893 traversed the Atlantic to visit the Chicago World's Fair, and to discover the country and its most significant cities, this awareness has spread to other circles and generalized interest in the productions of American architects.

Hinckeldeyn, for whom Richardson remained unsurpassed in all respects, underlined the originality of American approaches:

> Unlike the educated layman, who strives to assimilate the building to be judged to a particular style, and who finds

18. Two pages illustrating the architecture of Henry Hobson Richardson (1838–86) in F. Rudolf Vogel, *Das amerikanische Haus*, Berlin, 1910. Canadian Centre for Architecture, Montreal

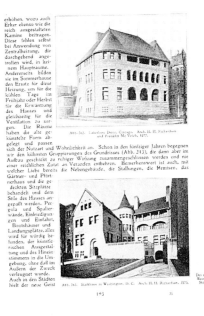

himself bewildered by the absence of such surface indications, today's professional architect does not consider style a priority, but proceeds with a more general assessment of the extent to which the means at his disposal reflect the building's uses and significance. Viewed in this way, the recent productions of American architecture can only inspire a favorable assessment, such is their practical, natural, truthful and spontaneous character.[100]

Hinckeldeyn lingered on American housing, where he saw women as exercising their benevolent influence—he thought public buildings uninteresting. Reiterating some of Paul Sédille's remarks, he saw American domestic architecture as "a happy combination of rational exteriors and efficient interiors across the spectrum, from the most modest naïveté to the most exalted beauty and dignified gravity." He also praised lively surfaces obtained "in the nature of the materials."[101] The Berlin architect Hermann Muthesius, who, in the course of six years as technical attaché at the German Embassy in London had amassed material for his three-volume *Das englische Haus*, a work that had considerable impact on his contemporaries, visited America on the occasion of the 1904 St. Louis Exposition commemorating the Louisiana Purchase, as did Gustave Umbdenstock, future professor of architecture at the École Polytechnique in Paris.[102]

The success of Muthesius's book on English housing led to the publication, in 1910, of *Das amerikanische Haus*. This was comparable in scope to the earlier work, though in the end only one volume, devoted to building history, was published.[103] Its author, F. Rudolf Vogel, exhausted himself in decades of observation, while his publisher's relative indifference failed to galvanize the results of these observations into a sufficiently ambitious format. As editor-in-chief of *Deutsche Bauhütte* and deeply interested in questions of construction and hygiene,[104] Vogel had discussed the model of the American single-family wooden cottage and the comfort of its fittings and storage facilities. In

I. Louis Hulot, student architect (1871–1959). *Project for the Prix de Reconnaissance des Architectes Américains: elevation of a convention hall for New York*, 1900. École nationale supérieure des beaux-arts, Paris

II. Attributed to Antoni Gaudí (1852–1926). *Hotel project: longitudinal section*, 1908. Archivo de la Cátedra Gaudí, Barcelona

III. Attributed to Antoni Gaudí (1852–1926). *Hotel project: transverse section of the room "Homenaje a América,"* 1908. Archivo de la Cátedra Gaudí, Barcelona

IV. Henri François, student architect (1875–?). *Project for the*

Prix de Reconnaissance des Architectes Américains: section of hallway and rooms of a California inn, 1902.

École nationale supérieure des beaux-arts, Paris

V. Charles-Louis Boussois,
student architect (1884–?).
*Project for the Prix
de Reconnaissance des Architectes
Américains: elevation of a major
newspaper building for
an American city, 1907.*
École nationale supérieure
des beaux-arts, Paris

VI. René Dubois, student architect
(1894–?). *Project for the Prix
de Reconnaissance des Architectes
Américains: elevation
of a university campus, 1921.*
École nationale supérieure
des beaux-arts, Paris

Das amerikanische Haus, Vogel retraced the evolution of American domestic architecture, identifying genealogies leading to the designs of Frank Lloyd Wright, which were thus presented to German architects before Wright arrived in Berlin, distancing himself from troubles in his native land.

Hendrik Petrus Berlage's 1910 visit to America awakened Dutch architects' lively interest in the Chicago School.[105] Berlage, a long-standing admirer of Richardson, toured Germany in 1911 and delivered a memorable series of lectures in Europe, notably before an audience of architects and engineers in Zurich, on the work of Sullivan and of Wright, "this master who has been able to create a building which has no equal in Europe."[106] Berlage made no bones about his favorable impressions:

> I have tried to give you a brief glimpse of modern American architecture by describing the works of the two greatest American architects of our time. . . . During my short stay in America . . . I concerned myself primarily with the work of Sullivan and Wright . . . I came back from America convinced that a new architecture is growing. . . . We Europeans certainly have no reason to regard American architecture as inferior. On the contrary, the designs of the best American architects show an originality and an imagination which promise a great evolution in the future. . . . American architecture should be accorded the high estimation which it really deserves.[107]

The discovery of new professional figures was not the sole factor in the development of Americanism after 1900. Continuous improvements in the construction and fitting out of buildings filled the columns of European reviews. Each new "tall building" was inserted into the changing picture of the competition for the city skies. German, British, French, Italian, and Russian reviews all contributed their commentary. The rapid evolution in metal techniques was not the only phenomenon; experiments with reinforced concrete also received considerable coverage, be they in Ernest

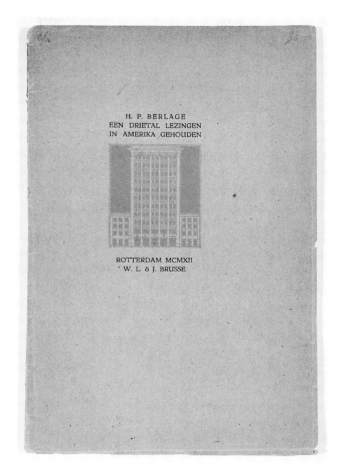

19. Cover of Hendrik Petrus Berlage (1856–1934), *Een drietal lezingen in Amerika gehouden*, Rotterdam, 1912. Canadian Centre for Architecture, Montreal

Ransome's factories[108] or Edison's procedures for houses molded in one piece, which Le Corbusier was still discussing in the twenties.[109]

Thematic changes in the yearly École des Beaux-Arts competitions for the Prix de Reconnaissance des Architectes Américains reflected growing interest in American programs, and its entries increasingly placed the latest construction techniques in an urban setting. Some briefs even required this. The 1908 competition for a "bridge at the gates of a commercial city" referred more or less explicitly to New York, and Alfred Levard's entry included a sectional plan set against a vertical city backdrop including the Flatiron Building.[110] Noteworthy among the more exotic competition briefs were the "great factory in Alaska" of 1893, with its snowy renditions; the 1894 "popular

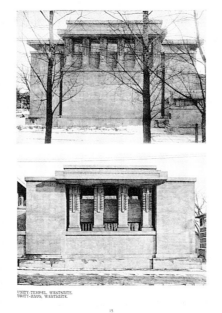

UNITY-TEMPEL UND UNITY-HAUS
OAK PARK ILLS.

UNITY-TEMPEL, WESTSEITE
UNITY-HAUS, WESTSEITE.

14

15

20. Two pages illustrating the Unity Temple by Frank Lloyd Wright (1867–1959) in *Ausgeführte Bauten*, Berlin, 1911. Canadian Centre for Architecture, Montreal

library with public baths and restaurants"; and the 1900 "New York convention building." The brief for the latter assumed "that an immensely rich New Yorker has launched a competition for the construction of an edifice devoted to large-scale meetings."[111] Both Louis Hulot and Charles-Ernest Duval presented domed buildings in the railway station vein, with accompanying belfries. In fact, tall buildings were something of a rarity, and did not surface again until 1907, with "the building of a great newspaper in an American city," in response to which Gaston-Émile Lauzanne and Charles-Louis Boussois combined the theme of a tower lighting up the city with that of a "luminous" newspaper. All in all, given their scale, detail, and graphic contextualization, these projects furnish a reliable picture of young Parisian architects' knowledge of the American scene.

The Hotel as Commonplace

Among the prizewinning competition entries, Henri François's 1902 "Californian travelers' hotel" included

a log façade and, in section, a restaurant in the form of a rotunda and sumptuous bedrooms—a mark of travelers' and architects' fascination with American hotels. From the outset of the nineteenth century, the prodigies of hotel life constituted a major social characteristic of the country, and life in the great hotels became what Daniel Boorstin has called "emblematic of the fluidity of dynamic America."[112] As Paul Morand pointed out, Chateaubriand had already shown interest in the inns of America, at a time when they housed travelers in conditions that could only be described as primitive. Chateaubriand wrote of his stupefaction upon seeing "an enormous bed, built round a central pole; [where] each traveller took his place, feet to the center and head outwards . . . so that the sleepers were symmetrically arranged like the spokes of a wheel or the sticks of a fan."[113] In an account of American travels, the Briton Alexander Mackay wrote that "nowhere in the world is the network of hotels carried to such an extent as in America";[114] in 1842, Charles Dickens described them in detail.[115] In 1852 the *Illustrated London News* published a view of the Mount Vernon Hotel at Cape May, commenting that "the building is so large that it contains 125 miles of gas pipes, or enough to supply a town of moderate size."[116] On his return to New York, Henry James was astonished at the sight of its "glass towers"; but it was at the Waldorf-Astoria that he discovered the "unprecedented use and value" of the hotel:

> . . . you are in presence of a revelation of the possibilities of the hotel—for which the American spirit has found so unprecedented a use and a value; leading it on to express so a social, indeed positively an aesthetic ideal, and making it so, at this supreme pitch, a synonym for civilization, for the capture of conceived manners themselves, that one is verily tempted to ask if the hotel-spirit may not just *be* the American spirit most seeking and most finding itself.[117]

Hotel briefs were doubtless the first to have directly challenged the ingenuity of European architects. In

1853 the French visionary Hector Horeau published a view of "an American hotel" situated on the corner of rue Faubourg Saint-Honoré and what is now boulevard Haussmann—a sketch remarkable, moreover, for the sheer scale of its glass façade, beneath which the horse-drawn omnibus seems absolutely tiny, though the distributions behind it seem more complex.[118] Twenty years later, in what may be considered the first handbook on hotel architecture, the Swiss Édouard Guyer pointed out the size of the collective spaces and vertical distributions to be found in American city hotels, for reasons linked apparently to the division of the sexes:

> In America the dining rooms are usually to be found on the first floor, whereas the sheer scale of these establishments would make it possible to place them on the ground floor, while the kitchens are housed either in a

vast basement, or on the ground floor, or next to the first-floor dining rooms. The reason for this is that, in America, quite special circumstances have to be taken into account. Gentlemen's habits require a considerable number of ground-floor bars (buffets), billiard rooms, and smoking rooms, whereas ladies and children require complete isolation, while being able to communicate freely between their private apartments and the public lounges reserved for families.[119]

At the outset of the twentieth century, images of the grand American hotel began to spring up in Europe, and notably in France. It revealed itself to be a primary example of the productions admired by tourists and professionals alike, and was deemed worthy of importing. In his monumental 1911 work, *L'Amérique moderne*, Jules Huret, who was writing for the general reader, opened his account with an inven-

INTERIEUR VAN HET
KANTOORGEBOUW
LARKINFABRIEK
TE BUFFALO.   No. 2

WRIGHT
ARCHITECT

HET „STRIJKIJZERGEBOUW".   No. 3

TE NEW-YORK
BROADWAY AND 5TH AVENUE

21. Two pages illustrating American architecture in Hendrik Petrus Berlage, *Amerikaansche Reisherinneringen*, Rotterdam, 1913, Canadian Centre for Architecture, Montreal

LE HALL JARDIN, avec ses larges baies, ses colonnes de marbre, et son double étage de balcons, est d'une somptuosité vraiment incomparable.

Les salles à manger des hôtels de New-York sont en général très luxueuses.

Les salons des hôtels sont admirablement meublés, décorés avec goût, et aussi luxueux que des salons de milliardaire.

Rien ne manque à ces gigantesques caravansérails, pas même des salles de spectacle parfaitement organisées.

Des alambics spéciaux, pour la fabrication du café absorbé à chaque repas, sont installés dans les sous-sols des grands hôtels américains.

LE BUREAU D'UN GRAND HOTEL est, à New-York, aussi vaste qu'une administration d'État en Europe.

Planche 11.

22. The Waldorf-Astoria Hotel, New York, in Jules Huret, *L'Amérique moderne*, Paris, 1911. Collection Jean-Louis Cohen, Paris

tory of the resources of the Waldorf-Astoria, "one of these colossal institutions such as can only be seen in America . . . a monster worth depicting":

> The veranda marking the entrance for cars and pedestrians comprises twelve large iron hoops covered with foliage; at night, it constitutes a veritable vault of electric light. The ground floor of the hotel consists of several immense and lofty dining rooms, each decorated in a different style and fitted out with small tables only, buffet suppers being unheard-of here . . . In every corridor of this gigantic caravansary, two rows of clients or passersby sit talking and smoking; anyone can frequent the saloons, the bars, the restaurants, the smoking parlors—everywhere is public. . . . And I shall not attempt to describe the incessant, antlike movement within the tea rooms, palmarium, café, bar, reception rooms, billiard room, or in the ladies' room itself, which is an exact replica of Marie-Antoinette's drawing room, with light colored upholstery, delicate, curved furniture, varnishes *à la* Martin, and Boulle furniture imitations.[120]

Even before the United States entered the war in 1917, observers such as the French engineer-journalist Victor Cambon envisioned a new clientele flooding across the Atlantic, armed with requirements unprecedented for Europe. Cambon hoped that "our gentle hotel proprietors" might be "better prepared to receive the Americans than our governments were to receive the Germans." The "common spaces for meeting and discussion, open not only to residents but to anyone in the city of acceptable turnout and bearing" fascinated Cambon, not only for their level of comfort and services, but for the "multiplicity" and "instantaneity" of their worldwide telephone networks:

> All this is fairly easy to describe; but what is less so is the cleanliness, the sparkle, the splendid upkeep, the precision of service throughout the hotel. No one who has not witnessed this can appreciate it, and anyone who has basked in its splendors can comprehend how difficult it is for us to satisfy people used to living in such surroundings.[121]

Kafka made his colossal Western Hotel the symbol of the social relations and "gigantism" of his imaginary America, while Huret recorded—in American fashion—its economic parameters (floor areas, costs, employment figures, production capacities, tonnage of food, etc.). The hotel was long to remain the accepted focus for the literature of travelers to America. In *New York*, Paul Morand, like numerous observers, expressed amazement at how open the hotels were to the street, but also noted some idiosyncrasies in hotel service:

> They differ from European hotels in that the porter does not play a rôle of majordomo, postman, beadle, sganarelle, policeman, and father confessor; often, indeed, there is no porter, any more than there is a concierge in a New York house. One never rings for servants, orders being all given by telephone. Clothes are not brushed and shoes are not cleaned unless one provides oneself beforehand with a valet, paid separately. Page-boys are known as "bell-boys," and each floor had its own "room service." Finally, a detail unknown to Europeans which often gets them into trouble: tips are not given at departure, but every time a servant comes to your room, be it only with a letter or newspaper.[122]

Hotels caught the imagination of European architects throughout the prewar period. Commissioned by a group of American businessmen and drawn up in association with the sculptor Lorenzo Matamala, Antoni Gaudí's project for a New York hotel doubtless constitutes the most extraordinary response to this type of program. A dizzy stack of limestone accretions in façade, this 1908 project anticipates some of John Portman's design solutions by more than fifty years, in particular the deployment of rooms around a cylindrical shaft, which becomes a high vertical grotto.[123]

Europeans were fascinated not only by the overall form of American hotels or their services, but also by the fittings and sanitary arrangements. Huret painstakingly recounts the ten electric lights in his room—"three on the ceiling, two on either side of the mirror, one on the bedside table, one in the bathroom, one in the dressing-room." And though Georges Duhamel describes his room as "my own shelter, my own burrow, my own refuge from this crazy town," he did not reject its comforts out of hand, even if one does detect a strain of melancholy here:

> I have a fine bathroom, a tap of ice water, heat, light, a radio on the table by the bed with six feet of cord attached so that I can go and come, shave, write, read, sleep, and still listen. . . . I can also be accommodated with a typewriter. Oh, comfort! I have it, it has me, we have each other.[124]

In his denunciation of the materialism prevalent in the United States, Duhamel ironized over "that fabulous bathroom which the economists and the sociologists vie in praising. It is the noblest victory of American pride,"[125] and his friend Luc Durtain was no less skeptical of the "civilization of water-closets and bathrooms" which he liked to consider ubiquitous trans-Atlantic features:

> Surely the inevitable bathroom, as indispensable to the American as electricity or central heating, will end up by cleansing the human brain of whatever resembles a thought and may inadvertently have adhered to it in the course of the day?[126]

Jacques Gréber and French Reconstruction

Vital to the Allied victory over Germany, the American intervention in the Great War also affected the European peace. While experts from the Rockefeller Foundation were directly involved in rebuilding regions devastated by the Germans in France, the city planner George B. Ford was commissioned by the association La Renaissance des Cités to draw up plans for the reconstruction of Reims—a martyred city *par excellence*. Park and garden policies implemented there before the outbreak of war (the renovation of the Patte d'Oie and the Collège des athlètes in Pommery Park) had already made Champagne's capital a testing ground for urban planning techniques; as Edmond Joyant pointed out in his *Traité d'urbanisme* (1923), postwar Reims was again at the forefront of planning initiatives following the passing of the Cornudet Law in 1919.[127]

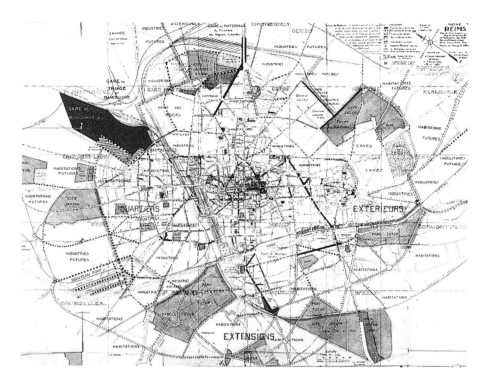

23. George Burdett Ford, architect (1879–1930). *Proposal for the reconstruction of Reims, showing the outskirts of the city and garden cities,* 1920. Direction de l'Urbanisme, Reims

the rise of automobile transport along American lines. Following approval of the plan for Reims, some critics began to consider Ford a counterpart to Major Pierre L'Enfant, who had crossed the Atlantic with his plan for Washington.[129]

Meanwhile, reconstruction involved another aspect of the American experience, the rationalization of construction yards for emergency housing. Policies of standardization based on first-hand observations of American examples were implemented by authorities in charge of "devastated regions."[130] In 1919, having been sent to America on two occasions, by the Commissariat général des Affaires Franco-Américaines and the Ministère des Régions Libérées respectively, Jacques Gréber gave a lecture at the Société des Architectes diplômés par le Gouvernement, the Beaux-Arts alumni club (under the chairmanship of Jacques Hermant, pioneer of Americanism), on the "organization of architectural works in the United States."[131] Gréber trusted that the Americans would pay back "a small part of the great services" rendered by France in furnishing a "brilliant breeding-ground of architects from the Beaux-Arts school." The main idea was that France would benefit from the experience of American architectural firms (which were much larger than their French counterparts) in such fields as component standardization and the forward-planning and management of construction sites.

A former Beaux-Arts student, Ford became interested in urban planning when he saw Hegemann's exhibitions in Berlin and Düsseldorf. A consultant for several American cities, he was one of the architects of the 1916 New York Zoning Ordinance and the theorist of change from City Beautiful to "City Scientific." For Reims, Ford proposed to doubly restructure a city flattened by months of shellfire.[128] While his introduction of diagonal thoroughfares was essentially Haussmannian, his division of the periphery into functionally distinct zones, and his siting of the industrial zones so as to provide direct access to railways and canals, were inspired by reforms carried out in American towns. With the publication of his *Aide-mémoire de l'urbanisme* (City planning primer) and a manual entitled *L'Urbanisme en pratique* (City planning in practice), both originally written versions of lectures to American soldiers returning from the front, Ford gave the French public a clear and concise overview of American planning principles. In particular, he underlined the importance of road networks, anticipating

If Gréber, who graduated from the Beaux-Arts in 1909—some years after the Prix de Rome generation that had devoted its energies to the invention of city planning as a discipline—is considered a pioneer of "urbanism" in France, it is less because of his contribution to French knowledge of America than as a result of his planning and teaching activities.[132] Gréber left for America in 1909, where until 1913 he worked as a landscape architect, first under architect

Guy Lowell, then under Horace Trumbauer. For Lowell, Gréber designed the gardens of the MacRay House at Roslyn, Long Island; for Trumbauer, he laid out the gardens of the Miramar House in Newport, Rhode Island, and the Widener House in Elkins Park, Pennsylvania. In 1913 he was commissioned (along with compatriot Paul-Philippe Cret, Trumbauer, and Clarence Clark Zantzinger) to design the Fairmount Parkway, which had been envisaged for Philadelphia since 1900. Gréber's designs gave rhythm to the new diagonal introduced in the plan for the city. In 1917 he was involved in the drawing up of a program for the global embellishment of the capital city.

In 1920 Gréber published the two volumes of his *L'Architecture aux États-Unis*, whose subtitle, *Preuve de la force d'expansion du génie français* (Evidence for the dynamic expansion of French genius) mirrors its narcissistic horizons.[133] Concerned both to serve the art and interests of France and to give France the benefit of American advances, this work offered, so to speak, a modern, trans-Atlantic equivalent of the Beaux-Arts school's Rome prizes. *L'Architecture aux États-Unis* was neither a treatise nor a methodical study, but rather a narrative—dictated direct, on the author's own admission—with illustrations in the form of somewhat static plates. In the preface, Victor Cambon, the discoverer of "modern countries,"[134] underlined Gréber's demonstration of the close cooperation between architects and engineers in America, and deplored the "powerful prejudice" that still prevailed in France on this subject:

> More than anyone, a French architect having practiced his art for any length of time in the United States should demonstrate the necessary *rapprochement* between the laws of technique and architectural principles. For in America (as in most countries) the architect's work, though clearly distinct from that of the engineer, resembles it in many respects, given the

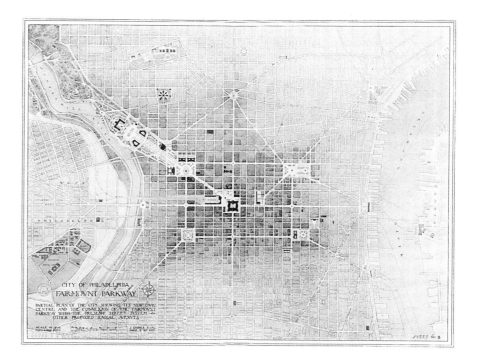

increasing role of mechanics, electricity, central heating, lighting, and ventilation in modern constructions.[135] Cambon underlined Americans' "emotion" upon seeing French historical monuments during the Great War, concluding that "since America has cut a figure in the world, all its architecture has been the daughter of our classical architecture." Recalling, however, the new significance of scientific management, "whose consequences will transform the conditions of labor throughout the world," he praised Gréber for depicting a living American reality to an archaic, insalubrious France, though he criticized him for failing to include "some of the beautiful athletic types which [American] architecture comprises":

> Browsing through these pages, not only architecture, but all American life unfolds before our eyes:
>
> Life of the first Puritan immigrants from Europe;
>
> Private life of Americans today, with their comfortable homes and sumptuous villas; [social] life, with its hotels, clubs, libraries, athletic sports; public life, with its realizations, both useful and superb, of universities, museums, parks, and zoological gardens.

24. Jacques Gréber, architect (1882–1962). *The Fairmount Parkway: plan*, Philadelphia, 1917. From *The Fairmount Parkway 1904–1919*, Philadelphia, 1919. Canadian Centre for Architecture, Montreal

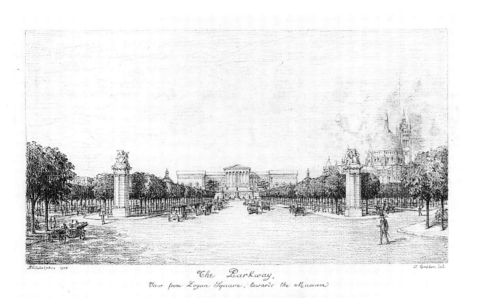

The Parkway,
View from Logan Square, toward the Museum

25. Jacques Gréber, architect (1882–1962). *The Parkway, view from Logan Square toward the Art Museum,* 1918. The Commissioners of Fairmount Park, Philadelphia

26. Two pages illustrating garden cities in Jacques Gréber, *L'Architecture aux États-Unis,* Paris, 1920. Canadian Centre for Architecture, Montreal

Gréber saw America as remaining culturally dependent on France, and American architects on the teachings of the Beaux-Arts. He shouldered the work's pragmatic typological approach cheerfully, acknowledging that he had not respected "the order of a theoretical treatise" in a strenuous attempt "to highlight the points characteristic of the most striking manifestations seen in the life of the United States." The work's historical analysis is fairly limited, in that Gréber—who regrets that "the immense territory of the United States has not kept sufficient traces of Indian architecture"—considered only the "colonial" style, Spanish and Texan missions, and above all Richardson's "neo-Romanesque school."

For Gréber, "home" architecture which, in the United States, "plays a role of the first importance," furnished no "clear evidence of French influence; the home is far too individualistic a program, and clients' whims may influence architectural trends."[136] Gréber's analysis focused essentially on the qualities of usage and comfort in the home. He recorded the "amiably hospitable" impression of American domestic plans, the role of the library and music room, and the existence of original spaces such as the "sun room" or "dining porch." Addressing the "mistress of the house" ("if she should happen to read" his book), he spoke of the "enormous surface area devoted to cupboards" and expatiated at length on the bathroom:

> The bathroom is a masterpiece: congenial, low-lying tub; conveniently-placed towel-rails that warm your robes while you bathe; a shelf for accessories at a height calculated to avoid banging your head in the course of ablutions; speedily-operated faucets; pressurized hot water, of course—baths in America are not the drawn-out ceremonies they so often become in France, for the caprices of the water-heater are unknown there.[137]

Gréber also underlined the "care with which the plans of the kitchen and its annexes are designed." He emphasized the qualities of "residential districts" in some cities, notably the New York "apartment houses":

> When they are designed merely to offer the advantages of the hotel, while guaranteeing the privacy of private apartments, they are perfect and well-adapted to French usage. They comprise beautifully appointed bedrooms and an ideal bathroom, a living room and, occasionally, a dining area and kitchen where one can prepare breakfast or any other collation. It is assumed that the inhabitants of these apartments take their

meals at restaurants, as do almost all foreign visitors to Paris. Should they wish to stay at home or receive guests, a restaurant annex is there to supply them with all the meals they might desire. Services are everywhere simplified.

 . . . The advantages of the apartment house or *pied-à-terre* are essentially those of program and not of architecture. It would be interesting for Paris to have a number of such buildings, which would be immensely popular, above all if their architecture were less cold than that of comparable buildings in America.[138]

Turning to "collective housing," Gréber discussed garden cities such as Forest Hills Gardens on Long Island, created before the war by the Russell Sage Foundation, remarking on the inventive use of reinforced concrete there.[139] But above all, he was impressed by the "working-class towns" built during the war, with their economical construction techniques and the variety of their layouts (within which house plans varied little). He enumerated the characteristics of the American hotel, analyzing both bedrooms and collective spaces, celebrated the virtues of silent heating and "rapid, spacious" elevators, and described the techniques used to lay piping in minute detail:

Ducts are invisible, hidden behind wall coverings, and only decorative faucets are seen. Examination and repair of the piping is achieved by opening a sort of cupboard or shaft outside the bathroom, more generally in passageways located outside the bedrooms. The workers, therefore, do not have to enter the rooms; leaks do not generally require decorative repairs and can be identified at a glance through daily visits to these shafts. In some intelligently studied plans, the shaft rises throughout the building's height, through openings in the floors, so leaks do not leave stains on the ceiling below.[140]

In his discussion of the "struggle for life," i.e., business, Gréber described the transition from the quasi-Florentine "block" with its superstructures to the "tower." He drew attention to mechanical plant and

the elevators, and to the fact that floor occupancy was "entirely elastic" since it depended on the "client's wishes." He noted the extent to which skyscrapers "well depicted" this competitive environment:

These three factors: the high cost of land, time-saving, and planned yield are reflected better than anywhere else in the American commercial building. In New York in particular, another factor must be considered: the land is both dear and inelastic, for its business center is naturally located to the extreme south of the city,

27. Perspective of the Civic Centre of Ottawa, title page of chapter XIV in Jacques Gréber, *L'Architecture aux États-Unis*, Paris, 1920. Canadian Centre for Architecture, Montreal

hemmed in on three sides by the shores of Manhattan. In order to build sufficient office space upon this colossal ant-hill, it was therefore necessary to multiply in height what could not be obtained in surface area. The rocky geological base of New York has made it possible to construct veritable towers, which elsewhere would require exorbitant subterranean shoring operations.

To these strictly utilitarian programming conditions must be added a specifically American idea, yet one absolutely in character, which is *commercial pride* or the *need for self-publicity*. A large bank wanting to construct its own building, the floors of which can be let out to other business, is forced to build higher than its neighbor. Do we not have the same thing in France with our novelty stores, which multiply their annexes to the point where they touch each other?[141]

On the other hand, Gréber barely touched on factories, limiting his remarks to the Victor phonograph factory in Camden, New Jersey and the Duplan Silk Corporation (originally a French company), describing their efficiency, comfort, and equality, assuring us that "the worker on the shop floor finds the same comfortable arrangements as the President in his office: ventilation, heating, efficient lighting, sound construction, fireproofing, hygiene." Gréber noted, however, that such factors in no way compromised the profit motive, here echoing Benoit-Lévy's remarks in *Cités-jardins d'Amérique*:

> Finally, the factory's productivity is certainly doubled for (without wishing to plumb their deepest thoughts) it can be seen from their expressions that these well-treated workers are far more motivated to perform well than merely to promote the success of their bosses.[142]

Gréber viewed prosaic structures devoted to exchange and transportation as having the "monumental dignity" of "purely commercial" programs. In addition to Grand Central, he noted the quality of small suburban train stations planned as "elements of the landscape." He also discussed education—fundamental to the American "melting pot"—above all the universities (some of which became "veritable towns") with their studied monumentality. In particular, he analysed the plan of the Berkeley campus, initially drawn up by Émile Bénard, and that of MIT. At a time when the plan for the redevelopment of the Paris periphery included a project for a Cité Universitaire, French interest in the latter program was, moreover, reflected in the 1921 Beaux-Arts Prix de Reconnaissance des Élèves Américains competition. Fernand Chevalier and René Dubois's prizewinning entries were both a series of buildings on open plan principles, combining formalism and the picturesque.[143]

For Gréber, who discussed both the New York Public Library and the Widener Library at Harvard, libraries were "one of the most beautiful social works of modern America," as were museums, of which the only instance touched on was the Cleveland Museum. He also discussed religious and military architecture, and singled out the buildings of West Point. Of the hospitals he noted the "applied empiricism, the studied absence of theoretical principles which appear to furnish the ideal solution and which progress subsequently refutes and undermines." He saw American administrative architecture as being most strongly influenced by French models, citing as examples Washington's International Bureau of American Republics (now the Organization of American States), designed by his friend Paul-Philippe Cret with Albert Kelsey. As for urban planning, Gréber pointed out that "embellishment is not just a *luxury*, it is *sound business*":

> The necessary effort that all the large American towns have made in order to win the right to be called cities is already bearing fruit. Built too quickly, their random layouts are now being revised so as to avoid aggravating their disorder. Their (generally rectangular) plans are being corrected regardless of cost—even in the city centers—by superimposing plans of the Haussmannian type, involving the injection of diagonal arteries,

public squares, and boulevards, thus improving traffic flow *and* beautifying city interiors.[144]

Gréber also discussed the work of the Commission for the Plan for Washington and its "large French garden . . . [which] will serve as a framework for all the Federal public buildings, and will be, if not as beautiful, at least as harmonious as the park of Versailles." He even mentions his own work on the Philadelphia Parkway, "a little patch of greenery 400 meters wide" deep in the heart of the city, and the "acropolis crowned by the Fine Arts Museum"; he also expressed admiration for the implementation of Burnham and Bennett's plan for Chicago. He noted the role of commissions, forward planning, and transportation, though (unlike Hegemann) he made no specific mention of zoning. Rather than a general presentation of American architecture, Gréber's book was in fact designed with a view to perfecting architecture in France:

> Above all I have striven to highlight those aspects of American architecture that furnish lessons adaptable to French needs in the sphere of technical progress and which, down to the smallest detail, will confirm the unquestionable superiority of our architecture—the first and foremost of all in terms of design.[145]

He urged French architects to build in America, but also to find there an "invaluable complement to [their] studies":

> Let us therefore attentively follow the developments of the modern architectural school in the United States; let us analyze its advances so as to profit from them; and if the results of my study make some of my colleagues curious enough to see for themselves, if my photographs or my descriptions have not been colored by my arguments, then I shall have largely succeeded in these aims.[146]

Gréber was in fact hoping that the study of American architecture—as a fundamental means of confirming France's cultural hegemony—would bring "improved study of the problem of hygiene . . . more complete industrialization" and thus "an increase in our means of material production." Gréber's American

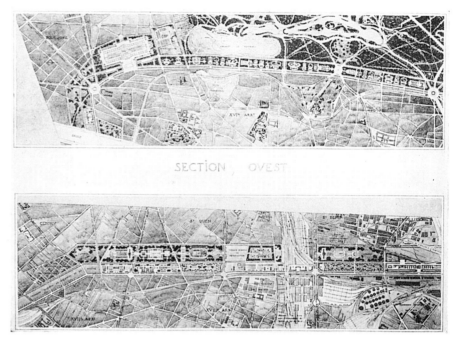

SECTION OVEST

ABOVE: PARKS AND HIGH CLASS RESIDENCES; BELOW: WORKMEN'S HOUSES AND PLAYGROUNDS—ACCEPTED PLAN FOR IMPROVEMENT OF OLD FORTIFICATION SITES OF PARIS.
Jacques Gréber, Architect.

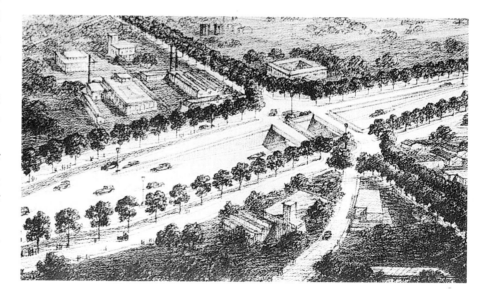

28. Jacques Gréber, architect (1882–1962).
Project for a boulevard on the fortifications of Paris, winning entry in the competition of 1919 for an extension plan for Paris.
From *The Architectural Record*, New York, January 1921.
Canadian Centre for Architecture, Montreal

29. Jacques Gréber, architect (1882–1962).
Crossing of the Marseille–Marignane autoroute in *Plan d'aménagement et d'exposition de Marseille, mémoire descriptif*, Paris, 1933.
Collection Jean-Louis Cohen, Paris

experiences informed his projects from the moment he returned to France. His plan for a circular boulevard, exhibited at the 1921 Salon des Artistes Français[147] and one of the most remarked-on entries of a competition held two years earlier for the extension plan for Paris, was rooted entirely in a system of "parkways," housing blocks, and public buildings replacing the obsolete fortifications.[148] As the author of *de luxe* "garden cities" in the image of what Forest Hills Gardens had become, Gréber incorporated his knowledge and experience of metropolitan America into plans for Lille and Marseille, and in his *magnum opus*, the plan for Ottawa (commissioned in 1937 when he was architect-in-chief for the Paris Exposition), in preparation for which he had studied Rockefeller Center.[149] On returning from America he entered the Musée Social and replaced Léon Jaussely as lecturer on "urban art" at the École des Hautes Études Urbaines, where he urged his pupils and those of the Beaux-Arts to visit America. Some episodes in his career, however, remain shrouded in mystery, for instance his role in the development of the Palos Verdes Estate in Los Angeles, or in the plan for St. Joseph, Missouri, for which he may have received a commission in the late twenties. On the other hand, he was certainly a consultant on the plan for the 1932 "Tri-State District" around Philadelphia, and for the 1939 New York World's Fair.

The Immeuble-Villas: Le Corbusier's Programmatic Americanism

The contradictory nature of European interpretations of American building types is evident in the migration of variations on the American grand hotel, which had received considerable attention from Gréber in 1920. One of these, the apartment hotel, inspired one of Le Corbusier's first manifesto projects. The mutual influences of hotel and apartment in America bore fruit at

30. Le Corbusier, architect (1887–1965). *Project for an immeuble-villas, axonometric and section* 1922. Fondation Le Corbusier, Paris

the outset of the twentieth century with the emergence of this building type, grouping two- and three-room apartments in a building equipped with common services. Designed for single persons and young couples, such projects were often designed by architects with hotel experience and were managed by hotel companies. They first appeared as a means of circumventing highway department regulations, which proscribed rental housing in certain residential areas of Manhattan, but which allowed hotels. A hybrid mix between large rental apartment buildings and hotels proper (Gréber regarded them as "a combination of travelers' hotel and home"),[150] residential hotels were innovative both because they offered the services of a grand hotel in a more stable environment, and also because they ushered in a phase of miniaturization in home equipment, in particular the kitchen, which, when it did not simply disappear, was reduced to the dimensions of the now-widespread "kitchenette." When the best examples were presented to the professional public, this program was assimilated both to the grand hotel and to investment property, under the vague category of "multiple housing block."[151]

Built in New York after a 1916 building height regulation authorizing progressive setbacks relative to street alignments, apartment hotels were located in large blocks, often on street corners, and exploited regulations to a maximum with superstructures as tall and slender as those of the great hotels. One Fifth Avenue by Helmle, Corbett, and Harrison; and Emery Roth's Drake Apartment Hotel rivaled the great New York hotels in both height and vertical structuring.[152] In his 1931 *Hôtels et sanatoria*, Gabriel Guévrékian hymned their virtues:

> Recent social upheavals have ushered in a new mode of existence inspired by hotel life, to the extent that hotels offer both private housing and the commonplaces of work, pleasure, and relaxation. Initial examples of "Apartment Houses" and "Collective Housing"

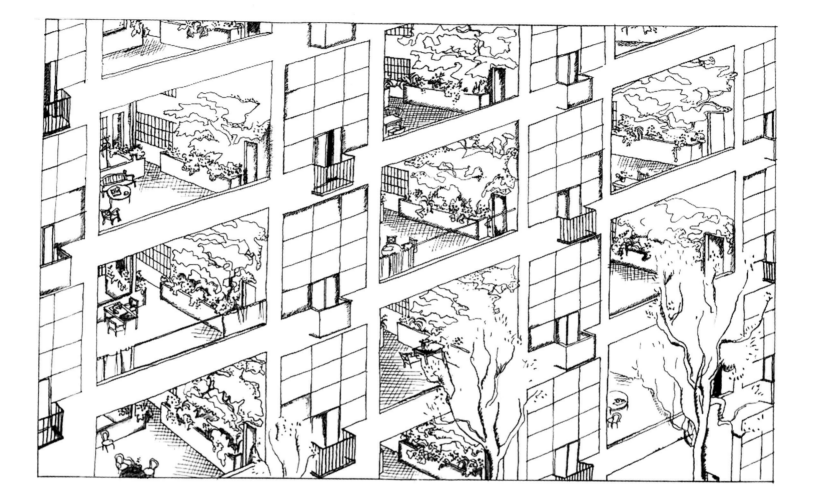

have proved most satisfactory, since the fact that they contain common services makes for lower costs, and less work for the inhabitants.[153]

"A New Formula for City Housing," Le Corbusier's *immeuble-villas*, was shown at the 1922 Salon d'Automne and he further developed it over several years. Far from being (as he later claimed) a "spontaneous" idea scribbled on a restaurant tablecloth, it was designed in response to a request from the Groupe de L'Habitation Franco-Américaine, which thus became the "sponsor" of his stand at the Salon. The group sought to construct cooperative buildings that would offer inhabitants "all the advantages of a hotel of the first order, together with those of a private apartment where they will feel perfectly at

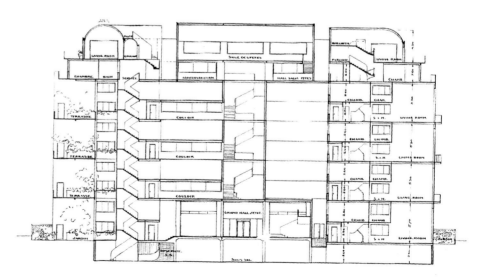

and pedestrian traffic, and in the principle of residential services as derived from the apartment hotel:

> On the roof of the building is a thousand-meter running track where people can exercise themselves in the pure air. There are also gymnasiums where instructors will help parents and children work usefully each day. There are solariums (the United States is winning the battle against tuberculosis through solariums). And there are party rooms which allow everyone to receive guests grandly and gaily at occasional moments in the year.
>
> There is no longer any *concierge*. Instead of seventy-two or a hundred and forty-four caretakers there are six valets on eight-hour shifts around the clock, who guard the house, receive and announce visitors by telephone and guide them to the lifts. They officiate in magnificent thirty-meter-long halls straddling the dual carriageway.[157]

For Le Corbusier, the "hotel organization manages collective services within the building and thus solves the domestic servant crisis (which is just beginning and is an ineluctable social fact)." The Groupe's buildings in Paris had hitherto been characterized by the extreme diversity of the apartment plans. Le Corbusier proposed to assemble, on these "closed alveolar subdivisions," 120 double-height units not unlike his 1921 Citrohan House type, with living room, mezzanine bedroom, and panoramic window. With his 1925 Pavillon de l'Esprit Nouveau, he succeeded in building a prototype of this "Franco-American system." His attempt to commercialize isolated units to be built on individual plots was a failure, though some elements later bore fruit, notably in the Wanner project in Geneva.

Received with both interest and skepticism by the press in 1922, the *immeuble-villas* were for Le Corbusier the starting point for a whole family of projects, in which the device of "hotel services" would remain intact despite variations in surface area or layout. His ideas were confirmed when he discovered "communal

ABB. 190. — NEW YORK. VORSCHLAG ZUR LÖSUNG DER VERKEHRSSCHWIERIGKEITEN
Architekten: Der Architekten-Ausschuß unter Leitung von Harvey W. Corbett. Vgl. Abb. 164—73.

DAS HOCHHAUS ALS QUELLE VON VERKEHRSSCHWIERIGKEITEN

New York war jahrhundertelang auf der Insel Manhattan zusammengedrängt, deren Gelände im Jahre 1626 den Indianern für 24 Dollar abgekauft wurde. Ihre Bodenwerte berechnen sich heute auf Milliarden von Dollar und das Chaotische der gesamten Entwicklung geht über die Grenzen des Glaublichen. Ein umfassender Stadtplan wurde im Jahre 1807 aufgestellt durch einen von der gesetzgebenden Versammlung des Staates New York eingesetzten Ausschuß. Der Plan war durchaus rechtwinklig und nahm keine Rücksicht auf das bewegte Gelände. In den sechziger Jahren machte der damals durch seinen Centralpark berühmt gewordene Olmsted einen Plan für das

Gebiet nördlich der 155. Straße, der allen damals erkennbaren Anforderungen des Geländes und des Verkehrs gerecht zu werden versuchte. Der Plan blieb unausgeführt; die geistlose Schachbretterweiterung wurde fortgesetzt und nur durch eingestreute Grünflächen gemildert.

Mit großen Hoffnungen wird dem neuesten und ehrgeizigsten städtebaulichen Unternehmen Amerikas, der Aufstellung eines „Planes für New York und Umgebung" entgegengesehen, das, von der gemeinnützigen Russel Sage Stiftung großartig finanziert, unter die Leitung des bekannten englischen Städtebauers Thomas Adams gestellt wurde. Es soll ein großer „Regionalplan" aufgestellt werden für den

44

31. Title-page illustration of a drawing by Harvey Wiley Corbett (1873–1954) entitled *New York. Vorschlag zur Lösung der Verkehrsschwierigkeiten* (New York, proposal for resolving traffic problems). From Werner Hegemann, *Amerikanische Architektur und Stadtbaukunst*, Berlin, 1927. Canadian Centre for Architecture, Montreal

home." Another promised combination was that of "style" or "French good taste" together with "the American sense of comfort."[154] In February 1922 the group announced the launch of a program of four buildings located in various Paris *quartiers*.[155] Acting on his own initiative, Le Corbusier proposed to create, on land lining the *boulevard extérieur* to the west of the city (on 400 x 200-meter plots replacing the razed city walls), a combination of housing and gardens.[156] The Americanist strain is perceptible both in Le Corbusier's vision of superimposed automobile houses" during visits to Russia in 1928 and 1929, and in lectures given in Buenos Aires in 1930 he insisted on the role of "communal services" in his projects, which he justified as being "common practice in all hotels of the world and on all seas."[158] In developing his projects Le Corbusier subsequently dissociated the notion of "hotel services" from the initial device of the *immeuble-villas*, in which each unit had its own private garden. With his projects for the industrialist Wanner the apartment units began to shrink in size, and this shrinkage went hand in hand with another line of research, involved *redents* or blocks that were tooth-shaped in plan, which had been foreshadowed in his 1922 *Contemporary City for Three Million Inhabitants*, and subsequently led to the type of "housing unit of proper size (*grandeur conforme*)."

32. Two pages of an article on traffic problems in America in Martin Wagner, *Städtebauliche Probleme in amerikanischen Städten und ihre Rückwirkung auf den deutschen Städtebau*, Berlin, 1929.

Collection Jean-Louis Cohen, Paris

Hegemann, Wagner, and Amerikanismus under the Weimar Republic

While French Americanists focused on city plans and specific architectural programs, German *Amerikanismus* was more complex from the start, and subsequently evolved. America's entry into the war in 1917 was viewed as a disaster by advocates of German-American *rapprochement*, Münsterberg for example. But this was not the case with radical artists like George Grosz, who at the time conceived of a mythical Far West where he had imaginary adventures, and in honor of which he wrote stirring poems.[159] His accomplice John Heartfield used a photograph of Daniel Burnham's Flatiron Building for the cover of the review *Neue Jugend* in 1917, as a means of criticizing advertising.[160] Grosz and Heartfield's 1919 collage *Dada-merika* assembled all the elements of the American "syndrome": office buildings, figures, electricity meters, but also businessmen's buttons and gloves.[161] Heartfield pursued this vein in cover designs for German translations of Upton

Sinclair. Subsequently, images of New York and Chicago buildings proliferated in the Dadaist and Constructivist collages, culminating in Paul Citroën's fantastic 1922 accumulation of skyscrapers, factories, and bridges, *Metropolis*.

Following German defeat, *Amerikanismus*—a phenomenon much discussed in the public forum—took on new significance in all spheres of German society, from intellectuals in revolt to statesmen.[162] The role of American capital in German industrial reconstruction, as consolidated by the Dawes Plan of 1924, provided a backdrop for the introduction of methods and cultural forms borrowed from the United States.[163] In this novel situation, prewar networks were reactivated. Werner Hegemann, who had spent part of the war in the United States, collaborated with the landscape architect Elbert Peets in collecting materials for a book on urban planning, *The American Vitruvius: An Architect's Handbook of Civic Art*, published in 1922,[164] the title of which was taken from Colen Campbell's eighteenth-century *Vitruvius Britannicus*. Interestingly, while Peets[165] crossed Europe in search of documentation on the urban spaces of the old continent, Hegemann went off to America in a literary collaboration coming in the wake of his study of the garden city at Wyomissing Park in Ealing, Pennsylvania.[166] Hegemann and Peets also worked together with Joseph Hudnut, future dean of the architecture schools at Harvard and Columbia. On returning to Europe, Hegemann became editor of *Wasmuths Monatshefte für Baukunst der Städtebau*.

The most remarkable result of Hegemann's reflections on America was the superb and exhaustive work entitled *Amerikanische Architektur und Stadtbaukunst*. Published in 1925, on the occasion of an exhibition of the same name in Berlin, this was simply an elaboration on the panels of the 1923 urban planning exhibition held at Gothenburg in Sweden, which had covered a large number of national scenes, and for which Hegemann had edited a more modest catalogue.[167] The presentational method of *Amerikanische Architektur und Stadtbaukunst* differs from Gréber's. Hegemann developed techniques he acquired in creating exhibitions and abandoned the use of autonomous plates, instead combining images and plans on the same page, thus permitting simultaneous comparative, synchronic, and critical analysis. The visual material was discussed in lengthy legends, which Hegemann justified by arguing that "brief, inelegant paragraphs beneath the legends may facilitate the hurried reader's task."[168] This impatient consumer may well have been none other than the architect in a hurry to find useful precedents and configurations.[169]

In *The American Vitruvius*, Hegemann and Peets reflected on the "plaza and court design in Europe" and "the grouping of buildings in America" at some length, including a discussion of fairs, campuses, hospitals, and civic centers. They also commented on architectural designs for streets and gardens, and highlighted urban plans they considered "unified projects." The aesthetic conservatism of their approach can be gauged by the fact that Washington D. C.'s plan formed the the book's sole appendix; but its title alone is enough to convince us of the historical scope of the American works presented:

> The spirit that guided Colen Campbell and the century following Christopher Wren is responsible for all indigenous art in the United States. It is the spirit of this evolution which the present volume is intended to serve. To this evolution America with her colonial art, her university groups, world's fairs, civic centers and garden cities, has made valuable contributions and is promising even greater ones through the development of the skyscraper, of the zoned city, and of the park system.[170]

The book's progressive approach is comparable to that of technical manuals on the "art of constructing cities" such as the classic *Der Städtebau*, published by Josef Stübben in 1890. On the basis of simple elements—the street and the square—Hegemann and Peets discussed configurations of increasing complexity—groups of squares or large public institutions—culminating in the notion of "unified design." Even if some of the plates were practically identical, the presentation was in diametrical opposition to Hegemann's *Amerikanische Architektur und Stadtbaukunst*, which targeted a European (mainly German) public. Hegemann focused first on urban plans—checkerboard or radial-concentric—then the civic centers, skyscrapers, crossroad intersections, pictorial unity of the street, links with the past. Then he discussed world's fairs and campuses, traditional houses and their heritage, garden cities, gardens, returning finally to architecture. Here, Hegemann's traditionalist stance again surfaced, as he vaunted the compositional and decorative qualities of large buildings by McKim, Mead, and White, while holding Frank Lloyd Wright's productions up to ridicule, for instance comparing the Larkin Building to photographs of ancient Chinese architecture. Hegemann thus set well-managed, metropolitan modernity against what he viewed as suspicious gesticulation. He also noted the German influence on American neo-Gothic architecture (as opposed to Gréber, who sought signs of Beaux-Arts influence), without, however, going to the chauvinist extremes of Stroh, whom he criticized.

The broad spectrum of German *Amerikanismus* can be measured by the gulf separating Hegemann (and critic Walter Curt Behrendt)[171] and Berlin's Social Democratic city planning director, Martin Wagner. A driving force behind the "social construction programs" inaugurated in the first years of the Weimar Republic and a nemesis for Hegemann, who mounted a campaign against his project for the Berlin Expo, Wagner initiated the *Siedlungen* programs built by Bruno Taut in the German capital during the twenties. In his *Amerikanische Bauwirtschaft* (American Building Economy), published following a trade union-financed visit to America in September–October 1924, Wagner studied the practical aspects of rationalization within the American building industry, regretting that the forms of socialization he had been elaborating since 1918 were only timidly applied there.[172]

In 1929, when Wagner returned to America accompanied by fellow Social Democrat Ernst Reuter, Transportation Director for the city of Berlin, he became involved in negotiations with American investors for the construction of housing estates in Berlin (in 1927 he had negotiated the Chapman project for the construction of 14,000 housing units at Schönberg). Wagner also took an active interest in the transformations of Berlin, developing the idea of specialized districts (which had begun to appear before 1914), while at the same time attempting to define new relations between space financed pri-

vately and that financed by the public sector. During his 1929 travels he studied the mechanisms involved in the "production" of American cities, notably traffic management and the notion of the rapid obsolescence of commercial buildings, two questions relevant to the development of the *Weltstadt* (world city) which Berlin aimed to become, before it suffered the terrible effects of economic crisis.[173]

33. Cover of Walter Curt Behrendt, *Städtebau und Wohnungswesen in den Vereinigten Staaten* (Urban planning and housing in the United States), Berlin, 1926. Collection Jean-Louis Cohen, Paris

An American industrial presence in European cities was already evident before the Great War. Symptomatically (and illegally) in St. Petersburg, the sphere atop the Nevsky Prospect's tallest structure—the Singer Building— rose above the Winter Palace's cornice. In the decade after the war, the reconstruction and modernization of Europe called not only for the reorganization of its industries on American lines, but for a generalization of the machine age paradigm. In the "vacuum-cleaning" process (to use Amédée Ozenfant's words) embraced by the radical architects, American industry was influential in terms of both its buildings and its organizational methods. Celebrations of the American machine featured in the discourse of all the European avant-gardes, from Paris to Frankfurt to Berlin to Moscow.

American Industrial Buildings and the Avant-Garde

With an article published in the 1913 *Jahrbuch* of the Deutsche Werkbund, Walter Gropius became one of the very first architects of the rising generation to discuss American industrial construction techniques. The photographic documentation for this text (until then unpublished in Europe) appears to have been given to Gropius by Karl Benscheidt, the industrialist who had recently commissioned him to build the Fagus Factory at Alfeld-an-der-Leine—a building which, with its wide bays and glazed corners, the strong horizontal lines of its yellow brick courses and metal acroterion, conjured up the large American factories published in the *Jahrbuch*. In his article, Gropius discussed not only the grain elevators (Rudyard Kipling, passing through Buffalo in 1889, had seen these "nightmare buildings"),[174] but a whole range of American industrial monuments:

Walter Gropius (1883–1969) and Adolf Meyer (1881–1929), architects. *Fagus Factory, Alfred/Leine: perspective from the southwest*, 1910–11. The Busch-Reisinger Harvard University Art Museums, Cambridge, Mass.

The "Motherland of Industry"

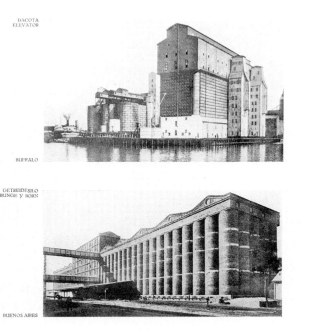

34. Photographs of industrial buildings illustrating the article by Walter Gropius "Die Entwicklung moderner Industriebaukunst" (The development of modern industrial architecture), in *Die Kunst in Industrie und Handel, Jahrbuch des deutschen Werkbundes*, Iena, 1913. Canadian Centre for Architecture, Montreal

Germany seems to have gained the lead in the field of artistic factory buildings in comparison with other European countries. But in the motherland of industry, in America, there are industrial complexes whose unknown majesty surpasses even the very best of our German buildings of this kind. The grain elevators of Canada and South America, the coal bunkers of the big railroads, and the most recent work halls of the North American industrial corporations impress one as having a monumental strength that can almost stand comparison with the buildings of ancient Egypt. They have an architectural image of such convincing impact that the spectator cannot help but grasp the meaning of the building. What these buildings are is self-evident, and their monumental effect cannot be explained as inherent in their size. It seems that their designers have retained an independent, healthy, and pure feeling for massive, compact, and integrated forms. Therein lies for us a valuable hint: that we should abandon our historical nostalgia and any other intel-lectual considerations which dim our modern European artistic creativity and obstruct our artistic immediacy.[175]

Gropius's commentaries on the grain elevators and factories of Buffalo and Detroit marked the beginnings of a new monumentality that inspired his own industrial projects, such as the Fagus Factory and the model factory constructed for the 1913 Werkbund exhibition. A series of texts followed, principally by Le Corbusier in *L'Esprit nouveau* and *Vers une architecture*, and Moisei Ginzburg in the Moscow review *Arkhitektura* and in his book *Stil i Epokha*. The images of industrial America circulated well outside radical circles and even reached conservative architects, particularly in Germany.[176] Nor were such images an architectural monopoly. As Reyner Banham pointed out in his study *A Concrete Atlantis*,[177] the art historian Wilhelm Worringer, writing in 1927, also regarded the Buffalo silos as modern echoes of the monuments of ancient Greece.[178]

The Expressionist Erich Mendelsohn also reflected on American industrial architecture; from 1914 he sketched a series of imaginary factories, docks, and railroad stations that was exhibited in 1919 at Paul Cassirer's gallery in Berlin. On this occasion he gave a lecture entitled "The Problem of a New Architecture" before the Arbeitsrat für Kunst, a group formed after 1918. First contrasting slides of large metallic market halls built at the turn of the century with his own fantastic drawings, Mendelsohn then showed pictures of grain elevators and Wright's Larkin Building, vaunting the "expressive effects" of the former:

> The group of grain silos in Buffalo masters its spatial components by deploying within its spaces modern construction techniques and technical assemblages of large massings, which seem the result of mathematical pragmatism.

Though critical of the rigidity of the Buffalo constructions, Mendelsohn saw the intense spatial effects of Wright's building as expressing a collective power that transcended the narrow-mindedness of modern Functionalist architecture:

On the building's exterior, the brick masses of staircase towers draw light into the vertical niches, their undivided rise pulling all the floors up evenly into their angular tendency toward stone.

In the interior the thrust of the piers rises up to just under the glass ceiling. Here the clarity of the construction, its apparent severity, points to the usefulness of calculated functionality in creativity, for it draws exterior and interior into its rhythm, and the lighting and metal furniture of the hall are drawn into a successful relation of mass and light.

Such endeavors give evidence of the spontaneity of the yearning for form that is no longer the privilege of an individual talent, but is already the instinct of a society that is struggling for its future.[179]

Interest in the industrial buildings of the United States was not, however, restricted to Germany; a similar curiosity seems to have characterized French discourses of an anti-Germanic character, as when the poet Jean Cocteau conjured up the image of grain elevators and machinery in his 1918 publication *Le coq et l'arlequin*.

35. Walter Gropius, architect (1883–1969) and Adolf Meyer, architect (1881-1929). *Fagus Factory, Alfred/Leine: perspective from the southwest,* 1910–11. The Busch-Reisinger Harvard University Art Museums, Cambridge, Mass.

36. Walter Gropius
(1883–1969) and Adolf Meyer
(1881–1929), architects.
*Model factory and office building
for the Werkbund Exhibition,
Cologne: perspective,* 1914.
The Busch-Reisinger Harvard
University Art Museums,
Cambridge, Mass.

American plants and machinery resemble Greek art insofar as utility lends them a spareness and grandeur free of frills. But that is not art. The role of art involves grasping the meaning of these times, discovering in the spectacle of practical spareness an antidote to non-utilitarian beauty which only encourages frills.[180]

We know how keen Le Corbusier was to promulgate the virtues of the grain silos, which took on almost ethical status in his thought. In *L'Esprit nouveau* he compared the chaos of the suburbs with these ordered industrial cathedrals, reprinting some of the photographs used by Gropius in 1913. The illustrations for Le Corbusier's *3 rappels à MM. les architectes* were also quite familiar to some European architects, who were therefore much surprised to find them slightly modified. The row of triangular pediments atop the silos at Buenos Aires had been painted over in gouache, an act for which Le Corbusier's accomplice, Amédée Ozenfant, claimed credit. In his *Mémoires,* Ozenfant recalled their mutual interest in grain elevators, and

claimed to have been given photographs of them by the writer Henri-Pierre Roché on his return from America. Like Gropius and Worringer, he, too, emphasized the Egyptian character of "these monumental edifices, at the time quite unknown in French artistic circles":

I was struck by their majesty, some of them almost having the size and impact of the temples of Luxor, as well as being admirably sober in form—very purist, though unintentionally so. This was not the work of artists, but of anonymous engineers. *Function* was greatly satisfied thanks to excellent cooperation between the forces involved in the equation *function* and *construction.* This willing association produced satisfactory forms like many of those Nature created on her own. Here and there, of course, these powerful batteries of monumental cylinders—like so many castle keeps—were crowned with Greek-style pediments. The engineer, or some architect hanging around the drafting table, must have wanted to "embellish" the technicians' pure work, as though one could embellish an egg . . . I eliminated these outgrowths with gouache, so that everything attained—or rather returned to—its pure state.[181]

One of Le Corbusier's more assiduous readers, Moisei Ginzburg, who in 1923 celebrated the plastic qualities of the grain elevators of Detroit in the pages of the review *Arkhitektura*, found similar virtues in American factories: in his book *Stil i Epokha*, published the following year, they take on the status of *Gesamtkunstwerke* (total artworks) of the machine age:

> The factory is the most natural consequence of the development of the machine. It unites within itself a whole assembly of machines, which are sometimes homogeneous, but always bound together by one and the same common purpose. Such an assembly of machines is imbued by a movement that is infinitely more intense than that of each individual machine; at the same time, the heterogeneous machines that are united by one common purpose are an example of an even more striking and orderly compositional organization.[182]

According to Ginzburg, the rhythms that take hold of these machine assemblies reflected a "monumental movement" which, however, was not restricted to the internal spaces of industrial shelters:

> The factory envelops this monumental movement, representing a grandiose envelope for it, and must certainly express all of its characteristic aspects. On the other hand, it already represents a kind of housing—true, a housing more for labor and machines than for man, but housing nevertheless—i.e., a veritable work of architecture, with all its spatial characteristics; hence, an analysis of such industrial structures should be of great importance to us.[183]

The factory's relationship to the environment gives rise to a dimension of collective utility which Georges Benoit-Lévy had noticed and commented on in *Cités-jardins d'Amérique*, in which he waxes lyrical over General Electric's factory "park" at Schenectady.[184] This admiration found an echo in

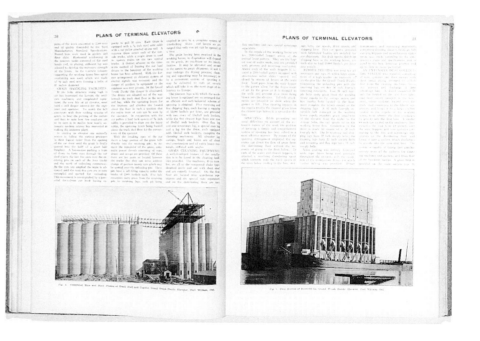

37. Silos and grain elevators in Canada. From Le Corbusier, "Trois rappels à MM. les Architectes. Le volume," in *Vers une architecture*, Paris, 1923. Canadian Centre for Architecture, Montreal

38. Two pages illustrating grain elevators in the *Grain Dealer Journal*, Chicago, 1913, Collection Marc Dessauce, New York

39. Two images of grain elevators in the city of Buffalo. From Moisei Ginzburg, "Estetika sovremennosti," in *Arkhitektura*, 1923. Getty Center, Resource Collections, Santa Monica

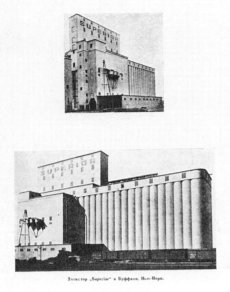

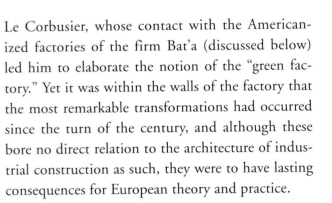

40. Iakov Chernikhov, architect (1889–1951). Elevator and grain factory, 1923. From *Konstruktsiia arkhitekturnykh i mashinnyk form* (Construction of architectural and mechanical forms), Leningrad, 1931. Canadian Centre for Architecture, Montreal

Le Corbusier, whose contact with the Americanized factories of the firm Bat'a (discussed below) led him to elaborate the notion of the "green factory." Yet it was within the walls of the factory that the most remarkable transformations had occurred since the turn of the century, and although these bore no direct relation to the architecture of industrial construction as such, they were to have lasting consequences for European theory and practice.

Taylorism and Architecture

The dangers of the accelerating rhythms of labor in the United States were perceived before the end of the 19th century. Friedrich Nietzsche wrote that "The Americans, worn out, worn out too fast, perhaps only seem a future world power."[185] Elsewhere he commented:

> There is an Indian savagery, a savagery peculiar to the Indian blood, in the manner in which the Americans strive after gold: and the breathless hurry of their work—the characteristic vice of the New World— already begins to infect old Europe, and makes it savage also, spreading over it a strange lack of intellectuality. . . . And just as all form obviously disappears in this hurry of workers, so the sense for form itself, the ear and the eye for the melody of movement, also disappear.[186]

More than factory exteriors, photographs of which flooded reviews in Germany, Paris, and Moscow (to a certain extent giving the lie to Nietzsche's remarks) it was the organization of Taylorized and Fordized enterprise that fashioned architectural thinking in the wake of the Great War. "Scientific management" as pioneered by Frederick Winslow Taylor, whose early texts had been translated throughout Europe before the war, was henceforth combined with a Fordist wave sparked off by the Detroit industrialist's autobiography, whose message engulfed all industry.

Some improvements in industrial production had certainly been achieved before Taylor's experiments; in the last thirty years of the 19th century, considerable effort had been made to bring methods of study and calculation to the shop floor.[187] A global analysis of pre-Taylorist rationalization policies in the industrial sphere and architects' perceptions of those policies has yet to be carried out.[188] Here, I shall simply recall the basic doctrinal principles underlying Taylorist and Fordist rationalization, briefly pointing out some distinctions between the two.

The fruit of experiments carried out by Taylor in industries located in the eastern United States,[189] and informed by Frank Gilbreth's work on diagrams of movement, "scientific management" infused all the industrialized nations in the years previous to the Great War, which itself played a decisive role in disseminating the new methods.[190] Such techniques were quickly adopted by all the belligerents, given the vital strategic importance of the industrial front as a whole. Also significant was the massive influx of female workers more amenable to adapting to new production modes than the old working classes, whose hostility to "organized overwork" (the title of a 1913 French Socialist broadsheet) is well documented. As Olivier Pastré has pointed out, Taylorism reflected a reality both precise and somewhat vague:

> At the micro-economic (or micro-social) level, Taylorism can be defined as a dual division of labor, both horizontal (the separation of tasks) and vertical (the distinction between design and execution). . . . This primary definition can be considered a subset of the broader idea of Taylorism as a mode of social regulation. This second definition is resolutely macro-economic (or macro-social), and underlying it is the implicit hypothesis that the organization of labor is not restricted to that of production tasks. Historically speaking, a given mode of labor organization is as much characterized by social relations taking place outside the workplace as by the way tasks are articulated within the company.[191]

Taylor's proposals, based on his earlier notion of "systematic management," which had centered on rationalization at the level of top management, broadened to include the company as a whole, culminating in the creation of a new "state of mind." It took on board some earlier doctrines and management techniques (e.g., Henry L. Gantt's charts), and underwent several modifications in Taylor's own lifetime, for instance as a result of Gilbreth's research into diagrams of movement, which Jean Prévost viewed as a "humanism of labor," and which were successfully adapted to architectural design.[192] Another important feature of Taylor's work was the elaboration of strategies for the dissemination of his discoveries, an integral part of his approach; this "self-marketing" called on *ad hoc* professional organizations like the Taylor Society, the press, and publishing. This explains the speed

41. View of the factory park at the Schenectady electrical power station, in Georges Benoit-Lévy, *Cités-jardins d'Amérique*, Paris, 1905. Collection Jean-Louis Cohen, Paris

Fig. 20. L'entrée de l'Usine Parc.
Usine d'électricité de Schenectady.

with which the functional diagrams of his "scientific management" spread in Europe before 1914, being used by Ernst May in Frankfurt and by Ginzburg in Moscow.

Frequently confused with Taylorism, Fordism is a mode of labor organization based on the introduction of the assembly line and mass production on the one hand, and on the other, a generous wage policy that creates a mass consumer market for manufactured goods. The spread of Fordism in Europe and the world was to a large extent due to translations of Ford's own books, which were immediate and lasting bestsellers.[193] Moreover, accounts of direct American experiences, such as *Standarts* by Hyacinthe Dubreuil,[194] who became a close friend of Le Corbusier, hastened the dissemination of a myth to which René Clair paid a cinematographic tribute in his 1932 film *A nous la liberté.*

The Russian situation is especially remarkable in that the spread there of Taylorism was not halted by the 1917 revolution. Moreover, by 1920 Fordism had to all intents and purposes become a mythical image. In Russia, the development of capitalism involved widespread assimilation of the new methods of production and management evolved in Western Europe and the United States. As early as 1909, rapidly executed translations familiarized Russian engineers and industrialists with Taylor's research into the rationalization of industrial production.[195] A. V. Pankin, professor at the Academy of Artillery, and L. A. Levenshtern, a mining engineer, translated and commented on Taylor's principal publications[196] and furnished accounts of both Gilbreth's experiments and Gantt's work.[197] A large number of commentaries and experimental accounts accompanied the dissemination of the original American texts, and technicians such as Walter Polakov,[198] who emigrated in the wake of the

1905 revolution, also studied how modernization strategies involving mass production processes were rooted theoretically and empirically in America.

Russian Social Democrats closely followed the emergence of Taylorism, and in 1913 the philosopher Aleksandr Bogdanov published a commentary on the effects of the new doctrine.[199] Lenin himself wrote in *Pravda* of "a 'scientific' system to squeeze the worker."[200] But an analysis published in the same newspaper less than a year later revealed that he had begun to view improved capitalist exploitation in a different light: "the Taylor system . . . is preparing a time when the proletariat will take over all social production."[201] Like the majority of the Russian "technical" intelligentsia, the Bolsheviks were in fact beginning to view America as the image of an industrial future hitherto identified with Germany.

Even before the civil war of 1917–22, Lenin seems to have been keen to establish direct relations with American industrialists, and to import American equipment in preference to that of other nations.[202] Indeed, Lenin's new "organization" signified nothing less than implementing Taylor's "scientific management."[203] Some weeks after the October Revolution, Lenin underlined the urgent need to implement Taylorist principles—at any price—in a now-celebrated text, *Immediate Tasks of the Soviet Government:*

> The Taylor system . . . is a combination of the refined brutality of bourgeois exploitation and a number of the greatest scientific achievements in the field of analyzing mechanical motions during work, the elimination of superfluous and awkward motions, the elaboration of correct methods of work, the introduction of the best system of accounting and control, etc. The Soviet Republic must at all costs adopt all that is valuable in the achievements of science and technology in this field. The possibility of building socialism depends exactly upon our success in com-

bining the Soviet power and the Soviet organization of administration with the up-to-date achievements of capitalism.[204]

In the prevailing political and economic circumstances, Lenin's position concerning the April 1918 decree on labor discipline was clear: it "must make explicit mention of the introduction of the Taylor system, in other words the use of all the scientific labor processes that the system implies. . . . For the implementation of this system," he added, it would be suitable "to bring in American engineers."[205] Nor is Lenin the only "historic" Soviet leader to have underlined the importance of Taylorism; all Bolshevik leaders, left and right, were unanimous on this point. Trotsky, for instance, recommended the militarization of production and the introduction of Taylorism, which he regarded as both "the most advanced form of exploitation of the labor force" and "a system for sensible expenditure of human strength," and which he subsequently imposed on railroad shop production.[206]

During the twenties, Soviet literature devoted to Taylorism—now called *Nauchnaia Organizatsia Truda*, or NOT—abounded. A new generation of translations was published, both of Taylor[207] and of Clarence B. Thompson,[208] another theorist of scientific management. These came with original analyses by Russian engineers,[209] but also translations of German commentaries, and comparisons between Taylor's system and that of the French engineer Fayol.[210] More generally, Russian readings of Taylorism, and the development of NOT, reflected a trend towards "scientific" production, reproduction, and Soviet material culture as a whole. As such, they were not only part and parcel of the economic revolution, but also formed the basis of its cultural counterpart.[211] It is as if the Russian intelligentsia had suddenly turned its back on Germany and France and henceforth strove to build a second

America (as Blok recommended). In 1926, René Fülop-Miller remarked on this new passion:

Industrialized America became the Promised Land. At an earlier period, the "intelligentsia" still looked for their models in Europe; but, immediately after the Revolution, a wild enthusiasm for America started; the magnificent industrial works of Germany and the highly perfected plants of France and England, all at once appeared paltry to Soviet Russia; they began to dream of Chicago and to direct their efforts towards making Russia a new and more splendid America.[212]

Fordism and "Deurbanism" in Russia

Strange indeed was the ideal America proposed, towards the end of the twenties, by the Union of Contemporary Architects or OSA, which responded to the question of the territorial impact of industrialization with the doctrine of "deurbanism."[213] The group, led by Moisei Ginzburg, virtually inverted the arguments formulated in 1926 in favor of urban densification, which will be commented on below. Essentially involving the idea of decentralized production and housing, deurbanism's main reference was America. The movement's principal strategist, the sociologist Mikhail Okhitovich, made no mystery of the source for his theorized dissolution of cities:

Deurbanization is a centrifugal process, a rejection. It is based on an identical trend in the technical sphere. Despite inauspicious circumstances related to private land ownership, Ford has extended his production through specialization linked to the proximity of primary materials: the finished product is born of the "encounter" of parts on the shop floor, and the workshops are themselves subject to centrifugal law.[214]

The allusion to Ford was in no way fortuitous. After the death of Lenin in 1924 the memoirs of

42. "Deurbanist"
project for Magnitogorsk
by Mikhail Okhitovich, illustration
in "Zametki po teorii rasselenia,"
in *Sovremennaia Arkhitektura,*
1930. Canadian Centre
for Architecture, Montreal

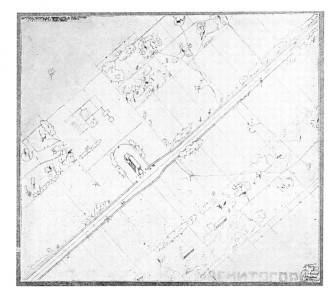

this figurehead of American industry sold almost as well as the work of the Soviet Union's founder, fueling renewed admiration for inventors and entrepreneurs such as Benjamin Franklin, Robert Fulton, and Thomas Edison.[215] To the astonishment of Western travelers, who remarked on his popularity in the remotest corners of rural Russia,[216] Ford was as famous as Charlie Chaplin, and the vein of Fordist literature inexhaustible.[217] As with Taylor, a number of analyses were translated from German authors of leftist Social Democrat or Communist leanings,[218] but there were also travel-

43. Dining hall with conveyor
belt inspired by Fordized
factories. From V. I. Velman, ed.,
*Tipovye proekty i konstruktsii
zhilishnogo stroitelstva*
(Typical housing project and
constructions), Moscow, 1929.
Collection Jean-Louis Cohen, Paris

Чертеж 50 ПЕРСПЕКТИВНЫЙ ВИД СТОЛОВОЙ И КОРИ-
ДОРА-БАЛКОНА В НЕЙ.

ogues like those of the poet Vladimir Maiakovsky, and other first-hand accounts. Unlike literature on Taylor, which was not read by the public at large, biographies and critical studies of Ford sold massively in the kiosks.[219] One American noted in 1940 that "though Lenin is today the God of Russia, Ford is her Saint Peter."[220] Addressing the chairman of the American Chamber of Commerce, Stalin expressed the extraordinary wish that "Heaven preserve him."[221] Seemingly, Ford had become Uncle Sam personified.

The Fordson tractor, first marketed in 1915 by Ford's Tractor Division, was produced in the workshops of the former Putilov factories in Leningrad from 1923 to 1932.[222] The Fordson, which had been a key factor in the modernizing of rural America,[223] was now used (along with equipment from the International Harvester factory, which had never been closed by the Soviets) to mechanize Russian agriculture, and large-scale model farms were ceded to Germans and Americans with a view to training Russian farm laborers. The Fordson was so popular that Sergei Eisenstein included a ballet of tractors in his film *The General Line*, and it became a byword among farm children, who affectionately nicknamed it *Fordsonichka*. By the end of the 1920s three-quarters of all Russian tractors were American, most of them Fords.[224]

The territorial schemes of the "deurbanists" were based on Ford's decentralized model (as would be Frank Lloyd Wright's *Broadacre City*, to a certain extent). But these far-flung systems, exemplified in the provisional proposals for Magnitogorsk, were also indissociable from another component of Fordism: extensive use of the automobile. Okhitovich, who was well aware of the long-term effects of favoring individual transportation, declared that "the automobile is an ephemeral necessity (in a time of transition) between the city's existence and its disappearance, and will forge seamless links with the countryside," adding that it was "the indispensable companion to an industry not yet spread out in space."[225] Yet given that Soviet automobile production was purely nominal, Okhitovich's stance was premature to say the least, even if it was shared by several members of the Communist Academy during urban development discussions held in 1929, when more than one participant alluded to America. Okhitovich himself paid a heavy price for his commitment when, denounced by a number of conservative architects, he fell prey to Stalin's purges.[226]

The study of motion within buildings informed the OSA's Constructivist design solutions, in coherence with Gilbreth's observations. Knowledge of the work of Frank and Lillian Gilbreth in the USSR, which dated to before 1914, deepened with the publication of several translations of their work, and as the Russians became interested in film as a means of measuring movement in the workplace.[227] Russian architects were less interested in Gilbreth's studies of the bricklaying process[228] than the idea of customizing space for repetitive movements. In 1927 Ginzburg abandoned his initial view of the link between mechanization and the architectural envelope, and adopted the "functional method" of design (*Tselevaia ustanovka*). He proceeded to forge two complementary tools: *grafik dvizhenia* (graph of movement), and *skhema oborudovania* (diagram of equipment), which together made it possible to design the architectural envelope of any program "in the most radical way possible." These two devices were based on Ford's analysis of factory space. Ginzburg cited a lengthy passage from *My Life and Work*, on the positioning of machines on the shop floor, in order to clarify his own intentions. For Ginzburg, the factory could serve as a baseline model for the analysis of any building type whatsoever:

The functional program, often expressed in a single word—factory, club, housing, etc.—must, after meticulous study, be materialized by the architect and related by him to a precise system of *productive and social processes.*

Productive or labor processes are generally associated with images of the workshop or factory; *social processes*, with housing and collective buildings. There are no fundamental differences here.

In any industrial enterprise, the production process culminates in a given product. It is dynamic, coherent, and moves in a precise direction from start to finish. The process is uniform and where possible uninterrupted, but is nonetheless clearly divided into distinct sequences. The dynamics of the production process can easily be represented in a *graph of movement*. The division of the process into distinct phases makes it possible to describe its dynamics in terms of a *static system* of separate but interdependent production operations, each of which corresponds to a particular piece of equipment.

In the contemporary factory, the *graph of movement* is the path taken by the assembly line, and describes the whole process from start to finish, from one machine to the next.

The equipment diagram shows the system of machines and tools required to carry out the various stages of production. The method of positioning this equipment determines the spatial configuration of the whole, depending on the type of production and the principle of the economy of labor.[229]

In the sphere of housing, Ginzburg considered the most efficient combination of minimal movement and maximum equipment to be the cabin of an ocean liner or the American hotel room with its foldaway beds, which he included in his illustrations. His observations inspired studies that were

THE "MOTHERLAND OF INDUSTRY"

carried out at the end of the twenties, under the aegis of the Stroikom (Building Commission). At the same time, M. Barshch and V. Vladimirov's research into the economics of movement and facilities aimed to establish a rational collective housing typology, and doubtless constituted OSA's most coherent body of experimentation. Architects working for the Stroikom were directly inspired by German research programs, such as those of Bruno Taut or Ernst May's Frankfurt team. But indirectly (via the German literature) it was the American methods that were used, as witnesses the slogan of the Constructivist V. Kuzmin, who pleaded for the "scientific organization of daily life."[230] Ivan Nikolaev's communal housing for textile students reflected the Spartan ideal of the ship's cabins or train sleeper compartments. In his last book, *Zhilishche* (1934), Ginzburg, reflecting on his research, gave an overview of communal dwellings but said nothing about their industrial origins.[231]

The "Organisation Scientifique du Travail" in France

Generally speaking, the effects of Taylorism on architecture involved the reorganization of work on construction sites on the one hand, and the design of buildings' interiors on the other. Whether or not this in turn ushered in a quasi-Fordist approach to production, leading to the rationalization of the work station, or a restructuring of internal departments and design within the workplace, "scientific management" was quickly assimilated by the generation of founders of the Modern movement. In France, the classics of Taylorist literature were translated some years before its assimilation by architects.[232] Rechristened as the "scientific organization of labor,"[233] French Taylorism was first implemented in a few of the war industries, then in

metallurgical production, before being applied on some construction sites.[234] However, the world of American enterprise had long since been described by tourists, journalists, and urban reformists such as Georges Benoit-Lévy.

As early as 1916, Le Corbusier, who was quite untouched by romantic delusions concerning Taylorism, regarding it as a harbinger of the "horrid, inevitable life of the future," attempted via the Société des Applications du Béton Armé (Society for the Applied Uses of Reinforced Concrete)—which he himself founded—and the Société d'Entreprises Industrielles et d'Études (Society of Industrial Enterprise and Analysis) to build a garden city at Saint-Nicolas d'Aliermont and several utility buildings at Saintes, Challuy, and Garchisy, all based on the notion of economy of scale. But not until he began building the 54 houses of the Quartiers modernes Frugès at Pessac, in 1924, was he able to integrate the principles of mass assembly:

Mass-production is based on analysis and experiment.

Industry on the grand scale must occupy itself with building and establish the elements of the house on a mass-production basis.

We must create a mass-production spirit. The spirit of constructing mass-production houses.

The spirit of living in mass-production houses.

The spirit of conceiving mass-production houses.

If we eliminate from our hearts and minds all dead concepts in regard to the houses and look at the question from a critical and objective point of view, we shall arrive at the "House-Machine," the mass-production house, healthy (and morally so, too) and beautiful in the same way that the working tools and instruments which accompany our existence are beautiful.[235]

Le Corbusier, who was involved in the reflections of the *Redressement français*, a business club for the dissemination of Taylorism and Fordism in France, contributed to technocratic reform in the name of the "machine age," and associated technical solutions on the construction site with what he regarded as the necessary reworking of urban form:

> If we are to industrialize and Taylorize the building industry, urban planners must first design new street systems, broad thoroughfares permitting the organization of vast construction sites where factory-built components (metallic frames), machines, rational handling techniques, and specialist teams can intervene.[236]

For Le Corbusier, who knew of Taylor's work with concrete, Pessac represented a clear opportunity to implement Taylorist principles. Apart from failed experiments such as the use of a cement cannon, his attempts to rationalize the construction process involved using an extremely limited range of components (a single type of reinforced concrete beam, a single type of internal staircase, a single type of window), thus achieving "architectural unity through [the use of] standard elements."

At this time Le Corbusier incessantly strove to convert the automobile industrialists to his viewpoints. This choice was not a random one, nor did it merely reflect the role of the automobile as fantasy-object for the architects of his generation. In fact, it was in the automobile and associated industries that Taylorism and Fordism developed most quickly in France. André Citroën was particularly active in this domain, while Peugeot owed the rationalization of its factories to the engineer Ernest Mattern.[237] For his part, André Michelin published scores of propaganda cartoons designed to persuade "François," the French worker, to accept solutions that had been so positive for "Sam," his American counterpart, as efficient as he was prosperous.[238]

A decade after failed attempts to persuade Peugeot or Citroën to sponsor his plan for Paris, followed by the successful courtship of Gabriel Voisin, Le Corbusier's faith in the automobile led him to ask once more for Citroën's support for his new Parisian projects and his ambition to rationalize the construction process:

> For 10 years I have carried in me this affirmation: that big industry must attend to building. That Citroën, Renault, Schneider must attend to building. I mean that their workshops, where the most perfect industrial organization prevails, should be used to build a consumer product of unlimited scope: the dwelling. And the dwelling should be produced not with stone and mortar, but with iron, wood, etc. . . . Automobile constructors exhaust themselves with sterile rivalries; they saturate the country with undesirable consumer objects (far too many automobiles for insufficient road and street networks). We must therefore develop the urban networks, and consequently develop the cities. To develop the cities we need mass production, with costs two, three, four times lower than current costs.[239]

Le Corbusier was not the only Parisian architect interested in rationalized production; witness the somewhat heavy-handed insistence with which Marcel Lods installed a Ford-inspired conveyor belt (for his concrete components) on the site of the La Muette housing project (built 1932–34). In the urban planning sphere, questions of global rationalization began to be posed after 1918, as regards both the reconstruction of "devastated" regions, where the sheer scale of the construction program entailed new methods,[240] and the extension of the Paris region, for which a competition was held in 1919. The winner of the competition's regional section, Léon Jaussely (whose project was based on the rationalization of rail, road, and river networks), stressed the pressing need to extend Taylorist principles to management of the metropolitan area, which he was the first to perceive as a unique economic system:

> Cities . . . are essential organic components in the national equipment. Consequently, it is necessary to

44. Lillian Gilbreth,
Study of a "Taylorized" kitchen.
From *La Construction moderne*,
1930. Canadian Centre
for Architecture, Montreal

"maximum yield" within the house, campaigned against "vampiric distances" and "exhausting materials," and proposed rational solutions in their stead. She regarded piping as "an essential factor of civilization" and recommended the mechanization of housekeeping. She saw positive examples of this in certain projects of the Modern movement, not only those of Le Corbusier, but also in the domain of hotel architecture, and published articles in *La Construction Moderne* on hotel design in the United States.[242] In her 1928 pamphlet *Si les femmes faisaient les maisons* (If women built houses), she regarded the apartment-hotel as a solution to the problems posed, and cited the specific instance of the Résidence Palace in Brussels, "a deluxe apartment-hotel where one can live as one wishes, collectively or in private, and where the mistress does the housekeeping when and as she so desires."[243]

Paulette Bernège praised the architect Paulet's project for a "rationalized housing block," an "immense skyscraper" giving "the working classes all the comforts of a luxury hotel, with all the social services which a modern housing project ought to possess." Clearly inspired by American production models, Paulet's project took the form of an immense skyscraper, cruciform in plan, designed to house five thousand people in apartments that would all be equipped "with cold and hot running water, baths, a main sewage system, garbage chute, elevator, electricity, heating, refrigerator, vacuum-cleaning systems, telephone, intercoms, etc.":

study development and extension plans that view the city as an economic organism whose equipment must be perfectly organized so as to maximize its economic yield. The principle is a simple one: primary materials are to be efficiently transported, without superfluous handling, they are to be exported from the factories without loss of time; the problem is for city consumers to get what they need with a minimum of handling. In short, the problem is one of large-scale Taylorization.[241]

In the housing sector, Paulette Bernège, a propagandist for domestic management, became interested in

The axial tower superimposes various social amenities, central lobbies, restaurants, movie theater, theater, gymnasium, library, amphitheater, etc.; the five lower stories of each of the lateral wings, surrounded by arcades, will house offices and public administration; above these, in the twenty-five tooth-shaped floors, families will generally live in apartments with three of their façades open to the sky, while the

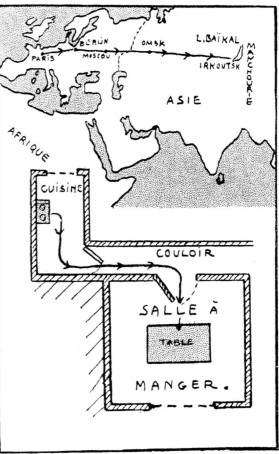

LES DISTANCES VAMPIRES

8 mètres de distance entre ma cuisine et ma salle à manger, m'obligent, en 40 ans, à parcourir la distance de Paris au lac Baïkal.

46. Paulette Bernège. "Les distances vampires." From *Si les femmes faisaient les maisons* (If women built houses), Paris, 1928. Collection Jean-Louis Cohen, Paris

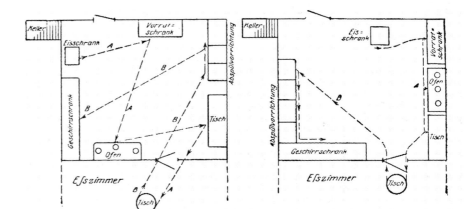

Abb. 47. Christine Frederick: Ganglinien in der Küche bei falscher (links) und richtiger Einrichtung (rechts)

L'ORGANISATION MÉNAGÈRE MODERNE

DEUXIÈME ÉDITION
du
TAYLORISME CHEZ SOI

par
Christine FREDERICK
Traduit de l'anglais par A. D. T.

PARIS
DUNOD
92, RUE BONAPARTE (VI)
1927

45. Title page of Christine Frederick, *L'Organisation ménagère moderne, 2e édition du Taylorisme chez soi*, Paris, 1927. Collection Marc Dessauce, New York

47. The "Taylorized kitchen," after Christine Frederick, 1913. From Bruno Taut, *Die neue Wohnung*, Berlin, 1924. Canadian Centre for Architecture, Montreal

fourth will house internal distributions, elevators, and service stairs.[244]

Bernège's idea, which she saw as an "experiment in housekeeping," took the form, so to speak, of a *petit-bourgeois* Waldorf-Astoria. Architects were impressed enough to invite her to the 1929 Congrès Internationaux d'Architecture Moderne (CIAM) in Frankfurt, the theme of which was minimal housing. But her ideas were to be without practical effect, as the ambitious housing programs funded by the 1928 Loucheur Law were compromised by the Depression.

Rationalization in Germany

Taylorism and Fordism, which penetrated all of Europe in the wake of the Great War, were subject to varying interpretations depending on the country involved. As with Paulette Bernège in Paris, American industrial doctrines transformed the thinking of German architects interested in the rationalization of domestic space, including Bruno Taut, Ernst May and, to some extent, Walter Gropius. The distribution analyses published by Taut in the pages of *Die neue Wohnung* in 1924, when he became involved in the construction of large-scale garden cities on the outskirts of Berlin, were based on "movement diagrams" published in 1913 by the pioneer of American domestic management reform, Christine McGaffey Frederick.[245]

In 1925, Ernst May built up a truly multidisciplinary team of architects, engineers, sociologists, and draughtspersons within the municipal services of Frankfurt am Main. The building program on which he worked until his departure for Berlin in 1930 promoted the scientific organization of labor in Weimar Germany on two fronts. On the one hand, May strove to industrialize the construction process, introducing factory-produced or prefabricated fittings such as doors and doorframes, windows, and some furnishings; on the other, he carried out detailed studies (largely involving Taylorist techniques) of the way housing was "used." The dazzling result of this dual strategy was the celebrated *frankfurter Küche* (Frankfurt kitchen), a design elaborated under the direction of Grete Schütte-Lihotzky and based, like Bernège's own studies, on research by the American social engineer Lillian Gilbreth and publications by Christine Frederick. This radical experiment reflected the ergonomics of movement and trajectory as well as the standardized production of furniture and equipment. Extremely compact (occupying a surface area of from four to six square meters), the Frankfurt kitchen was a truly Taylorist work station.

As director of the Weimar Bauhaus from 1919, Walter Gropius turned from America's grain elevators and factories and concentrated instead on its industrial production of houses.[246] Whereas May's Frankfurt experiments were largely Taylor-inspired, Gropius's work was essentially in line with Ford. Above all, Gropius wanted to promote an industrial model based on a parallel between the ever-diminishing costs of automobile production and those of housing, which were stagnant. At the instigation of the Berlin industrialist Adolf Sommerfeld, for whom he had built a curious log cabin in 1920, Gropius proposed lightweight houses in wood or metal mass-produced with the techniques of automobile production.

It would be a mistake to regard Fordist or Taylorist ideas as the exclusive domain of the German Functionalists, who were far from being the only ones to aim at space-saving and industrial processes. The theme of the *Minimalwohnung* (minimal apartment), so dear to the CIAM, was also adhered to by the traditionalist Alexander Klein, who proposed a grid for the analysis and classification of housing along "scientific management" lines. Such Taylorist architectural experiments culminated in Ernst Neufert's 1936 handbook, *Bauentwurfslehre*. Formerly Gropius's assistant and a professor at the Bauhochschule, which replaced the Weimar Bauhaus at the end of the twenties, Neufert was soon sacked for his *Baubolchewismus* (architectural Bolshevism). Yet he took his revenge with his 1936 manual, doubtless the architectural bestseller of all time. The dimensional systems elaborated by Neufert were based on three types of devices. The first addressed the problem of the objects and instruments to be stored in the home, from saucepans to grand pianos. The second concerned human movement in domestic and public spaces. The third took the form of plans deemed efficient and drawn from the vast repertory of projects designed in Weimar Germany. The influence of Taylor was most marked in the second of these, above all in ideas of motion control and in the definition of conditions of access to living and storage spaces.[247]

A generation of architects concerned with shaking up architecture's traditional value-systems—in the name of "function" and use—could not fail to employ doctrines like Taylorism, which held out the promise of increased mastery of both space and time. More than this, by guaranteeing mastery of the body as practiced on the shop floor, it opened up a dual prospect for the future. First, a new space-saving strategy (indispensable in a period of large-scale public housing policies) became possible, based not on simply shrinking the surface area of apartments, but on creating new spatial formats reflecting "objective" scale. But moreover, designers with recourse to dimensions based on observation also had the advantage of "naturalizing" functional architecture by forging new links with the human

figure—not in its ideal proportions, but this time with reference to movement.

Another consequence of Taylorism, in the sphere of industrial command and control, was reflected in the reorganization of the shop floor. The scientific organization of labor also entailed a reassessment of the relations between hierarchy and execution, by giving priority to the definition, distribution, and the monitoring of tasks. The spread of such techniques to construction immediately brought changes in the work of architects, affording them new production planning tools that surpassed relatively primitive drawings and estimates. Henceforth, architects were not so much designers or builders as planners and organizers. Indeed, they strenuously identified with this image, made possible by the final assimilation of Taylorism in the large-scale reconstruction of the second postwar era.

The Migrations of the American Factory

Radical architects' interest in the modern factory, which went hand in hand with a fascination for ocean liners (whose improved performance greatly increased the number of visitors to America), automobiles, and airplanes, is best illustrated by Le Corbusier's jubilation upon seeing the autodrome on the roof of Lingotto's Fiat factory, on the outskirts of Turin, in 1925. This eight-hundred-meter-long building was not only one of the first examples of American methods of labor organization in Europe, but also of a building as a total technical object.

This colossal project, designed from 1915 by the engineer Giacomo Matté-Trucco, originated in the experiences of Fiat's founder, Giovanni Agnelli, during travels to the United States in 1902 and 1912, which formed the basis of elaborations by senior

48. František Gahura, architect (1891–1958). The Bat'a complex, Zlín, Czechoslovakia, 1936. State Archives of Zlín

company executives. The Turin building involved solutions used in the Ford factory at Highland Park in Detroit, but this time on such a scale that it was seen as an object lesson for the original inventors:

> America will no longer pave the way in the field of such colossal industrial establishments, and [this] bold Italian design will henceforth be an example to American industry.[248]

While many automobile factories in Europe had wide recourse to Taylorism, most were developed without an architectural brief (and fewer still to a monumental one), instead being modeled on market fluctuations and real estate prices.[249] But the Lingotto factory gave the impression of a wholesale transfer of American production methods and industrial architecture. It goes without saying that the test track, which literally "crowns" the building, inverted the rationale of the assembly line in the boldest possible way, in its role—as Banham has pointed out—of dynamic visual image, not of the factory's (questionable) functionalist virtues, but rather of the bosses' commitment to modern consumer strategies. The factory thus became a showpiece where products could be presented and endorsed by visitors, architects, and statesmen. Moreover, the Communist leader Antonio Gramsci regarded Lingotto as a beachhead of Americanism, claiming that it would promote "the intelligence of the current situation in a large number of states on the old continent."[250] The critic Edoardo Persico regarded the "example of the structure of laws" set by the factory as revealing "an order expressive not of human will, but of a wisdom subject first and foremost to the law."[251] Twenty years after the completion of the Lingotto factory, Benito Mussolini, who had long since been converted to Americanism,[252] inaugurated the new Mirafiori factory; its designer, the engineer Vittorio Bonadè Bottino, had worked at Albert Kahn Associates before setting up an in-house design department at Fiat with a structure based on that of Kahn's Detroit office.

As was the case with Agnelli, increased familiarity with the American factory led other branches of production to create veritable industrial colonies in Central Europe. The Moravian Tomaš Bat'a, who had worked as a laborer in the shoe factories of Lynn, Massachusetts in 1904, and who visited America with his factory's executives in 1919–20, was to create one such colony. The overall plan for this private republic centered on the small town of Zlín, situated a hundred or so kilometers from Brno, was to a massive extent based on Fordist production principles. The "unknown dictator" (as Bat'a was dubbed by his detractors)[253] also integrated his production and marketing activities both horizontally and vertically, setting up a network of shops on the franchise model throughout Europe, where he also multiplied his production sites. Yet the corporation's magnetic pole remained Zlín, where the firm's architect, František Gahura, built reinforced-concrete industrial constructions based on those that his boss had seen at Lowell, Massachusetts. In a building designed by the young Slovak Vladimír Karfík, who worked with Frank Lloyd Wright from 1926 to 1930, Bat'a installed his office in a colossal elevator so as to be able to move vertically throughout the administrative block and meet his employees. Karfík then extended the town along the valley floor, constructing rationalized worker housing estates and public buildings.[254] On a visit to this site some time after that of his friend Hyacinthe Dubreuil (who had been responsible for disseminating images of Ford's factories in France), Le Corbusier began to develop the theme of the "linear city."[255] Bat'a's "integral" approach, comprising American production, marketing, and distribution principles, was further completed with studies for skyscrapers designed to herald the corporation's presence throughout Central Europe.

The most spectacular reproductions of the material and architectural framework of American industry were not, however, to be found in the projects of industrialists like Agnelli or Bat'a, but in the young Soviet Union, where the reconstruction of manufacturing infrastructure was inextricably linked to foreign intervention. The civil war precluded Russia from carrying out industrial policies which had been drawn up by the Bolsheviks in 1917, involving the granting of concessions to foreign companies. Implementation effectively began in 1924, with initiatives ranging from limited contracts to mixed-capital corporations. In the three years that followed, one hundred fifty companies were granted charters, from Armand Hammer's modest pencil factory to large-scale industrial projects. At the same time, the oilfields of Baku—crucial to the Soviet economy and to foreign trade—resumed production as a result of an accord with the American company International Barnsdall. Modernized drilling techniques, the creation of a pipeline to the Black Sea, and the construction of cracking refineries were all made possible by American technology. The same was true of the coal mines, and the steel industry was radically transformed with the direct help of the Freyn Company of Chicago, which brought

49. Residential quarter of Zlín, dwellings of Bat'a employees, 1934. State Archives of Zlín

50. Giacomo Matté-Trucco, engineer (1869–1934). The Lingotto Fiat factories, Turin, Italy, 1915–1922. Photograph taken in 1932. Archivio Storico Fiat, Turin

51. Photomontage
of the Moscow automobile
factory (AMO) constructed
by Albert Kahn Associates, 1933.
From *L'URSS en construction*,
August 1933. Canadian Centre
for Architecture, Montreal

COMPLETED AUTOMOBILES

broad-strip rolling mills to the USSR. In the transportation sector, the Soviets were careful not to nationalize corporations such as Westinghouse Brakes until after they had assimilated their technologies.[256]

In 1929, Russian fascination with Ford's processes and products culminated in a wide-ranging agreement which led to the construction of a factory at Nizhnii-Novgorod and the modernization of the AMO factory in Moscow, whose turnover had been sluggish since its inauguration in 1917, and which was now rechristened ZiS.[257] This accord provided for the sale of a large quantity of equipment and parts designed to increase Soviet automobile production to a theoretical annual output of 100,000 GAZ-A units (i.e., the Ford Model A).[258] Trucks, too, were both the light and heavy

models from the Dearborn Company. At the same time, engineers from the Austin Company headed production at the Nizhni-Novgorod factory.[259]

Over and above the influence of Ford, at the end of the twenties the Russians were still interested in American installations and industrial constructions generally, and in the technicians capable of building them. Albert Kahn,[260] who worked on a considerable number of projects following an invitation from Amtorg, a New York-based trading company, was involved in the massive factory construction campaign launched as part of the Five-Year Plan.

The Russians were interested less in the fairly nondescript office building designs of Kahn (whom Oskar

Storonov described in a letter to Le Corbusier as an "engineering god" who was unfortunately also a "pig architect")[261] than in his factories and their mechanical installations. A group of twenty-five architects and engineers working under Albert's brother, Moritz Kahn,[262] designed 521 of the 951 industrial sites built by the Americans between 1929 and 1932, including factories based on Ford's River Rouge complex at Dearborn in Stalingrad and Cheliabinsk (which produced the Caterpillar tractor), and trained some four thousand Soviet technicians.[263] At the largest and most crucial of these rising factories—in particular at Stalingrad—metallic structures and machines were imported directly from the United States by boat and train.[264] On the construction site, American engineers were astonished by the work rate of the Russians, who accused the former of behaving like "Italians," i.e., of refusing to work in freezing temperatures.[265]

Following completion of this colossal program, some American *spetsi* (specialists) stayed on to teach Russians their working methods. This led to a certain idealization of the American engineer. Thus, John Calder—a living instance of exchanges between the two nations, who worked on the River Rouge complex and was involved on the Stalingrad site—would appear as the protagonist of Nikolai Pogodin's play *Tempo*, which ran in Moscow in 1930.[266] Alongside the Donbass miner and the female Kolkhozian farm worker, the American engineer became a central, though ephemeral, figure in Stalin's propaganda machine.

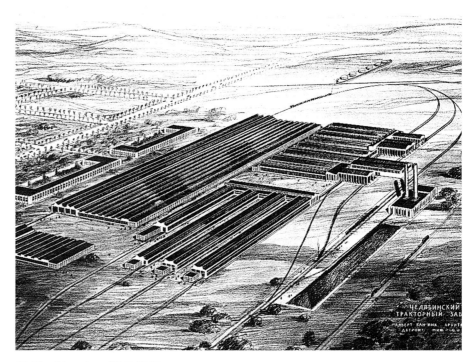

52. Albert Kahn, architect (1869–1942).

The Cheliabinsk Tractor Plant: bird's-eye view, 1930–33.

Albert Kahn Associates Inc., Detroit

53. Albert Kahn, architect (1869–1942).

The Cheliabinsk Tractor Plant: elevation and section of the forge, 1930.

Albert Kahn Associates Inc., Detroit

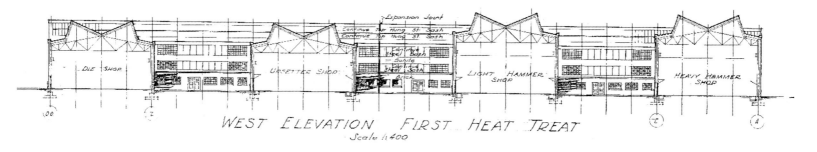

The wave of early publications and long-distance readings of the American scene was followed by a new phase in the 1920s, when it became easier to directly experience cities and architecture in the United States. As was the case with Soviet Russia, the trip to America came to be viewed as obligatory by writers and critics, who then could not fail to compare the two nations. Louis-Ferdinand Céline, who wrote of his American travels in his *Journey to the End of the Night*, was equally skeptical of American and Russian industrialization, stating bluntly that "all Fords are alike, Soviet or no";[267] and Georges Duhamel, who in 1928 had published a *Moscow Journal*, declared two years later that a sort of "communism" reigned in America.

In architectural circles of the late 1920s, images of America were assimilated through recapitulative or comparative anthologies, such as Ludwig Hilberseimer's *Großstadtarchitektur*, or *Die neue Baukunst in Europa und Amerika*, in which Bruno Taut still viewed grain elevators and Albert Kahn's factories as news.[268] But European architects gained more subjective perceptions through the travels of certain active protagonists in the new postwar culture. The camera replaced the sketchbook, and above all an earlier, idealized vision of America gave way to more complex visions of urban reality, with reactions ranging—sometimes in a single breath—from irony to outright hostility.

The Eye of Mendelsohn

The photographs published by Erich Mendelsohn in his 1926 *Amerika, Bilderbuch eines Architekten*, whether taken by him or, as we shall see below, by Knud Lonberg-Holm, were so forceful that they radically modified perceptions of the cityscapes of

Knud Lonberg-Holm (1895–1972). Construction of the Sheldon Hotel in New York, c. 1922. Reproduced in Erich Mendelsohn, *Amerika, Bilderbuch eines Architekten*, Berlin, 1926.
Nederlands Architectuurinstituut, Rotterdam

The Moderns

Discover

America:

Mendelsohn,

Neutra,

and

Maiakovsky

New York, Chicago, and Detroit. Mendelsohn's contradictory images pushed earlier views—including his own—onto the sidelines. In sketches made during the war period, he had imagined an industrial universe composed of cranes, hangars, factories, and silos, informed by rhythmic, Nietzschian perceptions quite unlike the generally static German views of America before WWI.[269] Travels undertaken in 1924 enabled him to compare his earlier notations with the reality of urban and rural America. The album published on his return reflects this encounter between ideal and real, juxtaposing intense views and ironic comment, but also lucid analysis within a saturated visual field.[270]

Mendelsohn embarked for New York in the fall of 1924, an experienced Berlin architect who had done much to reshape the architecture of the metropolis. In 1921 the German-born American critic Herman George Scheffauer had been the first to analyze the ideal projects of Mendelsohn,[271] whose career had been transformed by his Einstein Observatory at Potsdam and his Steinberg, Herrmann & Co. hat factory in Lückenwalde. In 1921–23 Mendelsohn and the young architect Richard Neutra added floors to the Jerusalemerstrasse headquarters of the daily *Berliner Tageblatt* for its Democrat editor Rudolf Mosse. Though Scheffauer pressed Mendelsohn to lecture in America as early as 1920, the latter hesitated, though he continued to study American production, and in 1923 accepted an invitation from the Dutch association Architectura et Amicitia to address the subject in a lecture on "Dynamics and Function." In it he showed slides of Mies van der Rohe's Berlin glass skyscraper project, comparing it with an aerial view of Manhattan and with entries of the Danish architect Knud Lonberg-Holm and the German Walter Gropius for the *Chicago Tribune* competition:

> If the close link between function and dynamics is valid for individual buildings, i.e., for cell structures,

it also obtains for the vast system of cells which is the city. Given that the smallest unit is in no way a passive observer but a dynamic participant, the street, which has to satisfy the need for rapid circulation, becomes a horizontal conduit leading from one pole to the next. The future city is in fact a system of points and, seen in a broader perspective, becomes fused with the spatial system, properly speaking.

> Seen in this way, the great contemporary city of today, unlike the marvelous spaces of the best cities of antiquity, is an inorganic agglomerate of most contradictory elements. And the cubic forms of isolated skyscrapers do nothing to alter this. Yet our time, more than any before it in history, needs to build totally new cities, or at least, to completely rethink [existing ones].[272]

A few months later, Mendelsohn was at last able to test his views on American soil, thanks to the good offices of Rudolf Mosse, himself an active Americanist, who commissioned him to write a column of "American notes" in the *Tageblatt*. On 9 October 1924 he left Cherbourg aboard the *Deutschland*, accompanied by the film director Fritz Lang, and during the crossing found time to note that the trans-Atlantic liner was not unlike those he had commented on in his lectures.[273] On 12 October he arrived in New York, "giddy" and "disturbed by the unforeseen dimensions of this colonial city," immediately noting "this disorderly wild growth in which, utterly undemocratically, individual financial wills to power have erected their twenty- to fifty-storey-high egos."[274] For his part, Fritz Lang was captivated by the nighttime atmosphere of the city. As he recounted forty years later, his "brief stay" in New York furnished the material for one of the great cinematographic masterpieces of the twenties:

> I first came to America briefly in 1924 and it made a great impression on me. The first evening, when we arrived, we were still enemy aliens so we couldn't leave the ship. It was docked somewhere on the West Side of New York. I looked at the streets—the glaring

lights and the tall buildings—and there I conceived *Metropolis*.[275]

Lang stayed in New York and Los Angeles, providing readers of the Berlin review *Film-Kurier* with images of the former's cinematographic potential:

Where is the film of these "stone Babels" which are American cities? . . . The mere sight of New York would be enough to place this beacon of loveliness at the center of a film. The lights glimmer and flash in a whirl of reds, blues, and luminous whites, mingled with loud greens, swallowed up in black nothingness, then suddenly reborn in a glorious interplay of colors. Streets which are shafts full of turning, swirling lights, crisscrossing each other in a frank acceptance of life. And above all this, soaring above the cars and overhead tracks, are blue and gold, white and purple towers; snatched from darkness by floodlights, advertising billboards rise higher still, up to the stars, alive in their continual and constantly renewed variations.[276]

The letters that Mendelsohn sent back to Europe, and occasional articles written on the spot, enable us to reconstruct the principal stages of his travels. He quickly decided to concentrate his energies:

Here in New York lies all America. One need not search far. But all America means an undreamed-of mass of material for study. For this reason the trip to California is off. It must be abandoned, because America is too big to be seized and mastered in one.

This journey is a voyage of investigation for eye and brain, very hard work and certainly an excellent massage. Once the field is known and can be assessed in accordance with its own premises and prospects—only then does it become ripe for one's own undertakings.[277]

Having delivered a lecture in New York on "The Laws of Modern Architecture," which broadly reiterated the themes of his 1919 lecture, he took a train to Buffalo, where he discovered Niagara Falls and suburban automobile civilization. He was also able to revise earlier views on Wright's Larkin Building, which he now deemed "more suitable for a sacred purpose than an industrial institution." He photographed the grain silos "like mad," but regarded them as "interim to [his] silo dreams." In Pittsburgh, Mendelsohn met the urban planner Frederick Bigger before moving on to Detroit, and reached Chicago at the end of October. There he met Knud Lonberg-Holm, who had been appointed to a teaching post at the University of Michigan at Ann Arbor following the success of his *Chicago Tribune* designs,[278] and who for two years had been submitting regular contributions to radical European reviews, such as the Constructivist Zurich bulletin *ABC Beiträge zum Bauen*.[279] Holm showed Mendelsohn Chicago's electricity plant and introduced him to the Finnish architect Eliel Saarinen, who had settled in Chicago following the *Chicago Tribune* competition.

In early November Mendelsohn accepted an invitation to visit Frank Lloyd Wright at his Wisconsin home, Taliesin—the culmination of his travels. Prior to arriving, he dutifully studied the work of Wright and his predecessors.[280] Neutra, who had been at Taliesin for several months, noted that "Wright was rather against him [Mendelsohn] but surely received an excellent impression of Mendelsohn's creative vitality."[281] Neutra officiated as interpreter and played a key role as mediator between the two men, skillfully playing down potential conflicts.[282] By mid-November Mendelsohn was back in Berlin, his head full of contradictory impressions. In January of the following year he published an article on New York in the *Berliner Tageblatt*,[283] and subsequently, two texts on the encounter with Wright and his architecture;[284] they remained on cordial terms until the fifties, even if Wright's name is not mentioned once in the pages of *Amerika*.

This album broke with the traditional iconographies of architectural literature, which had combined panoramic views of the cityscape with close-ups of

54. Two pages illustrating the Equitable Trust Building in Erich Mendelsohn, *Amerika, Bilderbuch eines Architekten*, Berlin, 1926. Canadian Centre for Architecture, Montreal

NEW YORK
EQUITABLE TRUST-BUILDING

isolated buildings. Instead, *Amerika* proposes a purely subjective itinerary. The reader is invited to accompany the architect on a tour, not of the habitual categories of urban building, nor of the "typical" and readily available phenomena of American civilization—its gigantism for instance—but rather, of the "grotesque" facets of the urban scene. The texts and photographs of *Amerika*, which sometimes seem to lead autonomous lives when detached from their original context, in combination manifest Mendelsohn's own contradictory impressions.

The large format of *Amerika* is striking, all the more so in that the margins are especially broad and the texts, to all intents and purposes, sparse.[285] The double-page spreads give the vertical photographs a soaring quality, and the use of heliogravure, a technique rare in architectural publications of the day, emphasizes the cities' dark corners and alleyways. Where Gréber and Hegemann published static photographs and plans, the snapshots of *Amerika* play down monumental effects and focus instead on the links and interstices between urban objects. Mendelsohn was hostile to the taxonomies of the urbanists, and his vision is also to be distinguished from the Modernist iconographies pioneered by Walter Gropius in his 1913 article on American industrial buildings. Though Mendelsohn, like Worringer before him,

evokes the pyramids, he is (in clear opposition to Gropius and Le Corbusier) most concerned to express the atmosphere in which the buildings are used, as one of his letters testifies:

Mountainous silos, incredibly space-conscious, but creating space. A random confusion amidst the chaos of loading and unloading corn ships, of railways and bridges, crane monsters with live gestures, hordes of silo cells in concrete, stone, and glazed brick.[286]

A refined aesthetic object, the album was intended not only for architects, but for a far wider intellectual public, and juxtaposes the facets of an America riddled with contradictions in its social system, in its spaces, and above all in its culture. Indeed, Mendelsohn underlines the "lack of culture" of this "nouveau riche" nation in a vengeful preface that puts the book more on a par with the numerous contemporary examples of anti-American literature than with wide-eyed *Amerikanismus*. Some of its commentaries echo the historian Oswald Spengler's warnings of the hazards to which *Kultur* was exposed in the face of a fundamentally materialist civilization. The ironic and occasionally cryptic legends of the photographs are largely based on Mendelsohn's initial impressions as he transmitted them to Europe in his correspondence; the approach is quasi-cinematographic. Taken with a small-format camera, the views of New York streets are edited into several sequences in which architectural contrasts unfold in a series of zoom shots along Fifth Avenue. The old urban *veduta*, which was already rigidly codified in the case of New York,[287] is here replaced by the instantaneous shot of the reporter, which Mendelsohn exploited to amplify his ambiguous vision. As we leaf through page by page, dark foregrounds with pedestrians and automobiles give way to luminous backgrounds filled by soaring skyscrapers, thus illustrating the stark contrast between the city's glacial order and the "embers" fueling the American melting pot. By alternating sequences of close-ups of construction sites and transportation systems with sordid views of backyards and ironic shots of eclectic activities, Mendelsohn pinpoints the "markers of a new culture" within the "jumble" of the city. Occasionally, an isolated image conveys the contradiction between the two registers of nouveau riche buildings and transport flow, as in the Park Avenue blocks built over the rail tracks of Grand Central Terminal.

As we now know, Fritz Lang would express his vision of America in the segregated, mechanized city of *Metropolis*, whose sets were designed by Erich Kettelhut. The cinematographic qualities of Mendelsohn's own *Amerika* were quickly perceived and commented upon. In "The Architect's Eye," an article appearing in the Russian technical review *Stroitelnaia Promyshlennost* only weeks following publication of the book, El Lissitzky paid homage to the "utterly uncustomary pictures. To understand some of them, you must hold the book over your head and turn it." In Lissitzky's view, Mendelsohn's "dramatic film" captured an America viewed not from a distance, but from the inside. Mendelsohn's eye revealed "the inner processes of things, enabling us to reflect on them."[288] On the other hand, Lissitzky regretted that the "crowds" had disappeared from the streets and sidewalks of *Amerika*, and pointed up Mendelsohn's disillusionment when confronted by a nation that had lost its soul:

> What then does the architect see, whose sight is clearer than his understanding? This eye is not blinded by the eccentricity of the sensations of the city that surround it; it sees and ascertains that real progress—really profound change in the very principles and forms of spatial division—is still very rare. On the other hand one finds much energy and very large dimensions. Everything grows elementally, like a tropical forest, depriving itself of light and air, consuming itself.[289]

The Constructivist Aleksandr Rodchenko, too, leafed through the pages of *Amerika*, and regarded it

55. Erich Kettelhut,
set designer (1893–1979).
*Sketch for the first version
of the set for the film* Metropolis
by Fritz Lang, 1925.
Fondation Deutsche Kinemathek,
Berlin

56. Otto Hunte,
set designer, *Recreation of the
set design for* Metropolis
by Fritz Lang, 1929. Deutsches
Filmmuseum, Frankfurt am Main

57. Aleksandr Rodchenko (1891–1956). Comparison of the visual approach of *Amerika, Bilderbuch eines Architekten* with the traditional approach in *Novy LEF*, 1928. Canadian Centre for Architecture, Montreal

as an instance of a new photographic approach, one diametrically opposed to the static tradition of American urban photography. In a lively debate with Boris Kushner over "the paths of modern photography" in 1928, Rodchenko compared two photographs taken from *Amerika* with commonplace views of the same subjects. Mendelsohn's *Woolworth Building* was an oblique, low-angle shot quite unlike the distant, frontal views common at the time;[290] similarly, the soaring verticality of his *Equitable Building* had nothing in common with the "stereotyped" views of contemporary American albums. For Rodchenko, unlike Americans and Europeans who followed "the laws of perspective" and offered viewpoints "at the belly-button level," Mendelsohn photographed "honestly, seeing buildings as the man in the street might do." Such shots had, however, been taken before, notably from the foot of the Eiffel Tower on the occasion of the 1889 Exposition Universelle; Le Corbusier, too, employed low-angle photography during his travels to the Far East in 1913.[291] But for Rodchenko, who would use comparable effects in his photographs of

Moscow at the end of the twenties, Mendelsohn's photographs triumphantly justified his own artistic theory:

> . . . in order to accustom people to seeing from new viewpoints it is essential to take photographs of everyday, familiar subjects from completely unexpected vantage points and in completely unexpected positions. New subjects should also be photographed from various points, so as to present a complete impression of the subject.[292]

Though Mendelsohn's album was rapidly incorporated into the Russian debate over architecture and the new photography,[293] another passionate "Americanist," Bertolt Brecht, reacted quite differently. At a time when he was writing his earliest plays, such as *Jungle of Cities* (which he began in 1924), Brecht viewed America as a land of naked exploitation and urban crisis. In the mid-twenties he began to regard business and consumer goods as determining the whole of American life, art and literature included. It was in this frame of mind that he discovered *Amerika*. Brecht was fond of primary sources, visual or literary, on the everyday life of American cities, and used images of the grain elevators in a play on cereal trade. But he also recognized the symbolic value of an "impressive photograph" found on plate 29 of the original edition of *Amerika*:

> I saw a photograph of the entrance to Broadway in New York (the gate of this cement gorge, over which "Danger!" is written) and tried hard to figure out what people will be able to say about the distractions of these cities when their time is up.[294]

Brecht was explicit on the usefulness of Mendelsohn's "extraordinary photographs," "which can be pinned up separately on the wall and give the (surely deceptive) impression that large cities are inhabitable."[295] Better than anyone, he understood *Amerika*'s warnings about the violence and menace represented in an urban environment—of which he had no direct experience until exile brought him to

Los Angeles in July 1941. Mendelsohn himself was well aware that *Amerika* lent itself to essentially negative readings, so much so in fact that when he sent a copy to Lewis Mumford, he expressed the hope, in a cover letter, that he would "perceive the positive side and not merely the sharp criticism of [his] country's historical vertigo."[296] Friendly relations with Mumford were one of the direct consequences of the 1924 trip. Mumford would remain attentive to the work of Mendelsohn, who in 1928 wrote him a letter recommending Walter Gropius on the occasion of the latter's first trip to America.

In Germany, Mendelsohn's book sold to readers well outside architectural and art circles.[297] More generally, European readers could not avoid comparisons between *Amerika* and earlier publications. Writing in the Russian Constructivist review *Sovremennaia Arkhitektura* (Contemporary Architecture), Aleksandr Pasternak contrasted Mendelsohn's vision with Hegemann's, regarding the former as conveying the "quintessence" of America, though he reserved the right to "draw [his] own conclusions" and corroborated the earlier view that there were two American architectures, the old conservative and the new based on standardization and the "scientific" organization of labor.[298]

Amerika was a dazzling success in the bookstores, and was reprinted several times in the year of its publication. The sixth impression (1928) was a complete reworking of the original edition. Several images were replaced, and others remounted.[299] Mendelsohn was also forced to acknowledge the fiction implicit in the absence of photographic credits; he now claimed responsibility for "most" of the illustrations, and attributed sixteen of the original photographs to Knud Lonberg-Holm.[300] True, the Dane had already marketed some of his photographs in Europe, which explains why he was credited with them long before

58. Photograph of Broadway in New York City. Plate 29 of Erich Mendelsohn, *Amerika, Bilderbuch eines Architekten,* Berlin, 1926. Canadian Centre for Architecture, Montreal

the revised edition appeared, and why he protested vigorously against Mendelsohn's "borrowings." In 1925, one year before *Amerika's* publication, László Moholy-Nagy obtained direct from America a "night-time view" included in Mendelsohn's book, and used it in his *Malerei Photographie Film,* a book extending his Bauhaus teachings.[301] Lonberg-Holm corresponded with the Dutch architects J. J. P. Oud and Cornelis van Eesteren, who in 1928 published his reflections and American photos in the review *i10*.[302] Morever, twenty-two of the twenty-six new photographs included in the 1928 edition of *Amerika* (of which three were replacements) were attributed to Erich Karweik, Mendelsohn's chief draughtsman, who had visited America in 1927.[303] Finally, it is possible that some documents were "borrowed" from photographic agencies, whose documentation of construction sites was especially prolific at the time.

Opposite:

VII. Knud Lonberg-Holm
(1895–1972). Photograph of
the Woolworth Building,
New York, 1923. Reproduced
in Erich Mendelsohn, *Amerika,
Bilderbuch eines Architekten*,
Berlin, 1926.
Estate of K. Lonberg-Holm,
New York

59. Knud Lonberg-Holm
(1895–1972). Construction
of the Sheldon Hotel in New York,
c. 1922. Reproduced in Erich
Mendelsohn, *Amerika, Bilderbuch
eines Architekten*, Berlin, 1926.
Nederlands Architectuurinstituut,
Rotterdam

60. Moisei Ginzburg
(1892–1946), Review of the
book *Amerika, Bilderbuch eines
Architekten* by Erich Mendelsohn,
in *Sovremennaia Arkhitektura*,
1926. Collection Jean-Louis
Cohen, Paris

61. "America, Reflections
by Knud Lonberg-Holm,"
an article illustrated with
photographs of American
factories, in *i10*, October 1928.
Canadian Centre for Architecture,
Montreal

While its polemic content was discussed by Brecht and Neutra, *Amerika* was used as a storehouse of images by a number of critics and architects, and thus constituted a primary source for novel readings of the modern metropolis, and even for unusual montages. In 1927 the critic Adolf Behne illustrated an article on advertising for *Das neue Frankfurt* with Fritz Lang's *Broadway at Night*; Lonberg-Holm's *New York, Madison Square*; and *Detroit, a New Street*."[304] In 1930 El Lissitzky used images from *Amerika* in his designs for a sports complex, and created two photomontages on the theme of "runners" in which a hurdler is set against a network of vertical lines, with *Broadway at Night* as backdrop.[305] For his book on Russian architecture published in the same year, Lissitzky used Mendelsohn's low-angle technique in his photographs of Moscow buildings.[306]

Mendelsohn's 1924 travels had an immediate impact on his own practice. His industrial building

X. Knud Lonberg-Holm (1895–1972). Photograph of the rear façade of the Tuller Building in Detroit, 1923. Reproduced in Erich Mendelsohn, *Amerika, Bilderbuch eines Architekten*, Berlin, 1926. Estate of K. Lonberg-Holm, New York

IX. Knud Lonberg-Holm (1895–1972). Photograph of the Cadillac Hotel in Detroit, 1923. Reproduced in Erich Mendelsohn, *Amerika, Bilderbuch eines Architekten*, Berlin, 1926. Estate of K. Lonberg-Holm, New York

VIII. Knud Lonberg-Holm (1895–1972). Photograph of the rear façade of the Statler Building in Detroit, 1923. Reproduced in Erich Mendelsohn, *Amerika, Bilderbuch eines Architekten* under the title *Hinterhof* ("rear court"), Berlin, 1926. Estate of K. Lonberg-Holm, New York

XI. El Lissitzky (1890–1941). *The Runners*, after 1926. Galerie Berinson, Berlin

XIII. Cover of the review *Chantiers* reproducing the Lovell House by Richard Neutra (1892–1970). From *Chantiers*, March–April 1934. Institut Français d'Architecture. Centre d'Archives d'Architecture du xxᵉ siècle, Paris

XII. Cover of Richard Neutra, *Amerika: Die Stilbildung des neuen Bauens in den Vereinigten Staaten*, Vienna, 1930. Graphic design by El Lissitzky. Canadian Centre for Architecture, Montreal

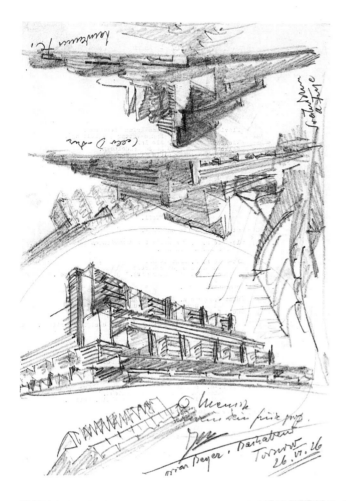

63. Erich Mendelsohn
(1887–1953). *Sketch
dedicated to Frank Lloyd Wright,*
1924. Kunstbibliothek,
Staatliche Museen zu Berlin,
Berlin

62. Erich Mendelsohn
(1887–1953). *Oskar Beyer,
Bachabend* (Oskar Beyer,
an evening of Bach) *Perspectives
drawn on the back of a concert
program,* 1926. Kunstbibliothek,
Staatliche Museen zu Berlin,
Berlin

64. Erich Mendelsohn
(1887–1953). *Sketch for an
American skyscraper,* 1924.
Kunstbibliothek, Staatliche
Museen zu Berlin, Berlin

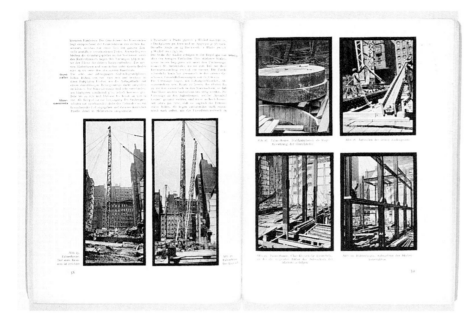

65. Two pages illustrating the construction of the Palmer House Hotel in Chicago, in Richard Neutra, *Wie baut Amerika?*, Stuttgart, 1927. Canadian Centre for Architecture, Montreal

programs, such as the textile mill at Leningrad, construction of which began in 1926, gained in complexity and scale, while commercial buildings such as the Schocken department stores at Stuttgart (1926) and Chemnitz (1929) included glazed corner cylinders that seemed to mock the timid ornament of American buildings. Before crossing the Atlantic, Mendelsohn had often associated his architectural fantasies with pieces by Bach or Brahms. He dedicated one of these sketches, entitled *American Skyscraper*—a design strongly cadenced by its parallelepipeds—to Frank Lloyd

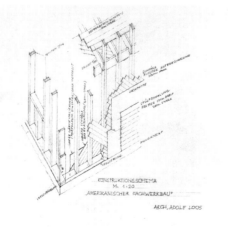

66. Adolf Loos, architect (1870–1933). *Axonometric for the "Amerikanischer Fachwerkbau" wood-frame construction of the Schnabl house*, Vienna, 1931. Graphische Sammlung Albertina, Vienna

Wright.[307] The success of *Amerika* encouraged further publication, and Mendelsohn now proposed a comparable book on Bolshevik Russia, which he discovered while his Leningrad building was under construction. But in 1929 he decided on a more complex enterprise involving a comparative study of the American, Russian, and European situations. In *Russland, Europa, Amerika*—a "cross-sectional" study showing American modernity in action—Mendelsohn is less reserved than in *Amerika*. He sees the Russians as having their feet in history and their heads in the clouds of inaccessible utopias—the offshoot of an America which Mendelsohn (among others) had helped make familiar. And he regards Europe as being caught in the middle.[308] In a sense, Mendelsohn's second work closed the first chapter of Americanism, for anti-American literature henceforth began to proliferate in Europe.[309]

Richard Neutra and the Chicago Construction Sites

Richard Neutra left Vienna for the United States in 1923, having learned of her charms from Adolf Loos. Neutra's American testimony would be substantially different from Mendelsohn's. He is the author of two books published within three years of each other: *Wie baut Amerika?* and *Amerika*. True, Neutra mediated Mendelsohn's encounter with Wright; but his views differed markedly from those of his former boss, whose opinions he attacked. In fact, Neutra was determined to make a success of his career in the Unites States at all costs.[310] Neutra regretted that in Mendelsohn's rather short tour, "[he] has formed a judgment about this country which is as negative as it is superficial. I don't think it is possible [he wrote to Frances Toplitz] to get a correct idea about this district of human civilization without paying the price as I do; to know it by patiently working here."[311]

Published in 1927, *Wie baut Amerika?* was directly inspired by such moody reflections. Turning his back on Mendelsohn's lyrical skepticism, Neutra lauded instead the positive American approach to design and construction. This version of the American lesson, which took on board the California which Mendelsohn had decided to neglect, centered on organization, technique, and standards.[312] The book reflects Neutra's long-standing preoccupation with "industrialized technology" in the United States (as inspired by Loos, who "would say that the most beautiful piece of cabinetwork was the oak toilet seat").[313] The book contains more than one direct reference to Loos's reflections on America, which Neutra had occasion to hear in the Viennese cafés. In his earliest correspondence with Rudolf Schindler (who had emigrated in 1914), Neutra requested documentation concerning "details of American construction."[314] Later, as draughtsman n° 208 at Holabird and Roche, he gained first-hand experience of the highly technical data that earlier travelers had neglected. He wrote *Wie baut Amerika?* in Chicago, Taliesin, and California, and sent it on to his in-laws, the Niedermanns, to negotiate with the publisher, who in turn modified its initial title, *Gegenwärtige Bauarbeit Amerikanischer Kreise* (Contemporary Building Work in American Circles).

Like Mendelsohn's, Neutra's book is an anthology based on experience—but one which, for the first time, was not *extrinsic* to American architecture, but instead tapped the resources of professional practice. A third of the work is devoted to the construction of the Palmer House Hotel in Chicago, with which Neutra had been directly involved at Holabird and Roche. Another distinctive feature is the book's geographic scope. Though he mentions New York briefly, the predominant scenes (for activity is discussed, in particular the construction sites) are Chicago and, for the first time, southern California.

Neutra's Americanism thus reflects a westward shift, with Los Angeles as a new epicenter. Though earlier books on Frank Lloyd Wright had furnished glimpses of his California houses, this publication opened up new horizons. In his introduction, Neutra denies having written "a literary work." In his view, "the public is not sufficiently informed concerning everyday matters and the real atmosphere surrounding the activities of the engineer-architect"; he dedicates the book to all men, "young and old," who strive and will strive "to develop constructions adapted to their epoch." *Wie baut Amerika?*'s technical content is clearly stated from the start:

> The lay reader is requested to be patient wherever technical matters are at issue. It is precisely from this point of view that a more precise understanding of architecture is to be achieved, and not from aesthetic prejudices, whatever their intrinsic value.[315]

The beginning of the book's first section, "Affirmation of the Present," is devoted to a fairly general consideration of machine age society and the American city. After remarking on questions of technique, housing policies, and traffic, he comes to railroad stations. Presenting his own designs for *Rush City Reformed*, a theoretical project motivated by metropolitan congestion and proposing a new urban model involving different levels of traffic flow, Neutra compares various types of terminals and through-stations, whether on the surface or underground. His treatment of the city culminates in a discussion of zoning, in which he cites the specific instances of New York and Chicago. He illustrates his view of the vertical mass of business centers with an image of the palace of Lhasa. Yet all this is designed to give weight to proposals for "tall, narrow blocks" as a model for his *Rush City Reformed*. The second part of the book is devoted to the grand hotel, which Neutra sees as an essential component of the business center—a particular example of the more general type of "composite multipurpose

67. Balloon-frame construction in Richard Neutra, *Amerika: Die Stilbildung des neuen Bauens in den Vereinigten Staaten,* Vienna, 1930. Canadian Centre for Architecture, Montreal

downtown structures,"[316] and a microcosm where all life can be lived.

In his description of design and construction processes, Neutra emphasizes the *efficiency* of American architectural offices. He discusses the division of labor as practiced at Holabird and Roche, and mentions, over and above the design office as such, the structural engineers, electricians, accountants, contract specialists, etc. He also enumerates the various types of detailed plans drawn up for each project, and notes the rigorous way in which the office's facilities (e.g. the library) are organized. He states that the structure represents an increasingly small proportion of overall costs, not only in large buildings but in houses, and cites a study by Henry Wright, who estimated that by 1970 it would represent no more than 15% of total building costs.[317] (This economic approach would also mark Neutra's subsequent publications.) The theme of *Skelett-konstruktion* leads seamlessly to that of domestic architecture, and here Neutra presents one of his own projects. He then proceeds to California and La Jolla, with a discussion of Schindler's 1923 Pueblo Rivera, built in concrete.

Neutra also discusses the cement blocks used in Wright's California houses with a rhetorical question concerning the excesses of machine age architecture and "formalism": "What can 'expressed structure' possibly mean?" He affirms the *"sachlich"* character and "clear form" of industrial buildings, and is of the opinion that technique will lead only to a gradual evolution in form, though he believes that its elements will be eventually more plentiful than at the time of writing. He cites the multivolume *Sweet's* catalogue of building components in a novel approach to the links between architect, industry, and the market. Finally, he tackles the question of construction in terms of the frame, detailing the advantages of industrial structures and tall buildings; for the latter he recommends close study of pueblos, considering their layout an alternative to "dishonest forms." The last image of the book, Lloyd Wright's hotel at Palm Springs, shows a far west that is at once deserted and alluring.

Wie baut Amerika? was warmly received in Europe and the United States,[318] as well as in Soviet Russia, the only country to publish a translation.[319] In 1930 Neutra published a second book, entitled *Amerika,* as part of the collection *Neues Bauen in der Welt* published under the direction of Josef Gantner, editor-in-chief of *Das neue Frankfurt.* The cover of Neutra's *Amerika*—like that of *Frankreich,* written by his brother-in-law Roger Ginsburger—was designed by El Lissitzky, whose study of Soviet architecture, *Russland,* completed the collection.[320] *Amerika* centered specifically on modern architecture, and introduced new figures such as Irving Gill ("Sullivan's office boy"), and Rudolf Schindler, Neutra's increasingly independent associate. Its structure differs from that of his previous book, in that the approach is more specifically historical. Neutra traces the development of American architecture from the 19th century. He follows Patrick Geddes, the Scottish town planning specialist, in differentiating between "paleotechnic" and "neotechnic" (a dissociation that would be reiterated by Lewis Mumford). He stresses the specific quality of "neotechnic"—standardization—and argues the advantages of steel over concrete, the former more precise and stable in its characteristics.

Neutra underlines the *obsolescence* of American buildings and discusses the question of investment and financial management. This treatment of economic and market questions was quite new at the time, and reflects a preoccupation shared with Martin Wagner. Neutra's historical account commences with William Le Baron Jenney's Home Insurance Building and culminates with Irving Gill, linked by discussions of buildings by Burnham, Sullivan, Root, and Wright. In his prophetic concluding remarks on the future of lightweight neotechnical structures, Neutra even mentions the Ringling Brothers' big top.

The impact of *Amerika* was even greater than that of *Wie baut Amerika?* and its novel vision would be pointed up in Le Corbusier's *L'Architecture d'aujourd'hui.* Julius Posener reported that ". . . Neutra shows us neither the skyscrapers of Manhattan, nor Frank Lloyd Wright's Californian castles," and praised the inclusion of "numerous reproductions of blueprints, views of Los Angeles's manufacturing district, and the hall of a Chicago skyscraper, with its "twin elevator banks."[321]

On the strength of these two books, Neutra was invited to participate in the 1930 CIAM in Brussels, where he presented a report on "tall, horizontal, and intermediate structures under American conditions"[322]—the first time American techniques had been discussed at this conference. Henceforth, Neutra was viewed less as a reporter than as a Euro-

68. Photomontage by El Lissitzky (1890–1941), in David Arkin, *Arkhitektura Sovremennogo Zapada*, Moscow, 1932. Getty Center, Resource Collections, Santa Monica

pean-born American architect—an exile in fact—which reveals the extent to which the intellectual's lot was fraught with difficulties during that time. Unlike Carlo Emilio Rava, who dismissed Neutra's work as an example of the "paradoxical Mediterraneity of American architecture," Anna-Maria Mazzuchelli, writing in 1935, described it as "evidence of the universality of European taste and a clear instance of stylistic coherence," adding that "his polemic approach and his exile are hallmarks of our destiny."[323]

Maiakovsky's Futurist Disillusion

Spaced ten years apart, travel accounts by the Russian poet Vladimir Maiakovsky and Le Corbusier were tinged with the same condescending attitude to the stark contrast between American cities and architectural works. In the two decades following the 1917 revolution, direct experience of America by Russian avant-garde intellectuals was rare enough for Maiakovsky's journey in 1925 to take on symbolic value. Four years earlier, Maiakovsky had regarded the GOELRO plan of 1920 (for the electrification of Soviet Russia) as evidence that America was invading the Russian villages, and countered the view that electrification was nothing but pie in the sky in the poem "Ranshe, teper":

> Just wait, *bourgeois*, there will be New York at Tetiushi, there will be paradise in Shuia.[324]

His 1920 poem "150,000,000" depicted conquering America with images of the monster Woodrow Wilson and scenes from a Chicago operetta.[325] This vision was, moreover, criticized by Trotsky for its lack of "class consciousness." In New York, he commented ironically on his earlier naïveté and mocked stereotyped accounts like Tverskoi's:[326]

> Russians in general, and Russian artists and Futurists in particular, depict America through various images that basically boil down to this: a vision of grandioseness. In peasant imaginations, this takes the form of prosperous, limitless meadows on which vast herds of fat cattle graze.
>
> For Futurists, it takes the form of a gigantic puppet of Woodrow Wilson, symbol of the American bourgeoisie.
>
> Chicago is a colossal city of 14,000 streets, each with six hundred arcades, all drowned in a sea of electric lighting that makes daylight seem like a feeble candle. No inhabitant is below the rank of general.[327]

Maiakovsky's voyage to New York followed that of Sergei Esenin in 1923. On his return, Esenin published *Zheleznyi Mirgorod,* an account of the trip marked by a romance with Isadora Duncan, in which he attacked the Futurists:

> On the sixth day, around noon, land appeared.
>
> An hour later, New York rose before my eyes. Mother of God, Maiakovsky's poems are so tame! How can the power of its iron and granite be expressed in words?! It is a speechless poem. Any description would be paltry. Oh you nice, silly Russian poets, whether home-loving, town-developing, or electrifying, with your "forges" and your "*Lef*"— you're placing [a provincial town like] Tula alongside Berlin or Paris!"[328]

On his arrival in New York, where he met up with his old Futurist companion David Burliuk, Maiakovsky decided to "verify" the Americanism in which his earlier Futurist positions had been grounded.[329] Like Maxime Gorky in 1906, he was struck by the power of money and proceeded to depict the many segregated Americas and alienated crowds which he encountered there. Nonetheless, he expressed admiration for the skyscrapers, and for the Brooklyn Bridge over the East River, built forty years earlier by John and Washington Roebling, which had already received considerable notice in the Russian popular press and technical reviews.[330] Maiakovsky immediately saw America as "confirming . . . the Futurism of naked technology, the superficial impressionism of cables and smoke, whose task has been to revolutionize conformist mentalities henceforth confined to the villages." He allowed himself the (typically Futurist) indulgence of turning up his nose at the Manhattan skyscrapers, regarding them as "a gigantic accident stumbled upon by children," thus anticipating Le Corbusier's provocative remarks by a decade:[331]

> No, New York is not modern. New York is unorganized. Mere machinery, subways, skyscrapers and the like do not make real industrial civilization. These are only the externals.

America has gone through a tremendous material development which has changed the face of the world. But the people have not yet caught up to their world. . . . Intellectually, New Yorkers are still provincials. Their minds have not accepted the full implications of the industrial age.[332]

Maiakovsky's 1926 poem "Broadway" depicts the New York skyscrapers and the surge of people which they absorb during the day and regurgitate in the evening. Elsewhere, he saw Broadway as a heap of ruins, setting it off against the collective spirit of the New Russia.[333] In 1925 he published impressions of New York, Chicago, and Detroit in *Moio otkrytie Ameriki*.[334] In this book, with a cover designed by Rodchenko, Maiakovsky ponders on the fact that his admiration for specific technical achievements (including the Brooklyn Bridge) had not been enough to convince him of the virtues of Soviet industrial civilization, one quite devoid of the "new" culture.

Rodchenko, on the other hand, got no further than Paris, where he helped to prepare the Soviet pavilion for the 1925 Exposition des Arts Décoratifs, and bitterly regretted staying in the "old-fashioned"[335] French capital, all the more so in that in 1924 he had taken part in one of the most picturesque literary manifestations of *Amerikanizm*, designing covers for Marietta Chaguinian's *Mess-Mend, or A Yankee at Petrograd*, a ten-volume adventure novel in the extraordinarily popular pre-Revolutionary genre, examples of which include the adventures of Nick Carter and *Nat Pinkerton, King of Detectives*. Viktor Shklovski and Vsevolod Ivanov also tried their hand at *Pinkertonshchina* with their novel *Mustard Gas*.[336] Chaguinian's novel was a response to demands published in *Pravda* by the Bolshevik leader Nikolai Bukharin (who had spent some of the war years in New York) for a "Red Pinkerton."[337] The book was published under

69. Photograph of Vladimir Maiakovsky (1893–1930) in New York, in *Sovremennaia Arkhitektura*, 1930. Canadian Centre for Architecture, Montreal

the pseudonym "Jim Dollar," a name so obscure that Bukharin himself was briefly thought to be the author. In this episodic "novel-tale" the hero, Arthur Rockefeller, discovers Russia in the throes of proletarian revolution. Rockefeller joins forces against the capitalists with a group of workers who, under the leadership of Mick Thingsmaster, excel at the quasi-magical art of inventing a multitude of electrical weapons and equipment.[338] All in all, the Soviet Union proved capable (at least in literary terms) of turning the weapons of technology back on the West, whose decline was deemed as inevitable in Moscow as it was by Oswald Spengler in Germany.

„MIASTO MŁYN ŻYCIA"

FOTOMONTAŻ NA STR. TYTUŁ. TYGODNIKA
„NA SZEROKIM ŚWIECIE" 1929.—

Along with modernization campaigns in European cities following the Great War came a change in the nature of Americanism. The transformation of city centers enabled a new generation of public and private economic agents to create the conditions for the introduction of tall buildings along American lines. While radical architects were often ignored in this process or marginalized in the organized competitions, this did not prevent them from theoretical elaborations. Whereas Chicago had been the prewar model, urban theory after 1918 centered essentially on New York City.

New York: New Horizons

By then the world's largest urban agglomeration, New York was closely observed both by correspondents writing for weekly illustrated magazines and by the town planners, who in 1924 held their second world congress there. Throughout the twenties, the urban transformation of New York usually involved the private sector in municipal initiatives, and European specialists were actively involved in this process. The 1916 Zoning Ordinance drawn up by George Ford regulated building heights through a system of setbacks. From 1921 to 1929, the banker Charles Dyer Norton, who had been one of the commissioners of Burnham and Bennett's plan for Chicago, organized the first Regional Plan, funded by the Russell Sage Foundation, and commissioned the Scottish planner Thomas Adams (who had hitherto worked in Canada) to draw it up.[339] Designed to combat urban congestion, the plan envisaged a "rational dispersion" of industry and housing throughout the region; it therefore recommended a strengthening of transportation infrastructure, and above all the creation of a network of highways linking

Kazimierz Podsadecki, artist. *The City—Mill of Life*, 1929.
Sztuki Museum, Łodz

Europe

Interprets

the

Skyscraper

70. E. Maxwell Fry (1899–1987). *Project for a city of the future, 1929–31.* From the *First Regional Plan for N.Y. and its Environs,* 1931. Regional Plan Association, New York

urban districts with the outlying counties, involving an ambitious program of tunnels and bridges.[340] The development of Manhattan was based not only on policies regulating zoning and usage (which had already been covered by the Zoning Ordinance), but also the transformation of the civic center and a program of monuments on both sides of the island. The plan was heterogeneous in character, with illustrations by George Ford, Francis Swales, and the British architect E. Maxwell Fry, the only one to envision radically modern solutions for the city. Harvey Wiley Corbett's suggestions were based on reformulations of his prewar studies of differential traffic levels, which were revised and illustrated by Hugh Ferriss.

The contradictions inherent in this plan were little remarked on in Europe, though its centralist hypothesis was attacked in 1922 by Raymond Unwin, the theorist and practitioner of the English garden city.[341] Suggestions by Lewis Mumford, who contested the plan's "colossal highway networks," the fetishism of its "ill-prepared pudding," and above all its failure to decentralize housing districts and thus allow for the creation of viable suburban municipalities, were studiously ignored.[342] The only decentralizing element to be implemented—the new town of Radburn, created by Henry Wright and Clarence Stein from 1927 on, and predicated on extensive use of the automobile—would not be fully discussed in Europe until the late thirties.[343]

On the ground, the most striking phenomenon was the renewed race for the sky in Manhattan. The Empire State and Chrysler buildings were analyzed in detail in the technical reviews of Europe.[344] The 1916 regulations had paved the way for a marked increase in the size of housing, offices, and hotels, accompanied by a gradual introduction of novel decorative themes. The drawings in which Hugh Ferriss explored the potential of the 1916 regulations (envisioning a rationalized "metropolis of tomorrow") figured among the most coherent and poetic expressions of the transformations then underway in the city; they carried enough conviction to become reference images both of the city as Corbett, Hood, and Ferriss themselves had imagined it, and of its built reality.[345]

European responses to these new urban programs were most clearly formulated in several competitions, which were doubtless more the fruit of symbolic ambitions than of real estate pressures.[346] The skyscraper, a central feature in the new architectural and urban landscape, thus became a sort of joker in the pack whose symbolic power, it was assumed, could solve the problem of urban congestion and conflict (which nonetheless went on, sometimes for decades).

From Friedrichstrasse to Chicago Tribune

The idea of a metropolis consisting of specialized districts, which had already been popular among planners before 1914, emerged in greater detail in the competitions and urban projects of the postwar years. Architects and urban reformers vied with each other in their desire to elaborate practical strategies. In 1914 in Berlin, where the crystalline fantasies of the Expressionists were associated with visions of metropolitan reform,[347] the architect Bruno Möhring, who had participated in the St. Louis Exposition in 1904 and had been an eminent candidate in the Berlin competition held in 1910, proposed a tall building for the triangular plot hemmed in by a branch of the river Spree, the Friedrichstrasse, and the central station. In 1920, acting on behalf of Berlin's business community, he attempted to persuade the Prussian interior minister to authorize exceptions to the regulation limiting building height throughout the capital to 22 meters. In 1921 his *Turmhaus Aktiengesellschaft* organized a competition for the construction of an office building eighty meters high, a symbolic "cry" in defense of the tall building.[348]

The entries were extraordinarily varied, a mark of the vitality of the German architectural scene and fascination with the skyscraper brief, as witness the explicitly Americanist theoretical designs published by K. Paul Andrae.[349] Though practically nothing was built in Germany at the time, the skyscraper seems to have galvanized the architectural profession as a whole.[350] For some, like Mies van der Rohe and Otto Kohtz, this challenge led to a series of reflections on the tall building within the city, whereas for others, such as Hugo Häring, Hans Poelzig, and Hans Scharoun, it represented no more than a short-lived episode in their work on the architecture of the metropolis. For the most part, the candidates interpreted Möhring's mandate in terms of the tripartite division of the commercial building, while adapting it to a most peculiar site. In many cases they designed a massive plinth, with various treatments of the superstructure.[351]

Mies van der Rohe's project, which marked his spectacular entry into the sphere of urban architecture, differed from all the other designs in its utter indifference to urban context (which was merely reflected in his glass facades) and in its transcendence of the modern structure/archaic facing dichotomy which Le Corbusier and El Lissitzky would denounce. The twenty-story prism, a steel frame en- cased in glass, had neither base nor crown, and was simply sliced off at its summit. It was to have occupied the totality of the triangular site; three "canyons" led from the street to the ground floor elevators and carried light to the upper stories.[352] At the 1923 *Grosse Berliner Kunstausstellung*, Mies exhibited a second skyscraper in which the angular glass surfaces of the competition entry were replaced with a continuous, undulating façade. Though diametrically opposed to contemporary American efforts in concept, both versions reproduced their "free" partitions, which, moreover, hallmarked Mies's studies for office buildings at the time. One critic, writing in the *Journal of the American Institute of Architects*, regarded Mies's 1923 project as "the image of a naked building descending the stairs," in response to Walter Curt Behrendt's analysis of German skyscraper designs:

> In technical construction the German projects will seem familiar to American architects, because in this respect they closely imitate the American model. Imitation, in this case, is fully justified, for it seems hardly possible to devise anything better than the American engineers' "steel-cage construction," which carries all loads independently of the external walls, thereby relieving these of all functions of support.

71. Ludwig Mies van der Rohe, architect (1886–1969). *Project for a skyscraper in the Friedrichstrasse: perspective*, Berlin, 1921. Bauhaus-Archiv, Berlin

72. Ludwig Mies van der Rohe, architect (1886–1969). *Project for a skyscraper in the Friedrichstrasse: east elevation*, Berlin, 1921. The Museum of Modern Art, gift of the architect, New York

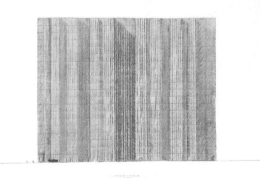

On the other hand, as regards planning and architectural treatment, German architects have evinced remarkable creative originality, and have perhaps surpassed the American models in various and entirely new directions.[353]

Behrendt analyzed not only Mies's project but also that of Poelzig, whose tectonic approach was altogether different. The three concave façades of his Y-shaped tower inscribed within a circle are punctuated by solid verticals, with openings cadenced in Berlin fashion. The project's "integral, predominantly architectonic organism" (in Hilberseimer's phrase)[354] was visible in its internal organization, with staircases slightly off axis relative to the openings on the façades. Apart from these two extremes of transparency and opacity, the competition entries were extremely varied, especially those of the Expressionists. Hans Scharoun designed differential volumes wrapped around a triangular courtyard, while Hugo Häring proposed two variant V- and Y-shaped plans, both draped in flexible outer skins. The Luckhardt brothers, who won second prize, ignored the shape of the site and proposed a large rectangular building with strongly accentuated horizontals. Martin Elsaesser, who like Mies opted for a prism, organized his façades (with their conventional openings) around a rectangular courtyard. He shared fourth prize with Otto Kohtz, who had long been fascinated with the theme of the skyscraper, and whose design was based on that of New York's Sheldon Hotel, which had recently been published in the German press. Kohtz proposed a free-standing, vertical structure reflecting earlier research, in particular his *Reichshaus* project.[355] Alfons Bäcker was awarded first prize for a relatively uninspired octagonal plan. The Berlin competition was followed by others held in various German cities on the theme of the skyscraper or large office building. Poelzig's designs for the Hamburg *Messehaus* competition (1924–25) figured among the most literal

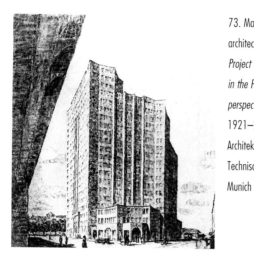

73. Martin Elsaesser, architect (1884–1957). *Project for a skyscraper in the Friedrichstrasse: perspective*, Berlin, 1921–22. Architekturmuseum Technische Universität, Munich

74. Hugo Häring, architect (1882–1958). *Project for a skyscraper in the Friedrichstrasse: perspective*, Berlin, 1921–22. Stiftung Archiv der Akademie der Künste, Berlin

75. Otto Kohtz, architect (1880–1956). *Project for office tower in the Friedrichstrasse at the corner of Karlstrasse: perspective*, Berlin, early 1920s. Plansammlung der Universitätsbibliothek der Technischen Universität, Berlin

76. Hans Poelzig, architect (1869–1936). *Project for a skyscraper in the Friedrichstrasse: perspective*, Berlin, 1921–19. Plansammlung der Universitätsbibliothek der Technischen Universität, Berlin

77. Walter Gropius, architect (1883–1969), with Adolf Meyer, architect (1881–1929). *Project for the* Chicago Tribune *Building: model*, 1922. Bauhaus-Archiv, Berlin

renderings, not of the isolated skyscraper, but of the American city skyline, with its tiered glass prisms.[356]

Only a few months after the Berlin competition, Chicago became the scene of the first Americanist export drive. The competition for new headquarters of the *Chicago Tribune*, in commemoration of its 65th birthday, was deliberately left open to all the architects on the planet. Despite the notable absence of Mendelsohn, Mies, and Le Corbusier, this competition was the occasion for the first massive European response to a specifically American brief, moreover one with ties to the first "tall buildings" of the nineteenth century.[357] Thirty-seven of the 265 entries (from twenty-three countries) were German, and one might be excused for regarding the competition as the second round of its Berlin counterpart, apart from the contribution of radical architects absent from the latter.

A measure of German architects' fascination with the New World is furnished by their massive representation in this competition, which demonstrated that the "radicals" were not the only Americanists.[358] The projects most representative of Weimar Germany were those of Walter Gropius and Adolf Meyer (parallelepipeds whose orthogonal grid was accentuated by the bladelike balconies), Ludwig Hilberseimer, and the Taut brothers. Hilberseimer removed all architectonic traces from his austere system of façades, which resemble George Grosz's contemporary paintings of buildings with dark window openings. Max Taut split his tower into prisms with a slender façade-grid, whereas the four corner pillars of Bruno Taut's tower rose to a pointed crown.

Classified among the French candidates (he lived in Nice at the time), Adolf Loos mocked eclectic strategies with a timeless, unfashionable, acontextual entry in the shape of an isolated Doric column in the Greek style, novel in that Roman examples were more generally used. Loos commented:

All those non-traditional forms were all-too-swiftly replaced by new ones, and the owner soon became aware that his building was not modern, since such forms change like ladies' hats.

So the only thing to be done was to invent the typical American skyscraper, examples of which were easy to identify at the beginning of the movement; but it is henceforth difficult for the uninitiated, on seeing a picture of a building, to tell whether it is located in San Francisco or Detroit.

This author consequently chose the column for his design. Tradition dictated the motif of a single, colossal column—Trajan's column was the model for Napoleon's column on Place Vendôme in Paris.

Architectural and aesthetic objections were raised to this idea—was it permissible to build an inhabited column? To which it might be replied that the finest skyscraper designs, those to which no similar objections could be made, were based on uninhabited monuments like the tomb of King Mausolus, used as a model for the Metropolitan Building, and a Gothic church, taken as a model for the Woolworth Building.[359]

Loos was certain that the column would one day be built, "if not in Chicago, then at least in another American city"; if not by him, "then at least by another architect." He stressed the stark contrast (surprising for the spectator) between the polished surface of the plinth and the column's grooved shaft. Loos's use of the term "column" indicated a humorous analogy between the architectural and the printed column—a reference to his earlier journalistic activities in America.

With the exception of Eliel Saarinen's "Gothic" skyscraper—a graceful telescopic design in response to the problem of the shift from squat base to slender summit, which won second prize behind John Mead Howells and Raymond Hood's designs and

80. Adolf Loos,
architect (1870–1933).
Project for the Chicago Tribune: *elevation,* 1922.
Graphische Sammlung Albertina,
Vienna

78. Adolf Loos, architect (1870–1933).
Project for the Chicago Tribune: *preparatory sketches,* 1922.
Graphische Sammlung Albertina, Vienna

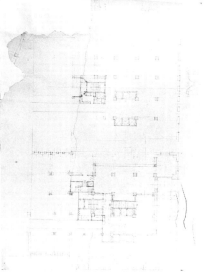

79. Adolf Loos, architect (1870–1933).
Project for the Chicago Tribune: *plan of ground floor and entrance,* 1922. Graphische Sammlung Albertina, Vienna

81. Eliel Saarinen, architect (1873–1950). *Project for the Chicago lakefront: perspective of the Chicago Tower, 1923. Cranbrook Art Museum, Bloomfield Hills, Mich.*

earned the praise of Louis Sullivan[360]—the foreign contributions were generally unremarkable. No Russians entered the competition; all five French entries, and most of the nine Italian designs, reiterated eclectic figures in the Beaux-Arts tradition, whose potential had been exhausted exactly thirty years earlier by Deperthes. Marcello Piacentini's knowledge of American architecture materialized in his façades, and his designs demonstrated a unity absent in those of his compatriots.[361] The most interesting Italian contribution to skyscraper design

came a few months later with the traditionalist Piero Portaluppi's project for New York. Set within a cityscape clearly modeled after Manhattan, his SKNE Building was, so to speak, carried in triumph by its four housing blocks, thus anticipating the midtown atriums of the 1980s. Portaluppi developed the theme of the cantilever in a theoretical project for Hellytown in 1926. The SKNE Building, with its soaring glass façades and vertical ribs, also anticipated solutions adopted for the Empire State Building.[362]

82. Eliel Saarinen, architect (1873–1950).

Project for the Chicago Tribune: *perspective,* 1922.

Courtesy of the Cranbrook Art Museum, Bloomfield Hills

XIV. Peter Behrens,
architect (1868–1940).
Architectural composition,
cover of *Das Plakat,* June 1920,
Canadian Centre for Architecture,
Montreal

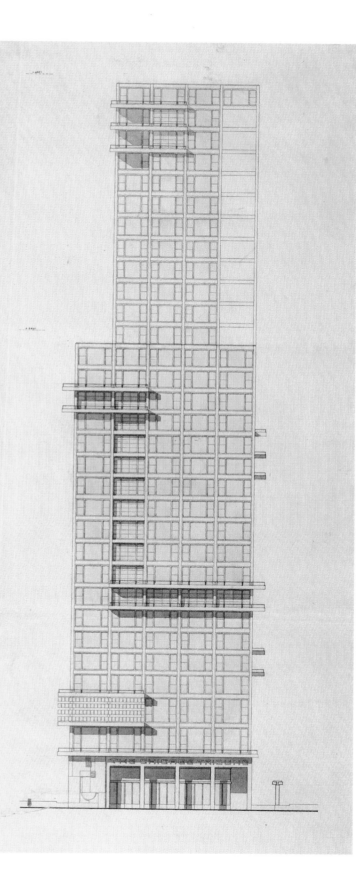

XV. Walter Gropius,
architect (1883–1969),
with Adolf Meyer,
architect (1881–1929).
Project for the Chicago Tribune:
elevation, 1922.
Courtesy of the Busch-Reisinger
Harvard University Art Museums,
Cambridge

XVI. Otto Kohtz,
architect (1880–1956).
*Project for Reichshaus: interior
perspective*, Berlin, early 1920s.
Plansammlung
der Universitätsbibliothek
der technischen Universität,
Berlin

XVII. Piero Portaluppi,
architect (1880–1967).
*Skyscraper for the SKNE
company: perspective,*
New York, 1924. Collection Arch.
Piero Castellini Baldissera, Milan

XVIII. Auguste Perret, architect (1874–1954),

with Charles Imbert, draughtsman (1865–?). *Tower cities*, c. 1922. Institut Français d'Architecture.

Centre d'Archives d'Architecture du xxᵉ siècle, Paris

Bernard Bijvoet and Johannes Duiker's skyscraper project, with superimposed horizontals at its base and Wrightian perspectives towards its summit, differed markedly from those submitted by the other Europeans. Their project underlined continuing Dutch interest in the skyscraper. The Berlagian Americanism of the 1900s had paved the way for a number of Utopian designs; in 1916 Hendricus Theodorus Wijdeveld published a "Millionenstad" and several other urban plans involving tall structures,[363] and in 1926 Cornelis van Eesteren produced theoretical designs for the "business district of a large contemporary city." Following Bijvoet's departure for Paris, where he worked with Pierre Chareau, Duiker researched the theme of tall structures with a plethora of design proposals,[364] while a number of other Dutch architects elaborated designs for the country's city centers. Knud Lonberg-Holm, who remained in close contact with van Eesteren throughout this period, did not submit his designs, instead publishing them elsewhere. Lonberg-Holm's project, which Paul Citroën used along with Gropius and Meyer's in his collage *Metropolis,* attracted Le Corbusier's approval; in 1925 he included it in his *Almanach d'architecture moderne,* along with Mies's glass skyscraper and two "towers" by Auguste Perret,[365] the first architect to fully exploit the reinforced concrete frame.

From Perret's "Tower-Cities" to Le Corbusier's Plan Voisin

From 1920 Auguste Perret designed a number of tall structures intended for several sites within Paris. This work had in fact begun before the Great War, following the completion of his apartment building at 25 *bis* rue Franklin in 1903. In an interview with a journalist held on its roof terrace only two years later, Perret spoke of the panoramic vistas obtained from such a height, which he compared with those of the first "floor" of the Eiffel Tower: " . . . in daytime, one can see the grandstand and the finishing post at Longchamp; I sometimes even follow the races from here. One can also take in Saint-Cloud, the Mont Valérien, the aqueduct at Marly, and the quarries of Saint-Denis."[366]

In 1921 Perret, pursuing this theme, invited readers of *Excelsior* to visit his roof terrace, "which overlooks the marvelous scene of the Champ de Mars, and whence one discovers all Paris. . . . From the top of the building, which is, however, no more than eight stories high, one no longer hears the noise of the city. . . . Is it so hard to imagine all the houses of a modern city built as tall and even taller?" Perret clearly signaled his intention to build "houses of the future" raised "on broad pillars firmly anchored in ground entirely covered by a thick layer of concrete, beneath which heavy carts [*sic*], trains, and subways will circulate":

> . . . avenues two hundred and fifty meters wide, lined on either side with houses touching the skies, towers if you like, well-spaced blocks linked by footbridges, such that inhabitants of the sixtieth floor can visit their neighbors without going up or down too far or blocking the traffic on the avenues.
>
> . . . My city is rooted in a floor built ten to twenty meters above street level, covering the utilities currently encumbering the ground . . . here we find terminuses of ultra-rapid subway lines leading to suburbs within a mean radius of a hundred kilometers and railroad intersections for direct access to the city.[367]

Perret thus aimed to position his tower-blocks above distinct traffic lines, based on principles of demarcation imported from America since 1913, though he took pains to criticize "the error of American skyscrapers, which are quite illogical, being situated at the side of insufficiently broad

L'ILLUSTRATION

L'AVENUE DES MAISONS-TOURS. — Un extraordinaire projet pour résoudre la question de l'habitation dans la région parisienne.
Composition de JACQUES LAMBERT, d'après les esquisses de l'architecte AUGUSTE PERRET.

85. Jacques Lambert, illustrator, after Auguste Perret, architect (1874–1954).

Avenue of residential towers. From *L'Illustration*, 12 August 1922. Canadian Centre for Architecture, Montreal

83, 84. Auguste Perret, architect (1874–1954); Charles Imbert, draughtsman (1865–?).

Tower cities, c. 1922. Institut Français d'Architecture.

Centre d'Archives d'Architecture du XXᵉ siècle, Paris

avenues."[368] Similarly, he justified the cruciform configuration of his buildings by stating that "we shall have to build skyscrapers, but not like the Americans . . . they will have to be cruciform in plan . . . [so that] light floods into all the apartments."[369]

This research, which Charles Imbert (who was preparing a theoretical treatise on "tower-cities" in Perret's office) transcribed in a series of exploratory designs, was illustrated in sketches which broadly evoke the decorative themes of Art Nouveau. These included seaport landscapes and buildings of various shapes, topped with clockface and candelabra figures. Perret's ideas were most fully articulated in his 1922 tower-city project, of which a rendering by Jacques Lambert provides the sole surviving illustration. The towers comprise two distinct registers. Plinths rising ten or so storeys high from ground level are linked together at their summit by footbridges or gangways; above these, the shafts of the housing blocks rise up around forty floors and are crowned with superstructures of various shapes. They are evocative of *King's Views of New York* and Andrae's urban views. Perret also imagined "the Taylorization and mechanization of the most down-to-earth tasks," adding that "in the third dimension, life is transformed far more positively than in the minds of sociologists. Placed above the level of noise and dust, man will enjoy immense horizons and vistas far more

moving than those of any boulevard Raspail."[370] Another of Perret's theoretical projects, published in *La Science et la vie* in 1925, combined a skyscraper with a port infrastructure, thus symptomatically reproducing the encounter between ocean liners and tall buildings as condensed in certain views of the Manhattan piers. Once again, the reference to New York was implicit in the proposal:

> The edification of such structures is no longer a *tour de force*. New types of cement have been invented since the first skyscrapers of New York and San Francisco, and may well render obsolete the tons of treated steel required to shore up the tall buildings of Manhattan.
>
> . . . The lower stories become department stores and the basements (the Woolworth [Building] has six underground floors, with restaurants and hairdressing salons) are large enough to house all possible services.[371]

Le Corbusier discussed these tower-cities as early as 1921 in the pages of *L'Esprit nouveau*; a year later he published his plan for a *Contemporary City for Three Million Inhabitants*. In his *Almanach d'architecture moderne*, the juxtaposition of Perret's 1922 and 1925 projects with those of Mies and Lonberg-Holm is indicative of the manner in which Le Corbusier's approach to the problem evolved. He now rejected Perret's notion of the "tower" and expressed a clear preference for the skyscraper (though he

86. Auguste Perret, architect (1874–1954). *A residential tower.* From *La Science et la vie*, 1925. Bibliothèque du CNAM, Paris

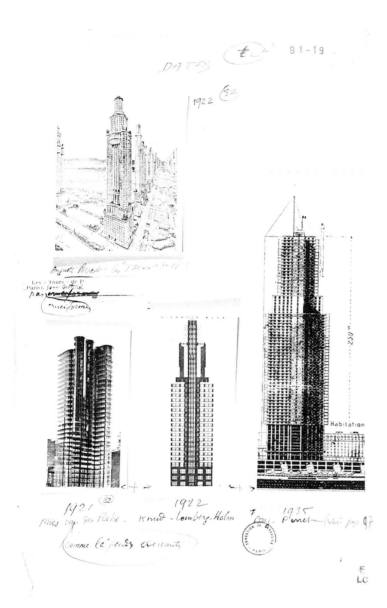

88. Paul Citroën, artist (1896–1983). *Metropolis*, 1923.

Rijksuniversiteit, Leyden, Netherlands

87. Le Corbusier, architect (1887–1965). Graphic design for the *Almanach d'architecture moderne*, 1925. Fondation Le Corbusier, Paris

regarded it as "fomenting disorder"), invoking views of Manhattan and the Woolworth Building:

> The *skyscraper*, an American term. An American building constructed (it is said) by the French; a building so tall that it scrapes the sky. There have been skyscrapers for twenty years. *Tower*, a term used in Paris to avoid saying "skyscraper." But to my mind the tower is a paltry thing. "Skyscraper" is a horrible word, but its meaning is more precise than "tower." *Tower* circumvents the question of origins.[372]

Though based initially on ideas formulated by Perret, Le Corbusier took up a critical position *vis-à-vis* skyscraper architecture, denouncing its excessive eclecticism in *Vers une architecture*, and its metropolitan absurdities in *Urbanisme*. With the plan for *Ville contemporaine* (1922) and the *Plan Voisin de Paris* (1925) he developed a new type of tall building, cruciform in plan, which he felt was more rational, and which was derived from Perret's initial proposals.[373] These projects for urban reorganization

—justly famous for their clarity and their radical character, which it would be superfluous to comment on here—incited many Europeans to further reflection, and established Le Corbusier's reputation as a bold innovator. Significant in this context was an article published in a contemporary Paris daily, which regarded the "dream of *L'Esprit nouveau*" as an appropriate vision of the capital "should Paris go American."[374]

Amerikanismus at Work in Berlin

In the capital of Republican Germany, Americanism was implemented on the two fronts of architectural projects and public administration. Duhamel claimed to have witnessed "the strangest 'Americanisms' in Germany, that country where the young men on returning from their first transatlantic trip, speak of New York as 'not bad but no longer American enough.'"[375] While Werner Hegemann pursued his journalistic activities, the idea of a global reorganization of Berlin's city center found its most radical formulation in Ludwig Hilberseimer's 1924 *Hochhausstadt* project, which owed as much to the stratified spaces of American urban designs as to Le Corbusier's ideas.[376] In *Großstadtarchitektur*, published in 1927, Hilberseimer presented a series of American high-rise buildings[377] and strove to justify his choice of rationally laid-out horizontal blocks (as opposed to Manhattan's skyscrapers) with intersecting transportation networks underground. In this context, Hilberseimer's evocation of Corbett's studies of split-level streets were explicit in *Großstadtarchitektur*, though his project emphasized rational planning more than a literal reading of American ad hoc solutions. In the project for a *Wohlfahrtsstadt* (welfare city), shown in Stuttgart in 1927, Hilberseimer proposed an extended city with a regular inner "City" of blocks crenellated or

tooth-shaped in plan at its center. By posing for the photographer in front of a model tower consisting of six buildings piled on top of each other, he ironically depicted himself as a builder of skyscrapers (which he refused to be), while at the same time conjuring up his *Chicago Tribune* designs.

Following his two field trips to America, *Stadtbaurat* Martin Wagner brought to Berlin notions of density and traffic flow and, above all, of the relations between public sector control and private investment. All paved the way for competitions on

89. Cornelis van Eesteren, architect (1897–1988); Louis-Georges Pineau, urban planner (1898–1987). *Building and traffic study for a commercial district in a large contemporary city, Paris, 1926.* Nederlands Architectuurinstituut, Rotterdam

90. Ludwig Hilberseimer,
architect (1885–1967).
High-rise city for Berlin:
east-to-west perspective, 1924.
The Art Institute of Chicago

91. Ludwig Hilberseimer,
architect (1885–1967).
Model for a "Wohlfahrtsstadt"
(Welfare City), presented
at the Wohlfarts-Ausstellung,
Stuttgart, 1927.
The Art Institute of Chicago

more complex urban themes. For Wagner—who, more than any other European architect, was interested in the economics of the American urban environment—the city (and with it the construction of tall buildings) had to be considered as a business enterprise and thus in terms of efficiency and productivity.[378] The offices and housing forming the theme of the competition for Berlin's Alexanderplatz can be seen as extending that of the Friedrichstrasse, in particular by reiterating the combination of transportation infrastructure and extensive business programs.[379] The most brilliant entries were those of Mies and the Luckhardt brothers (one of whom, Wassili, visited the United States in 1929).[380]

92. Martin Wagner, architect (1885–1957). *Project for the reconstruction of Potsdamer Platz and Leipziger Platz in Berlin: model, 1929.* Canadian Centre for Architecture, Montreal

Amerikanizm and Avant-Garde in Soviet Russia

Russian artists and architects tackled the question of the skyscraper from the early 1920s. Kazimir Malevich took up the challenge of the American city in sculptures he called "architectons," on one occasion superimposed on a photograph of Manhattan.

Russian Constructivists within the radical, avant-garde OSA group—namely, Ginzburg, Pasternak, and Leonidov—based their programs on skyscrapers, which they regarded as "social condensers" (but which they were, technically speaking, incapable of building). Pasternak first mentioned the American metropolis and the skyscraper in 1926, in an article on city planning published in the official organ of the OSA, *Sovremennaia Arkhitektura.* Pasternak (wrongly) deplored the absence of planning in the development of American cities, but above all he viewed the skyscraper as the very prototype of the "social condensers" by means of which the avant-garde intended to transform Soviet lifestyles in the

93. Peter Behrens, architect (1868–1940). *Project for the reconstruction of Alexanderplatz in Berlin:* model, Berlin, 1929. Canadian Centre for Architecture, Montreal

94. Kazimir Malevich
(1878–1935). *Architecton
against Manhattan
as background.* Illustration
in *Praesens,* Warsaw, September
1926. Sztuki Museum, Łodz

95. Nikolai Ladovsky.
"Skyscrapers of the USSR and
America," an article in *Izvestiia
ASNOVA,* 1926. Canadian
Centre for Architecture, Montreal

shortest possible time. To the extent that "social condensers [could] not, by definition, be dispersed or spread out in space, as far as possible it must be concentrated in a single point." Clearly, for Pasternak, who was of the opinion that "Americanism [would] leave its mark on the future cities" of Russia, that point had to be the skyscraper.[381] The engineer Boris Korchunov, who was also a member of the Constructivist group, followed Le Corbusier in favoring a skyscraper City in the heart of Moscow.[382]

The Rationalists—Krinsky, Ladovsky—strove to apply tectonic principles in their skyscraper projects of the early twenties. The problem of the skyscraper, which Malevich treated in a furtive, ironic manner, had been posed before 1914. With the first projects of the Commission for Painting-Sculpture-Architecture (*Zhivskulptarkh,* founded in 1919), the "communal housing" and "cathedrals of socialism" of Nikolai Ladovsky, Vladimir Krinsky, Nikolai Dokuchaev, and Georgi Mapu began to resemble Expressionist skyscrapers.[383] These architects, who in 1923 founded ASNOVA (Association of New Architects), pursued their research into the skyscraper through personal projects and teaching programs which they organized from 1920 at the Moscow VKhUTEMAS (Higher State Artistic and Technical Workshops).[384] Projects by Ivan Volodko and Sergei Lopatin, elaborated in 1924 and 1925 under Ladovsky's supervision, and Krinsky's study for the headquarters of the Higher National Economic Council, were critical architectural responses to the American ornamental treatment of façades. In the sole issue of *Izvestiia ASNOVA,* published in 1926, Ladovsky formulated pragmatic proposals concerning fire regulations for skyscrapers, daring to claim that "the skyscraper is no longer a problem for the USSR, but a reality." He deemed that "architecture should not camouflage structure, as in

XIX. Vladimir Krinsky
(1890–1971).
*Building for the Superior Council
of National Economy in Moscow:
detail of the façade, 1922–23.*
Shchusev Architectural Museum,
Moscow

XX. Aleksandr Rodchenko
(1891–1957).
The War of the Future, 1930.
Galerie Berinson, Berlin

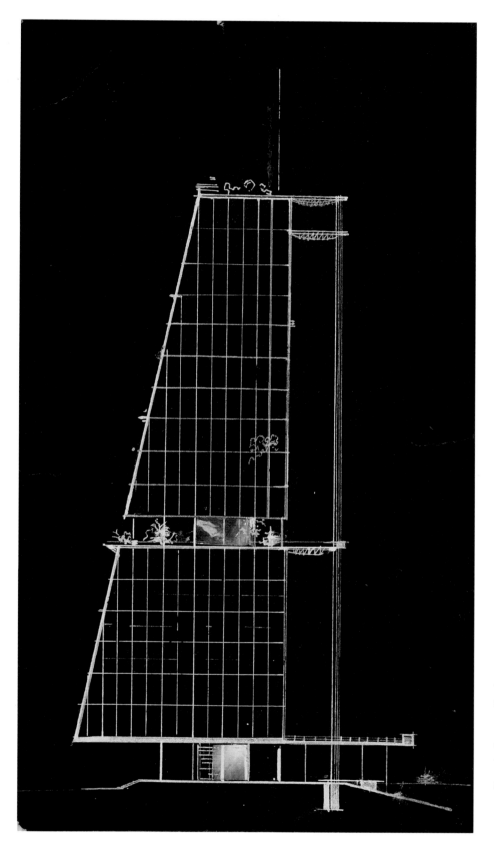

XXI. Ivan Illich Leonidov,
architect (1902–59).
*Competition project for the House
of Industry: glass-tower elevation,*
1929–30. Canadian Centre for
Architecture, Montreal

XXII. Iakov Chernikhov,
architect (1889–1951).
Architectural Fantasy with Diverse
Elements: Complex combination
of constructive volumes;
with pure decorative colors.
From *Architectural fantasies,*
Leningrad, 1933. Canadian
Centre for Architecture, Montreal

14
Архитектурная композиционная надуманность из многоразличных составляющих. Услож
ненная комбинация различных объемов сооружений с явной цветовой декоративностью.

XXIII. Iakov Chernikhov,
architect (1889–1951).
City of Giant Skyscrapers
in a Vertical Composition:
Warm orange and yellow tonal
range; conventional graphic
treatment of background.
From *Konstruktsia*
arkhitekturnykh i machinnykh
form (Construction of architectural
and mechanical forms),
Leningrad, 1931. Canadian
Centre for Architecture, Montreal

10
Город гигантов-небоскребов в композиции, выраженной по вертикали. Цветовая
гамма в теплых оранжево-желтых тонах. Условно-графическая фоновая обработка.

America; it must be 'sincere,'" adding, however, that "it would be naïve to believe that 'honestly' revealed structure alone could achieve architectural objectives." Stating that "the expression of height is the first of the skyscraper's problems," Ladovsky rejected the Americans' "Gothic" solutions, pointing out that bank directors of the twentieth century were not dressed like cardinals, and proposed instead a series of "plastic" solutions designed to lend direct architectural expression to the vertical and horizontal elements of skyscraper structure.[385]

Actual architectural responses to the problem of the skyscraper began to emerge with commissions from the state monopolies of the New Economic Policy. For the structural frame and suspended balconies of his initial designs of the *Izvestiia* Building in Moscow, Grigori Barkhin made use of a series of formal elements borrowed from another press-related project, Gropius and Meyer's entry into the 1923 *Chicago Tribune* competition. Boris Velikovsky, who designed a concrete office skyscraper for Gostorg, built its lower floors only, following a 1926 municipal regulation forbidding the construction of skyscrapers inside Moscow, which literally amputated all the projects then under study. However, this blow prevented neither Rodchenko from using the skyscraper ironically in his collages, such as *The War of the Future*, which showed an airship hovering dangerously above a Manhattan building, nor Iakov Chernikhov from indulging in his architectural reveries. Chernikhov based a number of his skyscraper designs on ASNOVA's formal procedures, and occasionally grouped them together to form a vaguely menacing skyline. His *Fundamental Principles of Contemporary Architecture* featured several variants of a "city-house" or "city-factory." Elsewhere, he proposed an agglomerate mass of buildings entitled "skyscraper city,"[386] a theme reiterated with the

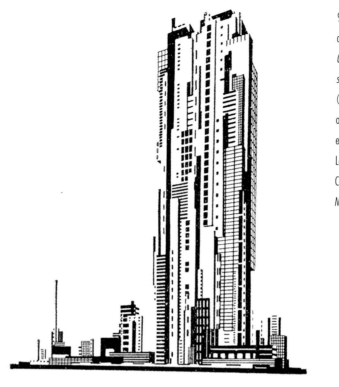

131 ВЕЛИКИЕ НЕБОСКРЕБЫ

96. Iakov Chernikhov, architect (1889–1951). *Giant Skyscrapers.* From *Osnovy sovremennoi arkhitektury* (Fundamental Principles of contemporary architecture, essay of experimental research), Leningrad, 1930. Canadian Centre for Architecture, Montreal

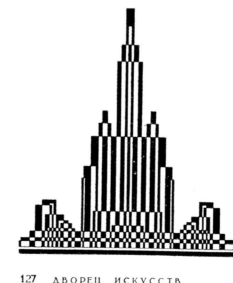

127 ДВОРЕЦ ИСКУССТВ
Двуцветная композиция из прямоугольников

97. Iakov Chernikhov, architect (1889–1951). The *Palace of Arts: Composition of bicolored rectangles.* From *Osnovy sovremennoi arkhitektury* (Fundamental Principles of contemporary architecture, essay of experimental research), Leningrad, 1931. Canadian Centre for Architecture, Montreal

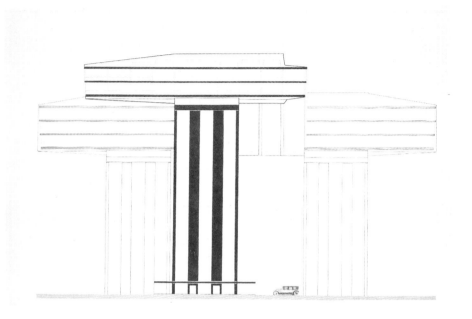

98. El Lissitzky (1890–1941). *"Wolkenbügel"* (skyhook) project in Moscow: elevation, 1924–25. State Tretyakov Gallery, Moscow

over subway stations, with the firm conviction that they are more beautiful than the original ones because they are ten times bigger. In New York and Chicago, engineers invented and constructed the fantastic steel skeletons of skyscrapers fifty storeys high, but the artist-architects, trained at the ancient Paris academy, clothed this living skeleton so skillfully with ostentatious embellishments that it was twenty years later before Europe recognized the crux of the matter.[389]

"city of giant skyscrapers" of his *Architectural Fantasies*,[387] which contains views of towers about to set themselves in motion. Chernikhov even situated a Suprematist-inspired project in America, the *Giant House in New York*.[388]

In the transfer of American themes to Russia via Germany, El Lissitzky was the crucial go-between, be it in terms of his own contribution to the architectural debate (as witnesses his *Wolkenbügel*, a "horizontal" skyscraper he drew up in several variations beginning in 1924) or through his critical observations on architecture in the United States. In 1925 he published a critique of *"Amerikanizm* in European Architecture" in the Moscow review *Krasnaia Niva*:

> In the Old World—in Europe—the words "America" and "American" conjure up ideas of something ultra-perfect, rational, utilitarian, universal. . . . Thus to the European mind New York became the new Athens, Manhattan the Acropolis, and the skyscrapers the Parthenon. It is true that New York itself knew nothing of this discovery. There they continue to build their temples to the Greek gods

Underlining the dichotomy between structure and ornament, which Le Corbusier had pointed up in *Vers une architecture* and which Maiakovsky had criticized during his travels in 1925, Lissitzky saw the "West" of the United States as the only remaining focus of innovation in the New World, ascribing this fact to Frank Lloyd Wright—"the only American architect. He has dared to turn his back on the precepts contained in manuals in order to forge a new housing type, which singles him out as the father of modern architecture." In fact, Lissitzky considered Europe to be "more American today than America itself" in its use of new materials, adding that "although Europe has adopted American principles . . . [it has] developed them in a new way," as witness European (and above all German) contributions to the *Chicago Tribune* competition. In 1926 Lissitzky published a technical analysis of the structural framework of industrial buildings and skyscrapers in the pages of *Stroitelnaia Promyshlennost*, the monthly review that kept its readers informed of "America under construction," in which he claimed that "Functionalism, Constructivism, horizontalism, verticalism, and above all Americanism are the watchwords of today's architectural thinking."[390] In this text he looked at the history of the skyscraper in the United States, taking in both the introduction of the metal frame that made lighter structures possible, with the concomitant use of various claddings (such as terra-cotta), and the standardization of materials. Lissitzky discussed the innovations of Sullivan and Wright, concluding that America was no longer the "center of gravity" of the new architecture, which (he claimed) was now to be found in the work of the Taut brothers, Mies van der Rohe, and Perret, and claimed that the problem of the skyscraper was now clearly posed in "our Union."

OSA was the most radical group in the Soviet Union, with theoretical orientations marked by the research of the first Constructivist artists.[391] The group was strongly interested in the American scene, be it from the standpoint of mechanization or that of skyscrapers and industrial buildings. Yet their analysis was a critical one and, in *Konstruktivizm*, published in 1922, Aleksei Gan expressed disdain for speculative commercial property built in America and Russia before the revolution, which was "haphazardly decorated to produce a flashy effect reflecting the eclectic whims of the owner, or given a veneer of stylishness reflecting some craze adopted by the builder himself, and usually [endowed] with a modern look" and which "multiplied by simple arithmetic, rising vertically in space."[392] In *Style and Epoch*, Moisei Ginzburg further criticized American production:

> . . . North America as a vital new power cannot, despite its own wishes, proceed along a course well-trodden by other cultures. An American tempo of life is emerging, utterly different from that of Europe—businesslike, dynamic, sober, mechanized, devoid of any romanticism—and this intimidates and repels a placid Europe. Nevertheless, wishing to be "as good as" Europe, America continues to import European aesthetics and romanticism as though they were commodities that had stood the test of time and been "patented," as it were. Thus, there emerges a single aspect of America: a horrifying mechanical mixture of new, organic, purely American elements with superficial envelopes of an outlived classical system "made in Europe."[393]

As we have seen, Ginzburg proposed to counter this "horrifying mixture" with the "industrial constructions" of America. Yet this presentation of American skyscrapers by Ginzburg and the OSA attracted criticism from the ASNOVA as a "leftist phase in architecture," especially as Constructivism's real home now appeared to be "capitalist America."[394] In fact, the OSA's arguments were based on the idea that one should not copy, and above all that Russian factories should be superior to American ones.[395] This presupposed a radical shift in design methods. For Ginzburg, the architect must cease to be the "decorator of life" and become "an organizer," i.e., a technician in the manner of the Taylorist "method engineers" at work in European and Russian factories. Ginzburg cited mathematical methods in the search for a new design approach, comparing architectural responses to program specifications with the search for the unknown factors of an equation.[396]

The Christopher Columbus Memorial, 1929

The competition organized by the Pan-American Union for a lighthouse commemorating Christopher Columbus at Santo Domingo furnished a new opportunity for European architects to design a tall structure with a minimal functional component. The Russians, deprived of direct contact with America (owing to the absence of diplomatic relations), and handicapped by the chaotic state of their professional institutions in the wake of the civil war, had not participated in the *Chicago Tribune* competition held seven years previously, though they certainly studied the entries; nor, since the USSR was not a member state, were Russian architects involved in the 1927 Geneva League of Nations Palace competition. Frustrated by this conspicuous

99. Frank J. Helmle,
architect (1869–1929),
Harvey Wiley Corbett,
architect (1873–1954),
Wallace K. Harrison,
architect (1895–1981),
and Viacheslav Oltarzhevsky,
architect (1880–1966).
*Christopher Columbus Memorial
lighthouse project: elevation.*
Shchusev Architectural Museum,
Moscow

100. Nikolai Ladovsky
(1881–1941). *Christopher
Columbus Memorial lighthouse
project: axonometric,* 1929.
Shchusev Architectural Museum,
Moscow

absence from the world stage, they took advantage of this new opportunity in large numbers. Yet despite the fact that the new competition offered a freer rein to the imagination, it would again be dominated by academic solutions.

The team of Helmle, Corbett, and Harrison (including the expatriate Russian Viacheslav Oltarzhevsky) figured among the ten selected for the second round by a jury whose members included Raymond Hood and Eliel Saarinen. The theme of the skyscraper was present in a wide variety of lighthouse designs (e.g. in the guise of the Tower of Babel, or associated with a terrestrial globe, or evoking the angular forms of a gigantic Art Deco paperweight). Some entries took the form of setback vertical structures in the post-1916 New York manner; others were syntheses of architectonic registers more closely resembling the earlier commercial structures. Of the Russian projects, that of the architect-artist Nikolai Lansere and the émigré Nikolai Vasiliev (both born in St. Petersburg) were remarked on by the jury. Apart from these two, the team of Georgi Krutikov and Ivan Varentsov, and the individuals Valdemar Tarasov, O. M. Kasianov, Andrei Belogrud, Andrei Bunin, Vladimir Krinsky, Nikolai Ladovsky, Konstantin Melnikov, and Ivan Leonidov all participated, thus reflecting a broad spectrum of Russian architectural culture, ranging from aficionados of American structures to proponents of abstract fantasies.[397] Several of their projects constituted significant stages in the development of radical approaches to the skyscraper and monumental architecture. This was true of designs by the rationalists Krinsky, Ladovsky, and the Krutikov team (the latter fresh out of the VKhUTEMAS), and by the Constructivist Leonidov; however, Melnikov's gigantic mobile double cone (as usual) defied categorization. While Leonidov's monument was a colossal antenna, prefiguring the era of telecommunications, he was nonetheless attracted to skyscraper themes. His almost simultaneous competition project for the House of Industry in Moscow was an audacious version of a tall building, a simple parallelepipedic tower with, on each floor, an open-plan work surface and a "serving" space for breaks and leisure activities—a configuration that was sharply criticized by the Rationalists.[398]

101. Konstantin Melnikov, architect (1890–1974).

Christopher Columbus Memorial lighthouse project, 1930.

Canadian Centre for Architecture, Montreal

Architecture to the Communist is another revolutionary weapon, or it would be more just to say, another evolutionary medium of expression to serve both a

98

Though Americanism furnished a considerable body of themes and images to radical groups, it also found its way into architectural circles far removed from the Modern movement. Those indifferent or hostile to Modernist orientations constructed their own visions of America, either through personal interpretation of America's images, or by elaborating alternatives in public competitions and commissions emanating from a wide variety of sources.

The Competitions
for the Triumphal Way in Paris

Developments in municipal policy led Perret, Le Corbusier, and other French architects to consider the question of tall buildings within Paris, a site on which Americanist influences had already left their mark. The giant Columbia Theater built for the 1900 Exposition Universelle was replaced three years later by Luna-Park—a direct reference to its Coney Island forbear. The "Devil's Wheel" and "Water-Chute" rides immediately became the main attractions of this popular amenity located within the zone *non aedificandi* on the edge of the city, the first in a series of leisure developments to be built there before 1940.[399] In 1930 Léonard Rosenthal, a dealer in fine pearls and an energetic developer of shopping arcades along the Champs-Élysées, financed a competition involving "architectural studies of the Place de la Victoire,"[400] with Maurice Boutterin, Henri Defrasse, André Granet, Le Corbusier and Pierre Jeanneret, Robert Mallet-Stevens, Émile Molinié and Charles Nicod, Auguste Perret, Albert Pouthier, Henri Sauvage, Victor Valensi, Émile-Louis Viret and Gabriel Marmorat, and the Russian Viacheslav Oltarzhevsky (doubtless standing in for Corbett) as invited candidates. This "competition of ideas" focused on the site encompassing the Porte Maillot and Luna-Park, of which Rosenthal was keen to secure the concession.[401]

Robert Camelot, architect (1903–93). *Construction of Radio City, New York*, 1932. Institut Français d'Architecture. Centre d'Archives d'Architecture du xxᵉ siècle, Paris

135

Models of the various projects, submitted on 1 April 1930, were exhibited the following year at the Salon d'Automne, in response to a brief emphasizing the role of the "Place de la Victoire" as the ultimate monument of Paris *intra muros*. It therefore had to "effect a junction between the Paris of yesterday and the Paris of tomorrow."[402] All the responses reflected Americanist influences, though to varying degrees. Rob. Mallet-Stevens imagined twin towers flanking an arch "brightly lit by night and ethereal by day, marking a future gateway to Paris."[403] The arch, a slender band of reinforced concrete, was to have dominated the avenue de la Grande Armée in a project whose continuous horizontals around the square were in opposition to its verticals.[404] Henri Sauvage proposed a definitive version of the stepped blocks which he had developed since before the war. Standing in isolation relative to the continuous blocks surrounding the square, a pair of large pyramid-shaped edifices with doorways six storeys high stood facing two obelisks, thus highlighting the project's Egyptian character. Elevator shafts broke up its sedimentary accumulations

and marked the vertical rhythms of its stepped blocks.[405] Auguste Perret, who initially advanced several hypotheses involving a "curtain" of tower-blocks,[406] settled in the end for a twin series of buildings hemmed in between the incisive horizontals of an elongated awning and a sharply angled cornice.

Le Corbusier's contribution to this tournament took the form of a raised, single-storey *Foch Esplanade*, upon which he positioned two skyscrapers inspired by his latest research (in particular his South American projects), with a network of access roads of freeway proportions, designed to facilitate the "perfect classification" of traffic. A "mausoleum" was "solemnly" positioned atop this raised platform, a "veritable forum" facing the avenue de la Grande Armée, constituting "an architectural landscape of the utmost modernism, the effect of which will be most striking by day or night."[407] Far from reinforcing the monumental axis of the Champs-Élysées and avenue de la Grande Armée, the *Foch Esplanade* was to have been an "organ for the classification, distribution, and derivation of traffic-flow—in a word, an articulation." The Porte Maillot, though linking up with the "*autostrada* at the edge of Paris," would reorient flow towards the new *Grande Traversée* to the north of the city. Rosenthal reacted to all these projects with extreme prudence. He was careful to hide them from public view, exhuming them only eighteen months later.[408]

In the following year, the competition for the development of the "Triumphal Way" from the Étoile to La Défense saw the earliest formulation of strategies for the vertical extension of the western outskirts—a development which finally materialized in the 1950s. This competition, concerning the axis from the Arc de Triomphe westward, was organized by the City of Paris and the Seine Department even before the results of the Rosenthal competition were made

102. Henri Sauvage, architect (1873–1932). *Project for the Rosenthal competition for the Porte Maillot: perspective, Paris, 1930.* Institut Français d'Architecture. Centre d'Archives d'Architecture du XXᵉ siècle, Paris

103. Auguste Perret, architect (1874–1954). *Project for the Rosenthal competition for the Porte Maillot: perspective*, Paris, 1930. Institut Français d'Architecture, Centre d'Archives d'Architecture du xxe siècle, Paris

known,[409] under combined pressure from certain elected representatives, including the city councilor Henri Gaillard, and from the main architectural bodies.[410] Entries were judged in February 1932. The competition was confined to "ideas," even if the brief was ultimately extended to include "the whole length of the axis leading from the Arc de Triomphe to the La Défense traffic circle."[411]

The brief stipulated treatment of the grand axis itself, two squares (the Étoile and La Défense) and the Porte de Neuilly. Thirty-five projects were submitted; some candidates had participated in the Victoire competition. Globally speaking, their treatment of form and program reflected deep-seated differences, notably concerning possible axial structures for the development of Porte Maillot. The prizewinning entries were remarkable for their realism. First prize went to Paul Bigot and the sculptors Landowski and Bouchard, who gave pride of place to La Défense as a "national Acropolis." Julien, Duhayon, and Chappey eschewed tall structures at La Défense, instead proposing a development principle similar to that of Molinié, Nicod, and Barbaud, and even to Perret's earlier proposal. Viret and Marmorat reduced the four towers of their Rosenthal entry to two, here positioning them upon a raised slab. Granet, too, reiterated some elements of his earlier rendering, but this time the two buildings parallel to the Porte Maillot axis were flanked by a "House of the Colonies" to the north

and a "large exhibition center" to the south, with the planned 1937 decorative arts exposition to be positioned along boulevard Maillot. Jacques Carlu's interest in the American scene was reflected in a series of elegant glass-faced skyscrapers at La Défense. As "urban art" jousts on a grand scale, the competitions of 1930–31 were symptomatic of the Americanism then ambient in Paris, whether in the projects of architects with first-hand experience of trans-Atlantic cities (such as Carlu or Labatut), or of those fascinated with skyscrapers and expressways from afar.

The Beaux-Arts and America

As these programs saw the theoretical emergence of (occasionally singular) skyscraper structures, the "Grand Tour" offered the best pupils of the Paris

Beaux-Arts school the chance to travel to America, in the footsteps of Jacques Gréber (who did not stay). Paul Cret and Jean Labatut were hired, respectively, by the universities of Pennsylvania and Princeton. Jacques Carlu, a friend of Raymond Hood at the Beaux-Arts and a teacher at MIT from 1924 to 1934, returned to Paris to build the Palais de Chaillot following his participation in the Triumphal Way competition. The novelty of the situation resided less in the fact that teaching in this vaguely modernized French academic institution moved closer to that in American schools (thus rendering the American students' trip to Paris superfluous) than in the fact that its best pupils traveled to America as well.

The "gratitude" of American Beaux-Arts pupils, initially expressed in a competition that they financed, now took the form of travel grants enabling the most brilliant French students to visit America—a geographical and historical inversion of the Grand Tour. Henceforth, it was the America of the future, and not the Europe of the past, that was to be explored.[412] Nonetheless, the methods by which the students explored and assessed America were often anchored in traditional practice. Thus Robert Camelot, who won the Second Grand Prix de Rome in 1933, had some difficulty in depicting the cranes of the Rockefeller Center with his insufficiently fluid watercolors (though he did succeed in collecting the blueprints of a large number of recent buildings in the course of his tour of American offices). The techniques used by Marcel Chappey, who won the Second Grand Prix de Rome in 1925, were somewhat different. Traveling the country armed with a camera, he amassed a series of worm's-eye views, selecting diagonals as the "vertical" axis to exaggerate the impression of height.[413]

Eugène Beaudouin, who won the 1928 prize, was less interested in images (as his timid photography well attests) than in traffic flow and construction methods. His comments, published in *L'Architecture d'aujourd'hui* in 1933, are similar to Le Corbusier's subsequent remarks regarding the adolescent aspect of American life:

> In the USA we find all the qualities and failings that made Rome great. A powerful organization at the service of immense political and financial resources has made it possible to build structures whose scale and perfect execution are astonishing, but their designs are invariably primitive. We are struck far more often by their quantity than by their quality, and by the repetition or scale of the undertaking far more than by the boldness of novel technical solutions.
>
> . . . As for construction methods, the rigorous management of construction sites and the various agents involved makes for extremely careful and often perfect execution.
>
> Yet paradoxical as it may seem at first sight, the existence of stringent, highly demanding yet outmoded building regulations leaves little room for architects to innovate. Technique quickly becomes routine. The resultant state of mind is hardly conducive to bold strokes. Perhaps regulations are like governments? A people gets those which it deserves. Perhaps such severity is merely that of a tutor towards an adolescent civilization.[414]

The principal lessons that Beaudouin took away with him (like Raymond Lopez, who would be the author of wide-ranging plans for the renovation of Paris in the 1950s, and who somewhat prosaically emphasized the "contrasts" present in this "country of extremes")[415] concerned the technical qualities of American buildings. The question of tall constructions was no longer the sole preoccupation, though it was still ever-present in the minds of architects and critics eager to modernize the city skyline. In 1934 Beaudouin, in collaboration with Marcel Lods and the engineer Vladimir Bodiansky, built the "first skyscrapers" of the Paris region at Drancy, completing the La Muette housing estate with a row of fourteen-

106. Robert Camelot, architect (1903–93). *Night view of Chicago*, 1932. Institut Français d'Architecture. Centre d'Archives d'Architecture du XXᵉ siècle, Paris

storey tower-blocks. As photographed by Lods, who was familiar with Neutra's illustrations, their skeletons resembled New York steel-cage structures towering above "defective" suburban plots.[416] Paul Nelson, who had been a pupil of Perret's at the Palais du Bois studio, was interested in an American program whose impact on European practice had as yet been little studied: the tall hospital building. His 1932 competition designs for a hospital complex in Lille reflected familiarity with large complexes such as the Cornell Medical Center, published during the twenties by Jean Badovici in *L'Architecture vivante*. Nelson's hospital project was associated with a freeway complex, and took the form of two tower-blocks using an architectonic steel and stone system more redolent of Le Corbusier's "Cartesian" skyscrapers than of the neo-Gothic façade of its New York state counterpart.[417] Meanwhile, the Office Technique pour l'Utilisation de l'Acier published regular reports on tall metallic structures, in which the technical performance, methods of calculation, and construction were explained at great length and in a detail that must have seemed surprising to anyone familiar with conditions then prevailing on French construction sites.[418] These disparities did not, however, prevent Louis Bonnier, the author of the 1902 regulation restricting building heights within Paris, from proposing designs far outstripping his own precepts,

107. Louis Bonnier,
architect (1856–1946).
*Study for a skyscraper near
Notre-Dame*, Paris, c. 1928.
Institut Français d'Architecture,
Centre d'Archives d'Architecture
du xxᵉ siècle, Paris

108. Louis Bonnier,
architect (1856–1946).
*Project for a setback building
in Paris (surpassing the building
height regulation of 1902)
including a part of the
rue de Rivoli and elevations
with templates: perspective*,
1934–38. Institut Français
d'Architecture. Centre d'Archives
d'Architecture du xxᵉ siècle, Paris

with sketches for stepped blocks on the riverfront, or for expanded variants of the Woolworth Building, juxtaposing them with Notre-Dame and the Place de la Concorde in photomontages. In this he yielded to arguments advanced in 1907 by the American correspondent of *La Construction moderne*, in response to adversaries of the "desecration" of Paris by "monstrous and unsightly" skyscrapers:

> No, Messrs. architects of France, do not spend your time grumbling and protesting; set to work, face up to conditions as they are. The time, the age of the skyscraper is upon you. Accept it for better or for worse; it is here to stay![419]

But French Americanism appears to have blossomed most freely in spheres of cultural or political influence farthest removed from Paris. The centerpiece of Donat-Alfred Agache's 1929 plan for the "remodeling" of Rio de Janeiro was to have been an office complex situated on the Praça do Castello.[420] New York imagery also guided the fantasies of the critic Léandre Vaillat. In the footsteps of General d'Amade, who had led the French invasion force in Morocco in 1907, and who was of the view that "before the end of the century, North African France will be the United States, and Casablanca, New York,"[421] Vaillat "almost expected to see a group of skyscrapers rise up of its own accord at the heart of this city of violent conquerors."[422] The debate over such buildings took distinc shape with zoning modifications in Morocco's harbor district and the drawing up of solutions in principle by Marius Boyer, most remarkable of the local architects.[423] Yet it was Lazare Goujon, the socialist mayor of Villeurbanne (adjacent to Lyon) who, in order to emphasize the town's autonomy, would build the only urban complex comparable to American models (and not without its delightful Art Deco references). The "skyscrapers" designed by Môrice Leroux and inaugurated in 1934 were indeed steel-cage constructions, which respected the system of setbacks prescribed by New York's 1916 Zoning

109. Guido Fiorini, engineer (1891–1965). *"Radiator" skyscraper: perspective,* 1930. Società Nazionale delle Officine di Savigliano, Turin

Ordinance. The two streets lined with stepped blocks had, at their entrance, two high towers which would bind the image of America to that of Social Democracy *à la Lyonnaise.*[424]

Le Corbusier's Journey to the Country of Timid People

In 1935 Le Corbusier in turn discovered New York, then in the grips of the Depression, and at once criticized the skyscrapers ("too small") and Central Park ("too big"), and went on to recommend "cellular reformation" of the metropolis. Published in 1937, his account of the trip mingled declarations of allegiance ("I am an American") with critical asides concerning Manhattan, which he saw as a "fairy catastrophe."

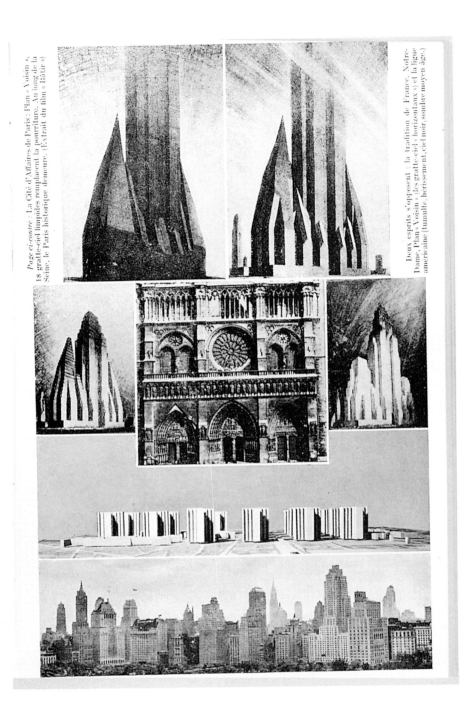

Page ci-contre : La Cité d'Affaires de Paris : Plan « Voisin », 18 gratte-ciel limpides remplacent la pourriture. Au long de la Seine, le Paris historique demeure. (Extrait du film « Bâtir »)

Deux esprits s'opposent : la tradition de France, Notre-Dame, Plan « Voisin » des gratte-ciel « horizontaux » et la ligue américaine (tumulte, hérissement, ciel noir, sombre moyen âge.)

110. Le Corbusier,

architect (1887–1965).

"Is Descartes American?"

Illustration in *Plans*, July 1931.

Canadian Centre for Architecture,

Montreal

The circumstances and vicissitudes of this journey are too well known to require further comment here.[425] However, it is useful to point out that Le Corbusier familiarized himself very early on with European descriptions of America, be it working class accounts (such as Dubreuil's *Standarts*) or economic studies. In the sphere of architecture, he read analyses published by Werner Hegemann, one of whose illustrations he published in *Urbanisme* (whereas Hegemann was critical of Le Corbusier's *Ville contemporaine*).[426] He continued his investigations of the modern skyscraper with a series of projects in which the steel cages remained visible behind their glass envelopes. A remarkable episode from this period was the preparatory work carried out from 1931 on the plan for Algiers, involving the Turin engineer Guido Fiorini (inventor of a structural principle known as Tensistruttura) and the metal construction firm Savigliano, resulting in several types of office skyscrapers shaped like radiators.[427]

From the early twenties, Le Corbusier was eager to drive out all signs of Beaux-Arts influence in America, deeming that only engineers were worthy of respect. Yet he remained unimpressed by the analyses of Jacques Gréber, and of the French in America only Jean Labatut found favor in his eyes. In 1935, following responses to the program of the Franco-American Housing Group, and having become an active campaigner in favor of Taylorism, he published a series of articles in the review *Plans* which posited the dilemma of modern society: "Americanize or Bolshevize?" In his own case, the Depression had made him an anti-capitalist—or at least hostile to the power of "money." In another text he advocated a more specifically architectural analysis of the "disorder" reigning in New York. He asked the question "Is Descartes American?" to justify his own "Cartesian" skyscrapers.[428] Having returned from America, where he gave so many lectures that he

142

111. *View of the* San Francisco Call *Building*. From Le Corbusier,
"Trois rappels à MM. les Architectes. Le volume," in *Vers une architecture*, Paris, 1923.
Canadian Centre for Architecture, Montreal

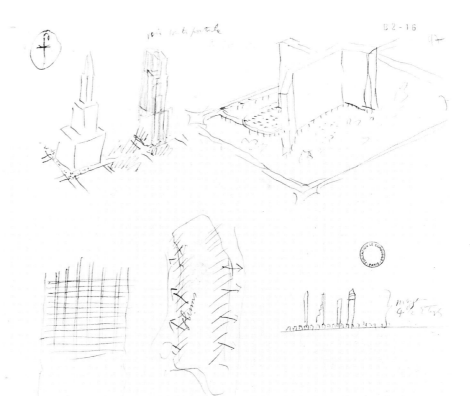

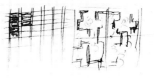

113. Le Corbusier,
architect (1887–1965).
Sketch for *When the Cathedrals
Were White*, 1937.
Fondation Le Corbusier, Paris

112. Le Corbusier,
architect (1887–1965).
Cover sketch for *When the
Cathedrals Were White*, 1937.
Fondation Le Corbusier, Paris

claimed to have produced "three hundred yards of drawings (six rolls of paper 50 yards in length)," Le Corbusier published in 1937 *Quand les cathédrales étaient blanches, voyage au pays des timides* (*When the Cathedrals were White*),[429] a heterogeneous collage of texts—articles from the review *Prélude*, travel notes, lecture notes, articles such as "What is America's Problem?" and his response to a questionnaire formulated by Percy Goodman—together with a series of explanatory drawings. The book's eclectic structure is a reflection of these materials; from the outset, Le Corbusier explains his troubles in France, and the account of his travels takes the form of events, anecdotes, and more ambitious analytical remarks.

Following the trans-Atlantic crossing on the *Normandie* (an "invigorating liner"), Le Corbusier echoes the amazement invariably expressed in the travelogues of the day in his description of the arrival in New York, "an image of incredible brutality and savagery," the opening scene of an experience which left him both indignant (like Duhamel) and enchanted. The chronological description of his travels describes his "conquests" and reiterates paradoxes concerning the excessive number and diminutive scale of skyscrapers and the timidity and outmoded habits of Americans (which the New York press cited in 1935).[430] He also describes his encounter at the Hartford Atheneum with A. Everett Austin, James Thrall Soby, Henry-Russell Hitchcock, "meteors . . . who play a hazardous and exhausting ride," and alludes to the work of Wallace Harrison with a curious mixture of sympathy and paternalism.

The title of his book is doubly enigmatic. In "Is Descartes American?" he contrasts the image of Notre-Dame Cathedral with that of the skyscraper. In *Cathedrals*, he is alluding to the moment when building resumed in the Middle Ages, when Europe "put on a white robe of churches."[431] Metaphorically,

however, the title refers to a period of intense energy, creativity, and purity. For Le Corbusier, the cathedrals of the twentieth century had yet to be built, and he was ready to do just that in the United States. The world is "to be put in order . . . as once was done before on the debris of antiquity, when the cathedrals were white."[432] Whiteness is here synonymous with novelty and a refusal to countenance disabling regulations. He states that "the cathedrals were white because they were new . . . when the cathedrals were white, there were no regulations." Here the allusion is to a lawsuit in which he had become embroiled over the technical solutions adopted for the Salvation Army's Cité de Refuge in Paris. He invokes the idea of collective forces at work in construction:

> Greatness is in the intention, and not in dimensions. When the cathedrals were white, the whole universe was raised up by immense faith in the energy, the future, and the harmonious creation of a civilization.[433]

For Le Corbusier, at this privileged moment in history "there was a common idea; Christendom was above everything else. . . . The journeymen masons paid no attention to being charming . . . no one thought that height was the sign of a degeneration of spirit . . . the spirit was triumphant." Today, on the other hand, "the cathedrals of France are black and the spirit is bruised."[434] He harks back nostalgically to a time when "there were no government diplomas; the crafts (and architecture) were practiced regionally in terms of local resources, raw materials, climates, customs. Controls were worked out in the midst of jobs to be done, within the corporations."

The second enigma concerns his "journey to the country of the timid": despite the fact that he everywhere encounters "a young people—sturdy and athletic," he is of the view that "American city planning in its very gigantism reflects a dangerous timidity, at a time when the problem is to react, and to act rightly." He claims to understand "the anxieties, the

XXIV. Robert Camelot,
architect (1903–93).
*Construction of Radio City,
New York*, 1932. Institut Français
d'Architecture. Centre d'Archives
d'Architecture du XXᵉ siècle, Paris

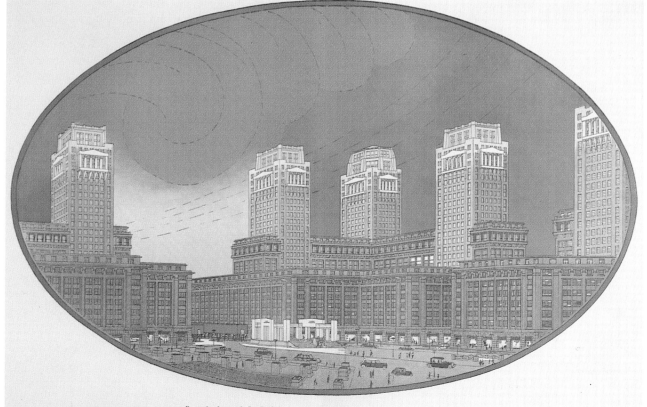

Perspectiva da praça do Castello idealisada pelo professor Alfred Agache como centro principal dos negocios

XXV. Donat-Alfred Agache,
architect (1875–1959).
*Planning project for the Praça
do Castello in Rio de Janeiro:
perspective*, 1929.
Collection Jean-Louis Cohen, Paris

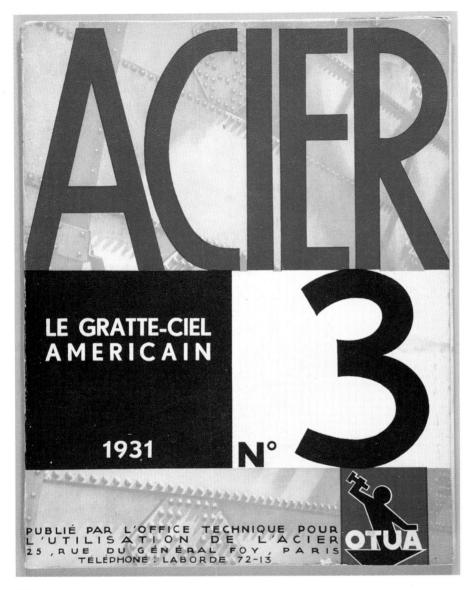

XXVII. Students of the VASI under the direction of Boris Korchunov (1885–1961). *Competition entry for the Peoples' Commissariat for Heavy Industry (NKTP) in Red Square: perspective*, Moscow, 1934. Shchusev Architectural Museum, Moscow

XXVI. Cover of *Acier* no. 3: "Le gratte-ciel américain," Paris, 1931. Collection Jean-Louis Cohen, Paris

XXVIII. Môrice Leroux, *Skyscraper, Villeurbanne*, 1934, cover of *Dix années de réalisations des municipalités socialistes, no. 2: Villeurbanne*, Lille, 1935. Collection Jean-Louis Cohen, Paris

XXIX. Boris Iofan,
architect (1891–1976).
*Rockefeller Center from
Fifth Avenue*, 1938. Canadian
Centre for Architecture, Montreal

timidities, and the brusque, reckless acts natural to youthful forces," but he perceives a certain "imbalance" at Vassar College where he witnesses girls studying Caravaggio. He recalls this in pictorial imagery mingling awe and fear of American industrial strength:

> The blinding light of the blast furnaces of Pittsburgh and the yellow brilliance of gold are accomplices of the green flames in the crypt of Caravaggio and on the altars of Surrealism, bleeding with sacrifices and roses.[435]

Much of the book is devoted to New York, which Le Corbusier regards as "the first city to be constructed on the scale of modern times" (whereas he treated the city with some condescension in previous texts on city planning published after 1922). "A vertical city," New York seen from the harbor resembles a pin cushion or a giant hedgehog. Unlike Paris, New York is "a great diamond, hard and dry, sparkling, triumphant." Central Park, "an immense treasure untouchable in the very center of Manhattan," is, however, "too large, a hole in the midst of buildings." The question of scale is a recurrent theme, and Le Corbusier never misses an opportunity to stress that "Manhattan reminds us that man is an ant or a bee subject to the necessity of living in a box." Yet over and above his observations of the city as a static entity, he identifies its crisis cycles, with particular reference to the evolution of Chicago. There are accents of Maxime Gorky in his denunciation of the city's "moral slums" and "gold . . . a crusher of hearts." In his discussion of the city's territorial expanse, he notes that the New York region is suffering from "encephalitis" yet he cannot hide his emotion when faced with the spectacle of everyday life, which he celebrates in terms evocative of Fritz Lang's vision. Broadway "streams with moving lights" at the heart of this "fairy catastrophe" which is at once a "lever of hope" and "diabolical."[436]

The question of the skyscraper is a major component of Le Corbusier's account. He regards it as both a "magnificent instrument" and a "proclamation" —but in technical terms only (an "acrobatic feat"). Though they are paralyzed by an elevator attendants' strike, he notes that "the elevators do work," unlike their Parisian counterparts. He considers constructions such as Howe and Lescaze's Philadelphia Saving Fund Society Building or Rockefeller Center as acceptable social amenities: to work in the complex built by Hood and Harrison is a mark of "self-respect."[437] Yet his disappointment is patent from the outset: alluding indirectly to the cupola of James M. Reid's *San Francisco Call* Building, which he had attacked in *Vers une architecture*, he states that "in contrast to our hopes the skyscrapers were not made of glass, but of tiara-crowned masses of stone." In a later passage he declares that "we laugh at the crowns of New York skyscrapers, which seem like chased decanter stoppers." The skyscrapers are "not big enough," though they are nonetheless "greater than the architects" of such misplaced fantasies, and represent mere "architectural accident . . . imagine a man . . . the torso remains normal, but his legs become twenty times too long." Finally, skyscrapers are "irrational from top to bottom." For Le Corbusier, this absurdity extends to the city as a whole; he (paradoxically) is in favor of an urban form which he also denounces: "here the skyscraper is negative; it kills the street and the city . . . it is a man-eating monster."[438]

His observations of the city's infrastructure are less clear-cut, given the fact that architects had been "dismissed" from such sectors of activity (as in the case of the George Washington Bridge). He admires this recent bridge, but also Grand Central, which he describes as "strong and rugged as a gladiator." Outside Manhattan, he reflects on the suburbs dotted with "a sinuous, charming, picturesque—and slightly arranged" system of parkways.[439] He rightly sees the suburbs as "reflecting Ford's lesson," contrasting them with the garden cities of Berlin, London, France, and

XXX. Boris Iofan, architect (1891–1976). *Project for the People's Commissariat for Heavy Industry: perspective*, Moscow, 1938. Canadian Centre for Architecture, Montreal

Morocco. The suburbs of New York and Chicago suffer from the "cancer" of the automobile. Unlike the "city of modern times," which has no suburbs, he sees the dilated urban agglomeration, with its "distended" garden cities, as the epitome of waste. The country is "on wheels" and "the family is cut in two . . . because the great cities are constructed against the grain."[440]

The American universities opened Le Corbusier's eyes to the human resources of the nation. He notes that "at the age of Olympic champion . . . athletic body, with a youthful heart at once strong and weak," the Americans are "every one an athlete," as against "the students of Paris, in poor shape physically and ill-fed." At Princeton he discovers "large, rich tribes encamped in the midst of greenery" yet is gripped by "a fear at seeing the doors open on the unknown of tomorrow." At the Cranbrook educational complex at Bloomfield Hills, Michigan (where he met its designer, Eliel Saarinen) he admires a "paradisaic retreat for disheartened combatants." In the course of his lecture tour, a savant in isolation, he visits the "young girls constantly renewed" of Vassar, which he describes as a "joyous convent," ambiguously singing the praises of the American woman as a "beautiful animal, a very beautiful animal" who "lives, in American society, by intellectual labor," but who frightens him to the point of preferring "the people eating cookies." He was doubtless more charmed by the "wax mannequins on 5th Avenue . . . idols on pedestals," revealing the "woman masters, with conquering smiles . . ."[441]

In his observations of American society as a whole, Le Corbusier meditates gravely on its history and its specific features, and identifies the United States with an awkward adolescent. This "tall young man afflicted by the obscure evils of his age" is "in a state of repression," and remains "strongly marked by the disciplines and irruptions of a society which in a sense just disembarked." With their "maladjusted hearts," the Americans have not yet "tasted the joys of (lively, active) thought . . . which contains the joy of a profusely flowered field."[442] He is not blind to divisions of race and class, and is mortified by Doctor Albert Barnes's refusal to let him visit his art collection at Merion, Pennsylvania, which le Corbusier regards as symptomatic of the "fat contentment of the men who have made America."[443] Elsewhere, "our millionaire" Rockefeller "is no more than a poor man whose name figures on the signpost for mountains of gold" (here Le Corbusier reiterates Mendelsohn's phrase), while he regards the "bosses" of the New Deal as no better "informed" than their French or Russian counterparts.

Le Corbusier is not content simply to observe and describe, interpret and criticize. As after all his travels, from Moscow to Latin America, he proposes practical solutions. In the first place, and unlike Gréber, he perceives instances of the "bankruptcy" of French "good taste" in America, though he also advocates cooperation—his watchword is "work together." Faced with competition from the skyscraper, which he acknowledges to be an idea specific to "these mad Americans," he wishes to correct its imperfections by eliminating noise (and the use of stone, for "in your eyries, you seem to be in cellars"). More generally, he aims to "rectify" New York by creating a new network for automobile traffic and renovating the riverside docks so as to render them "superb and pure." In order to "save" the city, he advocates a third metamorphosis, with the introduction of a new scale and new networks to reform its current "cellular state." Extrapolating earlier Parisian strategies in which he used exhibitions as a means of disseminating his ideas, Le Corbusier aims to use the 1939 World's Fair to make his positions known.[444] The program outlined in *Cathedrals* is designed to pave the way for a new Middle Ages in which everything will be rebuilt, at the same time abandoning the laissez-faire policies and waste intrinsic to autonomy. The idea was in fact to espouse the logic of the "right angle," which Le Corbusier deems "American," and which he would exploit fruitfully despite the fact that he returned from America more frustrated than stimulated.

Stalinist Urban Projects and America

While Americanism was taking on multiple and diffuse forms in Europe, the wind changed in Soviet Russia. The new trend was revealed at the organizational level by the creation, in 1932, of the Union of Architects, and in formal terms by the implementation of "Socialist" realism, as exemplified the following year in Boris Iofan, Vladimir Gelfreikh, and Vladimir Shchuko's victory in the competition for the Palace of the Soviets. The designs for this building underwent a decade of reconfigurations, in the course of which its affinities with American buildings were stressed on several occasions. Yet the clearest analogies between this project (which superimposed a colossal tower onto a domed hall) and American structures are to be found in the numerous comparable designs submitted to the 1929 Christopher Columbus memorial competition. Still another competition organized in 1934–35 for the Narkomtiazhprom (or People's Commissariat for Heavy Industry), revealed the limits of anti-modern censorship and the latent potential of Americanism. On this occasion Ivan Leonidov—the "child prodigy" of Constructivist architecture, and the first to be attacked by the "proletarian" movement— evinced his Americanist tendencies. In one of the last projects to reflect the OSA's aesthetic positions, Leonidov elaborated his skyscraper bordering Red Square with astonishing low-angle views of tall prismatic forms reminiscent of Mendelsohn's *Amerika* and the depictions of Moscow published in his *Russland, Europa, Amerika*. Leonidov's building was taller

114. Ivan Leonidov, architect (1902–59). *Project for the People's Commissariat for Heavy Industry: elevation*, Moscow, 1934. Shchusev Architectural Museum, Moscow

than its Manhattan counterparts, and soared rocket-like above the cathedral of Saint Basil.

Other entries for the Narkomtiazhprom reflected Americanist themes. The Vesnin brothers' designs resembled a hybrid mix between Albert Kahn's General Motors offices and a row of blast furnaces. Melnikov's project climbed dizzy heights, guiding its visitors through a giant turbine stator which resembled that of the dam across the Dnepr river. Just as Iofan's Palace of the Soviets project clearly invoked the Empire State Building, Stalin's Russia strove to Americanize the appearance of its cities, beginning with Moscow, by introducing not only tall buildings, but also new height regulations and park networks in the American manner.

The shift towards "Socialist" realism in her architecture did little to weaken Russia's interest in the American scene. The new phase which emerged was reflected in shifts in theme and emphasis in publications, but also in an intensification of Russian architects' direct contacts with America. The 1933

АРХИТЕКТУРА
ЗА РУБЕЖОМ
2
•1935• ИЗДАТЕЛЬСТВО ВСЕСОЮЗНОЙ АКАДЕМИИ АРХИТЕКТУРЫ

publication of Paul Cret's *Architectural Forum* text in the review of the Union of Architects, *Arkhitektura SSSR*, was designed to show that the Nazis were not the only ones to attack "Constructivist" and "Functionalist" architecture, which even Americans could criticize (although the editors of the Russian review expressed some perplexity vis-à-vis Cret's proposed "new classicism"). Interest in Wright was recurrent. Discussions of his work appeared in professional reviews and in the official party organ, *Pravda*. *Arkhitektura SSSR* interviewed him on his working methods,[445] while *Pravda* viewed his architecture as evidence of the crisis of capitalism. For his part, the critic David Arkin published Wright's postwar work in his 1932 book *Arkhitektura Sovremennogo Zapada*.[446]

Alongside numerous articles published in *Arkhitektura SSSR*, which thinned out towards the end of the thirties, a new publication devoted a large number of its cover illustrations and articles to the American scene: *Arkhitektura za rubezhom*. Given the difficulty of effecting skyscraper plans, American construction methods were now taken seriously. In 1934 Iofan, Gelfreikh, and Shchuko visited New York in order to gain first-hand experience of structural frames and facings.[447] Iofan, who was interested in the most recent skyscrapers (he later sketched Rockefeller Center from memory and photos), was favorably impressed by the parkway networks drawn up by Robert Moses for metropolitan New York. Shchuko published his own impressions of New York in *Pravda*.[448] David Arkin's *Arkhitektura Sovremennogo Zapada*, a study of the architectural and urban approaches of a relatively small group of Western practitioners, contained an extract from Neutra's *Amerika* under the title "Some Particularities of Recent American Architecture," and included views of *Rush City Reformed* and one of Lissitzky's photomontages.[449] Russian recognition of Neutra was reflected in the fact that the Russian architect Sergei

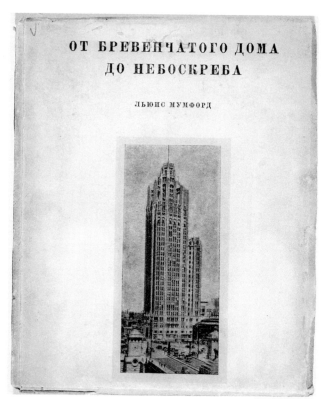

ОТ БРЕВЕНЧАТОГО ДОМА
ДО НЕБОСКРЕБА

ЛЬЮИС МУМФОРД

116. Lewis Mumford, *Ot brevenchatogo doma do neboskrioba, ocherk istorii amerikanskoy arkhitektury* (Russian edition of *Sticks and Stones*), Moscow, 1936. Collection Jean-Louis Cohen, Paris

Kozhin, a war prisoner liberated by the Americans in 1945, chose to work under Neutra in the United States, becoming his associate in the late forties.

In 1936 Arkin tackled the question of the link between aesthetics and the machine in his preface to a Russian translation (of a German translation) of Lewis Mumford's *Sticks and Stones*.[450] It should be recalled that in this book, Mumford corroborated Louis Sullivan's negative judgment of the 1893 Chicago Expo, underlining the key social role of architecture. Though Arkin claimed to appreciate Mumford's discussion of early nineteenth-century neoclassicism, a style corresponding to his own, he nonetheless contested the "pamphlet's" criticism of the machine age and its consequences, and compared Mumford's remarks to those of Oswald Spengler, roundly condemning both the "rejection" of the machine and machine age "fetishism," which he regarded Le Corbusier as exemplifying.[451]

115. *Rockefeller Center.* Cover of *Arkhitektura za rubezhom*, Moscow, 1935. Collection Jean-Louis Cohen, Paris

117. Viacheslav Oltarzhevsky, architect (1880–1965). *A New York Canyon: Pine, formerly King, Street, looking East,* in *Contemporary Babylon in Pencil Drawings,* New York, 1929. Canadian Centre for Architecture, Montreal

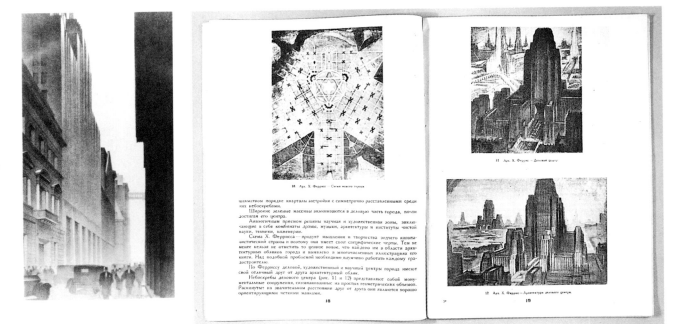

118. Hugh Ferriss, Two pages illustrating *The Metropolis of the Future,* in A. V. Shchusev and L. E. Zagorsky, *Arkhitekturnaya organizatsia goroda,* Moscow, 1934. Collection Jean-Louis Cohen, Paris

For the most part, however, Arkin praised American architectural culture, and even proposed a sort of study program, arguing that "nowhere has the capitalist city posed as many complex and contradictory architectural problems, nowhere have the very methods of architectural design and examples of architects themselves undergone transformations as wide-ranging as in America." He naturally saw the skyscraper as central to this culture:[452]

> Architecturally speaking the skyscraper, which is the dominant and even exclusive type of construction in America, comprises a whole series of complex and fundamentally new elements whose significance far transcends the limits of American experience.
>
> . . . A direct consequence of competition and land revenues—as if literally projected "in the air"—thus mirroring the contradictions inherent to the capitalist city, the skyscraper has nonetheless enabled the architect faced with problems of an unprecedented nature to broaden his thinking and his methods considerably.[453]

Arkin identified both the problem of the skyscraper's relationship with the street, evoking regulations concerning height, and technical innovations (such as the elevator) that made such tall buildings possible. Confirming the validity of the skyscraper experiment, he underlined the role of multifunctional buildings in the urban architectures of America, at a time when implementation of the 1935 plan for Moscow involved novel programs:

> One of the most important consequences of this experiment is doubtless this type of architecture in which the most varied activities are housed within a single structure. America has set the example in this type (first of all in its hotels, but also in its housing, its railway stations, etc.), in which housing, offices, concert halls, auditoria, libraries, business facilities, enormous restaurants are all contained within a single complex.[454]

Over and above this "extremely interesting" multifunctionality, Arkin celebrated the "culture of finish, furnishings, and facings" specific to American buildings. He also tackled the question of architectural form. Recalling the marginal nature of work by Sullivan or "the most recent of innovators, Frank Lloyd Wright," Arkin ironized over the "naïve" application to skyscrapers of the tripartite plinth/shaft/capital division in an echo of Lissitzky's earlier arguments.[455]

Ironically, at the spectacular 1937 Congress of Architects, which was supposed to mark "new directions" in Soviet architecture, it was Frank Lloyd Wright who followed Arkin in criticizing the eclecticism of early "tall buildings," singling out Iofan, Gelfreikh, and Shchuko's project (topped by a giant statue of Lenin).[456] Though carefully censored by *Pravda* and *Arkhitektura SSSR*, this speech did not prevent Wright from appearing on the sidelines in Iofan's company. On his return to America, he launched a retrospective view of Moscow's architecture "across the Pole," criticizing its gigantism but praising the human qualities of his interlocutors.[457] The most servile and cynical of these, Karo Alabian, went to New York to monitor construction of the Soviet Pavilion for the 1939 World's Fair,[458] an event that attracted wide publicity in Moscow.

The "socialist reconstruction" of existing cities brought with it renewed interest in Daniel Burnham's compositional methods and in the American park system. Henceforth, city planning treatises devoted much space to American projects and in particular to Utopian plans such as Hugh Ferriss's *Metropolis of Tomorrow*, which was regarded as incomparably more constructive than Le Corbusier's *Ville contemporaine* or Hilberseimer's *Hochhausstadt*. In their 1934 manual on the architectural organization of cities, Aleksei Shchusev and L. E. Zagorsky discussed Ferriss's designs in detail, regarding them as "far from uninteresting," and were especially attentive to the idea of a triangular configuration of urban "centers" demarcating science, art, and business activities:

> In Ferriss's view, artistic, scientific, and commercial centers must be differentiated architecturally. The skyscrapers of his business center are monumental constructions consisting of simple geometrical figures. The buildings of the scientific center differ from those of the business center. Positioned along streets that cross each other, they constitute isolated volumes corresponding precisely to their functional vocation. The scientific center is larger than the others. Its skyscrapers are taller towers housing laboratories, and the buildings stand closer together.
>
> The artistic center, too, has its own specific physiognomy . . . consisting of stepped blocks and lightweight circular towers that taper as they rise. These relatively few buildings are positioned freely, their architectural forms are richer, the roofs are flower gardens, and the principal streets are parks.
>
> The architectural and artistic principles formulated by Ferriss merit our attention, for they pose fundamental questions concerning the architecture of today's cities and furnish specific responses. It is true that his proposals are grounded in the American skyscraper with its tendentious symmetries, and as such are unthinkable as the basis for the global organization of a city. But it is clear that this architect, in his quest for the form of the "metropolis of tomorrow," has obtained some results.[459]

In their comparative and historical analysis of urban composition, Shchusev and Zagorsky were much preoccupied by architectural notions of contrast and unity, singling out the virtues of Washington's Mall in its subordination to the Capitol (here doubtless alluding to ongoing projects for approaches to the Palace of Soviets in Moscow). The principal author of the general plan for Moscow, Vladimir Semenov, was equally attentive to American city planning developments since 1914. In 1935 he reproduced and commented on the sketches published by Hegemann and Peets in *The American Vitruvius*.[460] In the same year, the Russians translated (though not without formulating some reservations in the preface) Thomas Adams's *Recent Advances in Town Planning* which outlined the Regional Plan for New York.[461] This interest in the American scene failed, however, to prevent the arrest and deportation of Viacheslav Oltarzhevsky on his return from ten years in the United States.[462] Though stimulating when carefully

119. Konstanty Gutschow,
architect (1902–1978).
*Project for a residential tower
for the Binnenalster in Hamburg:
elevation*, 1942.
Staatsarchiv Hamburg

120. Otto Kohtz,
architect (1880–1956).
*Project for a residential
skyscraper for Berlin: elevation.*
From Alfred Hugenberg,
Die neue Stadt, Berlin, 1935.
Collection Jean-Louis Cohen, Paris

filtered, knowledge of America remained ideologically hazardous in the eyes of the Soviet authorities, especially where comparisons of social structures were concerned.

America as Seen from Nazi Germany

Criticisms of the *Baubolschewismus* of radical groups in Hitler's Germany were no more efficient in stamping out Americanism than similar efforts in Russia—to the contrary, they seemed to give it renewed impetus. This convergence between the two national situations includes other common features that have led some critics to speak (often abusively) of a "totalitarian" architectural system.[463] In Germany, where designs were less clearly determined by Nazi political

and cultural orientations than they were by Stalin's Communist Party in Russia, Americanism in fact became a driving force behind the new regime's economic and territorial policies. Here, the principal legacy of the Third Reich was its motorway network which, though doubtless built with strategic considerations in mind, was clearly inspired by Fordist conceptions of production and consumption, in that it coincided with the launching of the German "people's automobile" (or *Volkswagen*)—a transposition of the Model T.[464] The idea of a network of carriageways independent of local traffic had already been the focus of propaganda operations between 1909, when the company AVUS was formed for the construction of a motorway in Berlin, and 1933, when Adolf Hitler implemented a program to which the Nazis had hitherto been opposed. Suspension bridges associated with this project were clearly drawn from American models, as witnesses the Elbe Bridge in Hamburg, whose piers were 150 meters high (like those of the George Washington Bridge), or the bridge over the Rhine at Cologne-Rodenkirchen, designed by the engineer Fritz Leonhardt (who had visited the United States). All in all, the new regime, attentive to the American-based strategies of its industries, implemented a "reactionary modernism."[465] In architecture, the best example of the "Americanocentrism" of the great industrial *Konzerne*, many bound up with Nazism to the point of active involvement in its concentration camp strategies, was furnished by Hans Poelzig, who in the last years of the Weimar Republic built the Administration Building of the chemical corporation I. G. Farben; one of its façades might be viewed as a dynamic reinterpretation of Albert Kahn's tooth-shaped General Motors building.

Both in its industrial policies and in its official manifestations, the Nazi regime tolerated and even encouraged the strategies pursued by modern architects and designers.[466] One of the earliest urban reform projects of the new regime was the *Neue Stadt*, a plan for Berlin drawn up under the impetus of the cinema and leisure magnate Alfred Hugenberg. For this project Hugenberg mobilized the forces of Otto Kohtz, who, in a reformulation of his earlier skyscraper studies, positioned quasi-Cartesian towers capped by Nazi eagles at the center of the city.[467] But the most radical tall building program was launched in Hamburg, the newly-dubbed *Führerstadt*, which was keen to convince passengers arriving in its port that the Reich was capable of building structures as tall as those of New York. A competition was held in 1937–38, and detailed studies were carried out by the architects Konstanty Gutschow and Fritz Leonhardt until 1942, when the project was abandoned due to the pressures of war.[468]

121. Boris Iofan (1891–1976), Vladimir Gelfreikh (1885–1967), Vladimir Shchuko (1878–1939), architects. *Project for the Palace of the Soviets: perspective, Moscow, 1934.* Shchusev Architectural Museum, Moscow

122. Iakov Chernikhov, architect (1889–1951). *Untitled,* c. 1933. From the unpublished series *Industrial Tales.* Collection Barry Friedman Ltd., New York

In the wake of Nazi defeat in 1945, the renewed triumph of American industry and organization guaranteed the United States' technological and cultural hegemony in Western Europe. Jeeps, Dakotas, and other equipment supplied via Lend-Lease agreements were seen as far afield as the USSR. German and French reconstruction was profoundly shaped by American models—reinforced by field studies, experimental constructions, and exhibitions. Propaganda operations were carried out throughout newly liberated Europe by the Americans. In the case of Italy, where the neorealists were deeply influenced by American culture, Bruno Zevi proceeded to vaunt Wright's architecture in his books[469] and via the political activities of the Associazione per l'Architettura Organica. In Rome, America's information services financed the publication of a *Manuale dell'architetto* with a view to rationalizing design and construction methods throughout Italy.[470] *Built in USA*, an exhibition organized by the New York Museum of Modern Art, toured Germany and underscored the impact of lectures by Walter Gropius, henceforth a representative of American architecture. In 1945 Otto Kohtz (who had stayed in Germany) designed a series of skyscrapers absolutely identical to those he had projected a decade previously, as part of his proposal for the "reconstruction of a metropolis"—except that now the necessary demolitions had indeed been carried out. In general, however, Germany came to know the United States more gradually and more durably, through a system of grants that enabled her best students to study in American schools. Other architects found their own way to America in the footsteps of Mendelsohn and Neutra, seeking out Frank Lloyd Wright in his Scottsdale retreat (for example Frei Otto in 1951).[471]

The United Nations Organization, whose creation in 1945 laid the foundations of the new world

View of the entrance to the *Exposition des Techniques Américaines de l'Habitation et de l'Urbanisme,* Paris, Grand Palais, 1946.
Ministère de l'Équipement, des Transports et du Tourisme, Paris

The Second World War and European Reconstruction

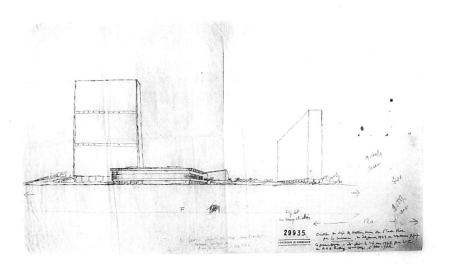

123. Le Corbusier,
architect (1887–1965).
*United Nations Building:
perspective*, New York,
27 March 1947.
Fondation Le Corbusier, Paris

order, at last furnished the occasion for the collaborative work foreshadowed in the competitions of the twenties, and on terrain that had inspired the most dynamic Americanist themes: Manhattan. In *When the Cathedrals were White*, Le Corbusier alludes to the team for the planning and execution of Rockefeller Center, with its committee of technical experts.[472] In 1946 he engaged in this form of collective work on an international committee for the construction of the UN headquarters, which included Oscar Niemeyer, Ernest Cormier, and Sven Markelius. Le Corbusier also called on the services of Vladimir Bodiansky, who joined a group of consultants including Hugh Ferriss, Matthew Nowicki, Gilmore D. Clarke, Louis Skidmore, and Ralph Walker. In the course of the group's meetings, Wallace K. Harrison succeeded in gaining support for a project based on Niemeyer's development of an initial idea by Le Corbusier, who nonetheless waged a vigorous campaign against the final project, in particular its façade. Notwithstanding some bitterness, however, the building as executed by Harrison incorporated a large number of proposals elaborated within the working group of 1946–48. The UN Building can be regarded as signaling international recognition of America's capacity to formulate a new architecture of

the skyscraper based on prewar models, even if Walter Gropius and Mies—as former German nationals—were excluded from the consultation process.[473]

American Models for Russia in the Wake of Destruction

Russia was represented in the UN project group by the unexceptional Nikolai Basov. Meanwhile, ideas for Russian reconstruction included the hypothetical construction of American-style suburban housing estates, while Andrei Burov proposed rebuilding Yalta on lines similar to those of Miami Beach. From 1941 to 1945, while American planes, trucks, and other equipment crossed the Atlantic *en masse*, Russian architects became particularly interested in American techniques. *Arkhitektura SSSR*, which now appeared relatively infrequently in the kiosks, discussed the industrialized housing of American armaments workers and new methods of wooden construction.[474] In 1943, Burov advocated importing prefabrication plants for the reconstruction of urban areas destroyed in Russia.[475] Andrei Bunin's idea for the construction of a *One-Storey Russia*—based on the travelogue of the humorists Ilf and Petrof, *One-Storey America*—was taken seriously to the point where, in 1944–45, the Russian Academy of Architecture published three works by Roman Khiger on the various types of American housing. The first of these was prefaced by Karo Alabian, who was now chairman of the Academy's commission for scientific and technical problems of the reconstruction. In this role he was willing to reinvest his firsthand knowledge of American architecture:

> In this preparatory phase, it is imperative that the architects, engineers, and economists familiarize themselves with the best examples of construction in the United States, and that they study them in detail.[476]

Direct contacts continued unabated. Frank Lloyd Wright corresponded with Arkin and Alabian in 1943.[477] The most dynamic institution was the architectural commission of the National Council of American-Soviet Friendship, created in 1943 in New York, under the patronage of the American Institute of Architects and chaired by Harvey Wiley Corbett. The group's active members included Talbot Hamlin, the director of Columbia University's Avery Architectural Library, and the architects John W. Root, George Nelson, William Wurster, Knud Lonberg-Holm, and Joseph Hudnut. Simon Breines and Hans Blumenfeld were both in direct contact with Soviet architects.[478] The Americans received regular requests for information concerning their rapid construction methods.[479] Alabian underlined the need for accurate data on zoning and planning standards.[480] Appointed head of the Bureau of Scientific and Technical Information of the architec-

tural commission of the Soviet Council of Ministers (after having been freed from the gulag following the intervention of the American Embassy) Viacheslav Oltarzhevsky asked his old friend Corbett for information concerning plaster and wood construction systems, prefabricated bathroom installations, and the recycling of industrial waste.[481]

As secretary of the architectural section of the All-Union Society for Cultural Relationship with Foreign Countries and the conduit for all correspondence, Arkin noted that an exhibition entitled *Architecture in the USA* had been held in June 1944 at the House of Architects, with documents from various sources, and that Moscow "architectural circles" had interest "in new prefabrication methods, town and village plans, and the work of a number of remarkable American architects."[482] In the wake of a solemn meeting of this society, to mark

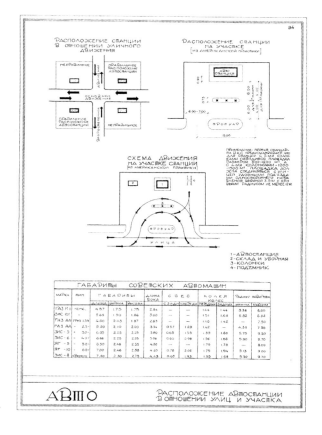

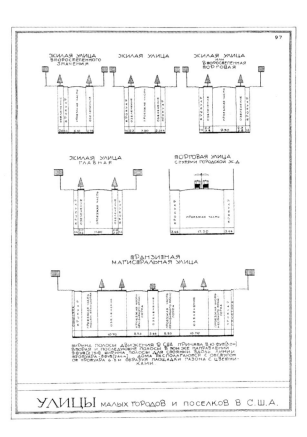

124, 125.
Viacheslav Oltarzhevsky, architect (1880–1965).
Plate for the manual
Gabaritnyi spravochnik arkhitektora, Moscow, 1947.
Canadian Centre for Architecture, Montreal

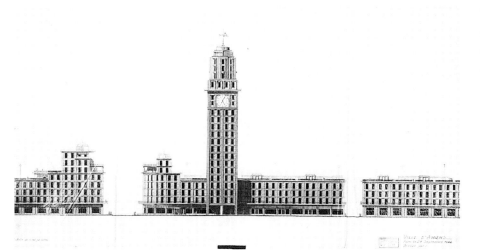

126. Auguste Perret,
architect (1874–1954).
*Project for the reconstruction
of Amiens: elevation*, 1934.
Institut Français d'Architecture,
Centre d'Archives d'Architecture
du XXᵉ siècle, Paris

the reception of documents forwarded by Corbett, a Russo-American construction meeting organized with the assistance of the Amtorg trading company was held at the New York Engineers' Society on 4 and 5 May 1945, with 300 participants.[483] The committee then organized a more ambitious exhibition, for which Frederick Kiesler designed a series of corrugated plywood panels (similar to those he used in the 1942 *Art of this Century* exhibition at the Peggy Guggenheim Gallery), where photomontages orchestrated a lyrical account of the origins of modern American architecture.[484]

In line with Roman Khiger, who regarded reconstruction as an "argument for the adoption of American examples," in 1947 Oltarzhevsky (again under the aegis of the Academy of Architecture) published a manual detailing the dimensions and "modules" used in American building practice. But even though his bibliography included the *Architectural Graphic Standards*, the *Time-Saver Standards*, and *Sweet's* catalogue, Corbett's former associate was careful to point out that "the examples drawn from [American and English] practice are furnished merely as references for given solutions, and cannot be used in the absence of critical appraisal."[485] The building programs analyzed included nursery and grade schools, sporting facilities, hospitals, agricultural buildings, hotels, shops, furniture, bathrooms, kitchens, streets, escalator systems, and gas stations "based on American practice."

But it was at Yalta that the strangest project of all came into existence (though it had nothing to do with the Allies' negotiations of 1945). Drawn up from 1941–45 under the direction of Moisei Ginzburg, who had been appointed planner-in-chief for the southern Crimea, Andrei Burov's reconstruction plan for this seaside resort did not employ the habitual compositional schemes, with two intersecting avenues on a monumental scale. Instead, it proposed a two-tier urban freeway that liberated the ground levels for pedestrians, and five different skyscrapers punctuating the shoreline.[486] The inspiration for the Yalta plan was none other than Miami Beach, which Burov had visited in 1930:

> An avenue lined with palm trees separates the beach from the city. On the other side of the road, there is a park planted with palm trees. Within the park and closer to the road, at intervals of two hundred yards or so, there are 42 ten to fifteen-storey hotel-towers, all built in the same year.[487]

But the bureaucrats in charge of Soviet architectural production regarded his project as a plan "ignorant of the practical problems of architecture and concentrating merely on its more formal aspect."[488] Opinions such as this one forced an increasingly "shameful" Russian Americanism to take refuge in skyscraper designs.

American Techniques in France

Some French reconstruction programs involved the resurrection of idealistic prewar projects, as was the case with those carried out at Le Havre and Amiens by Auguste Perret. In his initial plan for Le Havre,

Perret lined the southern seafront with tower-blocks situated in front of the moorings for trans-Atlantic liners, an echo of the "tower-cities" sketched a quarter of a century earlier.[489] But in the Amiens operation, the belfry would be the only tall structure. French architects and planners became especially interested in American experiments in prefabrication and regional planning, observing them in the course of field studies which, in the late forties, became "productivity missions" crucial to the modernization of the French economy. French architects largely absent during Nazi Occupation, from Free France or French circles in New York, were now particularly attentive to American wartime innovations. In fact, the century's second postwar period was characterized throughout Europe by the shift from theoretical *Americanism* to practical *Americanization*.

Several French architects had settled in New York before their country's defeat in 1940. Hector Guimard, a major proponent of Parisian Art Nouveau, died there in 1942, practically at the same time as Charles Siclis, the café and brasserie architect, who had unsuccessfully attempted to sell his ideas on camouflage to the Americans. Pierre Chareau, the architect of the Maison de Verre in Paris, had more luck than they: near New York he built a studio for the artist Robert Motherwell, his own house in East Hampton, and stage-sets for New York's Free French.[490] Architects and town planners among the wartime émigrés included both recent refugees and those who had decided to practice in the United States as early as the thirties. Maurice Rotival figured among the latter category. An engineer and town planner, Rotival had settled in America in 1937 and taught at Yale from 1939. Writing in the first issue of *L'Architecture d'aujourd'hui* following a five-year suspension of publication, he suggested the creation of a "Rhine Authority" in the manner of the Tennessee

Valley Authority (TVA), to coordinate the development of the Lotharingian waterway.[491] Rotival would also be active in the 1950s within the European Coal and Steel Community.

During the war, Jacques Carlu designed a 600-meter skyscraper for La Défense which resembled his 1931 project for the "Triumphal Way." A technical adviser to the 1943–44 Monnet delegation to Washington, Carlu was consultant for the internal layout of the United Nations building from 1950 to 1954.[492] André Remondet, who was awarded a Delano Grant in 1937, remained in the United States from 1940 to 1944 before returning to Paris, where he became co-director of an atelier at the École des Beaux-Arts with Auguste Perret.[493] Two of the most talented pupils of the first Perret atelier also spent the war years in America. Oscar Nitzchké (who had been

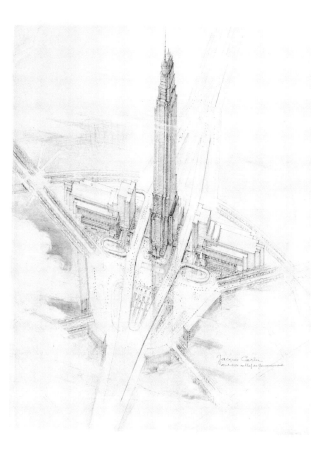

127. Jacques Carlu, architect (1890–1976). *Skyscraper project for La Défense: aerial perspective*, Paris, 1944. Canadian Centre for Architecture, Montreal

invited in 1938 by the architect of the Rockefeller Center, Wallace Harrison) taught at Yale with Rotival; together they drew up the plan for New Haven before again working with Harrison on the UN project.[494] Paul Nelson, who on returning to America had collaborated with Fernand Léger on a project for artists' studios in New York, joined the French diplomatic mission in Washington before returning to France to participate in the reconstruction.[495] Among the younger practitioners, Anatole Kopp, a former pupil of the École Spéciale d'Architecture, studied at MIT before teaching at Black Mountain College, where several former *Meister* of the Bauhaus were pursuing their research.

In 1945, Delano scholars selected from Beaux-Arts students again set out for the United States, and from 1948 to 1952, Gaston Leclaire, Jean Dubuisson, Henri Colboc, and Jean Willerval all effected their "Grand Tour,"[496] while Louis-Georges Noviant and others received newly-instituted grants from the Ministère des Affaires Étrangères. However, the most significant exchanges between American architecture and French reconstruction occurred outside academic circles. The French Ministry of Reconstruction and Town Planning (MRU) set up an office in London in 1944 and a year later in Washington, where it took over the task of analyzing construction issues from the Ministry of Industrial Production. Its three departments (town planning and architecture, documentation, purchasing and materials) acquired construction materials, imported prefabricated structures and, above all, drew up innumerable reports and memoranda.[497] The Ministry of Industrial Production delegation had been under the direction of Paul Nelson. One of his first tasks was to draw up a report on temporary housing, a particularly sensitive issue in the context of the first reconstruction operations directed by Colonel Antoine, the chairman of the

Union Nationale des Techniciens et Cadres, who declared his intention to create "provisional Franco-American communities in the disaster zones."[498] Nelson's manifold activities, which included the construction of the Franco-American hospital of Saint-Lô, culminated in an exhibition of American building techniques, which is discussed below.

In 1945, Raoul Dautry, the first minister of Reconstruction and Town Planning, at once sent delegations to America, doubtless recalling his own visit in 1912 as a young railway engineer.[499] One of his first envoys was Marcel Lods, who (if we are to believe André Chastel, then the architectural critic for *Le Monde*) returned to France yet a more radical "Modernist" with a "mission to inform."[500] A longstanding advocate of prefabrication and metal constructions, Lods was so filled with "euphoria and enthusiasm" that he hastened to give an account of his "bracing" travels at the Salle Pleyel, in a lecture entitled "Images of America." Emphasizing the "plenitude" and his "satisfaction" with Americans' "technical and human achievements," he appears to have considered their town plans, freeways, bridges, and (above all) prefabricated houses as the expressions of a "faith" which France lacked.[501]

In another lecture delivered on 20 December 1945 at the Institut Technique du Bâtiment et des Travaux Publics, Lods articulated a slightly different view of America. While acknowledging its "partial" successes, he rejected urban formations such as Los Angeles, a city which (reiterating Le Corbusier's phrase) he regarded as "the most beautiful of architectural catastrophes." He claimed to have learned the "lesson of America's failure":

> We are now in a position to announce that there exist houses accessible to all and capable of making life easier and more beautiful in the world.
>
> And yet they are merely temporary homes.[502]

EXPOSITION DES
TECHNIQUES AMÉRICAINES
DE L'HABITATION ET DE L'URBANISME
1939-194X
GRAND PALAIS
DU 14 JUIN AU 21 JUILLET 1946

XXXI. Paul Colin, poster designer
(1892–1985). *Poster for
the Exposition des techniques
américaines de l'habitation
et de l'urbanisme 1939–194X*,
1946. Archives nationales,
Centre des Archives
Contemporaines, Paris

XXXII. Andrei K. Burov, architect (1900–57).

Plan of the reconstruction of Yalta: elevation from the sea, 1945. Shchusev Architectural Museum, Moscow

XXXIII. Lev Rudnev, architect (1885–1956),
with Sergei E. Chernyshev (1881–1963),
P.V. Abrosimov (1900–61),
V.N. Nasonov, and A.F. Khryakov (engineer).
Moscow University, first version: overall perspective,
1948–53. Shchusev Architectural Museum, Moscow

XXXIV. Dimitri N. Chechulin,
architect (1901–81),
and M. Tigranov,
engineer (1904–52). *Zariadie*
office tower: panorama from
Red Square, Moscow, 1947–49.
Shchusev Architectural Museum,
Moscow

XXXV. Vladimir Gelfreikh
(1885–1967) and Mikhail A.
Minkus (1905–63), architects.
Ministry of Foreign Affairs:
façade, Moscow, 1948.
Shchusev Architectural Museum,
Moscow

XXXVI. Mikhail Posokhin
(1910–89) and Achot
Mndoyants (1910–66),
architects. *Residential building
on Vosstanaia Square: general
perspective*, Moscow, 1951.
Shchusev Architectural Museum,
Moscow

XXXVII. *Construction of the Ministry of Foreign Affairs by Vladimir Gelfreikh and Mikhail A. Minkus, Smolenskaia Place, Moscow. Cover for l'URSS en construction, 1949. Collection Jean-Louis Cohen, Paris*

Though he underlined the quality of these provisional dwellings, elsewhere in his lecture Lods stated that they could not resolve the question of prefabrication for permanent housing.[503] On the other hand, as a man passionately fond of aviation and aerial photography, he waxed lyrical over the splendors of the American landscape, in particular the airports:

As soon as they are free to do so (which is the case of the wartime munitions factories: Willow Run in Detroit, Beech Aircraft in Wichita, the provisional rehousing villages surrounding the factories and aviation schools on the plains), they proceed quite differently.

The aviation schools are marvelous, and seen from the air, their layout is wonderfully clear.

Seen from a height of two thousand meters, the runways, the housing for pupils and personnel, the hangars, and sportsgrounds—all bathed in greenery—give a splendid impression of the order, clarity, and elegance of the chosen design solution.[504]

Lods cited the TVA in his plea for a "wide-ranging plan" for France to make the data of the Monnet plan "applicable in space and time."[505] In the first issue that *L'Architecture d'aujourd'hui* had devoted to a modern architect, Lods hymned the virtues of Richard Neutra's lightweight California homes:

Neutra's message is infinitely precious.

Across the oceans, across another continent, we find an infinitely fresh, infinitely new architecture, one capable of convincing the skeptics that for a people that does not want to die, there is truly something other than repetition and proof (alas) that this is not the mere evocation of copies from past epochs.[506]

Lods emphasized how the "rough yet fertile ground of California seems to have been [Neutra's] preordained sphere of activity." But he was most impressed by Neutra's experiments with prefabricated metal elements and his research into the uses of aluminum. Moreover, Neutra's work soon became the focus of

heated debate in France. Conservative architects compared him unfavorably with Frank Lloyd Wright (whom they had recently "discovered"), while planners skeptical of modern forms, such as Gaston Bardet, pointed up contradictions between Neutra's intelligent technical solutions and the rigidity of his urban plans. A regular correspondent with Lewis Mumford, Bardet praised Neutra's teamwork yet compared him unfavorably with Lods, criticizing the former's failure to call into question the uniformity of his city plans and habits of "addition" instead of "composition."[507]

Shortly after Lods's return from America, a group tour was organized by the MRU. This included Michel Écochard, the architect of plans for Damascus and Beirut; Pierre-André Emery, a former assistant of Le Corbusier, who practiced in Algiers; Gérald Hanning, Le Corbusier's young assistant; André Sive, a former pupil of Perret; and Lods's former associate Bodiansky. Le Corbusier and Eugène Claudius-Petit (a future Minister of Reconstruction) were late in setting off and failed to rejoin the main group. The tour organized by the Museum of Modern Art took the group by automobile to Chicago and to the new towns of the Tennessee Valley.[508] Both in Algiers, where Émery, Sive, and Claudius-Petit engaged in public debates, and in Paris, the explorers shared many common views. On his return to Beirut, Écochard described the trip in a lecture at the American University, and compared Soviet Plans with American wartime policy. In his view, "the United States would not have been able to equip themselves with a merchant and naval fleet more powerful than all the others put together . . . and resupply the world had they not momentarily planned their economy."[509] He also alluded to the "Homeric combat" of those involved in the TVA program:

Contemplation of these works furnished some of the most fruitful lessons of my stay in the United States.

As an architect, the beauty of the dams and their infrastructure, the result of perfect collaboration between engineers and architects, satisfied me both aesthetically and practically.

As a town planner, the coordination between the nation's various traffic networks interested me deeply.

As a man, I saw a desolate country spring back to life and the human condition improve, and this is what moved me most.[510]

During their Atlantic crossing aboard the Liberty Ship *Vernon S. Hood*, the two latecomers Le Corbusier and Claudius-Petit cemented an undying friendship and the former put the finishing touches on his Modulor proportional system. Coming ten years after the disappointments of his earlier trip, this new "mission" gave Le Corbusier (and Lods and Écochard) the opportunity to discover America's great territorial developments. He later described his encounter with the aluminum magnate Kaiser, then responsible for the construction of three million houses yearly, and reiterated his earlier criticisms of endless suburban sprawl:

These houses are to be mass-produced, in other words they are to be family dwellings. They will cover a certain amount of ground; they will be erected along streets; these streets will not be in the towns, where there is no room, but in the country. The towns will be expanded to enormous size by suburbs, vast, tremendous suburbs. It will be necessary to create huge transport systems to make these suburbs accessible and mutually connected: railways, underground railways, trams, buses, etc. . . . This will involve the construction of innumerable roads, a huge network of mains (water, gas, electricity, telephone, etc.). What boundless activity, what wealth this will bring! Or don't you think so? I think this is just another example, carried to disastrous lengths, of the Great American Waste which I had already observed and analysed in 1935. No one is entitled to

breathe a word of warning in Mr Kaiser's ear, no one may even dream of calling a halt to his activities, no machinery is set on foot to channel his indomitable energy towards social and economic ends. . .[511]

In Knoxville Le Corbusier met David Lilienthal, director of TVA operations and author of a small book on this gigantic, government-owned enterprise which, thanks to the American information service, was already familiar to the French:[512]

. . . harmony is the aim of all Mr Lilienthal's work. His face lit up at the delightful thought of establishing a reign of harmony . . . by undertaking the most gigantic works and co-ordinating the most immense projects: water, motive power, fertilizers, agriculture, transport, industry. The end result: a territory as large as France was snatched from the grip of erosion, which, with a terrifying speed, was laying waste wide stretches of arable land. Now, victorious life was regaining possession of the salvaged land, performing upon it one of the greatest syntheses of modern organization.[513]

All in all, both groups perceived a changed America. Throughout the two previous decades, travelers had been fascinated by the urban density of Chicago and New York and their skyscrapers (and to a lesser extent by infrastructure); French leaders were now interested in the decentralization of industry and mass production, questions of suburban and regional development preoccupied the planners, and the architects took a long look at standardized and lightweight construction elements and the prefabricated detached house.

The subsequent careers of those participating in the MRU's early travels in America are worth discussing. Écochard became Morocco's town planning director, implementing his ideas in the plan for Casablanca, which he entrusted to Bodiansky. In step with Rotival's involvement in the Rhine valley operation, Sive worked with Georges-Henri Pingusson in the Saar.

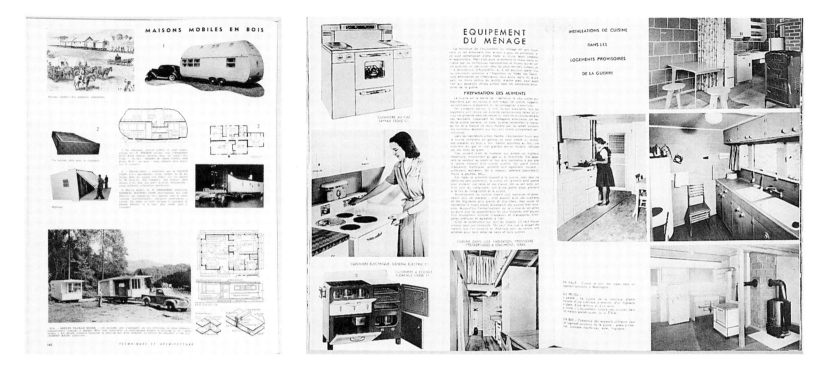

Lods, when commissioned to draw up plans for Mainz by that city's mayor, strove to introduce large-scale planning policies on Functionalist lines outlined in the Athens Charter, assisted by Gérald Hanning.[514] Claudius-Petit was Minister of the Reconstruction from 1948 to 1953. As mayor of Firminy, he commissioned Sive to draw up plans for a "priority urbanization zone," within which Le Corbusier built his third Unité d'habitation.

While a panoply of "sample" prefabricated houses were built on the experimental village created by the MRU at Noisy-le-Grand, Nelson's activities in the United States formed the basis of an exhibition inaugurated on 14 June 1946 by the Communist minister François Billoux, entitled *American Town-Planning and Housing Techniques, 1939–194X*. This exhibition was held beneath the vaulted glass roof of the Grand Palais, with photographic murals in lightweight frames, sample materials, catalogues of components, and full-scale examples of equipped houses.[515] Apart from Nelson and his assistant Fred-

erick Gutheim, the exhibition team included American architects and designers like Knud Lonberg-Holm, Gyorgy Kepes, and Ladislas Sutnar; young architects who had spent the war years in America, such as Anatole Kopp; and promising professionals such as Louis Kahn. Instead of presenting isolated architectural "works," the exhibition focused on structural components, equipment, and methods used on the construction site, all presented in an avant-garde exhibition format. Nelson explained this in *L'Architecture d'aujourd'hui*:

First of all, it should be stressed that this was not an exhibition of "architecture" or "urbanism" in the general sense of the terms, and that the choice of examples was not determined by aesthetic considerations, but by a concern to show the French public that *cheap* housing is *mass-produced* in America, that new materials are developed and applied there, and the extent to which Americans adapt to ever-changing conditions by constantly renewing their methods.

. . . Clearly, there can be no question of slavishly copying American methods in France; each country is

129. Two pages illustrating kitchen installations in American mobile homes in *L'Architecture d'aujourd'hui*, July 1947. Canadian Centre for Architecture, Montreal

128. Page showing American mobile homes in the journal *Techniques et architecture*, November 1945. Canadian Centre for Architecture, Montreal

130. View of the entrance to the *Exposition des Techniques Américaines de l'Habitation et de l'Urbanisme,* Paris, Grand Palais, 1946. Ministère de l'Équipement, des Transports et du Tourisme, Paris

131. General view of the *Exposition des Techniques Américaines de l'Habitation et de l'Urbanisme,* Paris, Grand Palais, 1946. Ministère de l'Équipement, des Transports et du Tourisme, Paris

132. Texas-style house, experimental postwar village, Noisy-le-Sec, 1946. Ministère de l'Équipement, des Transports et du Tourisme, Paris

subject to specific conditions, and industrialization must take these into account; nonetheless, certain principles are internationally valid, such as the development of standards essential to mass production and the coordination of all the factors of that production.

The exhibition revealed this general principle to the French architects and town planners. It also reassured them as to the so-called threat which standardization represents to design freedom: standardization does not restrict the architect's movements—it is a means of diversifying and constantly improving living standards.[516]

Though essentially devoted to the war years, the exhibition nonetheless showed examples of recent urban policies and architectural strategies. Town planning exhibits focused on experiments in urban "renovation" and regional planning initiatives— with the TVA naturally in the limelight—but also presented inexpensive housing projects. Architectural displays centered on technical matters, construction methods, the modernization of domestic equipment, and the use of prefabrication techniques on construction sites. Following Billoux's departure, Nelson, Roger Gilbert, and Charles Sébillotte built the remarkable Franco-American Hospital of Saint-Lô (1946–56), a symbol of trans-Atlantic cooperation, but also of collaboration between architects and artists: in 1955 Fernand Léger painted his last mural there.[517]

Following the initial field studies and the exhibition of 1946, professional circles involved in the reconstruction benefited from an uninterrupted flow of information from America. But it was not until 1949, with the creation of "productivity missions" in general and those of the MRU in particular, that the observation of techniques and production methods began to have a substantive effect on industry. James Silbermann of the U.S. Department of Labor, who met Jean Monnet during his visit to

Washington, set up "missions" enabling the French to learn more efficient methods of production and management. These commenced in 1950 and were organized by the Association pour l'Accroissement de la Productivité and the Comité National de la Productivité under Robert Buron.

According to Richard Kuysel's calculations, some three hundred missions involving twenty-seven hundred engineers, industrialists, workers, and civil servants visited the United States in the space of four years.[518] Their reports, which circulated widely, took a balanced view of American methods. Over and above their technical observations, the envoys brought back a strong awareness of the importance of human relations, marketing, and management. These discoveries coincided, moreover, with an era of political and trade union confrontation in France; the Communist-led Conféderation Générale du Travail refused to participate in the missions, and those trade unionists who made the journey were surprised to discover the high quality of working conditions and the influence of workers' organizations. Generally speaking, however, the envoys remained skeptical of the monolithic virtues of American consumer society.

Building missions organized from 1951 to 1954 concentrated on productivity, problems encountered on the site, finance, design, and specific trades. Their readings of American production were strongly marked by earlier field studies and exhibitions. The first of these missions studied "the structure and organization of the construction industry, labor relations, the organization of companies, relations between contractors and architects, contracts, building techniques, and all other factors of productivity, with a view to improving construction in France."[519] It remarked on the quality of domestic equipment and fittings, and on the integration of

construction and public works sectors within large corporations, which would be a *leitmotiv* of French policy when it came to build the country's *grands ensembles* (high-rise housing projects).

A further mission, entitled "Architects-Engineers-Contractors," set out in July 1951, led by Marcel Roux, a member of Claudius-Petit's cabinet at the MRU and former coordinator (with Sive) of town planning in the Saar region.[520] Professional encounters and visits to factories, construction sites, and recent buildings were the essential activities of this one-month mission covering the New York–Pittsburgh–Washington triangle. Its members were especially interested in relations between clients, designers, and contractors, and the quality and speed of construction (facilitated by "rational organization" of sites), noting that, proportionally, the United States built five times more housing than France. One chapter of its report underlined the "success" of Levittown, based on "typification," "planning," and "careful attention to detail."[521]

In their conclusions the envoys stated that it was "necessary and urgent to revise and codify French concepts and regulations in the field of economic housing [by simplifying] certain works," though the architect would not therefore have to "abandon his [artistic] conceptions." In particular, they insisted on reductions in "tasks performed by the housewife," "ceiling heights" (2.5 meters), and designers' safety coefficients. They further advocated increased cooperation with engineers in the design process, more detailed project studies, and a reduction in the number of on-site contractors. At the technical level they recommended increased mechanization of large- and small-scale tools and rationalization of the construction process. They underlined the need for large-scale programs so as to facilitate industrialized construction methods, alluding not without humor to "the excellent climate of cooperation between workers and bosses" in America. Further missions were devoted to specific questions, in particular that of prefabrication. This led to the development of prototypes destined for a brilliant future, such as the Levitt-inspired houses designed by Maisons Phénix in the 1950s.

The two generations of missions undertaken in the decade following the war were quite different in character. The first investigations centered on large-scale construction sites, infrastructures, and standardization, whereas later studies focused on production processes, know-how, and labor relations. Gradually, the emphasis shifted from technical to management aspects of the building industry. Nonetheless, the principal ministers of Reconstruction and Town Planning remained committed to the transfer of American technology, from Raoul Dautry, who instigated the first missions; Billoux, who sponsored Nelson's exhibition; or Claudius-Petit, who promoted the *grands ensembles*. But if each minister adopted his own specific American policy, each architect had *his* vision of America. Where Lods saw only prefabrication and large-scale territorial schemes, Bardet perceived the organic character of America's city plans; Noviant was captivated by the rational low-cost technologies and the ambition of urban compositions; while Remondet pinpointed more lyrical formal strategies.

The American tour legitimized "missionaries" and accelerated careers within official circles, but it also sharpened the strategies of innovative professional groups and accelerated *rapprochements* with some radical groups. Many of the practitioners involved in modernization operations in the Saar and Occupied Germany before 1949, and in Morocco and Algeria after 1950, had made the trip to America. What they shared was not so much the

cult of new heroes (Neutra; Mies; Skidmore, Owings, and Merrill) as sincere admiration for American methods of production.

The state-instigated urban plans for the Seine and Rhône valleys, which eventually led to the implementation of nuclear installations at Marcoule and Pierrelatte, were derived as much from research carried out during the Vichy regime or from Dutch and Soviet models as from American town-planning experiments. In the housing sector, systematic standards, rationalized construction methods, and the strategic use of *bureaux d'études* (engineering offices)—all recommended by the 1951 mission—had all been implemented by the end of the decade. Productivity policies determined the design and construction of the *grands ensembles*, which ultimately took the form of heavy rather than metal-only structures (which Lods continued to advocate for thirty years). And thus, the global idea of productivity-through-standardization would become hidebound in a single product: the reinforced-concrete housing development. Profound misgivings concerning this housing type had to be voiced before individual structures of the Levitt type and shopping centers began to invade the suburbs.[522]

Meanwhile, Americanization became a central political issue in France and the Communist party's unwavering defense of national culture carried considerable weight. Whether simplistic or complex, the anti-Americanist lobby rejected all United States initiatives out of hand, be it the massive influx of American credit with the Marshall Plan, or the Blum-Byrnes accord of 1946, which opened French markets to Hollywood movie production.[523] With the advent of the Cold War, the French Left brandished the threat of American hegemony, and in 1950, a debate over the supposedly harmful effects of Coca-Cola fired all sides of the Chambre des

Députés.[524] After the accounts of the Chicago Exposition and the literary impressions of the 1920s (Duhamel, Morand, Céline, Durtain, *et al.*), a new wave of contradictory texts inundated French bookshops, indicating a deeply divided intelligentsia: Jean-Paul Sartre, Simone de Beauvoir, and Roger Vaillant were firmly entrenched in the anti-American camp, while Raymond Aron (and much later, Jean-François Revel) headed the pro-Americans.[525]

The "Tall Buildings" of Moscow

Though postwar anti-Americanism found favor in Russia as in France, the debate dating back to the 1930s now led to the construction of a series of Stalinist "tall buildings" for Moscow. Built with the "technical" assistance of Viacheslav Oltarzhevsky, these buildings redefined the city's skyline, and made extensive use of the American constructional procedures and ornamental devices which the Soviet avant-garde had condemned two decades previously. Triumphal themes, already present in the monumental spaces of the 1935 plan for Moscow, gradually crystallized into designs that were singular given the silence in which the official programs matured, and the secretive way in which some architects drew up their designs. Iakov Chernikhov, for instance, designed a series of "Palaces of Communism" and "Pantheons," and the latter theme was studied by many architects who took refuge in Central Asia during the war years. In 1940, Iofan broached the idea of marking Moscow with a series of tall buildings:

> There are remarkable cities, such as Leningrad or Venice, which are implanted on flat sites. How has their skyline been formed? In Venice by its *campanili*, in Leningrad by its spires *(shpili)*. Things are quite different in Rome or Moscow, where architects have exploited the sites' geographical relief. In a city like Moscow, we should make use of variations in level and tall buildings.[526]

Conceptually speaking, post-1945 ideas for the design and implantation of skyscrapers were influenced by critical objections to American buildings raised in 1940 by Andrei Bunin and Maria Kruglova, former members of ASNOVA. In their town planning manual *Arkhitekturnaia kompozitsia goroda*, they formulated two types of criticism: in the first place, American skyscrapers were not sited in accordance with the correct rules of urban composition (i.e., of French classicism), but following the financial appetites of their builders, as shown in the "abysmal disorder" of the Manhattan skyline. Secondly, they lacked an artistic tradition and their proportions did not follow the principles Leon Battista Alberti laid down for *campanili*:

> The American skyline is something quite new. It has begun to emerge in the past thirty to thirty-five years, i.e., a period of marked regression in both creative and planning terms. Moreover, the cities of America have no artistic heritage. Their skyscrapers are the formal products of engineering rather than architecture, and the former is the blind servant of the capitalist economy. All this testifies to the fact that, in today's capitalist cities, and especially in America, the problem of the skyline holds no creative prospects for the future.[527]

Bunin and Kruglova regarded height difference between the various skyscrapers at the tip of Manhattan as insufficient, and that between the Empire State and Chrysler Buildings and their neighbors as excessive. Like Boris Iofan, they concluded that a program of tall buildings was required for Moscow. Their remarks were taken into account in the definition of the buildings' urban disposition and design. The French architect André Lurçat, who worked in the USSR from 1934 to 1937, had condemned the notion of building skyscrapers in Moscow:

> In most cases and in its current applications, the skyscraper is evidently a capitalist "disease." Its con-

struction involves major technical difficulties: lifts, water-supply at the upper levels, foundations, an adequate load-bearing structure. Now, in Moscow the ground-base is particularly poor. Since the whole city is collectively owned, why tackle such costly difficulties? The skyscraper is no longer necessary; it is preferable to use the surface area required for buildings of average height.[528]

The climate seems to have changed after 1945. In his 1952 treatise, *The Realist Foundations of Soviet Architecture*, Mikhail Tsapenko brandished the skyscraper as a weapon in the "fight against American imperialism":

> The socialist development of the USSR has attained such heights that it now constitutes a solid basis for new and decisive progress in our architecture, and a thorough search for new artistic and ideal models. What architects dreamed of many years ago, without being able to translate their dream into sound artistic principles, is now a reality.[529]

A new variant of the 1935 plan was drawn up after the war, and on 13 January 1947 the Soviet Council of Ministers decided to build a series of eight "multistorey houses":

> The architects and builders are faced with a great challenge, the creation of a series of buildings which will doubtless be unprecedented in height, technique, and architecture.
>
> . . .Their proportions and contours must be architecturally and artistically original. They must integrate Moscow's historical fabric and the silhouette of the future Palace of Soviets. These new buildings should not, therefore, be copies of well-known tall buildings abroad.[530]

Commissioned to work on this program in the role of consultant, Oltarzhevsky did not, however, succeed in building his own project for Vosstania Square. In 1953 he explained the traditional nature of the Moscow buildings and what distinguished them from their New York counterparts, which he knew well:

There is a solid and long-standing tradition of tall constructions in Russia. The various periods of the best classical Russian architecture produced remarkable instances of tall buildings which are extremely varied in character and in use. . . . [These] buildings have always been associated with the most significant historical events in the life of the nation and its people. Tall buildings confer on the old Russian cities (above all Moscow) their original and deeply expressive skylines.

. . . The tall buildings under construction in Moscow following the initiative and idea of comrade J. V. Stalin mark a new phase in the reconstruction of the capital and constitute a major world event in contemporary architecture. They give the city a new, expressive skyline and will pave the way for new architectural complexes corresponding to Moscow's role as the beacon of progressive humanity.

These tall buildings have been made possible by remarkable achievements in Soviet construction techniques, and in Soviet science and architecture.

The structural principles of Soviet tall buildings are diametrically opposite to those of the American "skyscraper," which is the result of unbridled capitalist competition and a capitalist attempt to extract maximum profit from each city plot. The interests of the majority of the population are thus sacrificed to the cupidity of the capitalists. Moscow's tall buildings are freely positioned at the most convenient points in the city and surrounded by sufficient green spaces; they serve the city as a whole, the Soviet people as a whole.[531]

Moscow's architect-in-chief Dimitri Chechulin coordinated construction operations. Six buildings (offices or housing) were built at strategic points in the city. These were the MID, or Ministry of Foreign Affairs, located on Smolenskaia Place, the hotels Leningradskaia and Ukraina, two housing blocks on Kotelnicheskaia Quay and Vosstania Square, and a mixed office- and housing block at the Krasnye Vorota subway station. Another very tall building was planned for the Zariadie district, close to the Kremlin. This network of towers, implanted on a curve corresponding more or less to that of the inner ring road, was completed with the construction of the solitary MGU (Moscow State University), relegated to the southwest of the city, where it dominated a new district envisaged in the 1935 plan.[532]

One is tempted to compare the specialized zoning of these skyscrapers—science to the southwest, government close to the center—with Hugh Ferriss's model, which Shchusev and Zagorsky commented on fifteen or so years earlier. In order to differentiate the Muscovite constructions from their American models, the spire atop the Kotelnicheskaia Building, which recalled the *shpil* of the Admiralty Building in St. Petersburg that pleased Stalin, was forced on all the others, and it was via these "hats" that the new buildings forged relations with the existing architectural repertoire. In 1947, Iofan also insisted on treatment of the middle sections of the buildings, which he felt the Americans were ignoring:

> The Americans take as their starting point the idea that the greatest care must be devoted to the upper and lower parts of the skyscraper. These are its most visible parts in American cities. But in Moscow, the tall buildings are visible from a great distance, and not only the "top" and the "bottom" but the building as a whole must therefore constitute a complete architectural work.[533]

Each of the buildings presented a comparable formal structure, modeled and differentiated in reference to the Russian past and recent American constructions. Moreover, though they were all designed as part of the new silhouette, highly specific correlations also had to be forged with street axes and adjacent blocks using rules formulated by Bunin and

Kruglova, which were in turn based on the German H. Maertens's research into "optical scale."[534] In his brief Iofan had been careful to detail such differences between the Soviet program and American realities.[535]

Vladimir Gelfreikh and Mikhail Minkus's Ministry Building on Smolenskaia Place—evincing similarities with the Coolidge Hospital in New York that should be underlined—is doubtless the most successful of the group. In its initial version it was capped with a vaguely Gothic crenellated crown, and its vertical styling was particularly dynamic. Two lateral wings jut out into the square in the manner of the lower floors of the Palace of Soviets, which Gelfreikh had helped design in the thirties. Within the building, a private elevator conveying the minister to his top-floor office was used for a quarter of a century by the former ambassador to Washington, Andrei Gromyko. Situated on the banks of the Moskva facing Kutuzovsky Prospect, the Hotel Ukraina was built by Arkadi Mordvinov, with the participation of Oltarzhevsky. The opposition between the upper floors of the building and the rest of the structure is reminiscent of the *fin-de-siècle* newspaper buildings of New York, and the rhythms of its avenue façade are particularly vigorous. The relations of the Hotel Leningradskaia to the surrounding urban fabric are somewhat different: built in the northeast on the Square of Three Stations, the hotel was designed by Nikolai Poliakov and Andrei Boretski, to some extent in echo of the Kazan Railroad Terminal, which Shchusev had begun to build before the revolution. It consists of a freestanding tower built over a broader base. The decor of the façades is in the style of what post-Stalinist Muscovites would mock as "neo-barrack" (rather than baroque) while its salons imitate those of old Russia.

The treatment of the façades of the housing

133. Robert Camelot,
architect (1903–1993).
*Project for La Défense:
perspective*, Paris, 1954.
Institut Français d'Architecture,
Centre d'Archives d'Architecture
du XXᵉ siècle, Paris

schemes is equally dynamic. The building overlooking Vosstania Place, to the west of the ring road, stands apart from the surrounding *kvartaly*, or apartment blocks. Designed by Mikhail Posokhin—who would be Moscow's architect-in-chief through the sixties and seventies—and Ashot Mndoyants, this building comprises three blocks articulated in an H-plan, each with its battery of elevators. The stepped configuration of its two lateral wings, which frame the central tower—the tallest of all—in the manner of bookends, is reminiscent of Rockefeller Center. The office and housing building built by Aleksei Dushkin and Boris Mezentsev above the Krasnye Vorota subway station, within a stone's throw of the Hotel Leningradskaia, lies tangential to the ring road, above which stands the office tower of the Ministry of Communications. The housing wings, which correspond in dimensions to the curtain of offices lining the boulevard, define a large rectangular courtyard. For the interiors Dushkin used metallic flutings in the pillars, an echo of the ribbed structure of the Maiakovskaia subway station, which he had built before the war.

The building on Kotelnicheskaia was built by Chechulin and Rostkovsky at the confluence of the Moskva and the Yauza rivers, and plays a dual role as a vertical landmark and an angular articulation between the lines of housing on the banks of both rivers. The base, faced in red granite, is taller than that of the other buildings, while the tower evokes design solutions adopted by McKim, Mead, and

White for the New York Municipal Services Building, constructed from 1907 to 1914. The Zariadie Building was designed by Chechulin alone. Located on the banks of the Moskva, facing the Kremlin, it houses an extremely dense office program extending the 1934 Narkomtiazhprom competition brief. The base blocks barely succeed in counterbalancing a tower that would have been far superior in section to the others—had it been built. Though the designs for the university building were initially entrusted to Iofan, whose Palace of Soviets (though greatly reduced during the war) was also to have been part of the network, in the end it was built by Lev Rudnev, Pavel Abrosimov, and Aleksandr Khryakov. This vast, predominantly vertical complex is flanked with solid annexes and in fact constitutes a fragment of urban fabric, thus prefiguring subsequent developments in the southwestern reaches of the city. In 1953, Boris Rubanenko would detail the artistic lessons of this undertaking in inflated rhetorical tones:

> The exuberant plastic treatment of the various volumes, the university's overall skyline, and the symphonic character of the whole makes it one of the most edifying and brilliant instances of creative development in the Russian town-planning tradition.[536]

In fact, these built skyscrapers crystallized all the architectural principles denounced by Ginzburg and Lissitzky thirty years earlier: their "living skeletons" were well masked behind heavy stone and terracotta facings, even if contemporary propaganda paraded the theme of the fitter atop a catwalk, braving the void in the manner of Lewis Hine's famous photograph.[537] Nonetheless, the architecture of Moscow's tall buildings was quickly exported to other nations of the socialist "camp" in reproductions adapted to diverse briefs, from Prague's Hotel International and the Palace of Culture in Warsaw to the Party's publishing house in Bucharest. In

134. Piero Martina, photographer, *Trucco aereo* (Carlo Mollino in flight over Manhattan), c. 1942. Biblioteca centrale di Architettura, Sistema bibliotecario Politecnico, Turin

somewhat attenuated form, similar "gifts" even reached China and Albania—symmetrical alternatives (so to speak) to the Americanization of Western Europe, whose vehicles were, however, far from devoid of American precedents.

Henceforth, skyscrapers were accepted well outside the "popular democracies" as elements in the grammar of urban transformations. Whereas Soviet Russia was most influenced by the eclectic American buildings of the years 1900–30, Western European architects were more attentive to internal changes in the American scene in their treatment of buildings designed to transform their metropolitan cityscapes. But tall buildings also became the object of controversy within the American-oriented cultures of Europe, as witnesses the opposition in 1957 to Gio Ponti's Pirelli Building and Belgiojoso, Peressutti, and Rogers's Torre Velasca, both in Milan. The same year, Robert Camelot sketched his initial plans for the development of the La Défense business district in Paris, the construction of which would begin a decade later and would reveal the French misunderstanding of Manhattan's urban structure.

The Marshall Plan and the Cold War transformed the nature of Americanism, which henceforth involved the direct introduction of American consumption patterns and suburban organization. The Americanization of European space replaced earlier accumulations of ideal references; America was now an ever-present factor in politics and consumer society. However, specific interests within the nations of Europe tended to diverge following the Second World War. France, for instance, was fascinated by problems of productivity and industrialization, while Russia imitated the skyscraper, and British architects became interested in the American landscape, popular culture, and technique in general.

Giedion's Mechanization Takes Command

One of the most remarkable manifestations of postwar Americanism was Sigfried Giedion's historical study, *Mechanization Takes Command*, published in 1948. This immediate and enduring bestseller traced the modes of emergence of American industry and the mechanization of agriculture and daily life with the care and patience characteristic of an author who combined the gifts of engineer, art historian, militant in favor of modern architecture, and entrepreneur.

Giedion's book was the fruit of research carried out in the United States, in the archives of corporations such as McCormick, Westinghouse, and General Electric, and in the records of the Patent Office, in which some original models that had survived the clearing-out of 1926 were studied with care. The book was written in 1941–45 while Giedion was in the United States, where he became actively involved in the debate concerning "new monumentality."[538] The idea of a global study of American industrial culture began to take shape during his project for an inquiry *Zur Entstehung des heutigen Menschen* (On

John McHale (1922–78).

Cover of *Machine Made America: A Special Number of the Architectural Review*, May 1957. Avery Architectural and Fine Arts Library, Columbia University, New York City (*idem* Plate XLII)

Americanization,

Mechanization,

Suburbanization

the origins of contemporary man), which he formulated from 1928 to 1936,[539] and which his American research brought to fruition from 1937. His *Bauen in Frankreich* (Building in France, 1928) showed an interest in "national constants" (including those of America), whereby the architecture of each country is a function of its "sociological structure" (he regarded the "constructive temperament" of the French as corresponding to the "organizational tendencies" of the Americans and the "craft mentalities" of the Dutch). In *Space, Time and Architecture* (1941), whose chronological structure was partly inspired by Neutra's *Amerika*, Giedion stressed the role of the balloon frame in the genealogy of the Chicago School's metallic constructions and proposed to reveal "this unfortunate schism between its thought and feeling which struck down the magnificent power of the nineteenth century."[540]

In *Mechanization Takes Command*, Giedion at once refers to postwar conditions, stating that "the coming period . . . must be a time of reorganization in the broadest sense" and has to "reinstate human values." Giedion therefore proposes to "go back to the

sources," since "the process leading up to the present role of mechanization can nowhere be observed better than in the United States, where the new methods of production were first applied, and where mechanization is inextricably woven into the pattern of thought and customs."[541] The book reformulates the notion of the "national constant" and focuses on "anonymous history," ignoring the habitual themes associated with that type of narration, even if the names of inventors and engineers are mentioned on occasion.[542]

Following the methods of presentation first used in *Bauen in Frankreich*, the visual component of *Mechanization Takes Command* is crucial, and incorporates captions designed for the "hurried reader"; Herbert Bayer and László Moholy-Nagy played a key role in the book's design. The visual arts are everywhere in evidence, doubtless inspired by the exhibition *Cubism and Abstract Art* held at the MoMA in 1936, even if visual comparisons between the paintings of Klee, Kandinsky, Calder, Léger, and Ozenfant or Buñuel's photograms on the one hand and the images of machines on the other occasionally seem a little forced.[543] Thirty years later, Hans Magnus Enzensberger would salute Giedion's "rare visual intelligence," comparing him with historical anthropologists such as Norbert Elias and Walter Benjamin.[544]

In *Bauen in Frankreich*, the "anonymous" dimension that had interested Giedion was construction, as architecture's "unconscious." In that earlier work he had written that the role played by the builder tended to be an "anonymous and collective" one.[545] In *Mechanization*, on the other hand, it was no longer a question of smoking out the engineer behind the architect, but of examining the "simpler things" that have "molded our present-day living."[546] Yet unlike Adolf Loos, who placed the most arresting anonymous products within tradition, Giedion focused on innovation.

He orients his inquiry "from the human standpoint," beginning with "the concept of Movement, which underlies all mechanization. There follows the hand, which is to be supplanted; and Mechanization as a phenomenon." The transition "takes place in America during the second half of the nineteenth century." Giedion states that "the elimination of complicated handicraft marks the beginning of high mechanization," giving rise to the assembly line, which is "an American institution. . . . The mechanization of the housewife's work . . . and other complex handicrafts . . . is best observed in America." In order to demonstrate the significance of such historical changes, Giedion adopts a "typological" or "vertical" approach, as opposed to a horizontal "history of styles." This "diachronic" approach prefigures Gilbert Simondon's analysis of the shift from concrete to abstract objects.[547] Giedion states:

We are interested in the growth of phenomena, or if you will, in reading their line of fate over wide spans of time. Vertical sections make it possible to trace the organic changes of a type.[548]

This affinity for long-term historical methods goes hand in hand with methodological positions comparable to those of *Passagenwerk* by Walter Benjamin (who was familiar with Giedion's writings), in particular the interest in links between institutions and objects.[549] Giedion's narratives often span several centuries. In his analysis of movement he compares the fourteenth-century bishop-mathematician Nicole d'Oresme (in his view "the first to represent movement in graphic terms" and "to recognize that movement can be represented only by movement, the changing only by the changing") with nineteenth-century pioneers of photography such as Etienne-Jules Marey and Eadward Muybridge, whom he regards as precursors of Frank Gilbreth (1868-1924), "the first to capture with full precision the complicated trajectory of human

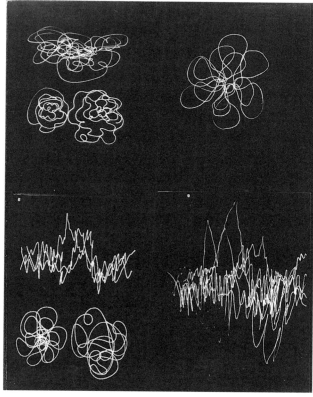

136. Frank Gilbreth, engineer (1868–1924). *Movement studies: 2 plates of 4 documents* (collected by Sigfried Giedion, May 1947). Institut für Geschichte und Theorie der Architektur (GTA), Zurich

137. Berenice Abbott, photographer (1898–1991). *View of a production line, May 1947. Inscription in the hand of Sigfried Giedion ("The chicken on the assembly line"). Institut für Geschichte und Theorie der Architektur (GTA), Zurich

138. Preparation of vegetables in the kitchens of the H. J. Heinz company (document collected by Sigfried Giedion, May 1947). Institut für Geschichte und Theorie der Architektur (GTA), Zurich

movement."[550] In his historical survey of mechanical processes, he contrasts the complex automata of the eighteenth century (especially those built by Vaucanson, whose innovations in the Lyon silk industry remained a dead end) with the purely "utilitarian" advances in the English cotton industry. Yet he deems America to be the geographical center of innovation for precise historical reasons which made the Midwest an unprecedented testing ground for mechanization:

> The dimensions of the land, its sparse population, the lack of trained labor and correspondingly high wages, explain well enough why America mechanized the complicated crafts from the outset.
>
> Yet an essential reason may lie elsewhere. The settlers brought over their European mode of living, their European experience. But from the organization of the complicated craft and the whole culture in which such institutions had grown, they were suddenly cut off. They had to start from scratch. Imagination was given scope to shape reality unhindered.[551]

It was in America that the rupture with the "mysteries" and monopoly of know-how by the guilds first took place, before the decisive developments of rationalization at the end of the nineteenth century and "the era of automation." Detailing the various stages in the mechanization process, Giedion traces Henry Ford's use of interchangeable parts and standardized production back to the invention of replaceable sawteeth fifty years earlier, and above all with Linus Yale's invention of the safety lock, following the step-by-step development from his "magic infallible bank lock" to his pin-tumbler cylinder lock, a process leading from "manual to mechanical fabrication."

Giedion sees antecedents of the assembly line and the scientific organization of labor as part of a continuous series of innovations, beginning with Oliver Evans's introduction into the grain milling process of the "endless belt," (which Thomas Jefferson held in low opinion, comparing the conveyor belt to "the screw of

XXXVIII. Stamo Papadaki, architect. *Jacket design for*
Mechanization Takes Command *by Sigfried Giedion:*
reclining chair and agricultural implement on a background of meat, May 1947.
Institut für Geschichte und Theorie der Architektur (GTA), Zurich

mechanization takes command

SIEGFRIED GIEDION

One of the leading figures in the promotion of modern architecture and art, Siegfried Giedion is well known in this country as a lecturer and as the author of *Space, Time, and Architecture*. Born in Switzerland in 1894, he was educated there and in Germany and Italy. At Weimar he was associated with Walter Gropius, with whom he played an important part in the introduction of modern architecture in Switzerland. He has been an active participant in the work of the Congrès Internationaux d'Architecture Moderne since its founding in 1928. In 1938 at Harvard University, he gave the Charles Eliot Norton Lectures upon which *Space, Time, and Architecture* was based.

In *Mechanization Takes Command*, Dr. Giedion takes the point of view that "Mechanization was misused to exploit both earth and man with complete irresponsibility. Often it penetrated domains that were by nature unsuited to it. . . . We have refrained from taking a positive stand for or against mechanization. We cannot simply approve or disapprove. One must discriminate between those spheres that are fit for mechanization and those that are not; similar problems arise today in whatever sphere we touch. . . . It is time that we become human again. . . .

"We are little concerned with the question whether man will ever attain a state of infinite perfection. We are closer to the ancient wisdom that saw in a possible moral evolution the course the world would take.

"This does not mean that we must resign ourselves to cruelty, hopelessness, or despair. Every generation has to find a different solution to the same problem: to bridge the abyss between inner and outer reality by re-establishing the dynamic equilibrium that governs their relationships."

--------------------ORDER FORM--------------------

$10.00 before May 13

ORDER NOW

.... 19

Oxford University Press
114 Fifth Avenue
New York 11, N. Y.

Gentlemen: Please send me...... cop...... of MECHANIZATION TAKES COMMAND by S. Giedion (Published price, $12.50)

NAME..

ADDRESS...

CITY.......................... ZONE...... STATE................

☐ Check enclosed   ☐ Charge my account

mechanization takes command

S. GIEDION

author of **SPACE, TIME, AND ARCHITECTURE**

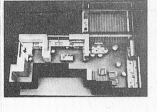

special price before publication

XXXIX. Promotional leaflet from the publisher of *Mechanization Takes Command*, 1948. Institut für Geschichte und Theorie der Architektur (GTA), Zurich

XL. Richard Hamilton
(b. 1922).
$he, 1958–61. Tate Gallery,
London/Art Resource, New York

XLI. Eduardo Paolozzi
(b. 1924). *Drink Dr Pepper*,
1948. Collection Sir Eduardo
Paolozzi, London

XLII. Cover of *Machine Made
America: A Special Number
of* The Architectural Review,
May, 1957. Canadian
Centre for Architecture, Montreal

XLIII. Ron Herron,
architect (1930–94).
*Instant City: Typical
Configuration—Santa Monica
and San Diego Freeway
Intersection, Los Angeles, 1969.*
Archigram Archives, London

Archimedes"). Evans's use of ancient techniques is underlined by Giedion, who narrates subsequent developments such as the partial mechanization of the assembly line in English biscuit manufacture (1804) or Bodmer's machine tools workshop (1840), which "by its layout and by the construction of its machines was to save movement, labor, and energy in conveyance." (Bodmer is also said to have introduced the first over-head cranes and conveyor belts for industrial production). But he regards the Cincinnati slaughterhouses of the 1860s (a panoramic painting of which was sent to the Vienna International Exposition of 1870) as laying the foundations of the modern assembly line. A large portion of the book is devoted to the mechanization of death, from its inception in Cincinnati (where a fascinated Frederick Law Olmsted had also observed the hog slaughtering and packing process) through the La Villette yards in Paris to Chicago's Union Stockyards, with detailed descriptions (though less picturesque than those of Upton Sinclair's *The Jungle*) of the slaughtering, cleaving, scraping, cutting, and trimming of livestock. Giedion is also attentive to concomitant changes in transport and marketing techniques, and recalls Armour and Swift's invention of refrigerator cars, the changed role of the butcher, and the introduction of corned beef.

Within the factory, he singles out three distinct rationalization strategies. Around 1900 Frederick Winslow Taylor innovated at the Midvale Steel Co. by introducing (in Taylor's own terms) "cardinal principles of the military type." Giedion compares Taylor with Freud (who was born in the same year) for his "unprecedented sharpness of analysis in revealing the inside of processes."[552] The second strategy was Frank Gilbreth's "visualization of space and time," using an ordinary camera and a simple electric bulb to "make visible the absolute path of movement." Giedion compares Gilbreth's "cyclographic" experiments with the work of the Futurists and Marcel Duchamp, and with Paul

Klee's ability "to give visible form to the innermost processes of the psyche." The third stage was obviously the assembly line installed in Henry Ford's Highland Park factory in 1914, which marked the beginnings of mass production and its corollaries: high wages and the democratization of the automobile.

The originality of Giedion's approach resides less in his industrial genealogies than in his study of the mechanization of organic processes, which he views as one of the constituent features of America, where specialization revolutionized agriculture:

> By the middle of the century, North America had earned the title of "a grand laboratory of nature for the production of new ameliorated fruit."[553]

Giedion omits the specifically architectural aspect of this "grand laboratory" in the Midwest, where agricultural production brought with it the construction of grain exchanges, hotels, train stations, and modern office buildings, and instead concentrates on the "reshaping" of tools such as the reaper, culminating in Cyrus McCormick's harvester, which he views as distinguishing "the pioneering spirit of the man of the Middle West from the European farmer."[554] The advent of the tractor and its tenfold increase in number in the years 1919–39—and with it "another source of mobile energy, the internal combustion engine"—ushered in a revolution comparable to that of "the compact electric motor [which] made it possible to mechanize domestic utensils."

At the other end of the food chain, Giedion analyses mass consumer products and the relations between industry and commerce. Bread production was revolutionized by the introduction of kneading machines, the use of baking powder for the fermentation of dough, indirectly-heated ovens, and slicing machines. The dough thus became "an organic body in perpetual movement." The effects on commerce were almost immediate, and Giedion justly claims that "mechanization has devalued the constant character of bread and turned it into an article subject to fashion, for which new-found charms must ever be devised."[555] In a passage concerning vegetable growth, Giedion alludes (not without misgivings) to the first uses of genetic techniques, and foresees the use of biotechnologies. The originality of this continuous chain of research makes America one of the great centers of human invention:

> Just as the origin of the planned Greek city is bound up with Ionia, the Gothic with the Île de France, and the Renaissance with Florence, so the mechanization of agriculture is indivisibly connected with the prairies of the Middle West.[556]

Giedion focuses his analysis of changes within human surroundings on American patent designs and models found in Washington or purchased in New York auction rooms. His historical survey is again an extended one, tracing the ancestry of the chair back to medieval "comfort" and posture. Giedion here adopts a dual approach. On the one hand, he attacks the "ruling taste" in the Empire period and the horrid "reign of the upholsterer," citing in opposition to these Henry Cole's *Journal of Design* and his attempts to "bridge the gap between the artist, the manufacturer, and the designer." On the other, he traces the gradual emergence of mobile furniture, from the "nomadic" Middle Ages to the "universal chest" (drawers, cupboards, etc.) and the typological specifications of modern furniture.

Giedion views the appearance of springs and mechanical parts in the eighteenth century as paving the way for the incipient "movability" of the nineteenth. Patent furniture then offered "revolutionary solutions": "Here the mechanical was used to aid and support the human organism. This furniture was constructed by engineers, not designed by upholsterers."[557] The emergence of mobile and adjustable furniture in America was embodied in the office chair, the barber's chair, and the dentist's chair. Convertible furniture—often grotesque in its available postures—was developed in

the sleeping cars of the transcontinental railways, and new "nomadic" models such as the folding bed or the hammock led to Alexander Calder's "mobiles." The tubular and bentwood furniture types developed by the European architects of the twentieth century were often pale copies of earlier American prototypes.

Within domestic space, Giedion naturally pays close attention to the kitchen and the bathroom, where mechanization had plenty of scope for innovation. He discusses the pioneers of domestic organization in America, Catherine Beecher and Christine Frederick, who were well known to the German architects of the day,[558] and traces the introduction of gas and electric ranges and new mechanized aids such as the vacuum cleaner, washing machine, dishwasher, refrigerator, and smaller appliances. As the question of aerodynamic form or "streamlining" became central to the debate, architects such as Frank Lloyd Wright proposed new types of layout for the kitchen and dining room. Giedion's watchword on this is clear: "What matters is to domesticate mechanization, rather than to let the mechanized core tyrannize the house."

His discussion of the mechanized bathroom takes much of its material from the exhibition that Giedion organized in Zurich in 1935, *Das Bad von Heute und Gestern* (The bath of today and yesterday). His long-term survey of "regenerative types" takes in the baths of antiquity and the Arab-Muslim *hammam*, but his account of the nineteenth century concentrates on hydropathy or the water cure. He then traces the typological developments of the "people's bath," or shower, and the invention of the mechanized American bathroom—a corollary of the grand hotel—in which "bedroom and bathroom eventually formed a unit."[559] In kitchen and bathroom alike, the "mechanical core" (as evinced in Buckminster Fuller's prefabricated bathroom of 1938) is advanced as an optimal solution for the future; here, Giedion's stance can be compared with the observations of French architects and engineers, in particular Jean Prouvé.

Despite Giedion's forward-looking and optimistic view of things, *Mechanization Takes Command* is skeptical of European technological innovations after 1945. In fact, Giedion advocates a "dynamic equilibrium" between mechanization and human values in a book that can be viewed as a homage to an "inventive spirit as common to America as the painter's talent in the Renaissance." Faced with American innovations, Giedion came to view his company Wohnbedarf's attempt to produce everyday objects as a sterile enterprise. Despite some adverse criticisms of the book (Arnold Hauser, for instance, regretted the arbitrary selection of examples),[560] European and American reactions were most favorable, as in this review by Marshall McLuhan:

> . . . a study of American life which has been rivalled, at a different level, only by De Tocqueville . . . in America in the nineteenth century the mind was least fettered by the depraved ruling taste which stultified the best insights of European architects and engineers . . . so that in the Midwest especially, the untrammeled engineer moved swiftly towards conceptions and objects which not only anticipated their European colleagues but which were in advance of the painters themselves.[561]

For his part, Lewis Mumford expressed satisfaction with the fact that, unlike Le Corbusier, Giedion had not adopted "an attitude of pious worship toward the machine."[562] Le Corbusier, on the other hand, who had now become entrenched in an inflexible anti-Americanism, appreciated the book Giedion had sent him but describes its title as "appalling, disturbing, American."[563]

Man Made America as seen from Great Britain

Giedion's images provoked a strong reaction in Great Britain, where they were analyzed in detail by (among others) the artists of the Independent Group. In the 1950s, the group's theoretical elaborations focused on the man/machine dichotomy posited in *Mechanization Takes Command*. During the seven years that separated two issues of *The Architectural Review: Man Made America* (1950) and *Machine Made America* (1957), British attitudes towards landscape, building, and culture underwent profound transformations.

The new Americanism broadened perceptions of the American city both geographically (with particular reference to California) and morphologically (taking in the phenomenon of suburbanization). As the automobile flooded into European markets, shopping centers and individual housing emerged based on the American suburban model. *The Architectural Review's* editorial team foresaw this process, at a time of change in economic and political relations between the United States and the old colonial power. Frank Lloyd Wright's visit to London in 1939 would remain stamped on the memories of architects, though Helmle, Corbett, and Hood's building operations in London were quickly forgotten. Despite considerable interest in industrial housing schemes analogous to those of Lods or Nelson, as evinced in Hugh Casson's 1946 work *Homes by the Million*,[564] British attitudes to the American scene were quite different than those of the French, doubtless because the former had been directly exposed to American lifestyles since 1942 and identified more closely with their American partners.

The Architectural Review—which numbered Nikolaus Pevsner, I. M. Richards, Gordon Cullen, H. de C. Hastings (*alias* Ivor de Wolfe), Helen Rosenau, James Stirling, Colin Rowe, and Reyner Banham among its contributors—combined a radical (but also critical and even ironic) Modernism with a scrupulous concern for history and urbanity. From this point of view, the articles published in *Man Made America* are indissociable from the *Townscape* ideal as first formulated in 1949.[565] For *Man Made America*, the review

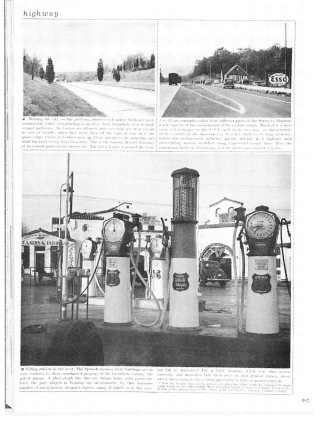

139. Page from the article "Scene" by Christopher Tunnard, in *Man Made America: A Special Number of the* Architectural Review, December 1950. Canadian Centre for Architecture, Montreal

140. Page from "Case Study: City," an unsigned article in *Man Made America: A Special Number of the* Architectural Review, December 1950. Canadian Centre for Architecture, Montreal

invited Henry-Russell Hitchcock, Christopher Tunnard (who taught at Yale),[566] and Gerhard Kallmann to depict a country fashioned by man's control of nature. The question of the scale of American productions was raised early, and editors were of the view that "giantism reveals a certain bigness of view (foreign to the British) which can make even squalor rather grand." In vertical terms, this "giantism" was of course embodied in the skyscraper, which Saul Steinberg gently mocked in his images of the American cityscape. Steinberg was described as the only American topographical artist "to have succeeded in portraying the New York scene . . . for he alone appears to realize that New York is not a modern city but only the dream of a modern city . . ." Horizontal gigantism was viewed with condescension, as reflected in America's "subtopias" and her apathetic reactions to urban chaos:

> The American people . . . easy, friendly, and highly democratic . . . have never developed a sensitivity to surroundings in the visual sense. A great fight has been won for better housing . . . at least, in this field a principle has been established. In planning, the "form-will" has yet to be developed.[567]

In fact, the review's questions reflected wider European anxieties concerning the American landscape, which it, too, regarded as presaging a common future:

> Where does the United States stand in this matter? Does it wish (as other communities in the world to-day have shown they do) to be directly instrumental in moulding its own environment, in such a way as to reflect a visual ideal—a concept of what constitutes order and propriety in the environment—or has the American community rejected a visual ideal, in favour of a laissez-faire environment—a universe of uncontrollable chaos sparsely inhabited by happy accidents?[568]

Here, too, the analysis focused on the country's scenic configuration. Tunnard cited Henry James's borrowed *bon mot* ("There is only one step from the sublime to the ridiculous")[569] before positing three distinct levels of perception:

Scene one gives a surface impression of a few outstanding characteristics of the American landscape, missing out the more obvious ones like Washington or New York. Scene two lifts the lid of some remarkable and typically American works of engineering genius which have had a fundamental though not immediately visible effect on the landscape. Scene three summarizes a few attempts that have been, or are being made to create or re-create propriety in the physical environment, with a passing glance at a city which seems intent on destroying it.[570]

This city was none other than Los Angeles, a "city un-beautiful" *par excellence,* and one oblivious to the Spanish episodes of its early history. Tunnard noted that "the Angelenos, who show little interest in the way their city politics are run, deserve to lose their past and to be visited by the plague of gritty smog, but it is tragic that the city's pursuit of the new has blinded her to the even more romantic past."[571] However, some planning initiatives, such as Levittown and Park Forest, found favor in Tunnard's thematic tour of the American urban landscape, a pictorial view taking the reader from the "street" to the "approach," from the "faubourg" to the "entrance to the city." Thus, he showed a "no-man's land—cities, towns, streets and backyards, into which the specialist rarely, if at all, makes a sortie."[572]

Hitchcock unrhetorically presented "things as they are," i.e., the new types of modern American architecture, and in particular "vernacular" programs such as motels. Winston Weisman pinpointed the speculative mechanisms underlying the Rockefeller Center development "as they are." Finally, Gerhard Kallmann presented "technology as is," and underlined the potential of the work of Mies and Buckminster Fuller, which he deemed America to have "ignored." All in all, the contributors were dismayed by the lack of "design" and absence of professional intervention underlying what they deemed the chaos of man-made America, symptoms not of a "civilized" nation, but on the contrary of one they found happy-go-lucky, neglectful, and blind:

. . . the U.S., having a bigger slice of the surface than Britain, has also more room for dirt. It will take longer—well into the twenty-first century, perhaps—for our brothers in dirt to make over the whole of that superb inheritance into a combination of automobile graveyard, industrial no-man's-land and Usonian Idiot's delight.[573]

141. The plan for Levittown, Pa., "grid" presented to the CIAM in Aix-en-Provence, 1953. Institut für Geschichte und Theorie der Architektur (GTA), Zurich

American Imagery and Pop Culture: the Independent Group

The young architects and artists of the postwar avant-garde effected a complete turnaround in British attitudes and approaches. Reviews and travel accounts brought images of metal techniques and a new contextual approach to landscape. Alison and Peter Smithson's Hunstanton School was vaguely inspired by Mies's IIT building, reproducing its massive envelope rather than the refinement of its detailing. Their subsequent work, in particular their *House of the Future,* a prototype designed for the 1956 Daily Mail *Ideal Home Exhibition,* reflected interest in the work of Buckminster Fuller. Each space was, so to speak,

142. Alison Smithson (1928–93) and Peter Smithson (b. 1923), architects. *Dwelling project presented at the exhibition* The House of the Future: *axonometric*, London, 1956. Canadian Centre for Architecture, Montreal

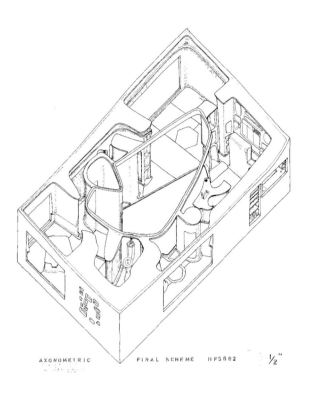

molded around its use, evoking Fuller's Dymaxion bathroom.[574] This generation was also influenced by Neutra's postwar buildings, as John Winter would emphasize in Neutra's obituary:

> I well remember the impact on us of the *Architectural Review*'s publishing the Tremaine House in 1950; at that time, sociology and Herts schools were *de rigueur* for AA students, and the very affluence of the Tremaine House made it seem a rather sinful, playboy's thing. But it could not be lightly brushed aside, because its imagery was so compelling and its siting so beautiful, and in any case had not the open-web joists of our beloved Herts schools been developed from those of Neutra's Lovell House and their single storey planning from Neutra's school at Bell?[575]

Reyner Banham, who had ignored Neutra's earlier work in his *Theory and Design in the First Machine Age*, came see new life in his postwar houses:

> They are romantic in the sense that the detail is a little less skinny, and the use of materials much less diagrammatic—you feel he begins to value brick or steel for their character as substances, not just their performance—and the living spaces within are intimately involved with the outdoors.[576]

Such enthusiasm was not, however, shared by all. In an account of his 1956 travels to California, James Ackerman seemed to regard Neutra's work in Los Angeles as tired and repetitive. For Ackerman, "The work of the better architects seems to be weakened by the need to be fashionable or photogenic." He saw Neutra's work as reflecting a "strong tendency to imitation," though legitimate to the extent that he "imitates himself (as of the thirties)."[577] The only building to earn his unqualified praise was Charles Eames's lightweight metal-frame house at the Pacific Palisades, part of the *Case Study Program* set forth by John Entenza. James Stirling saw this building in a 1949 visit to Los Angeles, and Lawrence Alloway discussed it in 1956.[578]

War-engendered technologies were especially in evidence in Great Britain, where the military, human, and technical presence of the United States was particularly marked. Despite the provisions of the Marshall Plan, Britain's postwar economy remained gripped by problems of penury, and rationing persisted until 1954. The 1943 London County Plan and the 1946 New Towns Act paved the way for reconstructions involving mediocre adaptations of Swedish models, while the 1951 Festival of Britain was inspired by fetishistic readings of continental Modernism. Richard Hamilton criticized the atmosphere of "pageantry" generated by the industrialists—"an aura of tradition, some scent of our royal heritage, is what makes our goods attractive to overseas markets."[579] Banham added that "the officer-and-gentleman establishment had, in historical fact, just caught up with a particular stylistic package that was about exhausted."[580] The *Britain Can Make It* exhibition held at the Victoria & Albert Museum in 1946 was different in emphasis and looked at the problem of the recycling of military techniques. A new working-class and anti-establishment generation, whether trained in the factories (Reyner Banham at Bristol-Siddeley) or at bomber controls (Nigel Henderson in the RAF), could not help but be attuned to the Cold War and (despite the threat of nuclear apocalypse) the *charme discret* of the B47 and B52. Bernard Myers commented in the magazine *Ark*:

> Some of the new American machines hit me in the solar plexus with their impression of power and purpose, comparable to the eighteenth-century gentleman's emotion of the "Sublime" on holding a Cyclopean-steam engine.[581]

Illustrated reviews, cartoon magazines, and images of everyday American life influenced the activities of the Independent Group, which formed in the wake of a series of lectures held from 1951 at the Institute of Contemporary Arts in London, and included the Smithsons, John McHale, Magda Cordell, Richard Hamilton, Nigel Henderson, Eduardo Paolozzi, Lawrence Alloway, and Reyner Banham. The combined product of a period marked by the end of penury and the "neo-Futurism" of the conservatives, the group's vision of the United States articulated production, consumption, and communication, as Lawrence Alloway later remarked:

> We felt none of the dislike of commercial culture standard among most intellectuals, but accepted it as fact, discussed it in detail, and consumed it enthusiastically. . . . Hollywood, Detroit, and Madison Avenue were, in terms of our interests, producing the best popular culture.
>
> . . . All the members of IG were basically in the humanities; we were not sociologists or anthropologists, although our interests extended into areas where they worked. We assumed an anthropological definition of culture, in which all types of human activity were the object of aesthetic judgement and attention.[582]

Apart from the advertising and illustrated magazines that John McHale, who had studied in America under Josef Albers, brought back in a trunk (earning himself instant celebrity),[583] the group was also sensitive to *Mechanization Takes Command* and the 1947 publication *Vision in Motion*, in which Moholy-Nagy declared:

> Social conditions, the arts, sciences, the development of an industrial technology with prefabrication, new materials, and new processes are the determining factors to realize the new architectural development. From them, the architect and planner will draw inspiration and factual knowledge, resulting in a changed conception of space.[584]

Moholy-Nagy was a partisan of the photographic image, and reflected on collage and photomontage, which the group also practiced. As if to illustrate popular analogies between the female body and "beautiful" automobile chassis, Paolozzi's photomontages juxtaposed pin-ups and images of advanced technology cut out from the advertising pages of American magazines, while Alloway pointed out the "links in science fiction between technology and sex."[585] In this context, McHale's reading of McLuhan's *The Mechanical Bride: Folklore of Industrial Man*, published in 1951, also constituted significant source material. The Smithsons' studies of machine and consumer images were the most lucid, with an irony that underlined the distance separating the group from the first Americanists:

> Gropius wrote a book on grain silos,
>
> Le Corbusier one on aeroplanes,
>
> And Charlotte Perriand—it was said—brought a new object to the office every morning;
>
> But today we collect ads.[586]

Richard Hamilton was especially interested in the notion of obsolescence.[587] His paintings and collages (in particular *$he*) were ironic comments on the servitude of mass consumption. Reyner Banham also addressed this topic (to which Martin Wagner had alluded in the twenties), but this time as regards the aging of buildings.[588] The Independent Group thus laid solid theoretical bases for a series of exhibitions for the London public, including three at the ICA: *Growth and Form* (1951) on themes tackled by Giedion; *Parallel of Life and Art* (1953) on those developed by Moholy-Nagy; and *Man, Machine and Motion* (1955), which combined both earlier themes.

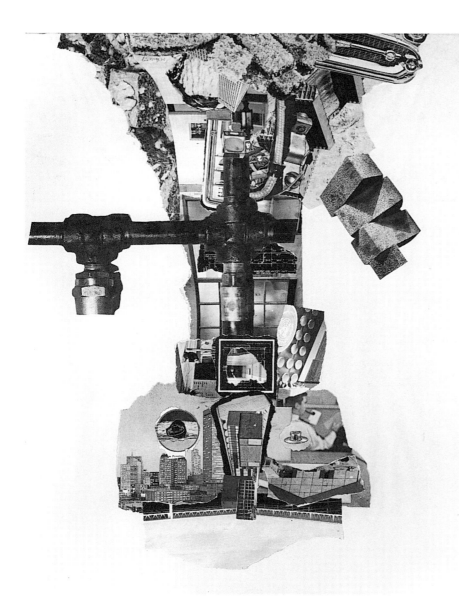

143. John McHale (1922–78).

Machine Made America, 1957.

Collection Magda Cordell McHale, Buffalo, N.Y.

In the following year Theo Crosby, then editor-in-chief of *Architectural Design*, organized *This is Tomorrow* at the Royal Festival Hall. This exhibition included work by the Independent Group and architects more open to the Constructivist aesthetic, such as Colin Saint-John Wilson, who roofed over part of the hall with Buckminster Fuller-inspired trelliswork. One of the stars of the film *Forbidden Planet* (which came out in England that year), Robby the robot, played an active role. Banham commented that "it was the first time an exhibition had been inaugurated by a robot." In fact, the presence of this mechanical/electronic King Kong once more revealed the extent to which images of the future were confused with those of America.

Machine Made America

The 1957 issue that *Architectural Review* devoted to "Machine Made America" revealed the extent to which canons of good taste that had still held sway seven years previously had now been stood on their head by the Independent Group. The review, within which Banham was exercising an increasingly authoritative role, now proceeded to reassess construction techniques and aesthetic choices in the American suburb, a territory where the only order henceforth considered possible was the curtain wall. The author of the photomontage on the cover was none other than John McHale, who at the time was analyzing the Eames House and the work of Buckminster Fuller:

> The cover personage, with the tetragram of power—Neutral, Drive, Low, Reverse—graven on his heart, was assembled from typical fragments of the cultural complex that he also symbolizes; Machine Made America. The source of material was one of America's favourite flattering mirrors, coloured magazine illustrations, and reflects a world of infra-grilled steak, pre-mixed cake, dream-kitchens, dream-cars, machine-tools, power-mixers, parkways, harbours, tickertape, spark-plugs, and electronics.[589]

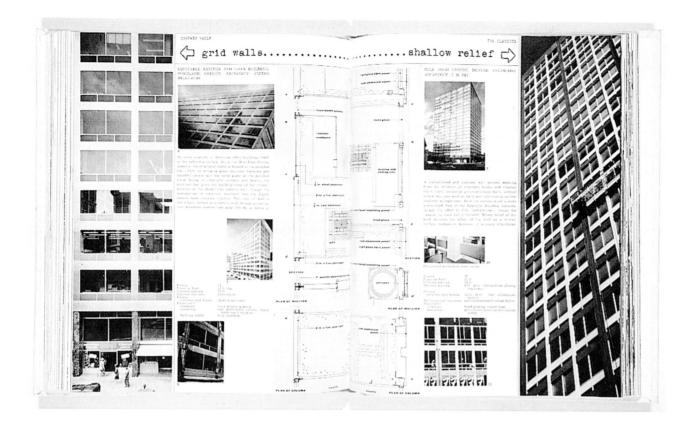

144. Two pages of the article "The Contribution of the Curtain Wall to a New Vernacular SYNTAX," in *Machine Made America: A Special Number of the Architectural Review*, ed. Ian McCallum, May 1957. Canadian Centre for Architecture, Montreal

The image of America forged by the group made it possible to tell "the success story of America which, through technology and prefabrication, has produced novel constructions in quantity." The key item of this predominantly glass-and-metal "architectural syntax" was the lightweight curtain wall, precedents of which were now traced. Its practical modalities, leading to a "new contemporary vernacular . . . [that has] completely transformed the face of urban America," were noted:

> The standardization of the external envelope in the form of curtain walls is beginning to bring a degree of order to much, that, since the breakdown of architectural discipline in the romantic movement, has been merely chaotic. At present, this standardization is piecemeal, experimental and sometimes ill-considered in design, but . . . its acceptance in America is beginning to give promise that a vernacular of modern architecture may be developing. Far from the results proving monotonous, there is surprising, and somewhat excessive, visual variety. This may well

calm down as production increases and the system is rationalized: the present period may then be considered as merely a first stage in which prototypes were produced and studied on their merits, and when variants were evolved for different types of buildings. From this brief American survey, it would seem that there are few types of building considered unsuitable for enveloping with one form or another of curtain wall.[590]

Forty architects, "from self-effacement to self-assertion, from Ivy League to grass-roots exuberance," including Mies, Louis Kahn, Philip Johnson, and Paul Rudolph, but also "provincials," illustrated various architectural interpretations of postwar industrial possibilities:

> It is a measure of U.S. vitality (and humility) that it is prepared not only to learn the relevant lesson from whatever quarter it comes, but also to accept the masters from wherever they come, and greatly and deservedly has it benefited from it. . . . The U.S. by adding to generosity and willingness to learn, wealth,

industrial potential and technological skill is beginning to add a new dimension to the adventure of today's architecture—quantity.

. . . It is to two faces of the American scene that this issue is devoted—to prefabrication in the form of curtain walls—resulting in a truly anonymous idiom—and to its necessary complement, creative originality among individuals. . . . It is the first time in the history of the modern movement that a common vocabulary of form, pattern, and proportion is becoming acceptable to architecture, builder, client and public.[591]

Faced with the ineluctable hegemony of steel, aluminum, and glass, the editorial team of the *Architectural Review* seemed to make a virtue of necessity in their plea in favor of a technique whose potential for diversification would only rarely be exploited in European architectural production. After having idealized building types such as the grand hotel, the Fordized factory, or the office skyscraper, Americanism now centered on a precise technical device such as the curtain wall. But *Machine Made America* also resembled a rallying cry and an attempt to encourage the timid application of advanced construction methods to Britain (whereas America had overcome its inhibitions). A pessimistic view of the architect's role in the city thus emerged—one quite different from the "townscape" illusions of *Man Made America*. Lawrence Alloway would give theoretical expression to this attitude on his return from America in 1959:

> The architect, accustomed to think of himself as the potential creator of environments, and encouraged to do so by so much architectural theory, has exaggerated the significance of his contribution to the city . . . Architects can never get and keep control of all the factors in a city which exist in the dimensions of patched-up, expendable, and developing forms.[592]

145. Ron Herron, architect (1930–94). *A Walking City*, New York, 1964. Archigram Archives, London

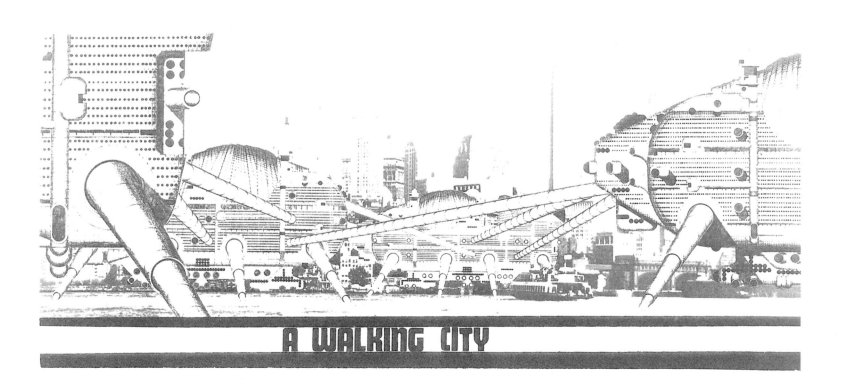

A WALKING CITY

Convinced of the potential role of "mass arts" in the city, Alloway also reflected on the role of "information theory" in American metropoles, thus prefiguring by more than three decades the telecommunications advances and "information highways" of the 1990s:

> The American City, more than most European cities at present, is geared to the communication systems of modern technology. In Los Angeles, advice about avoiding traffic jams is given from a helicopter and picked up on car radios. Broadcast at peak hours, "Operation Airwatch" is one of the most listened-to programmes in the area and includes commercials between traffic news. This compound of traffic signals and ads is characteristic of the symbol-thick environment of American cities and highways.[593]

Archigram: Drive-In America

This receptivity to the predominance of the image and communications networks within the city[594] led to Pop Art, but also to Archigram, whose theoretical designs pioneered the high-tech approaches of the sixties. Now analysis centered not on building as such, but on "gadgets" and their territorial mobility:

> The Genius of American ingenuity is the portable gadget: that unique piece of equipment that can be ordered by catalogue, sent through the mail (instructions enclosed) and easily used to transform some undifferentiated set of circumstances into a condition nearer human desires.[595]

The Independent Group's ironic collages and Banham's commentaries found their common vanishing point in the designs that Archigram elaborated in the decade or so following 1961.[596] In inspiration and in their expressive forms, these projects would to a large extent mark the outermost limits of Americanism. Postwar American consumer society constituted not only a backdrop for the group's urban "machines," but also a direct source of inspiration for their ultra-modern housing concepts. Notions of permanent change and planned obsolescence underlying projects such as Peter Cook's *Plug-in City* (1964–66) were derived from earlier analyses of urban management in America. A striking visual homage to New York was Ron Herron's *Walking City*, a collage in which moving buildings were set against a Manhattan backdrop (this time it was the launchpads of Cape Canaveral, and not the grain silos of Buffalo, that inspired a subversive design group, directly rather than through magazine images).[597]

Ron Herron's *Instant City* project, evoking an inflatable air-carried environment, marked a shift in the group's attitude to the American city, deploying its ephemeral urban "networks" in Los Angeles, the "city un-beautiful." (In 1970 Reyner Banham devoted one of his best books[598] to a city that *The Architectural Review* had attacked as early as 1950, by which time its role as an urban laboratory had already begun to be analyzed by the Independents.) *Instant City*, which was financed by Chicago's Graham Foundation and drawn up in Los Angeles, was planned for British suburban sites, though its aerial forms were seen to hover over the intersection of the Santa Monica freeway and the San Diego freeway, which Banham would regard as a "monument in the sky" and a "kinetic experience."[599]

But Archigram's amused visions of the Californian metropolis furnished far more than an anchorage for their inflatable structures. The major reference for David Greene and Michael Webb's 1966 *Drive-in Housing* system was the American automobile: each unit could be customized by virtue of a series of movable parts. Notions of flexibility and obsolescence also inspired Michael Webb's contemporary project *Rent-a-Wall*, the partitions of which were mail-order components, and whose graphic presentation aped the ads of D-I-Y magazines such as *Popular Mechanics*. Such projects marked a dual shift in Americanist iconographies, involving increasingly West Coast orientations, as well as thematic changes, insofar as consumer issues supplanted those of production.

POSTSCRIPT:
AMERICANISM AND ARCHITECTURAL "EXCEPTION"

The divergences in European readings of Americanism in the second postwar phase were wide. The French were fascinated by the notion of productivity, Russian leaders (belatedly and hypocritically) acted out their skyscraper fantasies, while British architectural groups saw in the "new vernacular" and popular culture the seeds of a new approach. The link between Americanism and modernity was inextricably bound up with that between Americanization and modernization. In this context, anti-Americanist positions (especially during the iciest years of the Cold War) constituted defensive (and somewhat hysterical) mechanisms against the American "menace," a menace invariably coupled with an irrepressible seductiveness.

Americanism expanded into new registers during this time. Apart from the shift in geographical emphasis from the east (New York, Chicago) to the west (Los Angeles) and south (Houston)—a shift, moreover, that coincided with the disappearance of the Tower of Babel myth in favor of an image of prosperous American suburbs as the Land of Milk and Honey—more contradictory themes emerged. In the realm of urban form, the long-standing interest in vertical development was now accompanied by a fascination with, and repulsion for, the underground city. As regards the relationship between architecture and technique, the fear of suffocation by industry gave way to a celebration of fetishist solutions like the curtain wall. Finally, as far as the links between architecture, visual culture, and art were concerned, unexpected affinities between buildings and objects emerged in critical images heralding the subversion of traditional hierarchies between structure, envelope, and internal equipment (which Neutra had predicted as early as 1927).

The late 1950s, when Team 10 (including its founder-members, the Smithsons) radicalized the crisis at the CIAM, also saw the emergence within America itself (as if echoing analyses published in the *Architectural Review*) of criticisms of urban development models adopted since 1945. As references to the European historical city were increasingly cited in arguments against Functionalism, whether by Jane Jacobs[600] or, to a certain extent, by Robert Venturi,[601] the Americanism of the first half of the century encountered its upper limit, leading to more complex and diffuse relations of dependence between the Old and New Worlds—the former took its revenge on the latter in Ron Herron's *Walking City*, whose metallic pseudopods trampled underfoot a Manhattan which, forty years previously, Kazimir Malevich had used flatly as a mere context for his *Architecton*.

Thirty years after Archigram's fantastic Americanist images, the United States still seems to be a major focus for debate concerning the urban future of societies. Transformations of the cities of Asia and Latin America are still based on West Coast models, with business concentrated in urban centers and housing in urban sprawl, while the construction of Russian capitalism highlights the intensity of the "Americanomania" that has invaded all sectors of post-Bolshevik culture in Moscow—thus corroborating Duhamel's vision of America as "the path that, willy-nilly, we must follow."[602] In the 1970s, the scope of Americanism continued to expand, and readings (for instance those of Reyner Banham and Rem Koolhaas) allying archeological precision and narrative fantasy reopened discussions of earlier configurations. Forty years after the first geographical investigations, Banham was the first to propose a serene and imaginative study of Los Angeles.[603] His lively analysis remains a seminal one, to the extent that he pinpointed the way in which landscape, roads, and buildings have formed the Californian metropolis.[604] Banham's last work, on the transference of American grain silos and concrete factories to Europe, used a combination of industrial archeology and discursive analysis to pinpoint the precise functional modalities of American buildings and smoke out European architects' erroneous readings. In particular, he demonstrated that technical and architectonic solutions joyously adopted by the avant-garde were already dated (if not obsolete) by 1920, and that in any case they were more often than not radically misinterpreted.[605]

As we have seen, European travelogues and research reflected successive fetishistic representations of America, from hotels to railroad stations and from skyscrapers to shopping malls, and largely ignored American urban reality, instead constituting a vast typological register comparable to Durand's *Recueil et parallèle*.[606] Banham's study of Los Angeles and Koolhaas's analysis of New York, instead of listing programmatic categories, were the first to describe the regularities and eccentricities of American urban form. This was doubtless due to the fact that the former was a trained aeronautics technician and a provocative journalist, while the latter had been trained as a scriptwriter. Koolhaas in particular was the first to transcend the analysis of individual buildings, to postulate the notion of "congestion," and thus grasp the unprecedented architectural effects of Manhattan's cramped situation since 1900. Attentive to the unpredictability, the structural adaptability, and the bold programmatic solutions of some of their skyscrapers, Koolhaas analyzed urban experiments which had hitherto been deemed unworthy of metropolitan culture, such as Luna Park on Coney Island (which Maxime Gorky found so distasteful), thus raising the redemption of popular culture (begun by the Independent Group) to the level of the city. Fifteen years later, Koolhaas invoked quite different urban experiences in a critical study of the "bigness" of Atlanta, in accents not unlike those of Alloway, for instance when he notes the incongruity of architecture's globalist pretensions.[607] As Koolhaas himself professes, only Le Corbusier's analysis is comparable in its acuity and its personal tone—a fact since confirmed by Hubert Damisch.[608]

Among the blind spots plaguing European visions of American architecture, one of the most surprising concerns building culture, with the diffusion of images of solid steel cages enveloped in impenetrable granite, ceramic, or glass facings. Despite the interest shown between

1945 and 1960 in the work of Richard Buckminster Fuller and Sigfried Giedion's research into the balloon frame, Europeans were mostly incapable of grasping the significance of lightweight wood or steel structures—the very expression of American nomadism. Whether rationalized by Levitt or assembled into unstable prismatic forms by Frank Gehry, wooden structures have been vectors both of ultra-flexible industrialization and of remarkable ingenuity. Moreover, the lightweight Californian structures of Neutra or Charles Eames were forgotten from the moment when the European (and more specifically French) cult of reinforced concrete ruled out all other alternatives.

To the effects of designs and buildings must be added those of American cultural institutions. The activities of American museums and publishing houses had little effect on Europe before 1945. But from the moment when the German, Swiss, British, and Italian public saw *Built in the USA* and other exhibitions by MoMA, and Old World architects became familiar with American metropolitan buildings and smaller urban projects, United States institutions began to exercise a discreet but efficient hegemony over Europe. The Museum of Modern Art became less a vehicle for the dissemination of new trends than an institution for the ratification of doctrinal positions associating architects on both sides of the Atlantic. The watercolor designs presented under the title *Architecture at the École des Beaux-Arts*, and the graphic labyrinths shown in the 1988 "Deconstructivist" show were diametrically opposite, in postulates and in content (though some of the exhibits shown in 1988 were graphically closer to the Academies than to the Russian avant-garde); yet their impact on Europe was equally strong.

The 1992 inauguration of Disneyland at Marne-la-Vallée, coming just before the controversies over "cultural exception" that marked the Uruguay Round of the GATT talks the following year, sparked off renewed irritation in the face of the "American threat." This was hardly symptomatic, but rather an isolated episode in the complex network of intellectual relations nurtured since the Chicago Exposition of 1893. It is, however, likely that things will change in the 21st century, given that European and American architects occupy essentially the same intellectual space, even if American hegemony may well persist in the sphere of mass culture. Finally (and inconclusively), though Americanism is part and parcel of the global cycle of industrial and post-industrial modernity, its significance in the architectural sphere is highly specific. The French, German, Italian, or Russian intellectuals contributing to such an immense and contradictory corpus of texts doubtless invoked images that the Americans would be loath to repudiate. But the significance of architectural problematics ranging from Mendelsohn's photographic mural to Archigram's scenarios go far beyond strategies designed to reduce the visual domain to the status of mere illustrations. They eschew reproductions and seek to bring anamorphic readings of American urban and architectural production to the European scene in a continuous process of critical evaluations and transformations.

NOTES

1. Henry James, *The American Scene*, New York: Harper, 1907.
2. Georges Duhamel, *Scènes de la vie future*, Paris: Mercure de France, 1930; Engl. trans.: *America: the Menace*, Boston: Houghton Mifflin, 1931.
3. Edward W. Said, *Orientalism*, New York: Random House, 1978.
4. Franz Kafka, *Amerika*, New York: Schocken Books, 1962.
5. These are brought together in organized form in "The New Babylon: The 'Yellow Giants' and the Myth of Americanism," in Manfredo Tafuri, *The Sphere and the Labyrinth: Avant-Gardes and Architecture from Piranesi to the 1970s*, Cambridge, Mass.,: MIT Press, 1987, pp. 171–99.
6. For the French case, see Denis Lacorne, Jacques Rupnik and Marie-France Toinet, eds., *L'Amérique dans les têtes; un siècle de fascinations et d'aversions*, Paris: Hachette, 1986; Dominique Jullien, *Récits du nouveau-monde; les voyageurs français en Amérique de Châteaubriand à nos jours*, Paris: Nathan, 1992; Jean-Philippe Mathy, *Extrême Occident; French Intellectuals and America*, Chicago and London: University of Chicago Press, 1993.
7. Jean-Louis Cohen and Hubert Damisch, eds., *Américanisme et Modernité, l'idéal américain dans L'Architecture*, Paris: Flammarion and École des Hautes Études en Sciences Sociales, 1993.
8. "Presentation," in ibid., p. 1.
9. William Taylor, "New York et l'origine du Skyline; la cité moderne comme forme et symbole," *Urbi*, III, March 1980, pp. III–XXI.
10. Jean Prévost, *Usonie; esquisse de la civilisation américaine*, Paris: Gallimard, 1939, pp. 143–188.
11. Walter Benjamin, "Premières notes," *Paris: capitale du XIXe siècle*, Paris: Éditions du Cerf, 1989, p. 856.
12. Charles Baudelaire, "Further Notes on Edgar Poe," *Selected Writings on Art and Artists*, Harmondsworth: Penguin Classics, p. 198.
13. Arnold Dudley Lewis, *Evaluations of American Architecture by European Critics 1875–1900*, Madison: 1962 (Ph.D. thesis, University of Wisconsin).
14. César Daly, "Introduction," *Revue générale de l'Architecture et des Travaux Publics*, vol. XIV, 1856, pp. 8–10.
15. *L'Architecture américaine*, Paris: André, Daly Fils & Cie, 1886 (these portfolios of photographs by Albert Lévy are divided into three series of plates: *Édifices publics et établissements privés; Habitation urbaines; Habitation suburbaines*).
16. Paul Sédille, "American Architecture from a French Standpoint," *The American Architect and Building News*, vol. XX, n° 559, 11 September 1886, pp. 122–124.
17. Werner Oechslin, "Deperthes' 'Maison genre New York', oder der Misserfolg des Skyscrapers à l'européenne," *Archithese*, n° 20, 1976, pp. 42–61. Annie Jacques, *La Carrière de l'architecte au XXe siècle*, Paris: Musée d'Orsay, 1986, p. 53.
18. U. A., "École des Beaux-Arts; Concours du 'Prix des Américains,'" *La Construction moderne*, 13 February 1892, pp. 219–221.
19. On the 1893 World's Fair, see especially Neil Harris, Wim de Wit, James Gilbert, Robert W. Rydell, *Grand Illusions: Chicago's World's Fair of 1893*, Chicago: Chicago Historical Society, 1993; James Gilbert, *Perfect Cities: Chicago's Utopias of 1893*, Chicago: University of Chicago Press, 1991. On European readings of Chicago: cf. Bessie Louise Pierce, *As Others See Chicago: Impressions of Visitors 1673–1933*, Chicago: University of Chicago Press, 1933.
20. Louis H. Sullivan, *The Autobiography of an Idea*, New York: Institute of American Architects, 1922, p. 325. Henry-Russell Hitchcock Jr., *Modern Architecture, Romanticism, and Reintegration*, New York: Payson & Clark, 1929, p. 110. On its impact in France, see Henri Loyrette, "Chicago: A French View" in John Zukowsky, ed., *Chicago Architecture 1872–1922: Birth of a Metropolis*, Munich: Prestel-Verlag and the Art Institute of Chicago, 1987, pp. 121–136.
21. Claude Lévi-Strauss, *Tristes Tropiques*, trans. John and Doreen Weightman, New York: Atheneum, 1975, p. 96.
22. E. W. Reed, "L'Auditorium Building à Chicago," *La Semaine des constructeurs*, 10 April 1890, pp. 170–172.
23. R. E., "Les grandes constructions américaines," *La Construction moderne*, 5 September 1891, pp. 568–569.
24. Adolphe Bocage, "La maison moderne et la situation de l'architecte aux États-Unis," *L'Architecture*, vol. 7, n° 41, 13 October 1894, pp. 334–339.
25. Jacques Hermant, "L'Architecture en Amérique et à la World's Fair," *L'Architecture*, vol. 7, n° 42, 20 October 1894, pp. 341–345; "L'Art à l'exposition de Chicago: L'Architecture en Amérique et à la World's Fair," *Gazette des Beaux-Arts*, September 1893, pp. 237–253; October 1893, pp. 416–425; November 1893, pp. 441–461. See: Thierry Kozak, *L'architecte Jacques Hermant (1855–1930)*, Paris: Université Paris–IV, 1993 (doctoral thesis under the supervision of Bruno Foucart), pp. 163–177.
26. Jacques Hermant, "L'Architecture et les industries qui en dépendent en Amérique et à l'exposition de Chicago," in *Exposition Internationale de Chicago en 1893, Rapports*, ed. Camille Krantz, Paris: Imprimerie Nationale, Comité 36 Génie Civil, Travaux publics, Architecture, 1894, p. 6.
27. The published plans only showed the building's "load-bearing points": A. Raguenet, *Maison rue Réaumur n° 132*, Paris: E. Ducher, 1901 (*Monographies de bâtiments modernes*, n° 151).
28. Julien-Azaïs Guadet, *Eléments et théorie de l'Architecture*, Paris: Librairie de "La Construction Moderne," undated (1901–1904).
29. On his return, Bing published *La culture artistique en Amérique*, Évreux, Imprimerie de Charles Hérissey, 1895. See Debora Silverman, *Art Nouveau in Fin-de-Siècle France: Politics, Psychology, and Style*, Berkeley: University of California Press, 1989.
30. Octave Uzanne (1852–1931), *Vingt jours dans le Nouveau Monde (De Paris à Chicago)*, Paris: May et Motteroz, 1893; "A Frenchman's impression of Chicago itself," *The American Architect and Building News*, n° 41, 1893, p. 176. Marquis de Chasseloup-Laubat, *Voyage en Amérique et principalement à Chicago*, Paris: 1893; "A Frenchman on the World's Fair and America," *The American Architect and Building News*, n° 39, 1893, pp. 58–60.
31. Paul Bourget, *Outre-mer, Impressions of America*, New York: Charles Scribner's Sons, 1895, pp. 117–118. Bourget also published his remarks in American magazines: Paul Bourget, "A Farewell to to the White City," *Cosmopolitan*, December 1893, pp. 133–140.
32. Friedrich Ratzel, *Sketches of Urban and Cultural Life in North America*, New Brunswick: Rutgers University Press, 1988.
33. See especially the writings of Ernst von Hesse-Wartegg: *Chicago: eine Weltstadt im amerikanischen Westen*, Stuttgart: Union Deutsche Verlagsgesellschaft, 1893; *Amerika als neueste Weltmacht der Industrie*, Stuttgart: Union Deutsche Verlagsgesellschaft, 1909.
34. J. W., "Briefe von der Columbischen Weltausstellung," *Deutsche Bauzeitung*, vol. 27, 10 June 1893, pp. 281–283; 17 June 1893,pp. 293–294; 28 June 1893, pp. 313–315; 19 July 1893, pp. 349–350; 29 July 1893, pp. 368–372; 19 August 1893, pp. 404–408; 23 September 1893, pp. 462–466; 11 October 1893, pp. 494–497.
35. Leopold Gmelin, "Architektonisches aus Nordamerika," *Deutsche Bauzeitung*, vol. 28, 15 September 1894, pp. 453–456; 29 September 1894, pp. 481–483; 3 October 1894, pp. 485–487; 6 October 1894, pp. 495–498; 20 October 1894, pp. 520–522; 27 October 1894, pp. 532–534; 17 November 1894, pp. 566–570; and 24 November 1894, pp. 582–583.
36. Werner Sombart subsequently published *Warum gibt es in den Vereinigten Staaten keinen Sozialismus?*, Tübingen: J. C. B. Mohr, 1906. Eng. trans.: *Why is there No Socialism in the United States?*, White Plains, NY: International Arts and Sciences Press, 1976. Münsterberg (1863–1916), a pioneer in the sphere of industrial psychology, had already published *Die Amerikaner*, Berlin: E. S. Mittler und Sohn, 1904. Eng. trans.: *The Americans*, trans. Edwin B. Holt, New York: McClure, Phillips & Co., 1904.
37. Paul Graef, *Neubauten in Nordamerika*, Berlin: Julius Becker, 1899. On German *Amerikanismus*, see Miles David Samson, *German-American Dialogues and the Modern Movement before the Design Migration 1910–1933*, Cambridge, Mass.: Harvard University, 1988 (Ph.D. thesis).
38. William Craft Brumfield, "Russian perceptions of American architecture 1870–1917," in *Reshaping Russian Architecture: Western Technology, Utopian Dreams*, ed. William Craft Brumfield, Cambridge and New York: Woodrow Wilson International Center for Scholars, Cambridge University Press, 1990, pp. 43–66.
39. Hans Rogger, "*Amerikanizm* and the Economic Development of Russia," *Journal of the Society for Comparative Study of Society and History*, 1981, p. 407.
40. Nikolai Melnikov, *Chudesa vystavki v Chicago (s 70 risunkami)*, Odessa, Tip. Odesskikh Novostei, 1893. A chemical engineer and polymath, Melnikov visited the Paris Exposition Universelle in 1889.
41. "Opisanie zdanii vystavki v Chicago:" *Nedelia stroitelia*, n° 1 & n° 3, 1893, pp. 2–3 and 10–11.
42. Vladimir Korolenko, "Fabrika smerti," *Sobranie sochinenii*, Moscow: 1956, vol. 10, pp. 146–156.
43. P. A. Tverskoi, *Ocherki Severo-Amerikanskikh Soedinionnykh Chtatov*, St. Petersburg, Tip. Skorokhodova, 1895, pp. 410–411.
44. Aleksandr Dmitriev, "Iz poezdki v Severnuiu Ameriku," *Zodchii*, vol. 34, 1905, n° 27, pp. 313–314; n° 28, pp. 321–324; n° 29, pp. 329–332; n° 30, pp. 337–339; n° 31, pp. 345–346; n° 35, pp. 381–385; n° 36, pp. 395–398.
45. Constantin Balmont, "Dva slova ob Amerike," *Zolotoe runo*, vol. 1, 1906, pp. 72–78. Aleksandr Blok, "Novaia Amerika," *Russkoe slovo*, 25 December 1913.
46. Maxime Gorky, *V Amerike, Ocherki*, Stuttgart: Dietz Verlag, 1906, Moscow: Foreign Language Publ. House, 1949. The text on New York was published simultaneously in America: "The City of Mammon, my impressions of America," *Appleton's Magazine*, August 1906, pp. 177–182. Stendhal had already remarked on the "tyranny of the dollar" in *La Chartreuse de Parme ...*
47. Burkhardt Rukschcio and Roland Schachel, *Adolf Loos Leben und Werk*, Salzburg and Vienna: Residenz Verlag, 1982, pp. 21–31.
48. Adolf Loos, "Der Silberhof und seine Nachbarschaft," *Neue Freie Presse*, 15 May 1898, cited in Rukschcio and Schachel, *Adolf Loos, Leben und Werk*, p. 24.
49. Robert Scheu, "Adolf Loos," *Die Fackel*, n° 283–284, 26 June 1909, cited in Rukschcio and Schachel, *Adolf Loos, Leben und Werk*, p. 30.
50. Richard Neutra, *Life and Shape*, New York: Appleton-Century-Crofts, 1962, pp. 160, 167.
51. See Richard Longstreth, ed., *The Mall in Washington, 1791–1991*, Washington, D. C.: National Gallery of Art, 1991.
52. Dugald MacFadyen, *Sir Ebenezer Howard and the Town Planning Movement*, Manchester: Manchester University Press, 1970 (1st edition 1933); Robert Beevers, *The Garden City Utopia: A Critical Biography of Ebenezer Howard*, New York: Saint Martin's Press, 1988, pp. 9–24.
53. Cf. Howard's autobiographical essay in the Frederic J. Osborn Collection, Central Library, Welwyn Garden City. On the impact of American reformists on Howard's own ideas, see Stanley Buder, *Visionaries and Planners: The Garden City Movement and the Modern Community*, New York and Oxford: Oxford University Press, 1990, pp. 3–53.
54. Patrick Geddes, *City Development; A Study of Parks, Gardens and Culture-Institutes*, Edinburgh, Outlook Tower, Bournville: The Saint George Press, 1904. On Geddes, see Philip Boardman, *The Worlds of Patrick Geddes, Biologist, Town planner, Re-educator, Peace-warrior*, London, Henley, and Boston: Routledge and Kegan Paul, 1978, pp. 166–178.
55. Georges Benoit-Lévy, *La Cité-jardin*, Paris: Henri Jouve, 1904.
56. Georges Benoit-Lévy, *Cités-jardins d'Amérique*, Paris: Henri Jouve, 1905, pp. 38–39.
57. See the role of Paris squares in Olmsted's reflections: *Frederick Law Olmsted, Public Parks and the Enlargement of Towns*, Cambridge, Mass.: American Social Science Association, 1870.
58. On the orientations of urban planning and parks policies in the United States, see M. Christine Boyer, *Dreaming the Rational City: The Myth of American City Planning*, Cambridge, Mass. and London: MIT Press, 1983, pp. 1–56. Galen Cranz, *The Politics of Park Design; A History of Urban Parks in America*, Cambridge, Mass. and London: MIT Press, 1982, pp. 3–100.
59. Jean-Claude-Nicolas Forestier, *Grandes villes et systèmes de Parcs*, Paris: Hachette, 1906, p. 5.

60. Bourget, *Outre-mer*, p. 274.

61. Forestier, *Grandes villes*, p. 22.

62. Jean-Claude-Nicolas Forestier, "Principes d'urbanisme," *Revue d'hygiène et de médecine préventive*, vol. 50, n° 3, March 1928, pp. 171–172.

63. Henri Luja, *Monographie du parc public de la ville de Luxembourg*, Luxemburg, 1950, p. 115.

64. Isaak M. Rubinov, "Evoliutsia domashney zhizni v Soedinennykh shtatakh," *Russkaia Mysl*, 1905, pp. 194–207; "Ocherki munitsipalnoi zhizni v Amerike," *Izvestiia Mosk. Gor. Dumy*, 1907, pp. 113–34 and 159–174.

65. Vladimir Semenov, *Blagoustroistvo gorodov*, Moscow: Tip. I. I. Riabushchinskago, 1912.

66. Giuliano Gresleri, Dario Matteoni, *La Città mondiale: Andersen, Hébrard, Otlet, Le Corbusier*, Venice: Marsilio, 1982.

67. Vereinigung Berliner Architekten, Architektenverein zu Berlin, *Anregungen zur Erlangung eines Grundplanes für die städtebauliche Entwicklung von Gross-Berlin*, Berlin: Ernst Wasmuth, 1908. In 1906 the Vereinigung published a document on Greater Berlin in which the American instance was already commented on.

68. Werner Hegemann, *Amerikanische Parkanlage: Zierparks, Nutzparks, Aussen-u. Innenparks, Nationalparks, Park-Zweckverbande*, Berlin: Ernst Wasmuth, 1911; *Der Neue Bebauungsplan für Chicago*, Berlin: Ernst Wasmuth, 1911; "Die Ausstellung für Städtebau und städtische Kunst in New York," *Der Städtebau*, vol. 6, 1909, n° 10, pp. 127–130; n° 11, pp. 146–148.

69. Hartmut Frank, ed., *Fritz Schumacher, Reformkultur und Moderne*, Stuttgart: Gerd Hatje, 1994.

70. On Werner Hegemann (1881–1936), see Christiane Crasemann Collins's introduction, "Hegemann and Peets, Cartographers of an Imaginary Atlas," in Werner Hegemann, Elbert Peets, *The American Vitruvius: An Architect's Handbook of Civic Art*, Princeton, Princeton Architectural Press, 1988 (originally published in 1922), pp. XII-XXII; and "A Visionary Discipline: Werner Hegemann and the Quest for the Pragmatic Ideal", *Center*, vol. 5, 1989, pp. 74–85; and Donatella Calabi, "Werner Hegemann o dell'ambiguità borghese dell'urbanistica, *Casabella*, 1976.

71. Boyer, *Dreaming the Rational City*, pp. 123–126.

72. Werner Hegemann, *Der Städtebau nach den Ergebnissen der allgemeinen Städtebau-Ausstellung in Berlin nebst einem Anhang: Die Internationale Städtebau-Ausstellung in Düsseldorf*, Berlin: Ernst Wasmuth, 1911 (vol. 1) and 1913 (vol. 2).

73. According to Christiane C. Collins, Werner Hegemann discusses the topic in his study published in *The Factory*, 1913.

74. Werner Hegemann, "European City Plans and their Value to the American City Planner," *Landscape Architecture*, vol. 4, 1913–1914, pp. 89–103.

75. Werner Hegemann, "Soll Berlin Wolkenkratzer bauen?," *Berliner Illustrierte Zeitung*, 1913.

76. Behrens's views were published in the *Berliner Morgenpost* of 27 November 1912.

77. Karl Scheffler, *Die Architektur der Großstadt*, Berlin: Bruno Cassirer Verlag, 1913, p. 14.

78. "Saving the Sunshine in the City's Valley of Shadow," *New York Herald*, 9 August 1909, quoted in Carol Willis, Georges R. Collins, *Visionary Drawings of Architecture and Planning 20th Century through the 1960s*, Cambridge, Mass. and London: MIT Press, 1979.

79. Harry M. Pettit, "The Cosmopolis of the Future," cover illustration for *King's Dream of New York*, New York: Moses King, 1908; Richard W. Rummell, "Future New York is preeminently the City of Skyscrapers," cover illustration for *King's Views of New York*, New York: Moses King, 1911. On these projects, see Cervin Robinson, "Wie wird man ein erfolgreicher Visionär?," *Archithese*, n° 18, 1976, pp. 5–12.

80. Henry Harrison Suplee, "The Elevated Sidewalk: How it Will Solve City Transportation Problems," *Scientific American*, 26 July 1913, p. 67.

81. "La ville future; une solution hardie du problème de la circulation, d'après le Scientific American," *L'Illustration*, n° 3676, 9 August 1913, p. 124; this article was reproduced two weeks later in Italy: "La circolazione futura e i grattanuvole a New York," *L'Illustrazione italiana*, 31 August 1913, p. 211. The project was also published in Russia: "Ulitsa v gorode budushchego," *Vokrug Sveta*, n° 36, 1913, p. 592.

82. Eugène Hénard, "Les villes de l'avenir," in *Town-Planning Conference*, London: 10–15 October 1910, Transactions, London: Royal Institute of British Architects, 1911, pp. 345–367.

83. Bernard Marrey, *Louis Bonnier (1856–1946)*, Paris: Institut Français d'Architecture, Liège, Pierre Mardaga, 1988.

84. The documents relative to these projects are in the Museum of the History of the City of Moscow. See Nina Smurova, "Urbanistische Phantasien in der künstlerischen Kultur Russlands Ende des 19., Anfang des 20. Jahrhunderts," in Selim Khan-Magomedov and Christian Schädlich, *Avantgarde 1 1900–1923; Russisch-Sowjetische Architektur*. Stuttgart: Deutsche Verlags-Anstalt, 1991, pp. 56–61.

85. These intersections first appeared in "New York: 1898–1908," *Scientific American*, vol. 99, 5 December 1908, p. 402, and are reproduced in Hegemann, *Der Städtebau nach den Ergebnissen der allgemeinen Städtebau-Ausstellung*, ill. 280. See also Thomas P. Hughes, "The City as Creator and Creation," in *Berlin New York Like and Unlike: Essays on Architecture and Art from 1870 to the Present*, ed. Josef Paul Kleihues and Christina Rathgeber, New York: Rizzoli, 1993, pp. 13–31.

86. Deborah Nevins, ed., *Grand Central Terminal: City within the City*, New York: Municipal Arts Society of New York: 1982.

87. P. Calfas, "La nouvelle gare centrale Terminus de New York" Le *Génie Civil*, vol. 63, n° 1613, 10 May 1913, pp. 21–26.

88. Umberto Boccioni, "Futurist Architecture: A Manifesto" in Ester Coen, *Umberto Boccioni*, New York: The Metropolitan Museum of Art, 1988, p. 250.

89. Antonio Sant'Elia, "Futurist Architecture" in *Programs and Manifestoes on 20th-Century Architecture*, ed. Ulrich Conrads, Cambridge, Mass.: MIT Press, 1970, p. 36.

90. The station was published in 1913: "La più grande stazione del mondo inaugurata a New York," *L'Illustrazione italiana*, 1 February 1913.

91. On Sant'Elia, see Luciano Caramel and Alberto Longatti, *Antonio Sant'Elia: The Complete Works*, New York: Rizzoli, 1987. *Antonio Sant'Elia; l'architettura disegnata*, Venice: Marsilio, 1991. Banham seems to have missed the American dimension of Sant'Elia's projects: Reyner Banham, *Theory and Design in the First Machine Age*, London: The Architectural Press, 1960, p. 132.

92. Pier Giorgio Gerosa, *Mario Chiattone, Un itinerario architettonico fra Milano e Lugano*, Milan, Electa, 1985.

93. Maurizio Scuderio and David Leiber, *Depero futurista e New York*, Rovereto: Longo, 1986.

94. *Carlo Mollino 1905–1973*, Milan: Electa, p. 87.

95. Harvey Wiley Corbett, "The Problem of Traffic Congestion, and a Solution," *Architectural Forum*, March 1927, p. 202; Carol Willis, "Drawing Towards Metropolis, in Hugh Ferriss, *The Metropolis of Tomorrow*, Princeton: Princeton Architectural Press, 1986, pp. 158-159.

96. Leonard K. Eaton, *American Architecture Comes of Age: European Reaction to H. H. Richardson and Louis Sullivan*, Cambridge, Mass.: MIT Press, 1972.

97. Karl Hinckeldeyn, "Henry Richardson und seine Bedeutung für die amerikanische Architektur," *Deutsche Bauzeitung*, vol. 26, 6 February 1892, pp. 64–66. On Hinckeldeyn, see Arnold Dudley Lewis, "Karl Hinckeldeyn: Critic of American Architecture," *The American-German Review*, vol. 27, no. 2, January 1961, pp. 10, 13, 37.

98. Paul Graef, *Neubauten in Nordamerika*, Berlin: Julius Becker, 1899 (preface by Karl Hinckeldeyn); some of the plates were republished in 1905.

99. *Ankundigung* (prospectus) for Graef, *Neubauten in Nordamerika*, 1899.

100. Karl Hinckeldeyn, preface to Graef, *Neubauten in Nordamerika*, pp. 1–2.

101. "Im Natur der Baustoffe." Compare the title of Henry-Russell Hitchcock's book on Wright: *In the Nature of Materials*, New York: 1942.

102. An album collection of Umbdenstock's drawings can be found at the Canadian Centre for Architecture.

103. F. Rudolf Vogel, *Das amerikanische Haus, Band I: Die Entwicklung der Baukunst und des amerikanischen Hauses*, Berlin: Wasmuth, 1910. In plan and layout, this work faithfully reproduces those of *Das englische Haus*. Further volumes were announced but never appeared.

104. F. Rudolf Vogel, "Der amerikanische Einfluss auf die moderne Baukunst," *Deutsche Bauhütte*, V, 1901, pp. 188–189, 201–202, and 254–256.

105. On links between the Netherlands and America, see A. W. Reinink, "American Influences on Late Nineteenth-Century Architecture in the Netherlands," *Journal of the Society of Architectural Historians*, vol. 29, 1970, pp. 163–174. Fons Asselbergs et al., *Americana*, Otterlo: Rijksmuseum Kröller-Müller, 1975 (exhibition catalog).

106. Hendrik Petrus Berlage, *Amerikaansche Reisherinneringen*, Rotterdam, 1913.

107. Hendrik Petrus Berlage, "Neuere amerikanische Architektur," *Schweizerische Bauzeitung*, vol. 60, 14 September 1912, pp. 148–150; 21 September 1912, pp. 165–167. Engl. trans.: "The New American Architecture," in D. Gifford, ed., *The Literature of Architecture*, pp. 615–616. Ten years earlier, the Swiss review had published an account of travels to New York, Chicago, Denver, San Francisco, and Seattle: F. Bluntschli, "Reiseeindrücke aus den V. S. von Nordamerika," *Schweizerische Bauzeitung*, vol. 38, 1901, pp. 23–260.

108. Reyner Banham, *A Concrete Atlantis: U.S. Industrial Buildings and European Modern Architecture 1900–1925*, Cambridge, Mass. and London: MIT Press, 1986, pp. 32–38.

109. Cyrille Simonnet, *Matériau et architecture, le béton armé: origine, invention, esthétique*, Paris: EHESS, 1994, pp. 332–333 (doctoral thesis).

110. École Nationale des Beaux-Arts, *Les Concours d'architecture de l'année scolaire 1908–1909*, 3e année, 2e série, Paris: Librairie Auguste Vincent, 1909, p. 5.

111. "Concours pour le 'Prix de reconnaissance des architectes américains'," *La Construction moderne*, 23 February 1901, p. 243.

112. Daniel J. Boorstin, *The Americans: The National Experience*, New York: Random House, 1965, p. 147.

113. François-René de Châteaubriand, quoted in Paul Morand, *New-York*: Paris: Flammarion, 1930, pp. 138–139. Engl. trans.: *New York*, New York: The Book League of America., 1930, p. 160.

114. Alexander Mackay, *The Western World Or Travels in the United States in 1846–47*, London: Richard Bentley, 1849, v. 1, p. 71.

115. Charles Dickens, *American Notes*, New York: St. Martin's Press, 1985, *passim*.

116. "The Mount Vernon Hotel, Cape May, New Jersey," *The Illustrated London News*, 17 September 1853, p. 228 (clipping held by Sigfried Giedion, GTA/ETH Zurich).

117. James, *The American Scene*, p. 102. In *The Golden Bowl*, James transposes his analysis to a Parisian hotel: Henry James, *The Golden Bowl*, New York: Scribner's, 1904.

118. Hector Horeau, "Hôtel Américain," *L'Illustration*, vol. XXII, 1853, p. 396.

119. Édouard Guyer, *Les hôtels modernes*, Paris: Veuve A. Morel, 1877, p. 52. (Original edition: *Das Hotelwesen der Gegenwart*, Zurich: Orell Füssli Verlag, 1874).

120. Jules Huret, *L'Amérique moderne*, Paris: Pierre Lafitte, 1911, p. 11.

121. Victor Cambon, "Le tourisme américain", *Notre avenir*, Paris: Pierre Roger, 1916, p. 236.

122. Morand, *New York*, p. 164.

123. Robert Descharnes, Clovis Prévost, *La vision artistique et religieuse de Gaudí*, Lausanne, Edita, 1969, pp. 189–197. Rem Koolhaas was quick to see the fantasmagoric potential of Gaudí's project in Rem Koolhaas, *Delirious New York, A Retroactive Manifesto for Manhattan*, New York: Rizzoli, 1978, pp. 87–89.

124. Duhamel, *Scènes de la vie future*, pp. 138–139.

125. Ibid., p. 203.

126. Luc Durtain, *Hollywood dépassé*, Paris: Gallimard, 1928, p. 35.

127. Edmond Joyant, "Reims," in *Traité d'urbanisme*, Paris: Eyrolles, 1929 (2d ed.), vol. 2, pp. 62–66.

128. See Ford's account of his French experiences: Georges B. Ford, *Out of the Ruins*, New York: The Century Co., 1919.

129. Pierre Bourdeix, "La reconstruction de Reims," *Le Nord et l'Est*, January 1926, cited by Marc Bédarida, "Compassion et aide américaines: la reconstruction de Reims (1918–1928)," in Cohen and Damisch, eds., *Américanisme et modernité*, p. 254.

130. G. La Flize, *Standardisation d'éléments de construction*, Paris: Union des Syndicats d'architectes des Régions dévastées, 1922.

131. Jacques Gréber (1882–1962), *L'Organisation des travaux d'architecture aux États-Unis*, Paris: Librairie Centrale des Beaux-Arts, 1919 (lecture delivered on 3 March 1919 at the École Supérieure des Beaux-Arts).

132. André Lortie, *Jacques Gréber architecte urbaniste 1882–1962: les aller-retour France-Amérique, une énergie cinétique au service de l'art urbain*, Créteil: Institut d'Urbanisme de Paris–Val-de-Marne, 1988 (postgraduate thesis).

133. Jacques Gréber, *L'Architecture aux États-Unis, preuve de la force d'expansion du génie français, heureuse association de qualités admirablement complémentaires*, Paris: Payot, 1920. The introduction was published in Jacques Gréber, "L'Architecture aux États-Unis," *Revue de synthèse historique*, vol. 29, 1919, n° 85–87, pp. 189–203.

134. Victor Cambon, *L' Allemagne au travail*, Paris: Pierre Roger, 1910; *Les derniers progrès de l'Allemagne,* Paris: Pierre Roger, 1914; *États-Unis–France*, Paris: Pierre Roger, 1917.

135. Victor Cambon, preface to Gréber *L'Architecture aux États-Unis*, v. 1, p. 9.

136. Gréber, *L'Architecture aux États-Unis*, v. 1, p. 35.

137. Ibid., p. 44.

138. Ibid., p. 100.

139. The Radical-Socialist mayor of Lyon, Édouard Herriot, echoed these comments in his own travel account: *Impressions d'Amérique*, Lyon, 1923, p. 81.

140. Gréber, *L'Architecture aux États-Unis*, v. 1, pp. 140, 146.

141. Ibid., v. 2, pp. 13, 16.

142. Ibid., p. 47.

143. École Nationale des Beaux-Arts, *Les Concours d'architecture de l'année scolaire 1921–1922*, Paris: Auguste Vincent, pl. 47–54.

144. Gréber, *L'Architecture aux États-Unis*, v. 2, p. 141.

145. Ibid., p. 159.

146. Ibid., p. 161.

147. Louis Dimier, "Les Salons," *L'Architecture*, vol. 34, n° 10, 25 May 1921, p. 1. On Gréber's lectures, see: *Bulletin de la SADG*, vol. 16, n° 13, 1st July 1921, pp. 159–163, and n° 15–16, 1st–15 August 1921, pp. 180–196.

148. Jacques Gréber, "The New Plans for Paris," *The Architectural Record*, January 1921, pp. 71–78.

149. Jacques Gréber, "New York 1933," *Urbanisme*, n° 13, April 1933, pp. 121–124.

150. Gréber, *L'Architecture aux États-Unis*, v. 1, p. 157.

151. Randolph William Sexton, *American Apartment Houses Hotels and Apartment Hotels of Today*, New York: Architectural Books Publishing Inc., 1929, p. 1.

152. For a detailed analysis of this program, see R. W. Sexton, "The Modern Apartment Hotel; Will it replace the private dwelling?," *The American Architect*, vol. 131, n° 2512, 5 January 1927, pp. 37–42; and "La maison de rapport américaine moderne," *La Construction Moderne*, vol. 42, n° 23, 6 March 1927, pp. 263–265. See also Paul Groth, *Living Downtown: The History of Residential Hotels in the United States*, Berkeley, Los Angeles, and London: University of California Press, 1994.

153. Gabriel Guévrékian, *Hôtels et sanatoria*, Paris: éditions S. de Bonadona, n.d. (1930), n. p.

154. "Les immeubles du Groupe de l'habitation franco-américaine," prospectus, Fondation Le Corbusier.

155. Groupe de l'habitation franco-américaine, letter to Daniel Niestlé, Paris: 8 February 1922, Fondation Le Corbusier.

156. Pierre-Alain Croset, "Immeubles-villas, les origines d'un type," in *Le Corbusier 1887–1965, une encyclopédie*, ed. Jacques Lucan, Paris: CCI and CNAC Georges Pompidou, 1987, pp. 178–189.

157. Le Corbusier, *Almanach d'architecture moderne*, Paris: G. Crès et Cie, 1926, pp. 125–126.

158. Le Corbusier, "Une cellule à l'échelle humaine," in *Précisions sur un état présent de L'Architecture et de l'urbanisme*, Paris: G. Crès et Cie, 1930, pp. 88–89.

159. On Grosz's epic dreams, see *"Asphaltcowboys* and *Stadtindianer:* Imagining the Far West," in Beeke Sell Tower, *Envisioning America: prints, drawings and photographs by George Grosz and his contemporaries*, Cambridge, Mass.: Busch-Reisinger Museum, 1990, pp. 17–36.

160. *Neue Jugend*, Berlin: n° 2, June 1917.

161. This collage, now lost, is reproduced in Peter Pachnicke and Klaus Honnef, eds., *John Heartfield*, Cologne: DuMont, 1991, pl. 2.

162. On the positions adopted by German critics, see Theodor Lüddecke, *"Amerikanismus* als Schlagwort und als Tatsache," *Deutsche Rundschau*, March 1930, pp. 214–221; Otto Basler, *"Amerikanismus,* Geschichte eines Schlagwortes," *Deutsche Rundschau*, August 1930, pp. 142–144.

163. On German-American relations in the twenties, see Ernst Fraenkel, ed., *Amerika im Spiegel des deutschen politischen Denkens*, Cologne and Opladen: Westdeutscher Verlag, 1959; Peter Berg, *Deutschland und Amerika; Über das deutsche Amerikabild der zwanziger Jahre*, Lübeck and Hamburg: Matthiesen, 1963; Charles S. Maier, *Recasting Bourgeois Europe: Stabilization in France, Germany and Italy in the Decade after WW I*, Princeton: Princeton University Press, 1988.

164. C. C. Collins, "Hegemann and Peets," in Hegemann and Peets, *The American Vitruvius*, p. XVI.

165. On Elbert Peets (1886–1968) see Caroline Shillaber, "Elbert Peets, Champion of the Civic Form," *Landscape Architecture*, vol. 72, n° 6, November 1982, pp. 54–59.

166. Werner Hegemann and Elbert Peets, *Wyomissing Park: The Modern Garden Suburb of Ealing, Pennsylvania, Reports and Plans*, Wyomissing: Wyomissing Development Corporation, 1919.

167. Werner Hegemann, "United States of America," in *International City and Town Planning Exhibition*, Gothenburg, 1923, pp. 351-387. See a discussion of Hegemann's contribution in Raymond Unwin, "The Gothenburg Intrenational Town Planning Exhibition and Conference, *Journal of the RIBA*, vol. 30, n° 19, 22 September 1923, pp. 521-622.

168. Werner Hegemann, *Amerikanische Architektur und Stadtbaukunst*, Berlin, Wasmuth, 1925, p. 9.

169. Three years later, Siegfried Giedion reiterated this declaration almost word for word to justify his choice of models in *Bauen in Frankreich:* Sigfried Giedion, "Vorbemerkung," *Bauen in Frankreich, Bauen in Eisen, Bauen in Eisenbeton*, Leipzig and Berlin: Klinkhardt und Biermann, 1928, n. p.

170. Hegemann and Peets, *The American Vitruvius*, pp. 2–3.

171. Walter Curt Behrendt, *Städtebau und Wohnungswesen in den Vereinigten Staaten, Bericht über eine Studienreise*, Berlin: Guido Hackebeil AG.

172. Martin Wagner, *Amerikanische Bauwirtschaft*, Berlin: Dreikellen-Bücher, 1925. This book was translated into Russian in 1928. On this politically-committed architect: Klaus Homann, Martin Kieren, Ludovica Scarpa, *Martin Wagner 1885–1957; Wohnungsbau und Weltstadtplanung; Die Rationalisierung des Glückes*, Berlin: Akademie der Künste, 1985.

173. Martin Wagner, *Städtebauliche Probleme in amerikanischen Städten und ihre Rückwirkung auf den deutschen Städtebau*, Berlin: Deutsche Bauzeitung, 1929.

174. For early instances see William J. Brown, "Walter Gropius and Grain Elevators," *History of Photography*, Autumn 1993, pp. 304–307.

175. Walter Gropius, "Die Entwicklung moderner Industriebaukunst," *Die Kunst in Industrie und Handel, Jahrbuch des Deutschen Werkbundes 1913*, Iena: Eugen Diederichs, 1913, pp. 21–22.

176. For a traditionalist view of American buildings see Werner Lindner, Georg Steinmetz, *Die Ingenieurbauten in ihrer guten Gestaltung*, Berlin: Wasmuth, 1923.

177. Banham, *A Concrete Atlantis*, pp. 204-205.

178. Wilhelm Worringer, *Ägyptische Kunst; Probleme ihrer Wertung*, Munich: R. Piper & Co, 1927. Engl. trans.: Wilhelm Worringer, *Egyptian Art*, London: G. P. Putnam's Sons, Ltd., 1928.

179. And quotation above: Erich Mendelsohn, "Das Problem einer neuen Baukunst," in *Das Gesamtschaffen des Architekten*, Berlin: Rudolf Mosse, 1930, pp. 16–17. Engl. trans.: Erich Mendelsohn, "The Problem of a New Architecture," in *Erich Mendelson: Complete Works of the Architect*, Princeton: Princeton Architectural Press, Inc., 1992, pp. 16–17.

180. Jean Cocteau, *Le coq et l'arlequin*, Paris: Éditions de la Sirène, 1918, p. 35.

181. Amédée Ozenfant, *Mémoires 1886–1962*, Paris: Pierre Seghers, 1968, pp. 112–113.

182. Moisei Ginzburg, *Style and Epoch*, Cambridge, Mass. and London: The MIT Press, 1982, pp. 107–08.

183. Ibid., p. 108.

184. "L'entrée de l'usine-parc," Benoit-Lévy, *Cités-jardins d'Amérique*, pl. 20.

185. Friedrich Nietzsche, *Aus dem Nachlass; Studien aus der Umwertungszeit 1882–1888*, Munich: Musarion Verlag, 1925 (*Gesammelte Werke*), vol. 17 , p. 373.

186. Friedrich Nietzsche, "Sanctus Januarius—The Joyful Wisdom Book IV," *The Complete Works of Friedrich Nietzsche*, ed. Oscar Levy, London: T. N. Foulis, 1910, Vol. 10, p. 254.

187. For an overview of these transformations, see David A. Hounshell, *From the American System to Mass Production 1800–1932*, Baltimore and London: The Johns Hopkins University Press, 1984, pp. 15–123.

188. In this context, the scope of Adrian Forty's analysis is not restricted to office design alone: Adrian Forty, "Taylorism and Modern Architecture," *Transactions of the RIBA*, vol. 5, n° 1, 1986, pp. 73–81.

189. Frederick W. Taylor, *Shop Management*, New York: Harper, 1904; and *Principles of Scientific Management*, London and New York: Harper, 1911. On Taylor himself, see Sudhir Kakar, *Frederick Taylor: A Study in Personality and Innovation*, Cambridge, Mass.: MIT Press, 1970.

190. On the consolidation and dissemination of Taylorism, see Judith A. Merkle, *Management and Ideology, the Legacy of the International Scientific Management Movement*, Berkeley: University of California Press, 1980.

191. Olivier Pastré, "Attention: un taylorisme peut en cacher un autre," in *Le Taylorisme*, ed. Maurice de Montmollin and Olivier Pastré, Paris: La Découverte, 1984, pp. 26–27.

192. Frank Bunker Gilbreth (1869–1924), *Bricklaying System*, New York and Chicago: The M. C. Clark Publishing Co, 1909; *Fatigue Study, The Elimination of Humanity's Greatest Unnecessary Waste, A First Step in Motion Study*, New York: Macmillan, 1918. Cf.: J. Prévost, *Usonie*, pp. 76–83.

193. Henry Ford, *My Life and Work*, Garden City: Doubleday, Page & Co, 1922; *Today and Tomorrow*, Garden City: Doubleday, Page & Co, 1926. German, Italian, etc., editions abound.

194. Hyacinthe Dubreuil, *Standarts; le travail américain vu par un ouvrier français*, Paris: Grasset, 1929. A Russian equivalent to this book is: S. G. Ledenev, *Za stankom u Forda*, Moscow: Gosudarstvennoe Izdatelstvo, 1927.

195. Merkle, *Management and Ideology*, pp. 103–129.

196. Frederick W. Taylor, *Administratvno-tekhnicheskaia organizatsia promyshlennykh predpriatii*, St. Petersburg, L. A. Levenshtern, 1912. *Nauchnye osnovy organizatsii promyshlennyh predpriatii*, St. Petersburg, L. A. Levenshtern, 1912 (in English, *Principles of Scientific Management*).

197. Frank Gilbreth, *Izuchenie dvizhenii kak sposob povysit proizvoditelnost pri vsiakoi rabote*, St. Petersburg, L. A. Levenshtern, 1913 (translated) and presented by A. V. Pankin and L. A. Levenshtern); initially: *Motion Study; a Method for Increasing the Efficiency of the Workman*, New York: Van Nostrand, 1911. Henry L. Gantt (1861–1919), *Sovremennye sistemy zarabotnoi platy i podbor rabochikh v sviazi s dokhodnostiu predpriatii*, trans. L. A. Levenchtern; presented by A. V. Pankin & L. A. Levenshtern, St. Petersburg, 1913. Initially: *Work, Wages and Profits, Their Influence on the Cost of Living*, New York: Engineering Magazine Co, 1910.

198. Among Polakov's major works, see: *Mastering power production; the industrial, economic and social problems involved and their solution*, London: Cecil Palmer, 1922; *Man and His Affairs from the Engineering Point of View*, Baltimore: Williams & Wilkins Co, 1925.

199. Aleksandr A. Bogdanov (Malinovskii), *Mezhdu chelovekom i mashiny; o Sisteme Taylora*, St. Petersburg: Priboi, 1913

200. Vladimir Ilich Lenin, "A 'Scientific' System of Sweating," in V. I. Lenin, *Collected Works*, Moscow: Progress Publishers, 1968, Vol. 18, pp. 594–595.

201. Lenin, "The Taylor System—Man's Enslavement by Machine," in *Collected Works*, Vol 20, pp. 152–154.

202. John Lewis Gaddis, *Russia, the Soviet Union and the United States: An Interpretive History*, New York: McGraw-Hill, 1978.

203. On Taylorism in the USSR, see Robert Linhart, *Lénine, les paysans, Taylor*, Paris: Le Seuil, 1976. Jean Querzola, "Le chef d'orchestre à la main de fer, Léninisme et Taylorisme," in *Le Soldat du Travail*, Paris: 1976, pp. 57–94 (*Recherches*, n° 32–33).

204. Lenin, "The Immediate Tasks of the Soviet Government," in *Collected Works*, vol. 27, p. 259.

205. Original version in ibid., vol. 42, pp. 68–83.

206. Leon Trotsky, *Sochinenii*, Moscow: Gosudarstvennoe Izdatelstvo, 1927, t. 15, pp. 92. See also Leon Trotsky, "nauchno-tekhnicheskaya mysl i sotsialisticheskoe khoziaystvo," *Izvestiia*, 2 June 1925.

207. Frederick W. Taylor, *Nauchnaia organizatsia truda*, Moscow: NKPS Transpechat, 1924; *Taylor o Taylorizme*, Leningrad, Moscow: Tekhnika Upravlenia, 1931.

208. Clarence B. Thompson, *Nauchnaia organizatsia proizvodstva, opyt Ameriki*, Petrograd, Petrogr. otd. Red.–izd. kollegi Narkomfina, 1920; original edition: *Scientific Management*, Cambridge, Mass.: Harvard University Press, 1914.

209. Arseni V. Mikhailov, *Sistema Taylora*, Moscow and Leningrad: Gos. Izd. 1928; *Sistema TsIT*, Moscow: Narkomat tiazh. prom., 1932. Ivan V. Rabchinskii, *O sisteme Taylora*, Moscow: Gos. Tekhnicheskoe izd. 1921.

210. Kurt Lewin, *Sotsializatsia sistemy Taylora*, Leningrad, Moscow: "Petrograd," 1925. Eduard Michel, *Kak proizvoditsia izuchenie rabochego vremeni (po Tayloru i Merricku)*, Moscow: Gos. Tekhnicheskoe Izd. vo, 1926. Yuri O. Liubovich, *Taylor i Fayol*, Riazan, 1924.

211. Richard Stites, *Revolutionary Dreams: Utopian Visions and Experimental Life in the Russian Revolution*, New York and Oxford: Oxford University Press, 1989, pp. 144–155.

212. René Fülop-Miller, *The Mind and Face of Bolshevism*, New York: Harper & Row Publishers, 1965, p. 22. Original edition: *Geist und Gesicht des Bolchewismus*, Zurich: Amalthea, 1926.

213. Recent texts on OSA include Hugh D. Hudson, Jr., "'The Social Condenser of Our Epoch': The Association of Contemporary Architects and the Creation of a New Way of Life in Revolutionary Russia," *Jahrbücher für Geschichte Osteuropas*, vol. 34, 1986, n° 4, pp. 557–583.

214. Mikhail Okhitovich, "K probleme goroda," *Sovremennaia Arkhitektura*, n° 4, 1929, pp. 130–134.
215. Henry Ford's memoirs went through four Soviet editions in 1924: Henry Ford, *Moia zhizn i moi dostizhenia*, Leningrad: 1924. Henry Ford, *Segodnia i zavtra; o SShA*, Moscow and Leningrad: Gos. izd., 1927.
216. E.g., Maurice Hindus, "Henry Ford Conquers Russia," *The Outlook*, 29 June 1927, p. 282.
217. On Ford's critical fortunes in the Soviet Union, see S. Shvedov, "Obraz Genri Forda v sovetskoi publitsistike 1920–1930–h godov: vospriatie i tranformatsia tsennosti chuzhoi kultury," in., *Vzaimodeistvie kultur SSSR i SChA XVIII–XX* vv., ed. O. E. Tuganov, Moscow: Nauka, 1987, pp. 133–142.
218. Jakob Walcher, *Ford ili Marx?*, Moscow: Izd. Profinterna, 1925; original edition: *Ford oder Marx, die praktische Lösung der sozialen Frage*, Berlin: Neuer Deutscher Verlag, 1925. Gilda Weiss, *Abbe i Ford; kapitalisticheskie utopii*, Moscow and Leningrad: Krasnyi proletarii, 1928.
219. N. Asov, *Genri Ford, Amerikanskii korol avtomobilei i traktorov; ego zhizn, dela i mysli, Populiarnyi ocherk*, Leningrad and Moscow: Petrograd, 1925. Naum Zinovevich Beljaev, *Genri Ford*, Moscow: Izd. Zhurnalno-gazetnyh obedinenizia, 1935. German G. Genkel (teacher and linguist), *Ford i fordizm (vpechatlenie)*, Leningrad, Kubuch, 1925; Nikolai S. Lavrov (prof. of technology), *Genri Ford i ego proizvodstvo*, Leningrad: Vremia, 1926. Boris S. Chikhman, *Ford i fordizm; ratsionalizatsia truda v Amerike*, Moscow: 1927.
220. Bernard Knollenberg, "American Business in Russia," *Nation's Business*, vol. 8, April 1930, p. 266, quoted by Parks, p. 186.
221. Erich Johnston, *We're All in It*, New York: E. P. Dutton & Co, 1950, pp. 81–82.
222. "Fordzon," in *Bolshaia Sovetskaia Entsiklopedia*, Moscow: OGIZ, 1936, t. 57, p. 131.
223. Reynold M. Wik, *Henry Ford and Grass-Roots America: A fascinating account of the Model-T Era*, Ann Arbor: University of Michigan Press, 1972.
224. Hindus, "Henry Ford Conquers Russia," pp. 280–283. Dana Dalrymple, "American Technology and Soviet Agricultural Development, 1924–1933," *Agricultural History*, July 1964; "The American Tractor comes to Soviet Agriculture: The Transfer of a Technology," *Technology and Culture*, n° 2, 1964.
225. Mikhail Okhitovich, "Zametki po teorii rasselenia," *Sovremennaia Arkhitektura*, n° 1–2, 1930, pp. 7–16.
226. Hugh D. Hudson, Jr., *Blueprints and Blood: the Stalinization of Soviet Architecture*, Princeton: Princeton University Press, 1994.
227. It was the engineer Ap. Ialovyi, senior member of the engineering factory at the Cinematographic Tekhnikum, who translated and presented one of their texts: Frank Gilbreth, *Prikladnoe izuchenie dvizhenii*, Moscow: Izd-vo VTsSPS, 1925.
228. Frank Gilbreth, *Sistema kladki kirpicha*, Moscow: Tekhnika Upravlenia, 1930 (translation of *Bricklaying System*, reprinted in the same year, 2d edition 1931).
229. Moisei Ginzburg, "Tselevaya ustanovka v sovremennoi arkhitekture," *Sovremennaia Arkhitektura*, vol. 2, n° 1, 1927, p. 4.
230. V. Kuzmin, "Problemy NO Byta," *Sovremennaia Arkhitektura*, vol. 5, n° 3, 1930, pp. 14–15.
231. Moisei Ginzburg, *Zhilishche*, Moscow: Gosstroiizdat, 1934.
232. Frederick W. Taylor, Sanford E. Thompson, *A Treatise on Concrete, Plain and Reinforced: Materials, Construction and Design of Concrete and Reinforced Concrete*, New York, J. Wiley and Sons, 1906.
233. Peter Hinrichs, Ingo Kolboom, "Wissenschaftliche Arbeitsorganisation (OST) in Frankreich zwischen Belle Epoque und Weltwirtschaftskrise," in *Absolut modern sein; Culture technique in Frankreich 1889–1937*, Berlin: Elefanten Press, 1986, pp. 75–90.
234. Olivier Cinqualbre, "France 1913–1925, Taylor dans le bâtiment, une idée qui fait son chemin," in *Architecture et industrie passé et avenir d'un mariage de raison*, Paris: CCI and Centre Georges Pompidou, 1983, pp. 198–206.
235. Le Corbusier, "Mass-Production Houses," in *Towards a New Architecture*, London: The Architectural Press, New York: Frederick A. Praeger, 1946, p. 210.
236. Le Corbusier, *Pour bâtir: standardiser et tayloriser*, supplement to *Bulletin du Redressement français*, 1 May 1928.
237. Yves Cohen, "Ernest Mattern chez Peugeot (1906–1916) ou comment peut-on être taylorien," *Le Taylorisme*, pp. 115–126.
238. *Prospérité ou Sam et François*, Clermont-Ferrand: Michelin & Cie, 1927.
239. Le Corbusier, letter to Etienne Gril, chief editor of the *Almanach Citroën*, Paris: 27 April 1934, Fondation Le Corbusier H 2(13) 36–37.
240. André Vaxelaire, "De l'usine urbaine à la cité scientifiquement aménagée," *L'usine et la Ville*, special issue of *Culture Technique*, Paris: Institut Français d'Architecture, 1986, pp. 21–42.
241. Léon Jaussely, "L'urbanisme au point de vue technique et au point de vue artistique," *Premier Congrès de l'habitation compte-rendu des travaux*, Lyon: Noirclerc et Fénétrie, 1920, pp. 10–37.
242. Paulette Bernège, "Les grands hôtels américains," *La Construction Moderne*, vol. 46, n° 16, 18 January 1931, pp. 249–255.
243. Paulette Bernège, *Si les femmes faisaient les maisons*, Paris: Mon Chez Moi, 1928, p. 41.
244. Ibid., p. 51.
245. Bruno Taut, *Die neue Wohnung, die Frau als Schöpferin*, Leipzig: Klinkhardt & Biermann, 1924. Christine Frederick, *Efficiency Studies in Home Management*, Garden City: Doubleday, Page & Co, pp. 1, 13; Frederick was also interested in consumer affairs: *Selling Mrs Consumer*, New York: The Business Bourse, 1929.
246. "Walter Gropius: From Americanism to the New World" in Winfried Nordinger, *The Architect Walter Gropius*, Cambridge, Mass.: Busch-Reisinger Museum, 1985, pp. 9–28.
247. Ernst Neufert, *Bauentwurfslehre*, Berlin: Bauwelt Verlag 1936. More than 300,000 copies were sold. Engl. trans.: *Architects' Data*, London: Crosby Lockwood & Son Ltd., 1970. See also Wolfgang Voigt, "Triumph der Gleichform und des Zusammenspassens; Ernst Neufert und die Normung der Architektur" in Winfried Nerdinger, *Bauhaus-Moderne im Nazionalsozialismus; Zwischen Anbiederung und Verfolgung*, Munich: Prestel, 1993, pp. 179–193.
248. "Fabbrica Italiana Automobili Torino 'Fiat'," in *Annuario della industria mineraria, metallurgica e meccanica in Italia 1916–1917*, Milan: n. d., p. 10, cited by Duccio Bigazzi, "Strutture della produzione: il Lingotto, l'America, l'Europa," in *Il Lingotto 1915–1939; L'architettura, l'immagine, il lavoro*, ed. Carlo Olmo, Turin: Umberto Allemandi, 1994, p. 284.
249. Olivier Cinqualbre and Yves Cohen, *Les usines dans l'action d'un grand industriel: Citroën, quai de Javel*, Paris: Inventaire Général, 1984.
250. See his seminal text on this: Antonio Gramsci, "Americanism and Fordism," in *Selections from the Notebooks of Antonio Gramsci*, ed. Quintin Hoare and Geoffrey Nowell, New York: International Publishers, 1971, pp. 277–320.
251. Edoardo Persico, "La Fiat: operai" (originally entitled "Fiat automobili—Via Nizza 250—Torino," *Motor Italia*, December 1927, republished in Edoardo Persico, *Tutte le opere (1923–1935)*, Milan, Edizioni di Comunità, 1964, pp. 4–5.
252. On Il Duce's cinematographic Americanism, see: Gian Piero Brunetta, "Il sogno a stelle e strisce di Mussolini," in *L'Estetica della politica, Europa e America negli anni Trenta*, ed. Maurizio Vaudagna, Bari: Laterza, 1989, 173–186.
253. Rudolf Philipp, *Thomas Bata, der unbekannte Diktator*, Vienna and Berlin: Agis-Verlag, 1928.
254. On the buildings of the corporation founded by Tomaš Bat'a (1876–1932), See: *Zavody Bat'a a.s. ve Zlíne, urbanismus, architektura*, Prague, Stavitel, 1935; Zdeněk Rossmann, *Zlín, mesto životni* aktivity, Zlín, Tisk, 1935; Vladimir Šlapeta, *Bat'a architektura a urbanismus 1910–1950*, Zlín, Státní Galerie v Zlíne, 1991.
255. Jean-Louis Cohen, "Nostro cliente è il nostro padrone, Le Corbusier e Bat'a," *I Clienti di Le Corbusier, Rassegna*, Milan, n° 3, June 1980, pp. 47–60. Se also Hyacinthe Dubreuil, *L'exemple de Bat'a, la libération des initiatives individuelles dans une entreprise géante*, Paris: Grasset, 1936.
256. Anthony Sutton, *Western Technology and Soviet Economic Development 1917 to 1930*, Stanford: Hoover Institution on War, Revolution and Peace, 1968, pp. 4–11.
257. Frank Ernest Hills, Allan Nevins, *Ford: Expansion and Challenge 1915–1933*, New York: Charles Scribner's Sons, 1957; Henry Ford, "Why I am helping Russian Industry," *Nation's Business*, vol. 18, June 1930, pp. 20–23.
258. Production reached 84,000 units in 1938 according to German souces cited by A. Sutton, *Western Technology and Soviet Economic Development*, p. 248.
259. Martin Greif, *The New Industrial Landscape, The Story of the Austin Company*, Clinton, N.J.: The Main Street Press, 1978, pp. 97 *et seq.*
260. Anatole Kopp, "Foreign architects in the Soviet Union during the first two Five-Year Plans," in W. C. Brumfield ed., *Reshaping Russian Architecture*, pp. 176–214. On Kahn, see Federico Bucci, *Albert Kahn, Architect of Ford*, Princeton: Princeton University Press, 1993, pp. 90–96.
261. Oscar Storonov, letter to Le Corbusier, 1932, Fondation Le Corbusier, Paris: cited by Jean-Louis Cohen, *Le Corbusier & the Mystique of the USSR* , Princeton: Princeton University Press, 1992, p. 198.
262. See Moritz Kahn, *The Design & Construction of Industrial Buildings*, London: Technical Journals Ltd., 1917.
263. See W. Hawkins Ferry, *The Legacy of Albert Kahn*, Detroit: The Detroit Institute of Arts,1970, pp. 24, 118–119; Grant Hildebrand, *Designing for Industry: the Architecture of Albert Kahn*, Cambridge, Mass. and London: MIT Press, 1974, pp. 128–130. "L'usine de tracteurs de Tchéliabinsk," *L'URSS en construction*, no. 8, August 1933.
264. I. Kassianenko, "Ispolzovanie amerikanskogo opyta v period stanovlenia sovetskogo promyshlennogo zodchestva (sotrudnichestvo s firmoi Alberta Kahna)," in O. E. Tuganov, *Vzaimodeistvie kultur*, pp. 111–120.
265. A. L. Drabkin, "American Architects and Engineers in Russia," *Pencil Points*, June 1930, pp. 435–440.
266. Maurice Hindus, "Pinch Hitter for the Soviets," *American Magazine*, April 1932, pp. 31–136. See the *Tempo* text in Eugene C. Lyons, *Six Soviet Plays*, New York: Houghton-Mifflin, 1934, pp. 157–224.
267. Louis-Ferdinand Céline, *Mea Culpa*, Paris: Denoël et Steele, 1936, p. 15.
268. Ludwig Hilberseimer, *Großstadtarchitektur*, Stuttgart: Julius Hoffmann, 1927; Bruno Taut, *Die neue Baukunst in Europa und Amerika*, Stuttgart: Julius Hoffmann, 1929; In English: *Modern Architecture*, London: The Studio, 1929.
269. Mendelsohn's interest in Nietzsche is reflected in correspondence with his fiancée, Louise, which is to be found at the Getty Center for the History of Art and the Humanities (information given by Fritz Neumeyer).
270. See my afterword to the French edition of this book: Erich Mendelsohn, *Amerika, livre d'images d'un architecte*, Paris: Éditions du Demi-Cercle, 1992, pp. 225–241.
271. Herman George Scheffauer, "Dynamic Architecture: New Forms of the Future," *The Dial*, n° 70, March 1921, pp. 323–328. On Scheffauer's contribution to *Amerikanismus*, see Herman George Scheffauer, *Das Land Gottes: Das Gesicht des neuen Amerika*, Hanover, P. Steegemann, 1923.
272. Erich Mendelsohn, "Die internationale Übereinstimmung des neuen Baugedankens oder Dynamik und Funktion ," *Architectura et Amicitia*, 2–9 February 1924, pp. 5–14, reprinted in *Das Gesamtschaffen des Architekten*, op. cit., p. 33.
273. Erich Mendelsohn, "Das Schiff," *Baukunst*, vol. 2, n° 3, April 1926, p. 92.
274. Erich Mendelsohn, "New York: 16. Oktober 1924, An Bord der *Deutschland*," in Oskar Beyer (introduction), *Erich Mendelsohn; Briefe eines Architekten*, Munich, Prestel-Verlag, 1961, p. 60. Engl. trans.: Oskar Beyer, ed., *Erich Mendelsohn: Letters of an Architect*, trans. Geoffrey Strachan, intro. by Nikolaus Pevsner, London, New York, and Toronto: Abelard-Schuman, 1967, p. 67.
275. Fritz Lang interviewed in Peter Bogdanovich, *Fritz Lang in America*, London: Studio Vista © Movie Magazine, 1967. Republished in New York: Praeger, 1969.
276. Fritz Lang, "Was ich in Amerika sah," *Film-Kurier*, n° 292, 11 December 1924.
277. Erich Mendelsohn, "New York: 16. Oktober," in Beyer, ed., *Erich Mendelsohn, Letters of an Architect*, pp. 67–68.
278. Initially close to De Stijl, active in Berlin in early 1920, Knud Lonberg-Holm (1895–1972) emigrated in 1923. A friend of Richard Buckminster Fuller, in the thirties he published the review *Shelter* in Philadelphia, before becoming research director for *Sweet*'s catalogue.
279. Knud Lonberg-Holm, "Amerika," *ABC Beiträge zum Bauen*, n° 1, 1924, p. 1.
280. In his memoirs, Lewis Mumford recalled having visited buildings of the Chicago School with Barry Byrne, who also showed them to Mendelsohn: Lewis Mumford, *Sketches from Life*, New York: The Dial Press, 1982, p. 429.
281. Richard Neutra, letter to Frances Toplitz, Taliesin, November 1924 in *Richard Neutra, Promise and Fulfillment, 1919–1932, Selections from the Letters and Diaries of Richard and Dione Neutra*, ed. and trans. Dione Neutra, Carbondale and Edwardsville: Southern Illinois University Press, 1986, p. 130.
282. Thomas Hines, *Richard Neutra and the Search for Modern Architecture; A Biography and History*, New York: Oxford University Press, 1982, p. 55.

283. Erich Mendelsohn, "New-York," *Berliner Tageblatt*, 3 January 1925, p. 5.
284. Erich Mendelsohn, "Besuch bei Wright," Baukunst, vol. 2, n° 1, 1926, p. 56; "Frank Lloyd Wright," in Henricus Th. Wijdeveld, *The Life-Work of the American Architect Frank Lloyd Wright*, Sandpoort, 1925, pp. 96–100; reprinted in *Wasmuths Monatshefte*, 1926, pp. 244–246.
285. Banham credits Rudolf Mosse with this "extravagance" (24 cm wide x 35 cm high): Reyner Banham, "Erich Mendelsohn, *Amerika, Bilderbuch eines Architekten*," *Journal of the Society of Architectural Historians*, vol. 38, 1979, n° 3, pp. 300–301.
286. Erich Mendelsohn, "Pittsburgh, 22. Oktober 1924," in *Briefe eines Architektens*, p. 67; cited in part in *Amerika*, p. 110.
287. Taylor, "New York et l'origine du *Skyline*."
288. El Lissitzky, "Glaz arkhitektora," *Stroitelnaia Promychlennost*, n° 2, February 1926, pp. 144–146. Engl. trans.: El Lissitzky, "The Architect's Eye," in *Photography in the Modern Era: European Documents and Critical Writings, 1913–40*, ed. Christopher Phillips, New York: Metropolitan Museum of Art/Aperture, 1989, pp. 221–226.
289. Phillips, ed., *Photography in the Modern Era*, p. 222. Lissitzky certainly had the opportunity to discuss Mendelsohn's travels when they met in Moscow in 1925: Letter to Sophie Küppers, Moscow: 18 October 1925, in Sophie Lissitzky-Küppers, ed., *El Lissitzky: Life, Letters, Texts*, London and New York: Thames & Hudson, 1980, p. 66.
290. The pagination is that of the 1926 edition of *Amerika*.
291. See photograph of the Saint Nicholas church in Malá Strana, Prague, published in Giuliano Gresleri, *Le Corbusier Viaggio in Oriente*, Venice, Marsilio, Paris: Fondation Le Corbusier, 1984, p. 133.
292. Aleksandr Rodchenko, "The Paths of Modern Photography," in Phillips, ed., *Photography in the Modern Era*, p. 261. Originally: Aleksandr Rodchenko: "Puti sovremmenoi fotografie," *Novyi Lef*, n° 9, 1928, p. 34. On Rodchenko's use of low- and high-angle shots, see Aleksandr N. Lavrentiev, *Rakursy Rodchenko*, Moscow: Iskusstvo, 1992, pp. 70–77, and Christopher Phillips, "Resurrecting Vision: The New Photography in Europe between the Wars," in *The New Vision: Photography between the World Wars*. New York: Metropolitan Museum of Art/Abrams, 1989, Rodchenko, pp. 82–85.
293. On this, see Christopher Phillips, "Twenties Photography: Mastering Urban Space," in Jean Clair, ed., *The 1920's: Age of the Metropolis*, Montreal, Museum of Fine Arts, 1991, pp. 209-225.
294. Bertolt Brecht, *Gesammelte Werke*, Frankfurt, Suhrkamp, 1967, vol. 15, p. 76, cited in Patty Lee Parmalee, *Brecht's America*, Miami: Miami University Press, 1981, p. 70.
295. Brecht, *Gesammelte Werke*, vol. 18, pp. 51–52.
296. Erich Mendelsohn, letter to Lewis Mumford, Berlin-Charlottenburg, 24 December 1925, published in Beyer, ed., *Erich Mendelsohn: Letters of an Architect*, p. 89.
297. Of the specialist review, see for example *Der Cicerone*, vol. 18, n° 5, March 1926, pp. 174–176; *Die Form*, vol. 1, March 1926, p. 132; Hermann Soergel, *Baukunst*, vol. 2, n° 4, 1926, p. 132; *Der Kunstwart*, vol. 40, September 1927, p. 408; E. Langlotz, *Zeitschrift für bildende Kunst*, vol. 61, 1927, supplt., p. H6; A. Stange, *Kunst und Handwerk*, vol. 77, 927, p. 44.
298. Aleksandr Pasternak, "Amerika," *Sovremennaia Arkhitektura*, n° 4, 1926, pp. 92–94.
299. 23 plates were added to the 77 of the first edition.
300. The mysterious origin of the photograph on page 131 was also elucidated, since Mendelsohn admitted that Fritz Lang.gave it to him.
301. László Moholy-Nagy, *Malerei Photographie Film*, Munich: Albert Langen Verlag, 1925, p. 129. This photograph is on page 77.
302. "America, reflections by Knud Lonberg-Holm," *i 10*, n° 15, October 1928, pp. 49–55.
303. Essentially Mendelsohn's office head, Karweik also designed personal projects, including the one which he entered into the 1925 competition for the development of the Unter den Linden district in Berlin. Karweik writes of his travels in correspondence with Lonberg-Holm: Lonberg-Holm Archives, New York.
304. Adolf Behne, "Kultur, Kunst und Reklame," *Das neue Frankfurt*, vol. 1, n° 3, January 1927, pp. 57–64. These correspond to pp. 77, 131, and 163 of *Amerika*. Behne credits Lonberg-Holm with photo 77 and Mendelsohn with 163, although he does not attribute 131.
305. Two of these collages are reproduced in *El Lissitzky (1890–1941) Architect, Painter, Photographer, Typographer*, Eindhoven: van Abbe Museum/New York: Thames & Hudson, 1990, pp. 178–179.
306. El Lissitzky, *Rußland, die Rekonstruktion der Architektur in der Sowjetunion*, Vienna: Anton Schroll u. Co, 1930, pp. 72, 77, 84, 85.
307. Bruno Zevi, *Erich Mendelsohn; Opera Completa*, Milan: Etas/Kompass, 1970, p. 110. Zevi underlines the "syntactic decomposition" of the city block in these sketches. Cf. Sigrid Achenbach, *Erich Mendelsohn 1887–1953; Ideen, Bauten, Projekte*, Berlin: Staatliche Museen Preussischer Kulturbesitz, 1987, pp. 58–59.
308. Erich Mendelsohn, *Russland, Europa, Amerika; ein architektonischer Querschnitt,* Berlin: Rudolf Mosse, 1929.
309. Of anti-American pamphlets, see esp. Adolf Halfelds, *Amerika und der Amerikanismus, Kritische Betrachtungen eines Deutschen und Europäers,* Jena: Eugen Diederichs, 1927.
310. The Swiss Werner Moser, who was working with Wright at the time, subsequently returned to Europe. In 1926 he published a Functionalist Chicago building designed two years previously: *ABC Beiträge zum Bauen*, 2d series, n° 3, 1926, p. 5.
311. Richard Neutra, letter to Frances Toplitz, 26 November 1924, cited in T. Hines, *Richard Neutra and the Search for Modern Architecture*, p. 55.
312. Richard Neutra, *Wie baut Amerika?*, Stuttgart: Julius Hoffmann, 1927.
313. Richard Neutra, *Life and Shape*, New York: Appleton-Century-Crofts, 1962, p. 189.
314. Richard Neutra, letter to Rudolf Schindler, Vienna, 15 July 1920, cited in Esther McCoy, *Vienna to Los Angeles: Two Journeys*, Santa Monica: Arts and Architecture Press, 1979, p. 127.
315. Neutra, *Wie baut Amerika?*, p. 1.
316. Neutra, *Life and shape*, p. 194.
317. Neutra, *Wie baut Amerika?*, p. 47.
318. Hitchcock compared Neutra to Gropius, Mies van der Rohe, and Le Corbusier: Henry-Russell Hitchcock, "How America Builds," *Architectural Record*, vol. 63, June 1928, pp. 594–595.
319. This translation was prefaced by the academician Aleksei Shchusev: Richard Neutra, *Kak stroit Amerika?*, Moscow: MAKIZ, 1929. In the controversy over urbanism and "deurbanism," the economist Georgi Puzis recommended the adoption of collective housing, as recommended by Neutra: "Sotsialisticheskii sposob rasselenia i sotsialisticheskii tip zhilia," *Vestnik komunisticheskoi akademii*, n° 37–38, 1930, pp. 344–388.
320. Richard Neutra, *Amerika; Die Stilbildung des neuen Bauens in den Vereinigten Staaten*, Vienna: Anton Schroll Verlag, 1930. On the collection as a whole, see "Neues Bauen in der Welt," *Rassegna*, n° 38, 1989.
321. Julius Posener, "L'Architecture nouvelle dans le monde entier," *L'Architecture d'aujourd'hui*, vol. 1, n° 5, April-May 1931, p. 80.
322. Richard Neutra, "Hoch-, Mittel- und Flachbau unter amerikanischen Verhältnissen, in *rationelle bebauungsweisen, ergebnisse des 3. internationalen kongresses für neues bauen (brüssel, november 1930)*, Stuttgart: Julius Hoffmann, 1931, pp. 58–63.
323. Anna-Maria Mazzuchelli, "Richard J. Neutra," *Casabella*, n° 85, January 1935, pp. 18–19.
324. Vladimir Maiakovsky, "Ranshe, teper," 1921, in *Polnoe sobranie sochinenii*, Moscow, 1955–1958, v. II, p. 98, cited in H. Rogger, "*Amerikanizm* and the Economic Development of Russia," p. 382. Tetiushi and Shuia are Russian provincial towns.
325. Carol Avins, *Border Crossings: The West and Russian Identity in Soviet Literature 1917–1934*, Berkeley and Los Angeles: University of California Press, 1983, pp. 48 *et. seq.*
326. Leon Trotsky, *Literatura i Revoliutsia*, Moscow: 1924, pp. 114–115. Cf. Charles Rougle, *Three Russians consider America: America in the works of Maksim Gor'kij, Aleksandr Blok and Vladimir Majakovskij*, Stockholm: Almqvist & Wiksell International, 1976, p. 115.
327. V. Seltsov, "Amerika v voobrazhenii russkogo, lektsia V. Maiakovskogo," *Novyi Mir* (New York), 8 October 1925, cited in Rougle, *Three Russians consider America*, p. 111.
328. Sergei Esenin, *Sobranie sochinenii v piati tomakh*, Moscow: 1962, v. 4, p. 258, cited in Rougle, *Three Russians consider America*, p. 117. Tula is the capital of Russia's metallurgical industries. On this trip, see: Gordon McVay, *Isadora & Esenin*, Ann Arbor: Ardis, 1980.
329. Semion Kemrad, *Maiakovsky v Amerike, stranitsi biografii*, Moscow: Sovetskii Pisatel, 1970, p. 17.
330. Vladimir Maiakovsky, "Brooklyn Bridge," in *Poems*, Moscow: Progress Publishers, 1972, pp. 60–63.
331. "Not Big Enough, Says Le Corbusier at First Sight," *New York Herald Tribune*, 22 October 1935, p. 21.
332. "Russia's Dynamic Poet Finds New York Tame; We're Old Fashioned, Unorganized, to Maiakovsky," *New York World*, 9 August 1925.
333. Vladimir Maiakovsky, "Broadway," *Polnoe sobranie sochinenii*, Moscow: Khudojestvennaia Literatura, 1955–1961, vol. 7, p. 57.
334. Vladimir Maiakovsky, *Moio otkrytie Ameriki*, Moscow: Gosudarstvennoe Izdatelstvo, 1926.
335. "Rodchenko v Parizhe: iz pisem domoi," *Novyi Lef*, n° 2, 1927, pp. 15–16.
336. Victor Shklovsky, Vsevolod Ivanov, *Iprit*, Moscow: Gosizdat, 1925.
337. Nikolai Bukharin, *Pravda*, 1923, cited in Avins, *Border Crossings*, p. 55. On Bukharin's stay in New York: see Stephen Cohen, *Bukharin and the Bolshevik Revolution; A Political Biography*, New York: Alfred A. Knopf, 1973, pp. 43–44.
338. Jim Dollar, *Mess-Mend, ili yanki v Petrograde, Roman-skazka*, Moscow: Gosizdat, 1924–25.
339. David Ward and Olivier Zunz, eds., *The Landscape of Modernity, Essays on New York City 1900–1940*, New York: Russell Sage Foundation, 1992.
340. Thomas Adams, *The Building of the City*, New York: Regional Plan of New York and its Environs, 1931. On the aims and methods of this plan, see Thomas Adams, *Planning the New York Region, an Outline of the Organization, Scope and Progress of the Regional Plan*, New York: Regional Plan of New York and its Environs, 1927. Cf. Michael Simpson, "Thomas Adams 1871–1940," in *Pioneers of British Town-Planning*, ed. Gordon E. Cherry, London: The Architectural Press, 1981, pp. 19–45.
341. Raymond Unwin, "New York and its Environs as a Regional Planning Problem from the European Point of View," in *Plan of New York and its Environs, Report of Progress*, New York: 1923, pp. 13–22.
342. Lewis Mumford, "The Plan of New York:" *The New Republic*, 15 June 1932, pp. 121–126 and 22 June 1932, pp.146–154.
343. Gaston Bardet, *Problèmes d'urbanisme*, Paris: Dunod, 1941, p. 55.
344. "Le gratte-ciel américain," *Acier*, n° 3, 1931 (published by the Office Technique pour l'Utilisation de l'Acier).
345. Hugh Ferriss, *The Metropolis of Tomorrow*, New York: Ives Washburn, 1929.
346. Gail Fenske, Deryck Holdsworth, "Corporate Identity and the New York Office Building"; Carol Willis, "Form follows Finance: The Empire State Building," in D. Ward, O. Zunz, eds., *The Landscape of Modernity*, pp. 129–159 and 160–187.
347. On this convergence, see M. Tafuri, *The Sphere and the Labyrinth*, pp. 219–233.
348. Hans von Poellnik, "Der Schrei nach dem Turmhaus," *Bauwelt*, vol. 12, n° 47, 20 November 1921, p. 1.
349. K. Paul Andrae, drawing, "Das grössere Berlin VIII," *Wasmuths Monatshefte für Baukunst*, vol. 7, 1922–1923, pp. 382.
350. On the role of the skyscraper in postwar German culture, see "Zur Entwicklung des Hochhauses in Deutschland," *Deutsche Bauzeitung*, vol. 55, 5 March 1921, pp. 89–95; Martin Mächler, "Zum Problem des Wolkenkratzers," *Wasmuths Monatshefte für Baukunst*, vol. 5, 1920–1921, pp. 191–194 et 241–244.
351. On this competition, see Florian Zimmermann, ed., *Der Schrei nach dem Turmhaus, Der Ideenwettbewerb Hochhaus am Bahnhof Friedrichstrasse Berlin 1921/1922*, Berlin: Argon-Verlag, 1988.
352. Mies van der Rohe, "Hochhäuser," *Frühlicht*, 1, n° 4, 1922, pp. 122–124; in Fritz Niemeyer, *The Artless Word: Mies van der Rohe on the Building Art*, Cambridge, Mass.: MIT Press, 1991, p. 240.
353. Walter Curt Behrendt, "Skyscrapers in Germany," *Journal of the American Institute of Architects*, September 1923, p. 366.
354. Ludwig Hilberseimer, "Architektur," *Das Kunstblatt*, n° 6, 1922, p. 132.
355. Otto Kohtz, "Das Reichshaus am Königsplatz in Berlin: ein Vorschlag zur Verringerung der Wohnungsnot und der Arbeitslosigkeit," *Stadtbaukunst alter und neuer Zeit*, 1920, pp. 241–245; *Büroturmhäuser*, Berlin:1921.
356. Hartmut Frank, "Melancholische, papierne Märchen; der Wettbewerb für eine Messehaus 1924–1925," in *Das ungebaute Hamburg*, ed. Ulrich Höhns, Hamburg: Junius Verlag, 1991, pp. 68–77.
357. On this revealing competition, see esp. Manfredo Tafuri, "The Disenchanted Mountain: The Skyscraper and the City," in Giorgio Ciucci, Francesco Dal Co, Mario Manieri-Elia, Manfredo Tafuri, *The American City from the Civil War to the New Deal*, trans. Barbara Luigia La Penta, Cambridge, Mass.: MIT Press, 1979, pp. 389–528. Robert Bruegmann, "When

Worlds Collided: European and American Entries to the *Chicago Tribune* Competition of 1922," in J. Zukowsky, *Chicago Architecture 1872–1922*, pp. 301–317.
358. *The International Competition for a New Administration Building for the* Chicago Tribune, Chicago: The Tribune Co, 1923.
359. Adolf Loos, *The* Chicago Tribune *Column*, Nice: self-published, 1922; cited in Heinrich Kulka, *Adolf Loos; das Werk des Architekten*, Vienna: A. Schroll Verlag, 1931, pp. 37–38.
360. Louis Sullivan, "The *Chicago Tribune* Competition," *The Architectural Record*, vol. 53, February 1923, pp. 151–157.
361. Giorgio Muratore, "Métamorphose d'un mythe: 1922–1943; le gratte-ciel américain et ses reflets sur la culture architecturale italienne," *Archithese*, n° 18, 1976, pp. 28–36.
362. This project was published in Piero Portaluppi, *Aedilitia*, Milan-Rome: self-published, 1927. Cf. Guglielmo Bilancioni, *Aedilitia di Piero Portaluppi*, Milan: CittàStudi, 1993.
363. Hendricus Theodorus Wijdeveld, "Inleiding voor de Torenhuis-projecten," *Wendingen*, n° 3, 1923, p. 3.
364. See Johannes Duiker, *Studie over hoogbouw*, Rotterdam: 1930.
365. Le Corbusier, "Dates," *Almanach d'architecture moderne*, Paris: G. Crès & Cie, 1925, p. 187.
366. P. de L., "Une maison de dix étages; terrasse fleurie; l'hôtel des sportsmen," *La Patrie*, 21 June 1905.
367. *L'Intransigeant*, 25 November 1920, p. 4.
368. Auguste Perret, cited by M. Pays, "Esthétique urbaine; l'adaptation des villes aux exigences de la vie contemporaine," *Excelsior*, 25 August 1921, p. 3.
369. Auguste Perret, cited by Raymond Cogniat, "La ville de demain, l'opinion de M. Perret," *Comœdia*, 29 August 1922, p. 1. Notwithstanding Perret's strenuous denials, the cruciform has been compared to American examples in Roberto Gargiani, *Auguste Perret; la théorie et l'œuvre*, Paris: Gallimard/Electa, 1994, p. 235.
370. Auguste Perret, cited by J. Labadié, "Les cathédrales de la cité moderne," *L'Illustration*, vol. 80, n° 4145, 12 August 1922, p. 132.
371. Auguste Perret, cited in J. Labadié, "À la recherche du 'home scientifique'," *La Science et la vie*, vol. 28, 1925, n° 102, p. 555.
372. Le Corbusier, "Dates," p. 186.
373. Francesco Passanti, "Le Corbusier et le gratte-ciel; aux origines du plan Voisin," in *Américanisme et modernité*, pp. 171–189.
374. A cutting from this unidentified paper was published in *Almanach d'architecture moderne:* Le Corbusier, "Dates," p. 188.
375. Duhamel, *Scènes de la vie future*, p. 245.
376. Richard Pommer, "'More a Necropolis than a Metropolis', Ludwig Hilberseimer's Highrise City and Modern City Planning," in *In the shadow of Mies: Ludwig Hilberseimer, architect, educator, and urban planner*, ed. Richard Pommer, Chicago: the Art Institute of Chicago/ Rizzoli, 1988, pp. 16–53. Marco De Michelis, ed., *Ludwig Hilberseimer 1885–1967*, Rassegna: n° 27, 1979.
377. Hilberseimer, *Großstadtarchitektur*, pp. 62–68.
378. Martin Wagner, "Ein Generalplan für Hochhäuser," 1929, reproduced in *Martin Wagner 1885–1957; Wohnungsbau und Weltstadtplanung*, pp. 108–110.
379. Ludwig Hilberseimer, *Das neue Berlin*: February 1929, pp. 39–40. See also Paul Westheim, "Umgestaltung des Alexanderplatzes," *Bauwelt*, vol. 20, n° 13, 1929, pp. 312–313.
380. Wassili Luckhardt, "Stand der moderner Baugesinnung in Amerika," *Bauwelt*, vol. 20, n° 46, November 1929, pp. 1118–1134; republished in: Achim Wendschuh, *Brüder Luckhardt und Alfons Anker*, Berlin: Akademie der Künste, 1990, pp. 123–125.
381. Aleksandr Pasternak, "Urbanizm," *Sovremennaia Arkhitektura*, n° 2, 1926, pp. 4–7.
382. Boris Korshunov, "Noveishie vzgliady na gorodskoe stroitelstvo," *Stroitelnaia Promyshlennost*, n° 12, 1925, pp. 874–875 and n° 2, 1926, pp. 147–148.
383. Selim Khan-Magomedov, *Pioneers of Soviet Architecture: The Search for New Solutions in the 1920s and 1930s*, New York: Rizzoli, 1987, pp. 141–143. Originally published as *Pioniere der Sowjetischen Architektur*, Dresden, VEB Verlag der Kunst, 1983.
384. These projects were published in *Arkhitektura, raboty Arkhitekturnogo fakulteta Vkhutemasa 1920–1927*, Moscow: Izd. Vkhutemasa, 1927, pp. 10, 12.
385. Nael (N. A. Ladovsky), "Neboskrioby SSSR i Ameriki," *Izvestiia ASNOVA*, n° 1 (the only issue), 1926, n. p.
386. Iakov Chernikhov, "Gorod neboskriobov," *Osnovy sovremennoi arkhitektury*, Leningrad, Izd. Leningradskogo O-va Arkhitektorov, 1930, ill. n° 100.
387. Iakov Chernikhov, "Gorod gigantskikh neboskriobov," *Arkhitekturnye fantazii*, Leningrad, Leningradskoe Ot. Vses. Poligraficheskogo Soiuza, 1933, ill. n° 10.
388. "Dom-gigant v Niu-Iorke," I. Chernikhov, *Osnovy*, ill. 223 a.
389. El Lissitzky, "'*Amerikanizm* v evropeiskoi Arkhitekture," *Krasnaia Niva*, Moscow, n° 49, 1925.
390. Lissitzky-Küppers, *El Lissitzky*, p. 369. Originally published as "Arkhitektura zheleznoi i zhelezobetonnoi ramy," *Stroitelnaia promychlennost*, n° 1, 1926, pp. 59–63.
391. On the Constructivists' initial theoretical positions, see Christina Lodder, *Russian Constructivism*, London and New Haven: Yale University Press, 1983. On OSA, see: S. Frederick Starr, "OSA: The Union of Contemporary Architects," in George Gibian, H. W. Tjalsma, *Russian Modernism, Culture and the Avant-Garde, 1900–1930*, London and Ithaca, NY: Cornell University Press, 1976, pp. 188–208; Hugh D. Hudson, Jr., "'The Social Condenser of Our Epoch': The Association of Contemporary Architects and the Creation of a New Way of Life in Revolutionary Russia," *Jahrbücher für Geschichte Osteuropas*, vol. 34, 1986, n° 4, pp. 557–583.
392. Aleksei Gan, *Konstruktivizm*, Tver, Tverskoe Idz-vo, 2ia Tipografia, 1922, in *Russian Art of the Avant-Garde: Theory and Criticism, 1902–1934*, trans. and ed. by John E. Bowlt, New York: Viking Press, 1976, pp. 214–225.
393. Ginzburg, *Style and Epoch*, p. 70.
394. Ivan Lamtsov and F. Shalavin were not slow to denounce OSA's Americanist tendencies: "O levoi fraze v arkhitekture (k voprosu ob ideologii konstruktivizma)", *Krasnaia Nov*, n° 8, 1927, pp. 226–239.
395. "Kritika konstruktivizma," *Sovremennaia Arkhitektura*, vol. 3, n° 1, 1928, p. 14. This unsigned article seems to have been written by Ginzburg himself.
396. On the Constructivists' "objective" methods, see Catherine Cooke, "Form is a Function X: The Development of the Constructivist Architect's Design Method," *Architectural Design*, n° 53, 1983, pp. 34–49.
397. Albert Kelsey, *Program and rules for second competition for the selection of an architect for the monumental lighthouse [. . .] to the memory of Christopher Columbus*, Washington, Pan-American Union, 1931.
398. "Dom promyshlennosti," *Sovremennaia arkhitektura*, vol. 5, 1930, n° 4, pp. 1–2, 9.
399. For a description of these, see G. Chalmarès, "Divertissements forains," *La Nature*, 3 July 1909, pp. 75–76.
400. Bertrand Lemoine, "Le déplacement des portes de Paris vers l'ouest, le concours de la porte Maillot 1931," *Les portes de la ville*, Paris: CCI and Centre Georges Pompidou, 1983, pp. 60–69.
401. Léonard Rosenthal, letter to Le Corbusier, Paris: 27 February 1930, Fondation Le Corbusier, R (3).1
402. L. R. (Léonard Rosenthal), "Transformation de la porte Maillot en une entrée monumentale de Paris," Société du Salon d'Automne, *Catalogue des ouvrages de peinture, sculpture, dessin, gravure...*, Paris: Impr. E. Puyfourcat, 1931, p. 309.
403. Rob. Mallet-Stevens, cited by Emmanuel de Thubert, "Le concours Rosenthal," *La Construction moderne*, 27 March 1932, p. 415.
404. Jean-François Pinchon, *Rob. Mallet-Stevens, architecture, mobilier, décoration*, Paris: Action Artistique de Paris: Philippe Sers, 1986, pp. 62–63.
405. Maurice Culot and Lise Grenier, *Henri Sauvage 1873–1932*, Brussells, Archives d'Architecture Moderne, 1976, 199–201.
406. Two sketches from this project are to be found in Jean-Louis Cohen, André Lortie, *Des fortifs au périf, Paris: les seuils de la ville*, Paris: Pavillon de l'Arsenal, Picard, 1992, p. 248.
407. Le Corbusier and Pierre Jeanneret, letter to Léonard Rosenthal, Paris: 2 April 1930, Fondation Le Corbusier, R (3) 1.
408. He justified his reserve by citing public opinion: Léonard Rosenthal, letter to Le Corbusier, Paris: 19 May 1930, Fondation Le Corbusier, R (3) 1.
409. Henri Descamps, "La démolition des fortifications de Paris: aménagement de la porte Maillot," *La Construction Moderne*, 1930–1931, pp. 187–191.
410. "Paris: aménagement de la porte Maillot," *L'Architecture*, 15 July 1931, p. 178.
411. Ville de Paris: département de la Seine, *Concours pour l'aménagement de la voie triomphale allant de la place de l'Etoile au rond-point de la Défense*, Paris: Editions d'Art Charles Moreau, n.d. (1932), p. 5.
412. On this point, see Isabelle Gournay, "L'École des Beaux-Arts et la modernità: il 'grand tour' americano (1926–39)," *Casabella*, n° 493, July–August 1983, pp. 40–47; Isabelle Gournay, *France Discovers America 1917–1939*, New Haven: Yale University, 1989, PhD thesis; and "Retours d'Amérique (1918–1940): les voyages de trois générations d'architectes français," Cohen and Damisch, eds., *Américanisme et modernité*, pp. 295–316.
413. Such views of the Chrysler Building were published in Marcel Chappey, *Architecture internationale II*, Paris: Vincent, Fréal & Cie, 1931, p. 57.
414. Eugène Beaudouin, "Urbanisme et architecture en USA," *L'Architecture d'aujourd'hui*, n° 9, November–December 1933, pp. 54–68.
415. Raymond Lopez, "1700 kilomètres à travers les États-Unis," *Bulletin mensuel de la SADG*, n° 11, 1 June 1936, pp. 183–185.
416. *Marcel Lods 1891–1978; photographies d'architecte*, Paris: CNAC Georges Pompidou, 1991, n.p.
417. Paul Nelson, *La Cité hospitalière de Lille*, Paris: Éditions *Cahiers d'Art*, 1933 (photographs by Man Ray).
418. See esp. "Procédés nord-américains de construction métallique d'immeubles," *Acier*, 1929, n° 3, Paris: Office Technique pour l'Utilization de l'Acier.
419. F. W. Fitzpatrick, "Les skyscrapers," *la Construction moderne*, 12 October 1907, pp. 19–21.
420. Donat-Alfred Agache, *La remodélation d'une capitale*, Paris: Société Coopérative d'Architectes, 1932.
421. Général d'Amade, letter prefacing Joseph Goulven, *Casablanca de 1889 à nos jours*, Casablanca, Flandrin, 1928.
422. Léandre Vaillat, *Le visage français du Maroc*, Paris: Horizons de France, 1931, p. 5.
423. See Jean-Louis Cohen and Monique Eleb, *Casablanca, laboratoire de la modernité architecturale et urbaine (1900–1960)*, Paris: Laboratoire Architecture, culture, société, XIXe–XXe s., Bureau de la Recherche Architecturale, 1993.
424. On this unique realization, see "Le centre urbain de Villeurbanne," *L'Illustration*, 9 June 1934, pp. 210–212. "Le nouveau centre de Villeurbanne," *Urbanisme*, n° 16, 1933, pp. 211–215; Georges-Henri Pingusson, "Le nouveau Villeurbanne," *L'Architecture d'aujourd'hui*, September 1934, pp. 6–13; and more recently, *Villeurbanne-gratte-ciel, où la banlieue devient ville*, Villeurbanne, Le Nouveau Musée, 1984.
425. Koolhaas, *Delirious New York*, pp. 235–282; Mardges Bacon, "Le Corbusier et l'Amérique: première rencontre" and Mary McLeod, "Le rêve transi de Le Corbusier: l'Amérique 'catastrophe féerique,'" in Cohen and Damisch, eds., *Américanisme et modernité*, pp. 191–207 and 209–227.
426. Le Corbusier, *Urbanisme*, Paris: G. Crès & Cie, 1925, p. 144; Werner Hegemann, letter to Le Corbusier, 12 March 1924, Fondation Le Corbusier, A 1(4).
427. Anna Maria Zorgno, *Fiorini-Le Corbusier 1931–1935*, Turin, Centre Culturel Français and Politecnico di Torino and SN delle Officine di Savigliano, 1988.
428. Le Corbusier, "Descartes est-il américain?," *Plans*, n° 7, July 1931, pp. 49–64.
429. Le Corbusier, *Quand les cathédrales étaient blanches, voyage au pays des timides*, Paris: Plon, 1937; Engl. trans.: *When the Cathedrals Were White*, New York: McGraw-Hill, 1964. (c) Reynal & Hitchcock, 1947.
430. "Not Big Enough, Says Le Corbusier at First Sight," *New York Herald Tribune*, 22 October 1935.
431. From Raoul Glaber's writings, as quoted in Le Corbusier, *Cathedrals*, p. 28.
432. Le Corbusier, *Cathedrals*, p. xxii
433. Ibid., pp. 20, 26.
434. Ibid., pp. 32, 37, 68, 111.
435. Ibid., p. 148.
436. On New York: see ibid., pp. 95, 36, 44, 89, 72, 192, 86, 156, 111, 42, 87, 91, 157, 84.
437. Ibid., pp. 41, 51, 63, 54.
438. Ibid., pp. 109, 112–13, 51, 59, 61, 189, 191, 89.
439. Ibid., pp. 76, 77, 136.
440. Ibid., 153, 214, 152.
441. Ibid., pp. 140, 139, 135, 110, 138, 134, 142, 144, 165–166. For the image of the American "girl" in French literature, see Theodore Zeldin, *France 1848–1945*, vol. 2: *Intellect, Taste, and Anxiety*, Oxford: Clarendon Press, 1977, pp. 129–138; and esp. Th. Bentzon, *Les Américaines chez elles, notes de voyage*, Paris: Calmann Lévy, 1895.
442. Le Corbusier, *Cathedrals*, pp. 105–107.
443. This chapter was excised from the American translation. In Plon's 1937 French edition *op. cit.*, it is found on pp. 153–56.
444. Le Corbusier, *Cathedrals*, pp. 56, 67, 185.
445. Frank Lloyd Wright, "Kak ia rabotaiu," *Arkhitektura SSSR*, vol. 2, n° 2, February 1934, pp. 70–71.

446. David Arkin, *Arkhitektura sovremennogo zapada*, Moscow: OGIZ-IZOGIZ, 1932.
447. Isaac Eigel, *Boris Iofan*, Moscow: Stroiizdat, 1978, p. 99. Boris Iofan, "Materialy o sovremennoi arkhitekture SShA i Italii," *Akademia Arkhitektury* n° 4, 1936, pp. 13–47.
448. Vladimir Shchuko, "Planirovka i arkhitektura, iz zagranichnykh vpechatlenii," *Pravda*, 20 April 1935, p. 2, reprinted in *Mastera arkhitektury ob arkhitekture*, ed. Mikhail Barkhin and Yuri Iaralov, Moscow: Iskusstvo, 1975, v. 1, pp. 268–272. Shchuko's diary is to be found at the Shchusev Museum in Moscow.
449. Arkin, *Arkhitektura sovremennogo zapada*, pp. 118–124.
450. Lewis Mumford, *Sticks and Stones: a study of American architecture and civilization*, New York: W. W. Norton & Co., 1924.
451. David Arkin, "Amerikanskaia arkhitektura i kniga Mumforda," preface to Lewis Mumford, *Ot brevenchatogo doma do neboskrioba, ocherk istorii amerikanskoi arkhitektury*, Moscow, Izd. Vses. akademii Arkhitektury, 1936, pp. 15–16. Originally Lewis Mumford, *Sticks and Stones; a Study of American Architecture and Civilization*, New York: Boni and Liveright, 1924.
452. When he republished his preface in 1941, Arkin entitled it "The Skyscraper": David Arkin, "Neboskriob," *Obrazy arkhitektury*, Moscow: Gos. arkhitekturnoe Izd. Ak. Arkh. SSSR, 1941, pp. 313–330.
453. Ibid., pp. 4–5.
454. Ibid., p. 7.
455. Ibid., pp. 10–11.
456. Frank Lloyd Wright, "Address to the Architects' World Congress—Soviet Russia 1937," *An Autobiography*, New York: Horizon Press, 1977, p. 573. This passage from Wright's intervention was included neither in *Izvestiia*, which published extracts on 26 June 1937, nor in *Arkhitektura SSSR*, which did the same in n° 7–8, 1937, pp. 49–50. On Wright's journey to the USSR, see Donald Leslie Johnson, "Frank Lloyd Wright in Moscow," *Journal of the Society of Architectural Historians*, March 1987, pp. 65–79; and *Frank Lloyd Wright versus America: The 1930s*, Cambridge, Mass. and London: MIT Press, pp. 209–230.
457. In this article, Wright juxtaposed criticisms of official Soviet architecture with praises of "comrade Stalin": Frank Lloyd Wright, "Architecture and Life in the USSR," *Soviet Russia Today*, October 1937, pp. 14–19, and *Architectural Record*, October 1937, pp. 59–60.
458. L. Karlik, *Karo Alabian*, Erevan, 1966. On this lost soul of architectural Stalinism, see Hudson, *Blueprints and Blood, passim.*
459. A. V. Shchusev, L. E. Zagorsky, *Arkhitekturnaia organizatsia goroda*, Moscow: Gosstroiizdat, 1934, pp. 17–20.
460. Vladimir Semenov, "Voprosy planirovki," *Akademia Arkhitektury*, n° 4, 1935.
461. Thomas Adams, Noveichie dostizheniia v planirovke gorodov, Moscow: Izd. Vses. *Akademii arkhitekturny*, 1935.
462. Where he published a series of plates at Corbett's instigation: W. K Oltar-Jevsky, *Contemporary Babylon in Pencil Drawings*, New York: Architectural Books Publishing Co, 1933.
463. Jan Tabor, ed., *Kunst und Diktatur; Architektur, Bildhauerei und Maleri in Österreich, Deutschland, Italien und der Sowjetunion 1922–1956,* Baden: Verlag Grasl, 1994.
464. Rainer Stommer, ed., *Reichsautobahn, Pyramiden des Dritten Reichs*, Marburg: Jonas Verlag, 1982.
465. Jeffrey Herf, *Reactionary Modernism; Technology, Culture, and Politics in Weimar and the Third Reich*, Cambridge, London, and New York: Cambridge University Press, 1984.
466. Winfried Nerdinger, "Modernisierung. Bauhaus. Nationalsozialismus," Nerdinger, *Bauhaus-Moderne im Nazionalsozialismus*, pp. 9–23.
467. Alfred Hugenberg, *Die neue Stadt*, Berlin: Verlag Scherl, 1935. On this project, see Hartmut Frank, "Des gratte-ciel pour le Führer, les constructions en hauteur du IIIe Reich," Cohen and Damisch, eds., *Américanisme et modernité*, pp. 389–392.
468. Hartmut Frank, "'Das Tor der Welt', die Planungen für eine Hängebrücke über die Elbe und für ein Hamburger 'Gauforum' 1935–1945," Höhns, *Das ungebaute Hamburg*, pp. 78–99.
469. Bruno Zevi, *Towards an Organic Architecture*, London: Faber & Faber, Ltd., 1950. Originally *Verso un'architettura organica*, Turin, Einaudi, 1945.
470. Mario Ridolfi, Cino Calcaprina, Aldo Cardelli, Mario Fiorentino, *Manuale dell'architetto*, Rome: Consiglio Nazionale delle Ricerche and USIS, 1945.
471. Frei Otto, "Ein Besuch bei Frank Lloyd Wright," *Bauwelt*, n° 2; 1952, pp. 24–26.
472. Le Corbusier, *Cathedrals*, p. 64.
473. See George A. Dudley, *A Workshop for Peace: Designing the United Nations Headquarters*, New York Architectural History Foundation, Cambridge, Mass.: MIT Press, 1994. Cf. Victoria Newhouse, *Wallace K. Harrison, Architect*, New York: Rizzoli, 1989, pp. 114–137.
474. V. Grossman, "Stroitelstvo voennogo vremeni v SShA i v Anglii," *Arkhitektura SSSR*, n° 1, 1942, pp. 26–32. L. Vrangel, "Novoe v arkhitekturnoi praktike SShA," *Arkhitektura SSSR*, n° 2, 1943, pp. 31–36.
475. Kirill Afanassiev, Vigdariia Khazanova, *Iz istorii sovetskoi arkhitektury 1941–1945; dokumenty i materiali, khronika voennikh let*, Moscow: Nauka, 1978, p. 86.
476. Karo Alabian, preface to Roman Khiger, *Maloetazhnye doma v SShA*, Moscow, Gosudarstvennoe Arkhitekturnoe Izd-vo Akademii Arkhitektury, 1944. By the same author, see *Planirovka posiolok v SShA*, Moscow: Gosudarstvennoe Arkhitekturnoe Izd-vo Akademii Arkhitektury, 1944, and *Mnogokvartirnye doma v SShA*, Moscow: Gosudarstvennoe Arkhitekturnoe Izd-vo Akademii Arkhitektury, 1945.
477. Frank Lloyd Wright, letter to David Arkin and Karo Alabian, 20 January 1943, in *Letters to Architects*, Fresno: California University Press, 1984, pp. 101–103.
478. Harvey Wiley Corbett, letter to Karo Alabian, New York: 2 May 1944, Lonberg-Holm Archives. See the announcement of the committee's creation: "Architects' Committee for American-Soviet Friendship, *Journal of the AIA*, May 1944, pp. 250–251.
479. Karo Alabian, Viktor Vesnin, Igor Grabar, letter to Harvey Wiley Corbett, Moscow: 25 April 1944, Lonberg-Holm Archives.
480. Karo Alabian, letter to Harvey Wiley Corbett, Moscow: n.d. (1944), Lonberg-Holm Archives.
481. Viacheslav Oltarzhevsky, letter to Harvey Wiley Corbett, Moscow: n.d. (1944), Lonberg-Holm Archives.
482. David Arkin, letter to Harvey Wiley Corbett, Moscow: n.d. (1944), Lonberg-Holm Archives.
483. Architects' Committee, National Council of American-Soviet Friendship, *News Bulletin*, n° 9, 25 July 1945. The minutes of the conference were published in *Architectural Forum*.
484. Kiesler's sketches and notes can be consulted in the Kiesler Estate Archives: Lisa Phillips, *Frederick Kiesler*, New York: Whitney Museum of American Art, W. W. Norton, 1989, pp. 67–68. The exhibition took the form of 40 flat panels of 4 x 6 ft. and 350 photographs selected by Douglas Haskell, editor of the *Architectural Record*, and covered the work of Holabird & Root, Frank Lloyd Wright, William Wurster, Albert Kahn, Corbett, Harrison, Hood, etc. The exhibition travelled to Moscow in 1945, though its existence was not recorded before January 1947: Architects' Committee, National Council of American-Soviet Friendship, *News Bulletin*, n° 11, 5 December 1945 and n° 14, 8 January 1947.
485. Viacheslav K. Oltarzhevsky, preface to *Gabaritnyi spravochnik arkhitektora*, Moscow, Izd-vo Akademii Arkhitektury SSSR, 1947.
486. "Eskiz proekta novogo Ialty," *Sovetskoe isskustvo*, 28 November 1944. A manuscript entitled *O Ialte i eio tsentre* is to be found in the archives of the Burov family. Raissa G. Burova, Raissa N. Blashkevich, Olga I. Rzhekhina, *A. K. Burov*, Moscow: Stroiizdat, 1984, pp. 98–106. Aleksei Tarkhanov, Sergei Kavtaradze, *Architecture of the Stalin Era*, New York: Rizzoli, 1992, pp. 99–105.
487. Andrei Burov, *Ob arkhitekture*, Moscow: Stroiizdat, 1960, pp. 142–143.
488. Simonov, "Preodolet serioznye nedòstatki v arkhitekture," *Sovetskoe Iskusstvo*, 26 March 1948.
489. See Guy Lagneau's sketch detailing the relationship between the quay and the tower: Gargiani, *Auguste Perret*, p. 257.
490. René Herbst, ed., *Un inventeur, l'architecte Pierre Chareau*, Paris: Éditions du Salon des Arts Ménagers, 1954. Marc Vellay, *Pierre Chareau architecte-meublier 1883–1950*, Paris: Éditions du Regard, 1984.
491. Maurice R., "Essai de réorganisation européenne avec le "planning" moderne," *L'Architecture d'aujourd'hui*, n° 1, May–June 1945, pp. 8–13. On Rotival, see Jean Alaurent, "Hommage à Maurice Rotival (1892–1980)," *Urbanisme*, vol. 49, n° 177–178, 1980, pp. 24–25.
492. On Jacques Carlu (1880–1976), see Isabelle Gournay, *Le nouveau Trocadéro*, Liège: Pierre Mardaga, 1985.
493. André Remondet, "Transformations de l'architecture américaine," *L'Architecture française*, vol. 7., n° 54, January 1946, pp. 29–33.
494. Gus Dudley, ed., *Oscar Nitzchké Architect*, New York: Cooper Union, 1985.
495. Terence Riley, *Paul Nelson, The Filter of Reason*, New York: Graduate School of Architecture, Columbia University, 1991.
496. Isabelle Gournay, "The Delano and Aldrich/Emerson Fellowship," Washington: American Institute of Architects, 1989.
497. See the reports and administrative memoranda kept in the Archives Nationales, fonds DG 943 MRU. Cf. Danièle Voldman, "A la recherche de modèles, les missions du MRU à l'étranger," *Images, discours et enjeux de la reconstruction des villes françaises après 1945*, Paris: Institut d'Histoire du Temps Présent and CNRS, 1987, p. 104.
498. Colonel A. Antoine, "Les ensembles d'habitations provisoires," *L'Architecture d'aujourd'hui*, n° 2, 1945, pp. 13–14.
499. Rémi Baudoui, *Raoul Dautry (1880–1951) le technocrate de la République*, Paris: Belfond, 1992.
500. André Chastel, "Où en est l'urbanisme français ?, II. Allons nous vers la cité idéale?," *Le Monde*, 14 June 1947, p. 4.
501. Marcel Lods, "Retour d'Amérique," *L'Architecture française*, n° 54, January 1946, pp. 23–28.
502. Marcel Lods, *Images d'Amérique*, lecture at the salle Pleyel, Paris: 1945.
503. Marcel Lods, "Expériences américaines," *Techniques d'Amérique, Techniques et architecture*, November 1945, p. 129.
504. Ibid.
505. Marcel Lods, *Demain l'Europe sera équipée; le serons-nous?, Cahiers de l'ITBTP*, n° 278, 15 December 1947, p. 11. On the TVA, see the following propaganda documents: John H. Kyle, *The Building of TVA: An Illustrated History*, Baton Rouge: Lousiana State University Press, 1958. Marguerite Owen, *The Tennessee Valley Authority*, New York: Praeger, 1970. See also the following critical studies: Philip Selznick, *TVA and the Grass Roots: A Study in the Sociology of Formal Organization*, Berkeley and Los Angeles: University of California Press, 1949. Preston J. Hubbard, *Origins of the TVA; The Muscle Shoals Controversy, 1920–1932*, Nashville: Vanderbilt University Press, 1961. Erwin C. Hargrove, *Prisoners of Myth: The Leadership of the Tennessee Valley Authority, 1933–1990*, Princeton: Princeton University Press, 1994.
506. Marcel Lods, "Visite à Neutra," *L'Architecture d'aujourd'hui*, n° 6, 1946, p. 5.
507. Gaston Bardet, "Le dilemme de Neutra ou l'urbanisme, antidote de la préfabrication," *L'Architecture française*, n° 83–84, 1948, p. 5.
508. Elisabeth Mock wrote on behalf of the MoMA to Mies van der Rohe on 8 October 1945, asking him to organize the four envoys' stay in Chicago (Mies van der Rohe Papers, Library of Congress, carton 40).
509. Michel Écochard, *La planification, condition de l'urbanisme*, conference given at the American University, Beirut, 9 May 1946, p. 5.
510. Ibid., p. 9.
511. Le Corbusier, *Modulor I and II*, trans. Peter de Francia and Anna Bostock, Cambridge, Mass.: Harvard University Press, 1980, pp. 53–53. Originally *Le Modulor*, Boulogne-Billancourt, Éditions de *L'Architecture d'aujourd'hui*, 1950.
512. David E. Lilienthal, *Construit pour le peuple: "TVA" – une expérience de la démocratie américaine*, New York: Les Éditions Transatlantiques, 1945. Originally: *TVA; Democracy on the March*, New York: Harper & Brothers, 1944.
513. Le Corbusier, *Modulor I and II*, p. 54.
514. On all these episodes, see Jean-Louis Cohen and Hartmut Frank, eds., *Les relations franco-allemandes 1940–1950 et leurs effets sur l'architecture et la forme urbaine*, Paris: École d'Architecture Paris-Villemin, Hamburg, Hochschule für bildende Künste, 1989.
515. "Exposition des Techniques Américaines de l'Habitation et de l'Urbanisme 1939–194X," *L'Architecture d'aujourd'hui*, n° 6, 1946, pp. 84–88.
516. Paul Nelson, "Précisions à propos de l'Exposition des Techniques Américaines de l'Habitation et de l'Urbanisme," *L'Architecture d'aujourd'hui*, n° 12, July 1947, p. 4.
517. Pierre Arrou, "L'Hôpital mémorial de Saint-Lô," *La Construction moderne*, August-September 1959, pp. 292–296; "Hôpital mémorial Franco-Américain de Saint-Lô," *L'Architecture d'aujourd'hui*, February-March 1957, pp. 50–55.
518. Richard F. Kuysel, "*L'American Way of Life* et les missions françaises de productivité," *Vingtième Siècle*, n° 17, January-March 1988, pp. 21–38. Cf. Luc Boltanski, "America America . . . Le plan Marshall et l'importation du management," *Actes de la recherche en sciences sociales*, n° 38, May 1981, pp. 19–41.
519. *Rapport des missions de productivité du bâtiment de France aux Etats-Unis*, Paris: Fédération Nationale du Bâtiment, 1951.
520. This team comprised the architects Calsat, Cammas, Herbé

and de Mailly, the engineers Meunier and Parinet and the contractors Arène, Maillard and Rivas.
521. Rapport de la Mission de productivité Architectes-ingénieurs-entrepreneurs, *Cahiers du CSTB*, n° 142, 1951, p. XLV.
522. Almost half a century after *Cités-jardins d'Amérique*, the indestructible Benoit-Lévy discussed the program of new towns launched by the Roosevelt administration in his "Villes vertes aux USA," *La Construction Moderne*, n° 9, April 1949, pp. 119–123. On the shopping centers, see Henri Colboc, "Le centre commercial, problème d'urbanisme," *L'Architecture française*, n° 145–146, 1954, pp. 4–5.
523. Georges Soria, *La France deviendra-t-elle une colonie américaine?*, Paris: Éditions du Pavillon, 1948 (preface by Frédéric Joliot-Curie). These episodes would give the GATT talks of 1993–1994 a flavor of *déjà-vu*.
524. Richard F. Kuysel, *Seducing the French: the Dilemma of Americanization*, Berkeley and Los Angeles: University of California Press, 1993, pp. 52–69.
525. On these controversies, see Marie Christine Granjon, "Sartre, Beauvoir, Aron: les passions ambiguës," in Lacorne, Rupnik, Toinet, *L'Amérique dans les têtes*, pp. 144–164; J.-P. Mathy, *Extrême Occident, passim.*
526. Boris Iofan, speech at the VII Plenum of the Union of Architects, published in *Arkhitekturnye voprosy rekonstruktsii Moskvy*, Moscow: Izd. Akademii arkhitektury SSSR, 1940, pp. 84–85.
527. Andrei Bunin, Maria Kruglova, *Arkhitekturnaia kompozitsia goroda*, Moscow: Izd. Akademii arkhitektury SSSR, 1940, p. 88. These analyses of American cities were based on *American Vitruvius* and Werner Hegemann's *Amerikanische Architektur und Stadtbaukunst.*
528. André Lurçat, quoted by Renée Michel, "Le Grand Moscou: une planification sans précédent dans l'histoire," *Russie d'aujourd'hui*, n° 35, November 1935, n.p.
529. Mikhail P. Tsapenko, *O realisticheskyh osnovakh sovetskoi arkhitektury*, Moscow: Gos. Izd. Lit. po Stroitelstvu i Arkhitekture, 1952, p. 352.
530. Council of Ministers of the USSR, *Sovetskoe Isskustvo*, 28 February 1947. Marina Astafieva-Dlugach, Yuri Volchok, "Rol proekta v razvitii obshchestvennogo soznania, k 40-letiu postanovlenia soveta ministrov SSSR 'o stroitelstve v Moskve mnogoetazhnykh domov'," *Arkhitektura i Stroitelstvo Moskvy*, February 1987, pp. 20–22.
531. Viacheslav K. Oltarzhevsky, *Stroitelstvo vysotnykh zdanii v Moskve*, Moscow: Gos. izd. Lit. po Stroitelstvu i Arkhitekture, 1953, p. 3.
532. Jean-Louis Cohen, "Il collettivo all'assalto del cielo," *Hinterland*, Milan: n° 2, March-April 1978.
533. Boris Iofan, "Mnogoetazhnye zdania stolitsy," *Moskovskii Komsomolets*, 19 August 1947.
534. Bunin, Kruglova, *Arkhitekturnaia kompozitsia goroda*, pp. 92–100.
535. Boris Iofan, "Arkhitekturnye problemy stroitelstva mnogoetazhnykh zdanii," *Arkhitektura i Stroitelstvo*, n° 3, 1947.
536. Boris Rubanenko, "Khudozhestvennye osnovy arkhitektury vysotnykh zdanii stolitsy," *Sovetskaia Arkhitektura*, vol. 4, 1953, p. 16.
537. See a photograph of this type on the cover of *l'URSS en construction*, n° 11, 1949.
538. Sigfried Giedion, Fernand Léger, José Luis Sert, "Nine points on Monumentality," 1943, Sigfried Giedion, *Architecture, you and me*, Cambridge, Mass.: Harvard University Press, 1958, pp. 48–52.
539. Sokratis Georgiadis, *Sigfried Giedion, an Intellectual Biography*, Edinburgh: Edinburgh University Press, 1993, pp. 153–155.
540. Sigfried Giedion, *Bauen in Frankreich*, Leipzig and Berlin: Klinkhardt and Biermann, 1928, and *Space, Time, and Architecture: The Growth of a New Tradition*, Cambridge, Mass.: Harvard University Press, 1949, p. 17.
541. Sigfried Giedion, *Mechanization Takes Command: a contribution to anonymous history*, New York: W.W. Norton & Company 1969, p.v. (Original edition: New York: Oxford University Press, 1948).
542. Dorothee Huber, Claude Lichtenstein, "Das Nadelöhr der anonymen Geschichte," *Sigfried Giedion 1888–1968, Der Entwurf einer moderner Tradition*, Zurich: Ammann Verlag, 1989; Martin Steinman, "Die Mechanisierung der Wohnung und die 'machine à habiter'," *Avant Garde und Industrie*, ed. Stanislaus von Moos and Chris Smeenks, Delft: Delft University Press, 1983, pp. 135–149.
543. There were 501 illustrations in the American edition, but only 367 in the French.
544. Hans Magnus Enzensberger, "Unheimliche Fortschritte," *Der Spiegel*, n° 6, 7 February 1983, pp. 196–201. In his afterword to the German edition, Stanislaus Von Moos compared the book to an "illustrated novel" on industrial culture: *Die Herrschaft der Mechanisierung*, Frankfurt-am-Main: Europäische Verlagsgesellschaft, 1982, pp. 781–816.
545. Giedion, *Bauen in Frankreich*, p. 10.
546. Giedion, *Mechanization Takes Command*, p. 42.
547. Gilbert Simondon, *Du mode d'existence des objets techniques*, Paris: Aubier, 1989 (original edition 1958).
548. Giedion, *Mechanization Takes Command*, pp. 10–11.
549. See the correspondence between Giedion and Benjamin, which is discussed in Huber, Lichtenstein, "Das Nadelöhr der anonymen Geschichte," *Sigfried Giedion*, p. 85
550. Giedion, *Mechanization Takes Command*, p. 25.
551. Ibid., pp. 38–9.
552. Ibid., p. 100.
553. Ibid., p. 132. Giedion is quoting from *The Rural Cyclopaedia*, Edinburgh, 1854, vol. 1, p. 222.
554. On McCormick, see Hounshell, *From the American System to Mass Production*, pp. 153–187.
555. Giedion, *Mechanization takes Command*, p. 207.
556. Ibid., p. 141.
557. Ibid., p. 393.
558. Catherine E. Beecher (1800–1878), *The American Woman's Home or Principles of Domestic Science*, Boston: H. A. Brown & Co, New York: J. B. Ford & Co, 1869. Christine Frederick, "The new domestic Economy," *Ladies Home Journal*, 1912. See also Dolores Hayden, *The Grand Domestic Revolution: a History of Feminist Designs for American Homes, Neighborhoods and Cities*, Cambridge, Mass.: MIT Press, 1981.
559. Giedion, *Mechanization takes Command*, p. 682.
560. Arnold Hauser, *The Art Bulletin*, 1952, pp. 251–252.
561. Marshall McLuhan, "Encyclopedic Unities," *The Hudson Review*, n° 4, 1949, pp. 599–602. See also Richard Neutra, *Arts & Architecture*, July 1948, and Mario Labò, "La meccanizzazione prende il comando ?" *Comunità* , n° 2, March-April 1949, pp. 39–41.
562. Lewis Mumford, "The Sky Line," *The New Yorker*, 15 May 1948, pp. 84–85.
563. Le Corbusier, letter to Sigfried Giedion, in *Homage à Giedion, Profile seiner Persönlichkeit: (Schriften und Dokumente von Sigfried Giedion sowie Beitrage der Freunde)*, ed. Paul Hofer, Basel and Stuttgart: Birkhäuser Verlag, 1971, pp. 50–51.
564. Hugh Casson, *Homes by the Million; An account of the housing achievement in the USA, 1940–1945*, Harmondsworth: Penguin, 1946.
565. Gordon Cullen, *Townscape,* London: The Architectural Press, 1961.
566. He reused the title of the issue in: Christopher Tunnard, Boris Pushkarev, *Man-Made America: Chaos or Control? An Inquiry into Selected Problems of Design in the Urbanized Landscape*, New Haven: Yale University Press, 1963. His other publications include *The City of Man*, London and New York: Charles Scribner's Sons, 1953; *American Skyline; The Growth and Form of our Cities and Towns*, New York: Houghton Mifflin Co, 1953; *The Modern American City*, Princeton: D. Van Nostrand Co, 1968.
567. *Man Made America, A Special Number of the Architectural Review*, London: December 1950, p. 359.
568. Ibid., p. 343.
569. James, *The American Scene*, cited in ibid., p. 345. The aphorism has also been attributed to Napoleon and Thomas Payne.
570. *Man Made America*, p. 351.
571. Ibid., p. 356.
572. Ibid., p. 385.
573. Ibid., p. 413.
574. Reyner Banham, "Things to Come (The Smithsons' House of the Future)," *Design*, June 1956, pp. 24–28.
575. John Winter, "Richard Neutra 1892–1970," RIBA Journal, June 1970, p. 245. The article cited is "House at Santa Barbara, Richard Neutra Architect," *The Architectural Review*, n° 641, May 1950, pp. 325–330.
576. Reyner Banham, *Los Angeles, the Architecture of Four Ecologies*, Harmondsworth: Penguin Books, 1971, p. 194.
577. James Ackerman, "Report on California," *The Architectural Review*, October 1956, p. 239.
578. Lawrence Alloway, "Eames' World," *Architectural Association Journal*, vol. 72, pp. 54–55, July–August 1956. On the Entenza program, see Elisabeth A. T. Smith, *Blueprints for Modern Living: History and Legacy of the Case Study Houses*, Los Angeles, MoCA, Cambridge, Mass.: MIT Press, 1989.
579. Richard Hamilton, "Inquest on the Festival of Britain," in *Collected Words 1953–1962*, London: Thames & Hudson, 1982, p. 148.
580. Cited by Charles Jencks, *Modern Movements in Architecture*, Harmondsworth and Middlesex: Penguin Books, 1973, p. 93.
581. Bernard S. Myers, "The Inclined Plane," *Ark*, no° 18, 1956, p. 35. Cited by David Mellor, "'A Glorious Techniculture' in Nineteen-fifties Britain," in *The Independent Group: Postwar Britain and the Aesthetics of Plenty*, ed. David Robbins, Cambridge, Mass. and London: MIT Press, 1990, p. 230.
582. Lawrence Alloway, "The Development of British Pop," in Lucy R. Lippard, *Pop Art*, New York and Oxford: 1966, pp. 32 and 36.
583. McHale emigrated to the to the United States in 1960; here he published his *The Future of the Future*, New York: Braziller, 1969. On his work, see Charlotta Kotik *et. al., The Expendable Ikon: Works by John McHale,* Buffalo, NY, Albright-Knox Art Gallery, 1984.
584. Laszlo Moholy-Nagy, *Vision in Motion*, Chicago: P. Theobald, 1947, p. 244.
585. Lawrence Alloway, "Technology and Sex in Science Fiction; A Note on Cover Art," *Ark*, Summer 1956, pp. 19–23.
586. Alison and Peter Smithson, "But Today We Collect Ads," *Ark,* November 1956, pp. 49–53.
587. Richard Hamilton, "Persuading Image" and "Artificial Obsolescence," in *Collected Words 1953–1962*, London: Thames & Hudson, 1982, pp. 135–146.
588. Reyner Banham, "Industrial Design e arte popolare," *Civiltà delle Macchine*, November-December 1955, pp. 12–15; in English, "Industrial Design and Popular Art," *Industrial Design*, March 1960, pp. 61–65; and "A Throw-Away Aesthetic," in *Design by Choice*, London: Academy Editions 1981, p. 90.
589. John McHale, in Ian McCallum, ed., *Machine Made America, A Special Issue of the Architectural Review*, May 1957, p. 293. See also John McHale, "Richard Buckminster Fuller," *Architectural Design*, July 1961, pp. 290–319; and *R. Buckminster Fuller*, New York: George Braziller, 1962.
590. *Machine Made America*, p. 323.
591. Ibid., pp. 295–297.
592. Lawrence Alloway, "City Notes," *Architectural Design*, vol. 29, January 1959, p. 34.
593. Ibid., pp. 34–35.
594. Reyner Banham, "1960 Stocktaking of the impact of traditions and technology on architecture today," *Architectural Review*, vol. 127, February 1960, pp. 94–96; "On Trial: 5. The Spec-Builders, Towards a Pop Architecture," *Architectural Review*, vol. 132, July 1962, pp. 44–45
595. Reyner Banham, "The Great Gizmo," *Industrial Design*, September 1965; *Design by Choice*, pp. 108–114.
596. See the anthology edited by Alain Guilheux, *Archigram*, Paris: Centre George Pompidou, 1994.
597. Warren Chalk, "An unaccustomed dream," in Peter Cook *et al., Archigram*, London: Studio Vista, 1973, p. 32.
598. Reyner Banham, *Los Angeles, the Architecture of Four Ecologies*, Harmondsworth: Penguin Books, 1971.
599. Ibid., p. 90.
600. Jane Jacobs, *The Death and Life of Great American Cities*, New York: Random House, 1961.
601. Robert Venturi, *Complexity and Contradiction in Architecture*, New York: Museum of Modern Art, 1966.
602. Duhamel, *Scènes de la vie future*, p. 220.
603. Banham, *Los Angeles.*
604. The only work to have avoided the ambient positivism of post-1980 research into Los Angeles, (many of which have struggled to "refute" Banham's thesis), is Mike Davis's *City of Quartz, Excavating the Future in Los Angeles*, London: New York: Verso, 1990.
605. Banham, *A Concrete Atlantis.*
606. Jean-Nicolas-Louis Durand, *Recueil et parallèle des édifices de tout genre, anciens et modernes, remarquables par leur beauté, par leur grandeur ou par leur singularité, et dessinés sur une même échelle*, Paris: 1799–1801.
607. Rem Koolhaas, *S, M, L, XL*, New York: The Monacelli Press, 1995.
608. Hubert Damisch, "The Manhattan Transfer," in *OMA–Rem Koolhaas Architecture 1970–1990*, ed. Jacques Lucan, Princeton: Princeton University Press, 1991, pp. 21–32.

taken in 1932. Archivio Storico Fiat, Turin

51. Photomontage of the Moscow automobile factory (AMO) constructed by Albert Kahn Associates, 1933. From *L'URSS en construction*, no° 1 (August 1933). Canadian Centre for Architecture, Montreal

52. Albert Kahn, architect (1869–1942). *The Cheliabinsk Tractor Plant: bird's-eye view*, 1930–33. Photographic print. Albert Kahn Associates Inc., Detroit

53. Albert Kahn, architect (1869–1942). *The Cheliabinsk Tractor Plant: elevation and section of the forge*, 1930. Pencil on linen, 77.5 × 116.8 cm. Albert Kahn Associates Inc., Detroit

54. Two pages illustrating the Equitable Trust Building in Erich Mendelsohn, *Amerika, Bilderbuch eines Architekten* (Berlin: Rudolf Mosse, 1926), pp. 2–3. Canadian Centre for Architecture, Montreal

55. Erich Kettelhut, set designer (1893–1979). Sketch for the first version of the set for *Metropolis* by Fritz Lang: perspective, 1925. Ink and pencil on paper, 31.5 × 38.6 cm. (image); 34.6 × 41.4 cm (sheet). Fondation Deutsche Kinemathek, Berlin
© Deutsche Kinemathek, Berlin

56. Otto Hunte, set designer. Recreation of the set design for *Metropolis* by Fritz Lang, 1929. Pencil on board, 73 × 51 cm. Deutsches Filmmuseum, Frankfurt am Main, Collection Otto Hunte
© Deutsches Filmmuseum

57. Aleksandr Rodchenko (1891–1956). Comparison of the visual approach of *Amerika, Bilderbuch eines Architekten* with the traditional approach, in *Novy LEF*, no° 9 (1928), pp. 33–34. Canadian Centre for Architecture, Montreal

58. Photograph of Broadway in New York. Reproduced in Erich Mendelsohn, *Amerika, Bilderbuch eines Architekten* (Berlin: Rudolf Mosse, 1926), pl. 29. Canadian Centre for Architecture, Montreal

59. Knud Lonberg-Holm (1895–1972). Construction of the Sheldon Hotel in New York, c. 1922. Reproduced in Erich Mendelsohn, *Amerika, Bilderbuch eines Architekten* (Berlin: Rudolf Mosse, 1926). Collection Van Eesteren, Nederlands Architectuurinstituut, Rotterdam

60. Moisei Ginzburg (1892–1946), Review of the book *Amerika, Bilderbuch eines Architekten* by Erich Mendelsohn, in *Sovremennaia Arkhitektura*, vol. 1, no° 1 (1926), p. 38. Collection Jean-Louis Cohen, Paris

61. "America, Reflections by Knud Lonberg-Holm," an article illustrated with photographs of American factories, in *i10*, no° 15 (October 1928). Canadian Centre for Architecture, Montreal

62. Erich Mendelsohn (1887–1953). *Oskar Beyer, Bachabend.* (Oskar Beyer, an evening of Bach). *Perspectives drawn on the back of a concert program*, 1926. Pencil on paper, 31.6 × 20.7 cm. Staatliche Museen zu Berlin, Kunstbibliothek
© Kunstbibliothek, Berlin

63. Erich Mendelsohn (1887–1953). *Sketch dedicated to Frank Lloyd Wright*, 1924. Brown pencil on onionskin paper, 23.1 × 30.8 cm. Staatliche Museen zu Berlin, Kunstbibliothek
© Kunstbibliothek, Berlin

64. Erich Mendelsohn (1887–1953). *Sketch for an American skyscraper*, 1924. Brown pencil on onionskin paper, 14.0 × 26.9 cm (13.0 × 25.9 cm). Staatliche Museen zu Berlin, Kunstbibliothek
© Kunstbibliothek, Berlin

65. Two pages illustrating the construction of the Palmer House hotel in Chicago, in Richard Neutra, *Wie Baut Amerika?* (Stuttgart: Julius Hoffman, 1927), pp. 38–39. Canadian Centre for Architecture, Montreal

66. Adolf Loos, architect (1870–1933). *"Amerikanischer Fachwerkbau," axonometric for the wood-frame construction of the Schnabl house*, Vienna, 1931. Pencil on paper, 46 × 64 cm (framed). Graphische Sammlung Albertina, Vienna
© VBK, Vienna, Austria, 1995

67. Balloon-frame construction in Richard Neutra, *Amerika: Die Stilbildung des neuen Bauens in den Vereinigten Staaten* (Vienna: Anton Schroll Verlag, 1930), p. 135, fig. 208. Canadian Centre for Architecture, Montreal

68. Photomontage by El Lissitzky (1890–1941), in David

Arkin, *Arkhitektura sovremennogo zapada* (Moscow: OGIZ-IZOGIZ, 1932). Getty Center, Resource Collections, Santa Monica

69. Photograph of Vladimir Maiakovsky (1893–1930) in New York, in *Sovremennaia Arkhitektura*, nos. 1–2 (1930), p. 2. Canadian Centre for Architecture, Montreal

70. E. Maxwell Fry (1899–1987). *Project for a city of the future*, 1929–31. Ink and wash on paper, 81.3 × 66.0 cm (framed). From the Regional Plan Association: *First Regional Plan for N.Y. and its Environs*
© Regional Plan Association

71. Ludwig Mies van der Rohe, architect (1886–1969). *Project for skyscraper in the Friedrichstraße: perspective*, Berlin, 1921. Charcoal and pencil on paper, 140 × 100 cm. Bauhaus-Archiv, Berlin

72. Ludwig Mies van der Rohe, architect (1886–1969). *Project for skyscraper in the Friedrichstraße: east elevation*, Berlin, 1921. Charcoal and pencil on brown paper, 55.3 × 87.5 cm. The Museum of Modern Art, New York. Gift of the architect
© 1994 The Museum of Modern Art, New York

73. Martin Elsaesser, architect (1884–1957). *Project for skyscraper in the Friedrichstraße: perspective*, Berlin, 1921–22. Pencil on tracing paper, 35.5 × 29.7 cm. Architekturmuseum Technische Universität, Munich
© Architekturmuseum der Technischen Universität München

74. Hugo Häring, architect (1882–1958). *Project for skyscraper in the Friedrichstraße: perspective*, Berlin, 1921–22. Stiftung Archiv der Akademie der Künste, Sammlung Baukunst, Nachlaß Hugo Häring, Berlin
© Akademie der Künste, Berlin, Collection Baukunst, Nachlaß Häring

75. Otto Kohtz, architect (1880–1956). *Project for office tower in the Friedrichstraße at the corner of Karlstraße: perspective*, Berlin, early 1920s. Ink and wash on tracing paper, 35.7 × 31.4 cm. Plansammlung der Universitätsbibliothek der Technischen Universität, Berlin
© Plansammlung der Universitätsbibliothek der Technischen Universität, Berlin

76. Hans Poelzig, architect (1869–1936). *Project for skyscraper in the Friedrichstraße*, Berlin, 1921–22. Charcoal on tracing paper, mounted on cardboard, 108.0 × 74.5 cm. Plansammlung der Universitätsbibliothek der Technischen Universität, Berlin

77. Walter Gropius, architect (1883–1969), with Adolf Meyer, architect (1881–1929). *Project for the* Chicago Tribune: *model*, 1922. Photograph. Bauhaus-Archiv, Berlin
© Bauhaus-Archiv, Berlin

78. Adolf Loos, architect (1870–1933). *Project for the* Chicago Tribune: *preparatory sketches*, 1922. Ink on paper, 154 × 64 cm. Graphische Sammlung Albertina, Vienna
© VBK, Vienna, Austria, 1995

79. Adolf Loos, architect (1870–1933). *Project for the* Chicago Tribune: *plan of ground floor and entrance*, 1922. Pencil on paper, 74 × 104 cm (framed). Graphische Sammlung Albertina, Vienna
© VBK, Vienna, Austria, 1995

80. Adolf Loos, architect (1870–1933). *Project for the* Chicago Tribune: *elevation*, 1922. Pencil on paper, 154 × 64 cm. Graphische Sammlung Albertina, Vienna
© VBK, Vienna, Austria, 1995

81. Eliel Saarinen, architect (1873–1950). *Project for the* Chicago lake front: perspective of the Chicago Tower, 1923. Pencil on tracing paper, 29.8 × 21.6 cm. Cranbrook Academy of Art Museum
© Cranbrook Art Museum

82. Eliel Saarinen, architect (1873–1950). *Project for the* Chicago Tribune: *perspective*, 1922. Photographic print, 98 × 50 cm. Courtesy of the Cranbrook Archives
© The Museum of Finnish Architecture

83. Auguste Perret, architect (1874–1954); Charles Imbert, draughtsman (1865–?). *Tower cities*, c. 1922. Stylographic pen on tracing paper, mounted on paper, 17.5 × 27.5, 23 × 31 cm. Institut Français d'Architecture. Centre d'Archives d'Architecture du XXᵉ siècle, Paris

84. Auguste Perret, architect (1874–1954); Charles Imbert, draughtsman (1865–?). *Tower cities*, c. 1922. Stylographic pen on tracing paper, mounted on paper, 21 × 16 cm. Institut Français d'Architecture. Centre d'Archives d'Architecture du XXᵉ siècle, Paris

85. Jacques Lambert, illustrator, after Auguste Perret, architect (1874–1954). *Avenue of residential towers*. From *L'Illustration* (12 August 1922), p. 133. Canadian Centre for Architecture, Montreal
© Auguste Perret 1994 /VIS*ART Droit d'auteur Inc.

86. Auguste Perret, architect (1874–1954). *A residential tower*. From *La Science et la vie*, vol. 28, no° 102 (1925). Bibliothèque du CNAM, Paris
© Auguste Perret 1994 /VIS*ART Droit d'auteur Inc.

87. Le Corbusier (1887–1965). Graphic design for the *Almanach d'Architecture moderne*, 1925. Collage and black ink on paper, 25.5 × 16.0 cm. Fondation Le Corbusier, Paris
© Le Corbusier 1994/ VIS*ART Droit d'auteur Inc.

88. Paul Citroën 1896–1983. *Metropolis*, 1923. Collage of printed matter on paper, 76 × 59 cm. Prints Collection, Rijksuniversiteit, Leyden, Netherlands
© Paul Citroën 1994/VIS*ART Droit d'auteur Inc.

89. Cornelis van Eesteren, architect (1897–1988), Louis-Georges Pineau, urban planner (1898–1987). *Building and traffic study for a commercial district in a large contemporary city*, Paris, 1926. Pencil, india ink, and photographic print on paper, mounted on cardboard, 114 × 74.5 cm; 117 × 77.5 cm (mounted). Nederlands Architectuurinstituut, Rotterdam, Van Eesteren Collection, Flucken Van Lohuizen Foundation, The Hague

90. Ludwig Hilberseimer, architect (1885–1967). *High-rise city for Berlin*: east-to-west perspective, Berlin, 1924. Watercolor on paper, 16.7 × 23.0 cm. Ludwig Hilberseimer Collection. Gift of George E. Danforth. The Art Institute of Chicago
© The Art Institute of Chicago

91. Ludwig Hilberseimer, architect (1885–1967). *Wohlfahrtsstadt* (welfare city), presented at the *Wohlfarts-Ausstellung: model*, Stuttgart, 1927. Ludwig Hilberseimer Collection. Gift of George E. Danforth. The Art Institute of Chicago
© The Art Institute of Chicago

92. Martin Wagner, architect (1885–1957). *Project for the reconstruction of Potsdamer Platz and Leipziger Platz: model*, Berlin, 1929. Canadian Centre for Architecture, Montreal
© Akademie der Künste, Berlin, Collection Baukunst, Foto Arthur Wagner, Inv. Nr. StB 4/95

93. Peter Behrens, architect (1868–1940). *Project for the reconstruction of Alexanderplatz: model*, Berlin, 1929. Canadian Centre for Architecture, Montreal

94. Kazimir Malevich (1878–1935). *Architecton against Manhattan as a background, Collage*. Illustration in *Praesens* (Warsaw), no° 1 (September 1926), p. 28. Collection Sztuki Museum, Łodz

95. Nikolai Ladovsky. "Skyscrapers of the USSR and America," an article in *Izvestiia ASNOVA*, no° 1 (1926). Canadian Centre for Architecture, Montreal

96. Iakov Chernikhov, architect (1889–1951). *Giant Skyscrapers*. From *Osnovy sovremennoi arkhitektury* (Fundamental principles of contemporary architecture, essay of experimental research), (Leningrad: Leningrad Society of Architects, 1930), p. 80, fig. 131. Canadian Centre for Architecture, Montreal

97. Iakov Chernikhov, architect (1889–1951). *The Palace of Arts: Composition of bicolored rectangles*. From *Osnovy sovremennoi arkhitektury* (Fundamental principles of contemporary architecture, essay of experimental research), 2d ed. (Leningrad: Leningrad Society of Architects, 1931), p. 82, fig. 127. Canadian Centre for Architecture, Montreal

98. El Lissitzky (1890–1941). *"Wolkenbügel"* (skyhook) *project in Moscow: elevation*, 1924–25. India ink, pencil, and collage on paper, 50.0 × 64.6 cm. State Tretiakov Gallery, Moscow

99. Frank J. Helmle (1869–1929), Harvey Wiley Corbett, architect (1873–1954), Wallace K. Harrison,

architect (1895–1981), and Viacheslav Oltarzhevsky, architect (1880–1966). *Christopher Columbus Memorial lighthouse project in Santo Domingo: elevation.* Pencil on tracing paper, 57.7 × 81.7 cm. Shchusev Architectural Museum, Moscow

100. Nikolai Ladovsky (1881–1941). *Christopher Columbus Memorial lighthouse project: axonometric*, 1929. Photographic print, 37.9 × 29.8 cm. Shchusev Architectural Museum, Moscow

101. Konstantin Melnikov, architect (1890–1974). *Christopher Columbus Memorial lighthouse project: elevation.* Published in Albert Kelsey, *Program and rules for the second competition for the selection of an architect for the monumental lighthouse which the nations of the world will erect in the Dominican Republic to the memory of Christopher Columbus*, Washington: Pan-American Union, 1930, p. 98. Canadian Centre for Architecture, Montreal

102. Henri Sauvage, architect (1873–1932). *Project for the Rosenthal competition for the Porte Maillot: perspective*, Paris, 1930. Pencil on tracing paper, 63 × 73 cm. Institut Français d'Architecture. Centre d'Archives d'Architecture du XXᵉ siècle, Paris

103. Auguste Perret, architect (1874–1954). *Project for the Rosenthal competition for the Porte Maillot: perspective*, Paris, 1930. Chalk on cardboard, 59.7 × 70.0 cm (matted). Institut Français d'Architecture, Centre d'Archives d'Architecture du XXᵉ siècle, Paris
© Auguste Perret 1994/VIS*ART Droit d'auteur Inc.

104. Jacques Carlu, architect (1890–1976). *Project for the Place de La Défense*, 1932. From *Ville de Paris, dépt. de la Seine, Concours pour l'aménagement de la voie triomphale de la place de l'Étoile au rond-point de La Défense* (Paris: Éd. d'Art Charles Moreau, n.d.), pl. 14. Canadian Centre for Architecture, Montreal
© Jacques Carlu 1995/VIS*ART Droit d'auteur Inc.

105. M. Chappey, L. Duhayon, M. Julien, architects. *Skyscraper project for the Place de La Défense*, 1932. From *Ville de Paris, dépt. de la Seine, Concours pour l'aménagement de la voie triomphale de la place de l'Étoile au rond-point de La Défense* (Paris: Éd. d'Art Charles Moreau, n.d.), pl. 46. Canadian Centre for Architecture, Montreal

106. Robert Camelot, architect (1903–93). *Night View of Chicago*, 1932. watercolor on paper, mounted on cardboard, 11.4 × 15.6 cm (image); 23.8 × 29.6 cm (mount). Institut Français d'Architecture. Centre d'Archives d'Architecture du XXᵉ siècle, Paris
© Institut Français d'Architecture

107. Louis Bonnier, architect (1856–1946). *Study for a skyscraper near Notre-Dame*, Paris, [c. 1928]. Photomontage, 23.8 × 14.0 cm. Institut Français d'Architecture, Centre d'Archives d'Architecture du XXᵉ siècle, Paris
© Institut Français d'Architecture

108. Louis Bonnier, architect (1856–1946). *Project for a setback building in Paris (replacing the 1902 regulation of building height) including a part of the rue de Rivoli and elevations with templates: perspective*, 1934–38. Watercolor and black pencil on paper, 72 × 107.5 cm. Institut Français d'Architecture. Centre d'Archives d'Architecture du XXᵉ siècle, Paris
© Institut Français d'Architecture

109. Guido Fiorini, engineer (1891–1965). *"Radiator" skyscraper: perspective*, 1930. India ink on tracing paper, 106.7 × 60.0 cm. Società Nazionale delle Officine di Savigliano, Turin
© Società Nazionale delle Officine di Savigliano, Turin

110. Le Corbusier, architect (1887–1965). *"Descartes est-il américain? (Is Descartes American?)".* Illustration in *Plans* nº 7 (July 1931), p. 63. Canadian Centre for Architecture, Montreal
© Le Corbusier 1994/VIS*ART Droit d'auteur Inc.

111. *View of the San Francisco Call Building.* From Le Corbusier, "Trois rappels à MM. les Architectes. Le volume." From *Vers une architecture* (Paris: G. Crès et Cie, 1923), p. 29. Canadian Centre for Architecture, Montreal
© Le Corbusier 1994/VIS*ART Droit d'auteur Inc.

112. Le Corbusier, architect (1887–1965). Cover sketch for *When the Cathedrals Were White*, 1937. Ink on paper, 21 × 27 cm. Fondation Le Corbusier, Paris
© Le Corbusier 1994/VIS*ART Droit d'auteur Inc.

113. Le Corbusier, architect (1887–1965). Sketch for *When the Cathedrals Were White*, 1937. Black ink on paper, 21 × 27 cm. Fondation Le Corbusier, Paris
© Le Corbusier 1994/VIS*ART Droit d'auteur Inc.

114. Ivan Leonidov, architect (1902–59). *Project for the People's Commissariat for Heavy Industry: elevation*, Moscow, 1934. Gouache on paper, 87 × 141 cm. Shchusev Architectural Museum, Moscow

115. Rockefeller Center, New York. Cover of *Arkhitektura za rubezhom* (Moscow), no° 2 (1935). Collection Jean-Louis Cohen, Paris

116. Lewis Mumford, *Ot brevenchatogo doma do neboskrioha, ocherk istorii amerikanskoy arkhitektury* (Russian edition of *Sticks and Stones*) (Moscow: Izd. Vses. Akademii Arkhitektury, 1936), pp. 15–16. Collection Jean-Louis Cohen, Paris

117. Viacheslav Oltarzhevsky, architect (1880–1965). *A New York Canyon: Pine, formely King, Street, looking East*, in *Contemporary Babylon in Pencil Drawings* (New York: Architectural Book Publishing Co., 1929). Canadian Centre for Architecture, Montreal

118. Hugh Ferriss, Two pages illustrating "The Metropolis of the Future," in A. V. Shchusev and L. E. Zagorsky, *Arkhitekturnaia organizatsia goroda* (Moscow: Gosstroizdat, 1934), pp. 18–19. Collection Jean-Louis Cohen, Paris

119. Konstanty Gutschow, architect (1902–1978). *Project for a residential tower for the Binnenalster in Hamburg: elevation*, 1942. Watercolor on paper, 30.5 × 45 cm. Staatsarchiv Hamburg, Gift of Konstanty Gutschow
© Staatsarchiv Hamburg

120. Otto Kohtz, architect (1880–1956). *Project for a residential skyscraper for Berlin: elevation.* From Alfred Hugenberg, *Die neue Stadt* (Berlin: Scherl-Verlag, 1935). Collection Jean-Louis Cohen, Paris

121. Boris Iofan, architect (1891–1976), Vladimir G. Gelfreikh, architect (1885–1967), Vladimir A. Shchuko, architect (1878–1939). *Project for the Palace of the Soviets: perspective*, Moscow, 1934. Pencil, watercolor, and pastel on paper, 167 × 194 cm (on 2 sheets). Shchusev Architectural Museum, Moscow

122. Iakov Chernikhov, architect (1889–1951). *Untitled*, c. 1933. From the unpublished series *Industrial Tales*. India ink and gouache on paper, mounted on cardboard, 10.4 × 10.4 cm. Barry Friedman Ltd., New York

123. Le Corbusier, architect (1887–1965). *United Nations Building: perspective*, New York, 27 March 1947. India ink and black and blue pencil on tracing paper, 38 × 66 cm. Fondation Le Corbusier, Paris
© Le Corbusier 1995/VIS*ART Droit d'auteur Inc.

124. Viacheslav Oltarzhevsky, architect (1880–1965). Plate from *Gabaritnyi spravochnik arkhitektora* (Moscow: Izd-vo Akademii Arkhitektury SSSR, 1947), pl. 94. Canadian Centre for Architecture, Montreal

125. Viacheslav Oltarzhevsky, architect (1880–1965). Plate from *Gabaritnyi spravochnik arkhitektora* (Moscow: Izd-vo Akademii Arkhitektury SSSR, 1947), pl. 97. Canadian Centre for Architecture, Montreal

126. Auguste Perret, architect (1874–1954). *Project for the reconstruction of Amiens: elevation*, 1934. India ink and pencil on paper, 68.5 × 108 cm. Institut Français d'Architecture, Centre d'Archives d'Architecture du XXᵉ siècle, Paris
© Auguste Perret 1995/VIS*ART Droit d'auteur Inc.

127. Jacques Carlu, architect (1890–1976). *Skyscraper project for the Place de La Défense: aerial perspective*, Paris, 1944. Pencil on tracing paper, 59.1 × 43.9 cm. Canadian Centre for Architecture, Montreal
© Jacques Carlu 1995/VIS*ART Droit d'auteur Inc.

128. Page showing American mobile homes in the journal *Techniques et architecture* (November 1945), p. 140. Canadian Centre for Architecture, Montreal

129. Two pages illustrating kitchen installations in American mobile homes in *L'Architecture d'aujourd'hui*, n° 12 (July 1947), pp. 52–53. Canadian Centre for Architecture, Montreal

130. View of the entrance to the *Exposition des Techniques Américaines de L'Habitation et de l'Urbanisme*, Paris, Grand Palais, 1946. Ministère de l'Équipement, des Transports et du Tourisme. Service de l'Information et de la Communication, Paris
© Ministère de l'Équipement, des Transports et du Tourisme, Paris

131. General view of the *Exposition des Techniques Américaines de L'Habitation et de l'Urbanisme*, Paris, Grand Palais, 10 June 1946. Ministère de l'Équipement, des Transports et du Tourisme. Service de l'Information et de la Communication, Paris© Ministère de l'Équipement, des Transports et du Tourisme, Paris

132. Texas-style house, experimental postwar village, Noisy-le-Sec, 1946. Ministère de l'Équipement, des Transports et du Tourisme. Service de l'Information et de la Communication, Paris
© Ministère de l'Équipement, des Transports et du Tourisme, Paris

133. Robert Camelot, architect (1903–1993). *Project for La Défense: perspective*, Paris, 1954. Ink on tracing paper, 66 × 110 cm. Institut Français d'Architecture, Centre d'Archives d'Architecture du XXᵉ siècle, Paris
© Institut Français d'Architecture

134. Piero Martina, photographer, *Trucco aereo* (Carlo Mollino in flight over Manhattan), c. 1938. Photographic print. Archivio Carlo Mollino, Biblioteca centrale di Architettura, Sistema bibliotecario, Politecnico, Turin

135. Sigfried Giedion, art historian (1888–1968). Photograph of the Manhattan Building (Chicago, 1891) by William Le Baron Jenney. Institut für Geschichte und Theorie der Architektur (GTA)—ETH Zurich
© Institut für Geschichte und Theorie der Architektur (GTA)—ETH Zurich

136. Frank Gilbreth, engineer (1868–1924). *Movement studies, 2 plates of 4 documents*, May 1947 (document collected by Sigfried Giedion). Silver prints mounted on paper, 25.7 × 20.3 cm. Institut für Geschichte und Theorie der Architektur (GTA)—ETH Zurich
© Institut für Geschichte und Theorie der Architektur (GTA) – ETH Zurich

137. Berenice Abbott, photographer (1898–1991). *View of a production line, May 1947*. Photographic print mounted on yellow onionskin paper with an inscription in the hand of Sigfried Giedion ("The chicken on the assembly line"), 29.5 × 20.9 cm. Institut für Geschichte und Theorie der Architektur (GTA)—ETH Zurich
© Berenice Abbott/Commerce Graphics Ltd., Inc.

138. Preparation of vegetables in the kitchens of the H. J. Heinz company, May 1947 (document collected by Sigfried Giedion). Institut für Geschichte und Theorie der Architektur (GTA)—ETH Zurich
© Institut für Geschichte und Theorie der Architektur (GTA)—ETH Zurich

139. Page from the article "Scene" by Christopher Tunnard, in *Man Made America: A Special Number of The Architectural Review*, vol. 108, no° 648 (December 1950), p. 356. Canadian Centre for Architecture, Montreal

140. Page from "Case Study: City," an unsigned article in *Man Made America: A Special Number of The Architectural Review*, vol. 108, no° 648 (December 1950), p. 362. Canadian Centre for Architecture, Montreal

141. The plan for the Levittown, PA, "grid" presented to the CIAM in Aix-en-Provence, 1953. Institut für Geschichte und Theorie der Architektur (GTA)—ETH Zurich
© Institut für Geschichte und Theorie der Architektur (GTA) – ETH Zurich

142. Alison Smithson (1928–93) and Peter Smithson (b. 1923), architects. *Dwelling project presented at* The House of the Future *exhibition: axonometric*, London, 1956. Ink on tracing paper, 92 × 72 cm. Canadian Centre for Architecture, Montreal
© Alison and Peter Smithson, Architects

143. John McHale (1922–78). *Machine Made America*, 1957. Collage, 73.6 × 58.4 cm. Collection Magda Cordell McHale, Buffalo, N.Y.
© Magda Cordell McHale
144. Two pages of the article "The Contribution of the Curtain Wall to a New Vernacular SYNTAX," in *Machine Made America: A Special Number of The Architectural Review*, ed. Ian McCallum, vol. 121, n° 724 (May 1957), pp. 309–10. Canadian Centre for Architecture, Montreal
145. Ron Herron, architect (1930–94). *A Walking City*, 1964. Collage, approx. 21 × 40 cm. Archigram Archives, London
© Ron Herron, Archigram, London

COLOR PLATES
I. Louis Hulot, student architect (1871–1959). *Project for the Prix de Reconnaissance des Architectes Américains: elevation of a convention hall for New York*, 1900. Pencil, wash, and watercolor on paper, 173 × 236 cm. École nationale supérieure des beaux-arts, Paris
II. Attributed to Antoni Gaudí (1852–1926). *Hotel project: longitudinal section*, 1908. Pencil on paper, 15.5 × 11 cm. Archivo de la Cátedra Gaudí, Barcelona
III. Attributed to Antoni Gaudí (1852–1926). *Hotel project: transverse section of the room "Homenaje a América,"* 1908. Pencil on paper, 13 × 10.5 cm. Archivo de la Cátedra Gaudí, Barcelona
IV. Henri François, student architect. *Project for the Prix de Reconnaissance des Architectes Américains: section of hallway and rooms of a California inn*, 1902. Sepia and watercolor on paper, 78 × 158 cm. École nationale supérieure des beaux-arts, Paris
V. Charles-Louis Boussois, student architect. *Project for the Prix de Reconnaissance des Architectes Américains: elevation of a major newspaper building for an American city*, 1907. 96.5 × 97.7 cm. École nationale supérieure des beaux-arts, Paris
VI. René Dubois, student architect. *Project for the Prix de Reconnaissance des Architectes Américains: elevation of a university campus*, 1921. India ink, watercolor, and airbrush on paper, approx. 104 × 372 cm. École nationale supérieure des beaux-arts, Paris
VII. Knud Lonberg-Holm (1895–1972). Photograph of the Woolworth Building, New York, 1923. Reproduced in Erich Mendelsohn, *Amerika, Bilderbuch eines Architekten* (Berlin: Rudolf Mosse, 1926), pl. 32. Estate of K. Lonberg-Holm, New York
VIII. Knud Lonberg-Holm (1895–1972). Photograph of the rear façade of the Statler Building in Detroit, 1923. Reproduced in Erich Mendelsohn, *Amerika, Bilderbuch eines Architekten* (Berlin: Rudolf Mosse, 1926), pl. 74, under the title *Hinterhof* (Rear court). Estate of K. Lonberg-Holm, New York
IX. Knud Lonberg-Holm (1895–1972). Photograph of the Cadillac Hotel in Detroit, 1923. Reproduced in Erich Mendelsohn, *Amerika, Bilderbuch eines Architekten* (Berlin: Rudolf Mosse, 1926), pl. 61. Estate of K. Lonberg-Holm, New York
X. Knud Lonberg-Holm (1895–1972). Photograph of the rear façade of the Tuller Building in Detroit, 1923. Reproduced in Erich Mendelsohn, *Amerika, Bilderbuch eines Architekten* (Berlin: Rudolf Mosse, 1926), pl. 73. Estate of K. Lonberg-Holm, New York
XI. El Lissitzky (1890–1941). *The Runners*, after 1926. Photographic print and collage, 12.0 × 21.4 cm. Galerie Berinson, Berlin
XII. Cover of Richard Neutra, *Amerika: Die Stilbildung des neuen Bauens in den Vereinigten Staaten* (Vienna: Anton Schroll Verlag, 1930). Graphic design by El Lissitzky. Canadian Centre for Architecture, Montreal
XIII. Cover of the review *Chantiers* reproducing the Lovell House by Richard Neutra (1892–1970). From *Chantiers*, vol. 2 (March–April 1934). Institut Français d'Architecture. Centre d'Archives d'Architecture du XXᵉ siècle, Paris
XIV. Peter Behrens, architect (1868–1940). Architectural composition, cover of *Das Plakat*, n° 6 (June 1920).

XV. Walter Gropius, architect (1883–1969), with Adolf Meyer, architect (1881–1929). *Project for the* Chicago Tribune: *elevation*, 1922. India ink and wash on paper, 151.5 × 75.8 cm. Courtesy of the Busch-Reisinger Harvard University Art Museums, Gift of Walter Gropius
© President and Fellows of Harvard College
XVI. Otto Kohtz, architect (1880–1956). *Project for Reichshaus: interior perspective*, Berlin, early 1920s. Pencil and watercolor wash on cardboard, 54.4 × 33.1 cm. Plansammlung der Universitätsbibliothek der Technischen Universität, Berlin
© Plansammlung der Universitätsbibliothek der Technischen Universität, Berlin
XVII. Piero Portaluppi, architect (1880–1967). *Skyscraper for the SKNE company: perspective*, New York, 1924. watercolor on paper, 102 × 64 cm. Collection Arch. Piero Castellini Baldissera
© Arch. Piero Castellini Baldissera
XVIII. Auguste Perret, architect (1874–1954); Charles Imbert, draughtsman. *Tower cities*, c. 1922. Blue fountain pen ink on onionskin paper, 21.0 × 16.0 cm. Institut Français d'Architecture. Centre d'Archives d'Architecture du XXᵉ siècle, Paris
© Auguste Perret 1994 /VIS*ART Droit d'auteur Inc.
XIX. Vladimir Krinsky (1890–1971). *Building for the Superior Council of National Economy in Moscow: detail of the façade*, 1922–23. Crayon on paper, 18 × 13 cm. Shchusev Architectural Museum, Moscow
XX. Aleksandr Rodchenko (1891–1957). *The War of the Future*, 1930. Collage, 51 × 35 cm. Galerie Berinson, Berlin
XXI. Ivan Illich Leonidov, architect (1902–59). *Competition project for the House of Industry: glass-tower elevation*, 1929–30. White ink on paper, mounted on cardboard. 29.8 × 18.5 cm. Canadian Center for Architecture, Montreal
XXII. Iakov Chernikhov, architect (1889–1951). *Architectural Fantasy with Diverse Elements: Complex combination of constructive volumes; with pure decorative colors*. From *Architectural fantasies* (Leningrad: Mezhdunarodnaia Kniga, 1933), pl. 14. Canadian Centre for Architecture, Montreal
XXIII. Iakov Chernikhov, architect (1889–1951). *City of Giant Skyscrapers in a Vertical Composition: Warm orange and yellow tonal range; conventional graphic treatment of background*. From *Konstruktsia arkhitekturnykh i mashinnykh form (Construction of architectural and mechanical forms)*, Society of Architects of Leningrad, Leningrad, 1931, pl. 10. Canadian Centre for Architecture, Montreal
XXIV. Robert Camelot, architect (1903–93). *Construction of Radio City*, New York, 1932. Watercolor on paper, mounted on cardboard, 11.4 × 15.6 (drawing); 23.8 × 29.6 (mount). Institut Français d'Architecture. Centre d'Archives d'Architecture du XXᵉ siècle, Paris
XXV. Donat-Alfred Agache, architect (1875–1959). *Planning project for the Praça do Castello in Rio de Janeiro: perspective*, 1929. Colored lithographic ink on paper, 35 × 50 cm. Collection Jean-Louis Cohen, Paris
XXVI. Cover of *Acier* n° 3: "Le gratte-ciel américain" (Paris: Office Technique pour l'Utilisation de l'Acier, 1931). Collection Jean-Louis Cohen, Paris
XXVII. Students of the VASI under the direction of Boris Korshunov (1885–1961). *Competition entry for the Peoples' Commissariat for Heavy Industry (NKTP) in Red Square: perspective*, Moscow, 1934. Pencil, india ink, and watercolor on paper, 143 × 140 cm. Shchusev Architectural Museum, Moscow
XXVIII. Môrice Leroux, *Skyscraper, Villeurbanne*, 1934, cover of *Dix années de réalisations des municipalités socialistes*, no° 2: Villeurbanne (Lille: 1935). Collection Jean-Louis Cohen, Paris
XXIX. Boris Iofan, architect (1891–1976). *Rockefeller Center from Fifth Avenue*, 1938. Charcoal and watercolor on cardboard, 75 × 55 cm. Canadian Centre for Architecture, Montreal
XXX. Boris Iofan, architect (1891–1976). *Project for Government House: perspective*, Moscow, 1938. Ink, watercolor, and pencil on paper, 42 × 37.4 cm. Canadian Centre for Architecture, Montreal

XXXI. Paul Colin, poster designer (1892–1985). Poster for the *Exposition des Techniques Américaines de l'Habitation et de l'Urbanisme 1939–194X*, 1946. Archives nationales, Centre des Archives Contemporaines (France)
© Paul Colin 1995/VIS*ART Droit d'auteur Inc.
XXXII. Andrei K. Burov, architect (1900–57). *Plan of the reconstruction of Yalta: elevation from the sea*, 1945. watercolor on paper, 60.5 × 158 cm. Shchusev Architectural Museum, Moscow
XXXIII. Lev Rudnev, architect (1885–1956); with Sergei E. Chernyshev (1881–1963), P. V. Abrosimov (1900–61), V. N. Nasonov, and A.F. Khryakov (engineer). *Moscow University, first version: overall perspective*, 1948–53. Pencil on paper, 182 × 350 cm. Shchusev Architectural Museum, Moscow
XXXIV. Dimitri N. Chechulin, architect (1901–81), and M. Tigranov, engineer (1904–52). *Zariadie office tower: panorama from Red Square*, Moscow, 1947–49. Pencil, ink, and watercolor on paper, 198 × 119 cm. Shchusev Architectural Museum, Moscow
XXXV. Vladimir Gelfreikh (1885–1967) and Mikhail A. Minkus (1905–63), architects. *Ministry of Foreign Affairs: façade*, Moscow, 1948. Pencil, india ink, and watercolor, 56.5 × 107 cm. Shchusev Architectural Museum, Moscow
XXXVI. Mikhail Posokhin (1910–89), Achot Mndoyants (1910–66), architects. *Residential building on Vosstania Square: overall perspective*, Moscow, 1951. Pencil and watercolor on paper, 127.6 × 168.7 cm. Shchusev Architectural Museum, Moscow
XXXVII. Construction of the Ministry of Foreign Affairs by Vladimir Gelfreikh and Mikhail A. Minkus, Smolenskaia Place, cover for *l'URSS en Construction*, no° 1, 1949. Collection Jean-Louis Cohen, Paris.
XXXVIII. Stamo Papadaki, architect. Jacket design for *Mechanization Takes Command* by Sigfried Giedion: *Reclining chair and agricultural implement on a background of meat*, May 1947. Silver print and ink on paper, mounted on cardboard, 25 × 33.4 cm. Institut für Geschichte und Theorie der Architektur (GTA)—ETH Zurich
(c) Institut für Geschichte und Theorie der Architektur (GTA)—ETH Zurich
XXXIX. Promotional leaflet from the publisher of *Mechanization Takes Command*, 1948. Two-color printing on paper, 25.4 × 20.5 cm. Institut für Geschichte und Theorie der Architektur (GTA)—ETH Zurich,
© Institut für Geschichte und Theorie der Architektur (GTA)—ETH Zurich
XL. Richard Hamilton (b. 1922). *$he*, 1958–61. Oil and collage on panel, 121.9 × 81.3 cm. Tate Gallery, London/Art Resource, N.Y.
© Richard Hamilton 1995/VIS*ART Droit d'auteur Inc.
XLI. Eduardo Paolozzi (b. 1924). *Drink Dr Pepper*, 1948. Collage on paper, 35.75 × 23.75 cm. Collection Sir Eduardo Paolozzi
© Tate Gallery, London 1995
XLII. John McHale (1922–78). Cover of *Machine Made America: A Special Number of The Architectural Review*, vol. 121, no° 724 (May 1957). Avery Architectural and Fine Arts Library, Columbia University, New York City.
XLIII. Ron Herron, architect (1930–94). *Instant City: Typical Configuration – Santa Monica and San Diego Freeway Intersection*, Los Angeles, 1969. Collage, approx. 21 × 27 cm. Archigram Archives, London
© Ron Herron, Archigram, London

CHAPTER OPENINGS

BIBLIOGRAPHY

Within each category, the works are listed in chronological order.

General Works

The International Competition for a New Administration Building for the Chicago Tribune, Chicago: The Tribune Co., 1923.

Kelsey, Albert, *Program and Rules of the second competition for the selection of an architect for the construction of a monument that the nations of the world will erect in the Dominican Republic in the memory of Christopher Columbus,* Washington: Pan-American Union, 1931.

Giedion, Sigfried, *Mechanization Takes Command: a contribution to anonymous history,* New York: W. W. Norton & Company, 1969. (Original edition: New York: Oxford University Press, 1948.)

Lewis, Arnold Dudley, *Evaluations of American Architecture by European Critics 1875-1900,* Madison, 1962 (Ph.D. thesis, University of Wisconsin).

Eaton, Leonard K., *American Architecture Comes of Age: European Reaction to H. H. Richardson and Louis Sullivan,* Cambridge, Mass.: MIT Press, 1972.

Ciucci, Giorgio with Francesco Dal Co, Mario Manieri-Elia, and Manfredo Turi, *The American City from the Civil War to the New Deal,* Barbara Luigia La Penta, trans., Boston: MIT Press, 1979. Orig.: *La città americana dalla guerra civile al New Deal,* Bari: Laterza, 1973.

Koolhaas, Rem, *Delirious New York: A Retrospective Manifesto for Manhattan,* New York: Oxford University Press, 1978.

Merkle, Judith, A. *Management and Ideology, the Legacy of the International Scientific Management Movement,* Berkeley: University of California Press, 1980.

Hounshell, David A., *From the American System to Mass Production 1800–1932,* Baltimore and London: The Johns Hopkins University Press, 1984.

de Montmollin, Maurice and Olivier Pastré, eds., *Le Taylorisme,* Paris: La Découverte, 1984.

Banham, Reyner, *A Concrete Atlantis: U.S. Industrial Buildings and European Modern Architecture 1900–1925,* Cambridge, Mass.: MIT Press, 1986.

Maier, Charles S., *Recasting Bourgeois Europe: Stabilization in France, Germany and Italy in the Decade after WWI,* Princeton: Princeton University Press, 1988.

Hughes, Thomas P., *American Genesis: A Century of Invention and Technological Enthusiasm,*

Harmondsworth: Penguin Books, 1990.
Cohen, Jean-Louis and Hubert Damisch, eds., *Américanisme et Modernité, l'idéal américain dans l'architecture,* Paris: Flammarion/École des Hautes Études en Sciences Sociales, 1993.

Dudley, George A., *A Workshop for Peace: Designing the United Nations Headquarters,* New York: Architectural History Foundation, Cambridge, Mass.: MIT Press, 1994.

France

Baudelaire, Charles, *Selected Writings on Art and Artists,* Harmondsworth: Penguin Classics.

Uzanne, Octave, *Vingt jours dans le Nouveau Monde (De Paris à Chicago),* Paris: May et Motteroz, 1893.

Bourget, Paul, *Outre-Mer, Impressions of America,* New York: Charles Scribner's Sons, 1895. Orig.: *Outremer, notes sur L'Amerique,* Paris: Plon, 1894.

Bing, Samuel, *La Culture artistique en Amérique,* Évreux: Imprimerie de Charles Hérissey, 1895.

Benoit-Lévy, Georges, *Cités-jardins d'Amérique,* Paris: Henri Jouve, 1905.

Forestier, Jean-Claude-Nicolas, *Grandes Villes et Systèmes de Parcs,* Paris: Hachette, 1906.

Huret, Jules, *L'Amérique moderne,* Paris: Pierre Lafitte, 1911.

Cambon, Victor, *États-Unis-France,* Paris: Pierre Roger, 1917.

Gréber, Jacques, *L'Organisation des travaux d'architecture aux États-Unis,* Paris: Librairie Centrale des Beaux-Arts, 1919

————*L'architecture aux États-Unis, preuve de la force d'expansion du génie français, heureuse association de qualités admirablement complémentaires,* Paris: Payot, 1920.

Le Corbusier, *Vers une architecture,* Paris: G. Crès & Cie., 1923.

Bernège, Paulette, *Si les femmes faisaient les maisons,* Paris: Mon Chez Moi, 1928.

Duhamel, Georges, *America: the Menace,* London: Allen and Unwin; Boston: Houghton Mifflin, 1931. Orig.: *Scènes de la vie future,* Paris: Mercure de France, 1930.

Ville de Paris: département de la Seine, *Concours pour l'aménagement de la Voie triomphale allant de la place de l'Étoile au rond-point de la Défense,* Paris: Éditions d'art Charles Moreau, s.d. 1932.

Le Corbusier, *When the Cathedrals Were White,* NY; McGraw-Hill, 1964. © Reynal & Hitchcock, 1947. Orig.: *Quand les cathédrals étaient blanches, voyage au pays des timides,* Paris: Plon, 1937.

Prévost, Jean, *Usonie; esquisse de la civilisation américaine,* Paris: Gallimard, 1939.

Le Corbusier, *Modulor I and II,* trans. Peter de Francia and Anna Bostock, Cambridge, MA: Harvard University Press, 1980. Orig.: *Le Modulor,* Boulogne-Billancourt: Editions de *l'Architecture d'aujourd'hui,* 1950.

Lacorne, Denis, Jacques Rupnik, and Marie-France Toinet, eds., *L'Amérique dans les têtes; un siècle de fascinations et d'aversions,* Paris: Hachette, 1986.

Gournay, Isabelle, *France Discovers America 1917–1939,* New Haven: Yale University, 1989, (PhD thesis).

Jullien, Dominique, *Récits du nouveau-monde; les voyageurs français en Amérique de Châteaubriand à nos jours,* Paris: Nathan, 1992.

Mathy, Jean-Philippe, *Extrême Occident; French Intellectuals and America,* Chicago and London: University of Chicago Press, 1993.

Kuysel, Richard F., *Seducing the French: The Dilemma of Americanization,* Berkeley and Los Angeles: University of California Press, 1993.

Germany/Austria

von Hesse-Wartegg, Ernst, *Chicago, eine Weltstadt im amerikanischen Westen,* Union Deutsche Verlagsgesellschaft, 1893.

Graef, Paul, *Neubauten in Nordamerika,* Berlin: Julius Becker, 1899.

Münsterberg, Hugo, *The Americans,* trans. Edwin B. Holt, New York: McClure, Phillips & Co., 1904. Orig.: *Die Amerikaner,* Berlin: E.S. Mittler und Sohn, 1904.

von Hesse-Wartegg, Ernst, *Amerika als neueste Weltmacht der Industrie,* Stuttgart: Union Deutsche Verlagsgesellschaft, 1909.

Vogel, F. Rudolf, *Das amerikanische Haus, Band I : Der Entwicklung der Baukunst und des amerikanischen Hauses,* Berlin: Ernst Wasmuth, 1910.

Hegemann, Werner, *Amerikanische Parkanlage: Zierparks, Nutzparks, Aussen-u. Innenparks, Nationalparks, Park-Zweckverbande,* Berlin: Ernst Wasmuth, 1911.

———Der Neue Bebauungsplan für Chicago, Berlin: Ernst Wasmuth, 1911.

———Der Städtebau nach den Ergebnissen der allgemeinen Städtebau-Ausstellung in Düsseldorf, Berlin: Ernst Wasmuth, 1911 (vol. 1) and 1913 (vol. 2).

———Amerikanische Architektur und Stadtbaukunst, Berlin: Ernst Wasmuth, 1925.

Wagner, Martin, Amerikanische Bauwirtschaft, Berlin: Dreikellen-Bücher, 1925.

Mendelsohn, Erich, Amerika, Bilderbuch eines Architekten, Berlin, Rudolf Mosse, 1926, revised ed. 1928.

Behrendt, Walter Curt, Städtebau und Wohnungswesen in den Vereinigten Staaten, Bericht über eine Studienreise, Berlin: Guido Hackebeil AG, 1926.

Hilberseimer, Ludwig, Großstadtarchitektur, Stuttgart: Julius Hoffmann, 1927.

Halfelds, Adolf, Amerika und der Amerikanismus, kritische Betrachtungen eines Deutschen und Europäers, Iena: Eugen Diederichs, 1927.

Neutra, Richard, Wie baut Amerika?, Stuttgart: Julius Hoffmann, 1927.

Mendelsohn, Erich, Rußland, Europa, Amerika, ein architektonischer Querschnitt, Berlin: Rudolf Mosse, 1929.

Wagner, Martin, Städtebauliche Probleme in amerikanischen Städten und ihre Rückwirkung auf den deutschen Städtebau, Berlin: Deutsche Bauzeitung, 1929.

Neutra, Richard, Amerika. Die Stilbildung des neuens Bauens in den Vereinigten Staaten, Vienna: Anton Schroll Verlag, 1930.

Hugenberg, Alfred, Die neue Stadt, Berlin: Verlag Scherl, 1935.

Fraenkel, Ernst, ed., Amerika im Spiegel des deutschen politischen Denkens, Cologne and Opladen, Westdeutscher Verlag, 1959.

Neutra, Richard, Life and Shape, New York: Appleton-Century-Crofts, 1962.

Berg, Peter, Deutschland und Amerika: Über das deutsche Amerikabild der zwanziger Jahre, Lübeck and Hamburg, Matthiesen, 1963.

Parmalee, Patty Lee, Brecht's America, Miami: Miami University Press, 1981.

Herf, Jeffrey, Reactionary Modernism: Technology, Culture, and Politics in Weimar and the Third Reich, Cambridge, London, and New York: Cambridge University Press, 1984.

Samson, Miles David, German-American Dialogues and the Modern Movement before the Design Migration 1910–1933, Cambridge, Mass.: Harvard University, 1988, (Ph.D. thesis).

Zimmermann, Florian, ed., Der Schrei nach dem Turmhaus, der Ideenwettbewerb Hochhaus am Bahnhof Friedrichstraße Berlin 1921/1922, Berlin: Argon-Verlag, 1988.

Tower, Beeke Sell, Envisioning America: Prints, Drawings and Photographs by George Grosz and his Contemporaries 1915-1933, Cambridge, Mass.: Busch-Reisinger Museum, 1990.

Kleihues, Josef Paul and Christine Rathgeber, eds., Berlin New York Like and Unlike: Essays on Architecture and Art from 1870 to the Present, New York: Rizzoli, 1993.

Nolan, Mary, Visions of Modernity; American Business and the Modernization of Germany, New York and Oxford: Oxford University Press, 1994.

Russia

Tverskoi, P. A., Ocherki Severo-Amerikanskikh Soedinionnykh Shtatov, St. Petersburg, Tip. Skorokhodova, 1895.

Gorky, Maxime, V Amerike, Ocherki, Stuttgart: Dietz Verlag, 1906, Moscow: Foreign Language Publ. House, 1949.

Semenov, Vladimir, Blagoustroistvo gorodov, Moscow: Tip. I. I. Riabushchinskago, 1912.

Ginzburg, Moisei, Style and Epoch, Cambridge, Mass. and London: The MIT Press, 1982. Orig.: Stil i epokha, problemy sovremennoi Arkhitektury, Moscow: Gosudarstvennoe Izdatelstvo, 1924.

Maiakovsky, Vladimir, Moio otkrytie Ameriki, Moscow: Gosudarstvennoe Izdatelstvo, 1926.

Arkin, David, Arkhitektura sovremennogo zapada, Moscow: OGIZ-IZOGIZ, 1932.

Bunin, Andrei, and Maria Kruglova, Arkhitekturnaia kompozitsia gorodov, Moscow: Izd. Akademii arkhitektury SSSR, 1940.

Oltarzhevsky, Viacheslav K., Gabaritnyi spravochnik arkhitektora, Moscow, Izd-vo Akademii Arkhitektury SSSR, 1947.

———Stroitelstvo vysotnykh zdanii v Moskve, Moscow: Gos. izd. Lit. po Stroitelstvu i Arkhitekture, 1953

Lissitzky-Küppers, Sophie, ed., El Lissitzky: Life, Letters, Text, London and New York: Thames & Hudson, 1980. Orig.: El Lissitsky Maler Architekt Typograph Fotograph, Dresden: VEB Verlag der Kunst, 1967.

Rougle, Charles, Three Russians Consider America: America in the works of Maksim Gor'kij, Aleksandr Blok and Vladimir Majakovskij, Stockholm: Almqvist & Wiksell International, 1976

Khan-Magomedov, Selim, Pioneers of Soviet Architecture: The Search for New Solutions in the 1920s and 1930s, New York: Rizzoli, 1987. Orig.: Pioniere der sowjetischen Architektur, Dresden, VEB Verlag der Kunst, 1983.

Starr, S. Frederick, Hot and Red: Jazz in the Soviet Union, London, New York and Oxford: Oxford University Press, 1983.

Tuganov, O. E., ed., Vzaimodeistvie kultur SSSR i SShA XVIII–XX vv., Moscow: Nauka, 1987

Stites, Richard, Revolutionary Dreams: Utopian Visions and Experimental Life in the Russian Revolution, New York and Oxford: Oxford University Press, 1989,

Brumfield, William Craft, ed., Reshaping Russian Architecture: Western Technology, Utopian Dreams, Cambridge and New York: Woodrow Wilson International Center for Scholars, Cambridge University Press, 1990

Italy

Hoare, Quinton and Geoffrey Nowell, eds., Selections from the Notebooks of Antonio Gramsci, New York: International Publishers, 1971.

Ridolfi, Mario, with Cino Calcaprina, Aldo Cardelli, and Mario Fiorentino, Manuale dell'architetto, Rome: Consiglio Naionale delle Ricerche/USIS, 1945.

Vaudagna, Maurizio, ed., L'estetica della politica; Europa e America negli anni Trenta, Rome and Bari: Laterza, 1989.

Olmo, Carlo, ed., Il Lingotto 1915-1939; L'architettura, l'immagine, il lavoro, Turin: Umberto Allemandi, 1994.

The Netherlands

Berlage, Hendrik Petrus, Amerikaansche Reisherinneringen, Rotterdam: 1913.

Asselbergs Fons, et al., Americana, Otterlo: Rijksmuseum Kröller-Müller,1975 (cat. d'exposition).

Great Britain

Dickens, Charles, American Notes, New York: St. Martin's Press 1985.

Cook, Peter et al., Archigram, London: Studio Vista, 1973.

Banham, Reyner, Design by Choice, London: Academy Editions, 1981.

Hamilton, Richard, Collected Words 1953-1962, London: Thames and Hudson, 1982.

Beevers, Robert, The Garden City Utopia; A Critical Biography of Ebenezer Howard, New York: Saint Martin's Press, 1988.

Robbins, David, ed., The Independent Group: Postwar Britain and the Aesthetics of Plenty, Cambridge, Mass. and London: MIT Press, 1990 (exhibition catalogue).

I N D E X

Photography Credits

Albert Kahn Associates Architects & Engineers, Detroit, Michigan: 52. State Archives of Zlín, Czech Republic: 48, 49.

Archivo de la Cátedra Gaudí, Barcelona: II, III. The Art Institute of Chicago, Chicago: 90, 91.

Bauhaus-Archiv, Berlin: 75.Bibliothèque nationale de France, Paris: 2.

CCA, Montreal, photography department: 5, 10, 11, 18, 19, 20, 21, 24, 26, 27, 28, 31, 34, 36, 38, 40, 42, 44, 45, 47, 51, 54, 57, 58, 61, 65, 67, 69, 85, 92, 93, 95, 96, 97, 101, 104, 105, 110, 111, 117, 124, 125, 127, 128, 129, 139, 140, 144, XII, XIV, XXII, XXIII.

Centre des Archives contemporaines, Paris, photography department: 130, 131, 132, XXI.

Marc Dessauce, New York: VII; VIII, IX, X.

École nationale supérieure des beaux-arts, Paris, photography department: 1, I, IV, V, VI.

Le Corbusier Foundation, Paris: 30, 87, 112, 113, 123.

Foto Saporetti, Milan: XVII. Gabinetto disegni e stampe, Pisa: 16, 17. Graydon Wood, 1989, Philadelphia: 25.

Harvard University Art Museums, Cambridge, Mass., Photo Services: 35, 36, XV.

Institute Français d'Architecture, Paris: 12, 83, 84, 106, 107, 108, XVIII, XXIX.

JIB Studio Professional, Turin: 134. Herman Kiessling, Berlin: XVI.

Museum Sztuki, Łodz, Poland: chapter openings 5, 94. Peter T. Muscato, Buffalo, N.Y.: 143.

Igor Palmin, Moscow: 100, 114, 121, XIX, XXVII, XXXII, XXXIII, XXXIV, XXXV, XXXVI.

The Print Studio at the Architectural Association, London: 145, XLIII.

Retina; Rotterdam: 59, 89. Peter Riesterer, Berlin: 55.

Pascal Stritt, photographer, Reims: 23. Sandrine Villain; Photo Studio Cnam, Paris: 86.

Studio Littré, Paris: 4, 6, 29, 32, 33, 41, 43, 46, XXV, XXVI, XXVIII